The Third Review
of
Special Education

LESTER MANN, *Editor*
Montgomery County Intermediate Unit
Blue Bell, Pennsylvania

DAVID A. SABATINO, *Editor*
Northern Illinois University
De Kalb, Illinois

GRUNE & STRATTON
A Subsidiary of Harcourt Brace Jovanovich, Publishers

New York   San Francisco   London

The Third Review of Special Education
is a book in the series edited by JSE Press.

©*1976 by Grune & Stratton, Inc.*

Grune & Stratton, Inc.
111 Fifth Avenue
New York, New York 10003

Distributed in the United Kingdom by
Academic Press, Inc. (London) Ltd.
24/28 Oval Road, London NW 1

Library of Congress Catalog Number 74-77379
International Standard Book Number 0-8089-0979-7
Printed in the United States of America

CONTENTS

PREFACE

As with its predecessors, *The Third Review of Special Education* has seen the light of day through the efforts of a number of people. Some of these are associated with the *Journal of Special Education* and JSE Press: Dr. Mann dealt with content editing and manuscript selection; Dr. Sabatino assumed responsibility for some of the author selection and contact; Dr. John Goodman handled the technical and copy editing; and Dr. Robert Kalapos was our liaison with Grune & Stratton, Inc., JSE's publisher. JSE's publications secretary, Nancy Schaaf, did yeoman service typing, keeping track of and harrassing authors for their manuscripts, and helping Dr. Goodman stay sane. None of us would have been able to function without the able direction of Mrs. Selma Carson, our Administrative Director. Finally, we would like to thank the staff of Grune & Stratton, who gave amply of their time and attention.

The Editors

INTRODUCTION

LESTER MANN

Montgomery County Intermediate Unit
Blue Bell, Pennsylvania

The Third Review of Special Education continues in the tradition of its predecessors. Rather than attempting systematically to scan and catalog the accomplishments of a field that is continually, if unevenly, expanding, we have attempted to examine and highlight certain select inquiries and issues. I believe that our choice has been most pertinent for 1976 and for the score of years beyond within which these topics will still be relevant.

In our first chapter Farley and Blom reexamine an old war horse—mental health consultation to schools. This was a very popular topic in the '50s and '60s, less so now but still extremely important. Our authors cover the topic well, defending while amplifying the traditional roles of mental health consultation in the context of the present day.

Moores' "Review of Education of the Deaf" does the field of special education a distinct service with its comprehensive views of theories and practices in deaf education. For the special educator who is not involved in deaf education it provides a sophisticated primer. For the educator of the deaf it should provide a welcome up-dating and reaffirmation of understanding within his field of expertise.

To those of our readers who are acquainted with Ivan Holowinsky's reviews of Soviet and Eastern European special education for the *Journal of Special Education,* and with his previous writings in these reviews, the reappearance of his name in *The Third Review* should be most welcome. So much that is conceptually important in special education is of Eastern European origins. Dr. Holowinsky in his current review of functional centers takes us beyond the peripheries of casual understanding into a direct interface with Soviet thinking on learning dysfunction.

The term "multiply handicapped" has a variety of meanings at the present stage of special education practice. In the review by Thurman, Langley, and Wood, it is applied in the traditional sense of "more-than-one-handicap."

Within our own experience we have found that the existence of sensory impairments in the mentally retarded child is often overlooked or given short shrift. Thurman et al. speak to these concerns by providing not only a thorough review of the literature of the past 25 years but recommendations for the study and programming of such children.

Categories have become unpopular in special education. Noncategorical special education smacks of democracy; categories of elitism, segregation, denial of service, etc. But taxonomy is a core approach to the management of behavior and essential to the scientific understanding thereof. Our understanding of what classification (i.e., taxonomy) means unfortunately is usually too scant to appreciate its true value, indeed its necessity, for the field of special education. Armstrong's review should do much to clear up some of the misconceptions about taxonomies and lead us to newer and better ones to guide our future research and practices.

Blanton, Sitko, and Gillespie have reviewed the issues and research relative to teaching reading to the mildly mentally retarded. This is not the first time that reading has been examined in detail in the Reviews, nor the last. For it will continue to be a prime, if not the major, focus of educational concern for a majority of special educators. Readers of the review by Blanton el al. will come away chastened but wiser from their re-encounter with the ever-present, ever-perplexing problems of teaching the retarded to read. Somewhat encouraged too, we would think, by the evidence that solid progress in understanding has been achieved.

Beth Stephens, in examining programs for the severely and profoundly retarded, gives our readership a cogent review of what has become one of the major areas of investigation and practice within the purview of special education. Professor Stephens approaches her topic as befits a veteran and a pioneer in this field while offering, in clear and concise form, her own personal views concerning the education and management of low functioning children.

The topic of teacher training in special education is one that we have to repeatedly and persistently examine and re-examine every several years or so. Shores, Burney, and Wiegerink approach the staggering task of understanding teacher education, and the efforts made to improve it, with vigor and thoroughness.

Institutionalization and mainstreaming are facets of the same issue: the same problem, the same opportunity. Our final two chapters of *The Third Review* address themselves to these topics. Vitello reviews institutional practices with the mentally retarded from a historical as well as topical vantage point. He examines some of the origins of our present patterns of treatment, along with contemporary research, and has some recommendations to make as to future courses of action.

Meisgeier's chapter on mainstreaming brings *The Third Review* to a close with certainly one of the most topical of present concerns in special education. He provides us with perspectives within what is still a rather inchoate area of inquiry. We are brought by Meisgeier from early stages of discussion about mainstreaming through concerns that are raised about the topic and then into current practices. A fitting coda for a volume that seeks to stabilize thought and research in the field of special education.

MENTAL HEALTH CONSULTATION TO SCHOOLS

Gordon K. Farley

University of Colorado Medical Center

Gaston E. Blom

Michigan State University

Within the past few years, mental health consultation to schools has taken on new importance and received increased attention. Several factors have contributed to these developments. First, school problems have become an increasingly frequent reason for referring a child for mental health services. Second, there has been growing recognition of the need to integrate and coordinate the dual efforts of education and mental health in helping handicapped children and their parents. Third, the current national emphasis on community mental health includes recognition of the school as an essential element of the community. A fourth contributing factor has been the recognition of the centrality of education in a child's life.

Hundreds of different projects have been undertaken by mental health personnel in order to help emotionally disabled children and their families in school settings. This paper summarizes and scrutinizes some of the more important efforts. The term, "mental health consultation" is used to encompass the consultation efforts of child psychiatrists, general psychiatrists, psychologists, social workers, and other mental health professionals involved with schools, directing their efforts to deal with emotional problems and issues. In addition, a "consultant" is defined as a professional who is not ordinarily a full-time employee of the school system but is, for the most part, an outsider to the system. Although they may vary in emphasis and orientation, these consultation efforts by different mental health professionals have more similarities than differences.

In this chapter we discuss: (*a*) the importance of schools in children's lives; (*b*) the changing school culture; (*c*) problems of entry, sanction, and maintenance; (*d*) the varied forms of school consultation; (*e*) the existing literature in school consultation; and (*f*) training in school mental health consultation.

THE IMPORTANCE OF SCHOOLS
IN CHILDREN'S LIVES

Mental health professionals have increasingly realized that a child's school experience is a crucial part of his or her emotional life. The teacher has come to be seen as an important, pivotal figure in the establishment and maintenance of a child's mental health. At the same time, the school has been indicted by some as a major contributor to mental health disorders (Glasser, 1969; Holt, 1969; Kozol, 1967; Kozol, 1972).

The extent of both emotional and learning disorders in children has come to the attention of mental health professionals. Surveys of school populations have shown the rate of emotional disturbance among school-age children to vary from 5 to 20% (Brandon, 1969; Lapouse & Monk, 1958; Moore, 1966; Rutter & Graham, 1965; Ryle, Pond, & Hamilton, 1965; Stennett, 1966; Wolff, 1967). In many inner-city school districts the percentage of children seen as having some degree of maladaption may approach 70% (Kellam & Schiff, 1967; Schiff & Kellam, 1967). The identification of "high risk" populations and the development of early and appropriate intervention programs has been stated to be an important national priority. Many mental health professionals have seen the school as a potentially therapeutic setting for children with emotional disturbances, even when other community or family resources are lacking, antitherapeutic, or seem to fail.

THE CHANGING SCHOOL CULTURE

For orientation to school consultation, it is important to have some understanding of the school as an institution of our culture. Moreover, a specific school may have a particular culture of its own, reflecting the children and families served as well as its leadership and staff.

While schools have been one of the most conservative and stable institutions in our culture, there is much evidence today that schools in general have been receiving criticisms, harassments, rejections, and suggestions for change from many sectors of our society through all forms of communication—legislation, press, television, lectures, letters, meetings, etc. Unfortunately, many of these communications are not rational or constructive and may miss the point. What is being attacked and criticized, in fact, are aspects of our society in which the school becomes a scapegoat. Owing to its basic nature and structure, the school system is less responsive to change than are other institutions. Because education has become increasingly politicized, the school is pulled by forces in our pluralistic society which may be regressive, progressive, egalitarian, paternalistic, prejudiced, or revolutionary. While some people wish to recapture "the good old days" in education, those days were not necessarily good for large numbers of children. Others do not want to differentiate the old in terms of what is desirable and what is not. So it is quite understandable that today the school is experiencing special, conflictful pressures, and one can identify with how school personnel feel in this situation. This does not mean that change should not occur, but it is important to understand that change is a psychosocial process, often poorly understood, recognized, and conceptualized. In his more recent writing, Sarason (1972, 1974) has focused on the study of institutions and the psychology of change, particularly in relation to schools.

It is difficult to consider all of the societal influences that are working both rationally and irrationally for change in our schools. Of major import are the attempts to desegregate schools in neighborhoods that have reflected segregation patterns and resisted change. The measures that have been taken, as well as the reactions to them, are very well known. As heterogeneity of children and their families within schools develops, individual schools lose their distinctive culture except as it is reflected by a school's particular staff.

Another influence at work is the different philosophies of education proposed by parents and by formal and informal groups. These philosophies can be characterized along a number of dimensions, including: (a) traditional to progressive; (b) basic-skills to total-child emphasis; (c) structure to exploration; (d) homogeneous to heterogeneous groupings; and (e) parental to professional control, among others. In response to these different opinions about educational goals and methods, alternative schools have been established where children are placed by parent choice.

A further trend is the increasing responsibility that schools are being asked to accept for various types of handicapped children. New legislation and funding at state and federal levels have supported more and better programs for such children. Some educators and parents have become concerned about the tendency to categorize and label children and to place them in special programs from which they may never return to the education mainstream. There has also been criticism of testing and diagnostic procedures whose results may have long-range educational and social implications. A growing viewpoint of normalization advocates that handicapped people should be entitled to the same rights as others within the scope of what is realistically possible. One can observe both integration and segregation of handicapped children within schools today, as well as the conflicting forces and emotional reactions to these alternatives.

Two more societal influences will be mentioned. One is professional accountability—exemplified in school records being made available to parents and older children and, further, in the rights of parents and their representatives to question, challenge, and participate in decision making. Schools, as well as other institutions, are far more open to scrutiny than ever before, and their effectiveness is being questioned. Professionals can no longer remain isolated, while their work and decisions go unquestioned.

A final influence of major import is the increased aggression, drug use, and sexual expression manifested in school settings. This is a reflection of what is going on in society at large, although the school is often blamed for it. The exposure to and experience with violence and other instinctual expressions at home, in our neighborhoods, and across the country are very well known. Television is but one highly important contribution to this environment. Instinctual manifestations in school settings pose special problems in management, help, and prevention. There are those within the community who claim these issues are not the responsibility of the school; yet schools cannot ignore them or deny their existence. Nor are simple solutions, such as expulsion or telling parents to rectify the situation at home, effective and relevant unless outside assistance is provided.

A school consultant must have some appreciation, then, for these cultural influences and the reaction of school professionals to them. Consultants will face them in their everyday work and may not have easy solutions available from their previous training and experience.

PROBLEMS OF SANCTION, ENTRY, AND MAINTENANCE

It has been pointed out that the problem of entry, i.e., introducing mental health services, is common to all types of mental health intervention within the schools (Levine & Graziano, 1972). Opposition to mental health efforts within schools has come from nearly every imaginable source—including superintendents, community principals, teachers—and has been based on both rational and irrational grounds. Schools have experienced ineffective services and unrealistic expectations from mental health professionals. It has been noted that acceptance within the school can be facilitated and partially assured if the mental health consultant is able to develop a strong relationship with an *informal leader* within the school or school system (Klebanoff & Bindman, 1962; Sarason, Levine, Goldenberg, Cherlin, & Bennett, 1966).

In an article entitled *What Help Can the Educator Expect from the Mental Health Specialist?* Berlin (1962) pointed out that school personnel and mental health specialists have many unrealistic expectations of each other and that these expectations interfere with collaboration. He noted that mental health specialists are often expected to use some special magic to solve the teacher's or administrator's problems, if only they would. Teachers often feel that the consultant should make what would more appropriately be an educational decision, e.g., whether a child should be passed or not. One area of difficulty between educator and mental health consultant is the educator's understandable fear that the consultant will analyze, pry, or otherwise meddle in the personal affairs and problems of the educator. Berlin sees the role of the mental health worker as including the following activities:

1. The consultant should be prepared to learn about the stresses and difficulties of the teacher's job.

2. The consultant is trained in the area of interpersonal relations and has special understanding of the causes and development of mental health problems in children. The consultant must use this knowledge to assess the degree of disturbance, evaluate the need for referral, and select the appropriate facility for referral.

3. Mental health consultation is an opportunity to communicate and demonstrate mental health principles to teachers.

Glidewell (1967) has written about differences in basic assumptions regarding the inducement of change in schoolchildren and in children in mental health institutions. He noted that the schools seek to induce change by appealing to the intellect, whereas mental health clinicians seek to induce changes in children by discussing and dealing with their feelings. Teachers are committed to working for the benefit of the total classroom, whereas mental health clinicians are equally committed to working in behalf of the individual child. These differences in basic assumptions and in the focus of commitment add to the difficulties in entry for the mental health consultant in the schools. These contrasts in goals, focus, views of behavior, approach to behavior, and value orientations have been amplified by Blom (1975).

Berlin (1962) also pointed out that mental health consultants should be open and candid and report to the consultees their own personal experiences of failure and frustration. This approach seems to be particularly useful in the opening stages of mental health consultation. Others have noted that the mental health consultant, in the initial consultative efforts with a school or a teacher, may often be presented with the most difficult child or the most unworkable situation in the school or classroom. The consultant's willingness to be involved in such a case often predicts his future success in consultative efforts regardless of his success or failure with the case.

Another obstacle to the effective use of consultation was discussed by Sarason (Sarason et al., 1966). He stated that, in general, teachers are relatively untrained in the use of mental health consultation and, similarly, mental health consultants are often seriously lacking in substantive knowledge concerning the classroom and education. Sarason noted, however, that mental health consultants to the schools have one particular advantage over teachers—i.e., not having the responsibility of handling a large group of children, thus being able to stand back a bit and view the problem somewhat dispassionately.

Several unique problems of the teaching profession led Sarason to suggestions regarding the role of the mental health consultant. He observed that the teacher is usually isolated in the classroom and thus has limited opportunities for contact with fellow teachers or other potentially helpful people. He noted that once a child is identified as "emotionally disturbed," a "hands-off" phenomenon takes place, and the teacher henceforth is unlikely to set appropriate limits or make the usual expectations of that child. Sarason also pointed out the role of the mental health consultant in helping to change a teacher's perception of a given problem. For example, with the consultant's help, a teacher may be able to see that a mildly retarded child, rather than being unable to learn, has, in fact, learning potential.

Blom (1972) noted that the mental health consultant in clinical and educational settings needs a wide variety of tools. He outlined conditions where the application of either behavior modification principles or mental health principles derived from psychoanalytic psychology may be used.

FORMS OF MENTAL HEALTH
CONSULTATION TO SCHOOLS

The oldest and still most frequently used form of mental health consultation to schools involves an individual child who is in treatment at a mental health facility. This consultation usually amounts to a visit to the school by a mental health professional for the purpose of exchanging information and sharing plans for treatment. Although common, this form of consultation is vastly underutilized. Studies have shown that the average number of visits to a school by a mental health clinic for a given child tends to be less than one visit per year of treatment (Berkowitz, 1968). Little has been written about this most commonly used interface between mental health and schools, other than to recite the difficulties in communication between the mental health person and the educator. There has been no attempt to determine whether this kind of communication is beneficial to either party or to the child who is the focus of interest.

Another common form of consultation utilizes the case review method—a detailed social history of the child and his family. Psychological testing is done, sometimes including projective testing; a child interview, as well as a physical exam, may also be performed; and, at the conclusion of an evaluation, a conference is held in which all the information is pulled together and presented, and some plans are made. Teachers have often complained that this type of study and conference are of little use to them for everyday classroom problems with disturbed and disturbing children.

Still another kind of consultation might be called setting consultation or system consultation. Here, the mental health professional attempts to define problems within the system and devise ways to alleviate them. These problems may range from an individual teacher's difficulty in controlling an unruly class to the superintendent of schools' failure to communicate effectively with the community.

On the individual-teacher level are reports of a number of apparently effective methods to improve the behavior of emotionally disturbed children. Behavior modification techniques have gained increasing popularity. Hewett (1970) stressed the importance of the "engineered classroom." There are many descriptions of effective methods for changing almost every conceivable behavior of individuals and groups one might encounter in the classroom (Bandura, 1969; Barnes, Wooton, & Wood, 1972; Edlund, 1971; Engelman, 1970; Graziano, 1971; Haring & Phillips, 1962; Krasner & Krasner, 1973; and Patterson, Cob, & Ray, 1972). Through consultation, teachers have been able to learn to offer more effective and consistent consequences for behavior in the classroom. Behavior modification techniques have been used to deal with talking out of turn, out-of-seat behavior, nonattentiveness, stealing, soiling, truancy, school phobia, anxiety,, underachievement, inhibition, depression, poor self-esteem, and a host of other conditions. Of all consultation methods, the usefulness of the consultant as a teacher of behavior modification seems to be the most clearly documented.

Sarason and his co-workers (Sarason et al., 1966) have frequently pointed out the classroom teacher's relative isolation within the school. One approach to mental health consultation within schools has been to form teacher groups. These groups have ranged from something resembling a "sensitivity group," through groups designed for problem solving, to groups that are primarily didactic and informational. These groups may be of relatively brief duration (8 to 10 weeks) or more extensive (1 to 2 years). They may be open and admit new participants within the course of the work, or they may be closed and admit no new participants after two or three sessions. Weiman (1969) reported examples of problem-solving groups led by a team consisting of a mental health professional and an experienced and trained teacher. The focus of discussion was on common, everyday classroom problems. Permission was given for teachers to express anger, anxiety, resentment, feelings of failure, and frustration. There was an emphasis on the sharing of common concerns, experiences, and of solving these problems. Others have attempted mental health consultation through teacher or principal discussion groups (Coleman, 1972; Rowitch, 1968; Sarason et al., 1966). Usually these groups have been well accepted by teachers, but

7

effectiveness evaluations noting more than consumer satisfaction have usually not been done.

Most often, mental health consultants in the schools have not provided direct services to emotionally disturbed children or their families but have seen themselves as acting through the teacher or some other regular school employee. There are some exceptions to this, however. Several mental health consultants have treated either children or their parents in groups in school settings. Barcai, Umbarger, Pierce, and Chamberlain (1973) report a comparison of three group approaches to underachieving children: Group remediation, group counseling, and art activity were compared in effectiveness. Remediation and counseling were found to be equally effective and both were superior to art activity in improving school performance. Tenenbaum (1970) noted improved grades as a consequence of group therapy for a group of nine students; no comparison group was used. Garner (1974) showed that behavior-disordered children can obtain some mental health benefits in the affective domain as a result of a group experience, although an influence on academic performance and learning was not evaluated. Gratton and Pope (1972) described the use of group screening and group treatment of children with emotional disturbances. The group treatment consisted of 12 1-hour sessions intended to modify the children's classroom behavior without producing "intrapsychic" changes. Success of a moderate degree was reported.

A large number of mental health consultants have helped emotionally disturbed children by treating their parents in groups. Gildea and her group reported considerable success in working with middle-class parents (Buchmueller & Gildea, 1949) but less success with parents from a lower socioeconomic class (Kahn, Buchmueller, & Gildea, 1951). In another example of a consultant's work with parents, group treatment of 30 parents for 6 weeks was reported to achieve good results, although data to support this conclusion was not presented (Hereford, 1963).

Still another method of providing mental health services to schools has been to teach school personnel the techniques of "life space" interviewing (Redl, Bernstein, Kitchener, Long, Morse, & Newman, 1963). This technique and modifications of it (Blom, 1971; Farley, Sadler, Duchesne, Prodoehl, & Weiman, 1975; Sadler & Blom, 1970) has been widely used and taught in public schools. Its purpose is to have a sensitive, empathetic person, trained in psychiatric interviewing, immediately available to a child in academic or emotional distress. Again, the impact of this type of help has not been rigorously evaluated.

A sparingly used approach to schools has been for the mental health consultant to attempt to help the school personnel be more creative and use their own resources in a more effective way in solving their own problems. This has usually necessitated gathering concerned personnel into working groups and asking such questions as, How would you like this school to be run? What would an ideal school for children be like? Ongoing discussions of this type have often resulted in clearer and more open communication between the teachers and principals within a school and the formulation of some specific recommendations for change and ways of carrying out those recommendations. This approach to school mental health consultation has in some instances reportedly resulted in increased job satisfaction, greater productivity of teachers, and improved abilities of the teacher to relate to emotionally disturbed children. Few objective measures of teachers' or children's gains have been attempted, however. Several descriptions of ways to carry out this type of program have been published (Ekanger, 1970; Sarason et al., 1966; Sarason, 1971). Sarason has emphasized the difficulties one would encounter in trying to effect change in a system.

Another important contribution of the mental health consultant may be in the early identification of children ''at risk'' for the development of later emotional and learning disabilities. Evidence has accumulated that these children can be identified early in their school careers. When appropriate and rapid intervention is arranged, they will show a smaller-than-expected incidence of such disturbances. Many types of early identification and intervention have been attempted, and only the better-known ones will be described.

Perhaps the largest national effort ever undertaken in the early identification and remediation of emotional problems has been Project Head Start, which began around 1965. Within Head Start centers a large number of checklists, observational protocols, and standardized rating scales were used to identify emotionally disturbed children (Comley & Hadjisky, 1967; Cowen, Dorr, Clarfield, Kreling, McWilliams, Pokracki, Pratt, Terrell, & Wilson, 1973; Graffagnino, 1967; Hotkins, Hollander, & Munk, 1968). Mental health consultation has been widely offered to and widely accepted by Head Start centers (Farley, 1971; Rosenblum, 1967; Shaw, Eagle, & Goldberg, 1968). Yet there have been few systematic attempts to evaluate the usefulness or impact of these consultations on Head Start centers.

The effectiveness of the Head Start experience itself in preventing either emotional or learning problems has been studied. Although the conclusions are ambiguous, it would appear that the results of the experience are at best disappointing in that one major study (Cicirelli, Evans, & Schiller, 1970) found little if any difference between treated and untreated children along a number of dimensions, including cognitive skills, self-esteem, racial tolerance, and ''emotional adjustment.'' Differences in the rate of success between types of programs were noted, however.

It has been known for some time that ''reproductive casualty'' can be linked with later emotional and learning disturbances, although in the interim between the time of the insult and the emergence of problems the child may look quite normal (Knoblock, 1960; Passamanick & Knoblock, 1966). Birch and his co-workers (Chess, 1968; Chess, Rutter, & Birch, 1963; Chess, Thomas, & Birch, 1967) have pointed out that behavior problems in school-age children can often be linked with certain identifiable patterns of "temperament" in infancy. These discoveries lead one to the conclusion that the identification of children at risk is of high importance in mental health consultation to schools. Children at risk can be identified in Head Start centers, preschools, and kindergartens through careful developmental and obstetrical history-taking and even later on school entrance. Children so identified can then be "tagged" and followed carefully during their school experience.

Intervention has been proposed in a number of ways. In the Woodlawn area of Chicago, community members listed the success of their children in school as their first mental health priority. The mental health center became active in offering mental health consultation to parents, schools, and children in an effort to reduce the incidence of learning and emotional disturbances evidenced within the classroom during early grades. In a careful evaluation of these efforts, not only was learning found to improve, but fewer children were diagnosed as disturbed or disturbing by teachers (Kellam, Branch, Agrawal, & Grabill, 1972; Kellam & Shiff, 1966, 1968).

Bower (1964, 1969) has pioneered attempts to identify emotionally handicapped children early in their school experience. He demonstrated the importance of helping children utilize the stresses experienced by them in school in order to make psychological gains.

Silver and Hagin (1972), using an interdisciplinary team, examined each first-grade child in a Lower East Side New York City school. The examinations included psychiatric, neurological, perceptual, psychological, and educational evaluations, which were then used for later preventive intervention. Such an effort may not be possible on a large scale, but it shows what can be done if resources are made available.

Because of the obvious undersupply of fully trained mental health professionals to meet the overwhelming mental health needs of school children, in recent years so-called nonprofessionals, paraprofessionals, nontraditional professionals, etc. have been increasingly used to fill the gap and provide more individual attention.

Cowen and his co-workers (Cowen, Zax, & Laird, 1966) described a program in which college student volunteers were used in an afterschool recreational and educational program for maladjusted children. Evidence as to benefit has been mixed. In one study (Cowen, Zax, Izzo, & Trost, 1966) of a 2-month treatment program, no differences between treated and untreated groups were noted, whereas in a later study (Cowen, Carlisle, & Kaufman, 1969), treatment for a 5-month period was shown to be beneficial. Goodman (1972) described a program in which college students have been used as therapists for emotionally disturbed elementary school-age boys. Results of this effort are difficult to evaluate. High school students having school adjustment problems themselves have been used by McWilliams and Finkel (1973) to help children who were experiencing adjustment problems in the primary grades.

The use of the so-called housewife therapist has been described by Rioch (1967) in most kinds of settings, among them, schools. Studies of their effectiveness have indicated a high level of competence. The use of mothers in the classroom to help with disturbed children has also been well described by Cowen (1969). Often nonprofessionals, including retired persons, custodial personnel, and ex-delinquent children, have been brought into the classroom in an attempt to help the teacher with problem children.

One program of importance used paraprofessionals in the area of primary prevention. In the Rochester Primary Mental Health Project (Cowen, Dorr, Izzo, Madonia, & Trost, 1971), after massive screening of first-graders, housewife child-aids were used to work either individually or in small groups with children identified as deviant. In a fairly rigorous study of the effectiveness of this method, treated children were shown to make significant gains, and these gains were shown to endure over time (Cowen, Dorr, Trost, & Izzo, 1972). Nonprofessionals have also been used in consulting roles in such programs (Cowen, Trost, & Izzo, 1973). Cowen and Schochet (1973) have studied children who benefit more from nonprofessional intervention versus those who benefit less with a goal of more effectively distributing limited resources. Efforts have also been made to identify specific types of problem children and to provide specific types of intervention (Lorion, Cowen, & Caldwell, 1974).

Since the Supreme Court decision on school integration, activity at every level has sought both to foster and impede its accomplishment. Mental health consultants in schools have generally felt that helping teachers, pupils, parents, and principals with feelings and behaviors that have arisen as a consequence of integration was within their competence and interest. Consultation efforts to schools either integrating or integrated have spanned the spectrum of possible interventions. Examples include providing a seminar on busing (Afield, 1972), arranging "confrontation" groups to ease racial tensions (Kranz, 1971), and on-the-spot assistance during times of racial crisis (Zegans, Schwartz, & Dumas, 1969).

COMMENTS ON THE EXISTING LITERATURE IN SCHOOL CONSULTATION

In looking at the different kinds of activity that school mental health consultants have been involved in, one is struck by its variety, scope, and range. Truly, mental health consultants have done everything imaginable in school

11

settings. The most serious criticism that can be leveled is that, despite their good intentions, a heavy expenditure of time and energy, and some courage, there is relatively little conclusive evidence that these consultative efforts have benefited school-age children.

The most popular type of evaluation (when it has been attempted) has been a consumer satisfaction evaluation. This assumes that if the consultee has been satisfied, then the consultation has been effective. There has been a belief that the process of consultation itself is intrinsically beneficial, and much effort has been expended in describing how the consultant begins and maintains the consultative relationship, as though the simple continuation of the process is evidence of benefit. While continuation of the relationship is probably a necessary condition for benefit, it may not be sufficient.

It has been frequently demonstrated that the more rigorous the evaluation of change, the less conclusive is the evidence of benefit. A few careful studies (Minde, Benierakis, Sykes, & Anderson, 1972; Minde & Werry, 1969) have failed to show any evidence of change as a result of intervention.

There is difficulty in categorizing the variety of consultative efforts, since the focus often seems to be chosen more as a result of the consultant's interests, whims, or convictions than anything else. At other times, the focus has been a result of a negotiation in which the consultant's competencies and the consultee's needs were looked at in a parallel fashion; then a type of activity was settled on as the result of an observed match.

Overall conceptualizing efforts have been presented (Berlin, 1966, 1969; Caplan, 1959, 1961, 1964, 1970; Newman, 1967; Sarason et al., 1966) but seem incomplete. Often the goals of the mental health consultant or the consultation are not clearly defined. Frequently a goal as vague and grandiose as ''the reduction of the prevalence of emotional disturbances in school-age children'' has seemed to be acceptable. There have been few limitations as to what the consultant sees within his general area of competency. Consultants have attacked with equal vigor hyperactivity, child abuse, school phobia, learning disabilities, and childhood psychosis.

Application of a psychopathology model to the school setting has often been used. At other times the consultant has viewed the school in family terms. Schools have been seen as sick or emotionally unhealthy. Many attempts to reduce the incidence or prevalence of emotional disturbances in children have merely moved such traditional treatment modalities as parent therapy, child therapy, group child therapy into the school setting. The assumption has also been made that consultants can perform effectively with the tools already at their disposal. Mental health professionals have felt that for successful school consultation one needs only training in psychiatry, psychology, or social work. Experience in individual treatment of disturbed adults and children has been deemed adequate to allow one to understand the complicated social system of the school and the classroom. Specialized training in school consultation, special knowledge of the school culture and curriculum, and special understanding of cognitive and learning issues have all been underemphasized.

At times mental health professionals have sought involvement in school consultation as a way to avoid deep and lasting emotional commitments to patients and as a way to distance themselves from the everyday difficulties of clinical practice. Yet one can make the point that some professionals are reluctant, inexperienced, or untrained in helping the kinds of children and their families who present major problems in schools. Such "professionals" may distance themselves through the act of consulting, may fear to be on the firing line, or apply limited experiences with cooperative families and less disturbing children to an expanded variety of situations.

TRAINING IN MENTAL HEALTH
CONSULTATION TO SCHOOLS

Since mental health consultation to schools is a relatively new endeavor, training until recently has been somewhat unsystematic and haphazard. The school psychologist has had a long tradition of helpfulness to the classroom teacher but has in many ways been seen chiefly as a diagnostician rather than a mental health consultant.

In recent years a number of school mental health training programs have developed. La Vietes and Chess (1969) wrote about a well-conceptualized and developed training program in what they term school psychiatry. They pointed out that school psychiatry training exposes the mental health consultant to the strangeness of the school setting and the differences in orientation between clinical and educational training. The training experience described included observation of normal children in a nursery school and kindergarten, assignment in a public school for ongoing observation, diagnosis and consultation, and assignment to a special school for disturbed children. A 10-session seminar was also included.

Lipton and Gilkeson (1966) and Pavenstedt (1966) emphasized the importance of the school setting as a training ground for mental health professionals. In their view, experience in a school setting provides a mental health trainee with important knowledge regarding normal behavior in children as well as a working knowledge of the classroom and the educational system.

Skurow and Dizenhuz (1973) described a program intended to sensitize people in child psychiatry training to schools and school problems. The training covered four phases, including: (a) information-oriented didactic sessions; (b) planned classroom observations of children, teachers, and the educational process; (c) problem-focused classroom experiences; and (d) individual conferences for the purpose of integrating the previous experiences.

School consultation experiences have been introduced during the beginning year in some psychiatric residencies (Powell & Mesmer, 1973). Again, this experience was felt to be crucial to the trainees' understanding of development and was also viewed as aiding the resident in learning to work with other professional disciplines. Bernard (1964) emphasized the importance of training in school settings and described a complete 5-year training program for "community child psychiatrists" that includes many school experiences in a number of varied settings.

Several authors (Altman, 1972; Brody & Schneider, 1973) have stressed the usefulness to the would-be school consultant of a teaching experience in an actual classroom. They pointed out, as a way of learning more about the school, the usefulness of a potential consultant experiencing the frustrations and anxieties of a classroom teacher firsthand. In both studies—the first in a normal classroom and the second in a classroom for disturbed children—empathy and common respect was the outcome for both clinicians and teachers. Blom (1975) has described how experiences in school settings can be integrated into a psychiatric residency.

SUMMARY

The authors have noted the increasing emphasis on mental health consultation to schools and tried to offer reasons for this. The central importance of the educational experience in a child's life was noted and discussed, as was the frequency of emotional disorders among school-age children. The changing school culture as well as changing school philosophies and responsibilities were mentioned.

Problems of entry into the schools and the maintenance of the consultative relationship were seen as common to all types of mental health interventions. Expectations and assumptions of the mental health consultant and teacher were compared. A variety of forms of mental health intervention within schools was discussed, including: teaching behavior modification techniques, early identification of children at risk, group counseling of teachers, direct services to children and parents (both individually and in groups), and "system" consultation, as well as other methods.

Comments on the existing school consultation literature noted that consultation efforts were often characterized by unclear goals and poor evaluation of benefits derived. Training in mental health consultation to schools was discussed. School consultation experiences have been regarded as valuable training for those in the mental health professions.

References

Afield, W.E. A mental health center seminar on busing. *Hospital and Communtiy Psychiatry*, 1972, **23**, 272-276.

Altman, M. A child psychiatrist steps into the classroom. *Journal of the American Academy of Child Psychiatry*, 1972, **11**, 231-242.

Bandura, A. *Principles of behavior modification*, New York: Holt, 1969.

Barcai, A., Umbarger, C., Pierce, T.W., & Chamberlain, P. A comparison of three group approaches to underachieving children. *American Journal of Orthopsychiatry*, 1973, **43**, 133-141.

Barnes, K.E., Wootton, M., & Wood, S. The public health nurse as an effective therapist-behavior modifier of preschool play behavior. *Community Mental Health Journal*, 1972, **8**, 3-7.

Berkowitz, H. A preliminary assessment of the extent of interaction between child psychiatric clinics and public schools. *Psychology in the Schools*, 1968, **5**, 291-295.

Berlin, I.N. What help can the educator expect from the mental health specialist? *California Journal of Elementary Education*, 1962, **31**, 7-15.

Berlin, I.N. Consultation and special education. In I. Phillips (Ed.), *Prevention and treatment of mental retardation*. New York: Basic Books, 1966.

Berlin, I.N. Mental Health consultation for school social workers: A conceptual model. *Community Mental Health Journal*, 1969, **5**, 280-288.

Bernard, V.W. Roles and functions of child psychiatrists in social and community psychiatry: Implications for training. *Journal of the American Academy of Child Psychiatry*, 1964, **3**, 165-176.

Blom, D. A nurse's experience with a standby program in an elementary school. *Journal of School Health*, 1971, **41**, 249-253.

Blom, G.E. A psychoanalytic viewpoint of behavior modification. *Journal of the American Academy of Child Psychiatry*, 1972, **11**, 675-693.

Blom, G.E. The training setting with special emphasis on schools. In L. Madow & C. Malone (Eds.), *The integration of child psychiatry into the basic residency program*. Hillsdale, N.J.: Townhouse Press, 1975.

Blom, G.E. Psychoeducational school communication and consultation. Unpublished manuscript, University of Colorado Medical Center, Denver, 1975.

Bower, E.M. The modification, mediation, and utilization of stress during the school years. *American Journal of Orthopsychiatry*, 1964, **34**, 667-674.

Bower, E.M. *Early identification of emotionally handicapped children in school*. Springfield, Ill.: Charles C Thomas, 1969.

Brandon, S. *An epidemiological study of maladjustment in childhood*. Thesis for the degree of Doctor of Medicine. University of Durham, 1960.

Brody, M., & Schneider, O.B. The psychiatrist as classroom teacher: School consultation in the inner city. *Hospital and Community Psychiatry*, 1973, **24**, 248-251.

Buchmueller, A.D., & Gildea, M.C.L. A group therapy project with parents of behavior problem children in public schools. *American Journal of Psychiatry*, 1949, **106**, 46-52.

Caplan, G. *Concepts of mental health and consultation*. U.S. Department of Health, Education and Welfare, Children's Bureau, Washington, D. C., 1959.

Caplan, G. *An approach to community mental health*. New York: Grune and Stratton, 1961.

Caplan, G. *Principles of preventive psychiatry*. New York: Basic Books, 1964.

Caplan, G. *Theories of mental health consultation*. New York: Basic Books, 1970.

Chess, S. Temperament and learning ability of school children. *American Journal of Public Health*, 1968, **58**, 2231-2239.

Chess, S., Rutter, M., & Birch, H.G. Interaction of temperament and environment in the production of behavioral disturbances in children. *American Journal of Psychiatry*, 1963, **120**, 142-148.

Chess, S., Thomas, A., & Birch, H.G. Behavior problems revisited: Findings of an anterospective study. *Journal of the American Academy of Child Psychiatry*, 1967, **6**, 321-345.

Cicirelli, V.G., Evans, J.W., & Schiller, J.S. The impact of Head Start: A reply to the report analysis. *Harvard Educational Review*, 1970, **40**, 105-129.

Coleman, R.F. Seminars for teachers of adolescents. *Journal of School Health*, 1972, **42**, 345-347.

Comly, H.H., & Hadjisky, M. One clinic's response to Head Start: A program of mental health appraisals. *Journal of the American Academy of Child Psychiatry*, 1967, **6**, 398-409.

Cowen, E.L. Mothers in the classroom. *Psychology Today*, 1969, **2**, 36-39.

Cowen, E.L., Carlisle, R.L., & Kaufman, G. Evaluation of a college student volunteer program with primary grades experiencing school adjustment problems. *Psychology in the Schools*, 1969, **6**, 371-375.

Cowen, E.L., Dorr, D., Clarfield, S.P., Kreling, B., McWilliams, S.A., Pokracki, F., Pratt, D.M., Terrell, D.L., & Wilson, A. The AML: A quick screening device for early detection of school maladaptation. *American Journal of Community Psychology*, 1973, **1**, 12-35.

Cowen, E.L., Dorr, D., Izzo, L.D., Madonia, A., & Trost, M.A. The Primary Mental Health Project: A new way to conceptualize and deliver school mental health service. *Psychology in the Schools*, 1971, **8**, 216-225.

Cowen, E.L., Dorr, D., Trost, M.A., & Izzo, L.D. Follow-up study of maladapting school children seen by nonprofessionals. *Journal of Consulting and Clinical Psychology*, 1972, **39**, 235-238.

Cowen, E.L., & Schochet, B.V. Referral and outcome differences between terminating and nonterminating children seen by nonprofessionals in a school mental health project. *American Journal of Community Psychology*, 1973, **1**, 103-112.

Cowen, E.L., Trost, M.A., & Izzo, L.D. Nonprofessional human-service personnel in consulting roles. *Community Mental Health Journal*, 1973, **9**, 335-341.

Cowen, E.L., Zax, M., Izzo, L.D., & Trost, M.A. Prevention of emotional disorders in the school setting. A further investigation. *Journal of Consulting Psychology*, 1966, **30**, 381-387.

Cowen, E.L., Zax, M., & Laird, J.D. A college student volunteer program in the elementary school setting. *Community Mental Health Journal*, 1966, **2**, 319-328.

Edlund, C.V. A reinforcement approach to the elimination of a child's school phobia. *Mental Hygiene*, 1971, **55**, 433-436.

Ekanger, C.A. The model schools project. Unpublished manuscript, University of Colorado Medical Center, Denver, 1970.

Engelman, S. Relating operant techniques to programming and teaching. In R.L. Jones (Ed.), *New directions in special education*. Boston: Allyn and Bacon, 1970.

Farley, G.K. Mental health consultation with a Head Start Center. *Journal of the American Academy of Child Psychiatry*, 1971, **10**, 555-571.

Farley, G.K., Sadler, J.E., Duchesne, E., Prodoehl, M., & Weiman, E. "Standby": The application of life-space interview techniques to public school settings. *Journal of the American Academy of Child Psychiatry*, 1975, in press.

Garner, H.G. Mental health benefits of small group experiences in the affective domain. *Journal of School Health*, 1974, **44**, 314-318.

Glasser, W. *Schools without failure*. New York: Harper and Row, 1969.

Glidewell, J.C. The education institution and the health institution. In E.M. Bower & W.G. Hollister (Eds.), *Behavioral science frontiers in education*. New York: Wiley, 1967.

Goodman, G. *Companionship therapy: Studies of structured intimacy*. San Francisco: Jossey-Bass, 1972.

Graffagnino, P.N. A Head Start school in a child psychiatric clinic. *Journal of the American Academy of Child Psychiatry*, 1967, **6**, 415-425.

Gratton, L., & Pope, L. Group diagnosis and therapy for young school children. *Hospital and Community Psychiatry*, 1972, **23**, 188-190.

Graziano, A.M. (Ed.), *Behavior therapy with children*. Chicago: Aldine-Atherton, 1971.

Haring, N., & Phillips, E. *Educating emotionally disturbed children*. New York: McGraw-Hill, 1962.

Hentoff, N. *Our children are dying*. New York: Viking, 1966.

Hereford, C.F. *Changing parental attitudes through group discussion*. Austin: University of Texas, 1963.

Hewett, F.M. Educational engineering with emotionally disturbed children. In R.L. Jones (Ed.), *New directions in special education*. Boston: Allyn and Bacon, 1970.

Holt, J. *The underachieving school*. New York: Pitman, 1969.

Hotkins, A.S., Hollander, L., & Munk, B. Evaluation of psychiatric reports of Head Start programs. In J. Hellmuth (Ed.), *Disadvantaged child*. Vol. 2. New York: Brunner-Mazel, 1968.

Kahn, J., Buchmueller, A.D., & Gildea, M.C.L. Group therapy for parents of behavior problems children in public schools. Failure of the method in a Negro school. *American Journal of Psychiatry*, 1951, **108**, 351-357.

Kellam, S.G., Branch, J.D., Agrawal, K.C., & Grabill, M.E. Woodlawn Mental Health Center: An evolving strategy for planning in community mental health. In S.E. Golann & C. Eisdorfer (Eds.), *Handbook of community mental health*. New York: Appleton-Century-Crofts, 1972.

Kellam, S.G., & Schiff, S.K. The Woodlawn Mental Health Center. *Social Service Review*, 1966, **40**, 255-263.

Kellam, S.G., & Schiff, S.K. Adaptation and mental illness in the first-grade classrooms of an urban community. In Psychiatric Research Report No. 21: *Poverty and mental health*. Washington, D.C.: American Psychiatric Association, 1967.

Kellam, S.G., & Schiff, S.K. An urban community mental health center. In L.S. Duhl & R.L. Leopold (Eds.), *Mental health and urban social policy*. San Francisco: Jossey-Bass, 1968.

Klebanoff, L.B., & Bindman, A.J. The organization and development of a community mental health program for children. *American Journal of Orthopsychiatry*, 1962, **32**, 119-132.

Knobloch, H. Environmental factors affecting human development, before and after birth. *Pediatrics*, 1960, **26**, 210-218.

Kozol, J. *Death at an early age*. Boston: Houghton Mifflin, 1967.

Kozol, J. *Free schools*. Boston: Houghton Mifflin, 1972.

Kranz, P.L. A racial confrontation group implemented within a high school. *High School Journal*, 1971, **55**, 112-119.

Krasner, L., & Krasner, M. Token economies and other planned environments. In C.E. Thoresen (Ed.), *Behavior modification in education: The seventy-second yearbook of the National Society for the Study of Education*. Chicago: University of Chicago Press, 1973.

Lapouse, R., & Monk, M. An epidemiological study of behavior characteristics in children. *American Journal of Public Health*, 1958, **48**, 1134-1144.

La Vietes, R.L. & Chess, S. A training program in school psychiatry. *Journal of the American Academy of Child Psychiatry*, 1969, **8**, 84-96.

Levine, M., & Graziano, A.M. Intervention programs in elementary schools. In S.E. Golann & C. Eisdorfer (Eds.), *Handbook of community mental health*. New York: Appleton-Century-Crofts, 1972.

Lipton, E.L., & Gilkeson, E.C. Utilizing a school for children to supplement the training of medical personnel. *Journal of the American Academy of Child Psychiatry*, 1966, **5**, 393-430.

Lorion, R.P., Cowen, E.L., & Caldwell, R.A. Problem types of children referred to a school-based mental health program: Identification and outcome. *Journal of Consulting and Clinical Psychology*, 1974, **42**, 491-496.

McWilliams, S.A., & Finkel, N.J. High school students as mental health aides in the elementary setting. *Journal of Consulting and Clinical Psychology*, 1973, **40**, 39-42.

Minde, K.K., Benierakis, C.E., Sykes, E., & Anderson, R.A. The response of school children in an upper-middle-class area to intensive psychiatric counseling of their teachers: A controlled evaluation. *Journal of Special Education*, 1972, **6**, 267-277.

Minde, K.K., & Werry, J.S. Intensive psychiatric teacher counselling in a low socioeconomic area: A controlled evaluation. *American Journal of Orthopsychiatry*, 1969, **39**, 595-608.

Moore, T. Difficulties of the ordinary child in adjusting to primary school. *Journal of Child Psychology and Psychiatry*, 1966, **7**, 17-38.

Newman, R.G. *Psychological consultation in the schools*. New York: Basic Books, 1967.

Passamanick, B., & Knoblock, H. Retrospective studies on the epidemiology of reproductive casualty: Old and new. *Merrill-Palmer Quarterly of Behavior and Development*, 1966, **12**, 7-26.

Patterson, G.R., Cobb, J.A., & Ray, R.S. Direct intervention in the classroom: A set of procedures for the aggressive child. In F.W. Clark, D.R. Evans, & L.A. Hamerlynck (Eds.), *Implementing behavioral programs for schools and clinics*. Champaign, Ill.: Research Press, 1972.

Pavenstedt, E. The nursery school, day care centers, and developmental studies. *Journal of the American Academy of Child Psychiatry*, 1966, **5**, 349-359.

Powell, G., & Mesmer, R. School consultation experience in a residency program. *Hospital and Community Psychiatry*, 1973, **24**, 170-171.

Redl, F., Bernstein, M., Kitchener, H., Long, N.J., Morse, W.B., & Newman, R.G. *The school-centered life space interview*. Washington, D.C.: Washington School of Psychiatry, 1963.

Rioch, M.J. Pilot projects in training mental health counselors. In E.L. Cowen, E.A. Gardner, & M. Zax (Eds.), *Emergent approaches to mental health problems*. New York: Appleton-Century-Crofts, 1967.

Rosenblum, G. A community mental health center's interaction with the Project Head Start program. *Journal of the American Academy of Child Psychiatry*, 1967, **6**, 410-414.

Rowitch, J. Group consultation with school personnel. *Hospital and Community Psychiatry*, 1968, **19**, 261-266.

Rutter, M., & Graham, P. Psychiatric disorders in 10 and 11 year-old children. *Proceedings of the Royal Society for Medicine*, 1965, **59**, 382-387.

Ryle, A., Pond, D., & Hamilton, M. The prevalence and patterns of psychologic disturbance in children of primary age. *Journal of Child Psychology and Psychiatry*, 1965, **6**, 101-113.

Sadler, J., & Blom, G.E. "Standby": A clinical research study of child deviant behavior in a psychoeducational setting. *Journal of Special Education*, 1970, **4**, 89-103.

Sarason, S.B. *The culture of the school and the problem of change*. Boston: Allyn & Bacon, 1971.

Sarason, S.B. *The creation of settings and the future of societies*. San Francisco: Jossey-Bass, 1972.

Sarason, S.B. *The psychological sense of community*. San Francisco: Jossey-Bass, 1974.

Sarason, S.B., Levine, M., Goldenberg, I.I., Cherlin, D.L., & Bennett, E.M. *Psychology in community settings*. New York: Wiley, 1966.

Schiff, S.K., & Kellam, S.G. A community wide mental health program of prevention and early treatment in first grade. In M. Greenblatt, P.E. Emery, & B.C. Glueck, Jr. (Eds.), *Poverty and mental health*. Washington, D.C.: American Psychiatric Association, 1967.

Shaw, R., Eagle, C.J., & Goldberg, F.H. A retrospective look at the experiences of a community child guidance center with Project Head Start. In J. Hellmuth (Ed.), *Disadvantaged child*. Vol. 2. New York: Brunner/Mazel, 1968.

Silver, A.A., & Hagin, R.A. Profile of a first grade: A basis for preventive psychiatry. *Journal of the American Academy of Child Psychiatry*, 1972, **11**, 645-674.

Skurow, N.R., & Dizenhuz, I.M. Teaching about teaching. *Journal of the American Academy of Child Psychiatry*, 1973, **12**, 354-365.

Stennet, R.G. Emotional handicap in the elementary years: Phase or disease. *American Journal of Orthopsychiatry*, 1966, **36**, 444-449.

Tenenbaum, S. School grades and group therapy. *Mental Hygiene*, 1970, **54**, 525-529.

Weiman, E.A. *Inservice training in classroom management for teachers and coordinators*. Denver: University of Colorado Medical Center Printing Services, 1969.

Wolff, S. Behavioral characteristics of primary school children referred to a psychiatric department. *British Journal of Psychiatry*, 1967, **113**, 885-893.

Zegans, L.S., Schwartz, M.S., & Dumas, R. A mental health center's response to racial crisis in an urban high school. *Psychiatry*, 1969, **32**, 252-264.

A REVIEW OF EDUCATION
OF THE DEAF

Donald F. Moores
University of Minnesota

Development of effective educational programs for the deaf has been hampered historically by a number of factors. Among the major obstacles to progress: (*a*) Deafness is a low-incidence condition, and (*b*) deafness imposes such severe communication limitations that specially trained personnel are required to deal with the problem. Deaf children represent the one group incapable of communicating effectively through the auditory-vocal channel, the primary means of instruction in the American educational system. Given the inflexibility of the educational establishment, only the exceptionally able (in terms of communication skills) deaf child is educated within the context of the neighborhood school. Short of a revolution in the value systems underlying education in general, the majority of deaf children will—and should—continue to be educated in special classes, day schools, and residential schools.

A third major obstacle to progress cannot be ignored. For a variety of reasons—mainly deriving from the fact that teaching deaf children is often a laborious, tedious, frustrating process—educators of the deaf have had a disturbing tendency to become embroiled in bitter controversies. The energies of the leading minds in the field have frequently been dissipated by their involvement in controversies made incapable of resolution because they have been presented in dichotomous, either-or terms. Thus, disagreement over issues such as "natural" versus "structured" language instruction, "mainstreaming" versus "segration," and early versus later reading have their roots in the 19th century and show no indication of early resolution. The most widely known schism among educators of the deaf, that involing the so-called oral-manual methods war, may be traced back even further, to the 18th century.

Given the above situation, it would be surprising to find that educational research has had any major impact upon education of the deaf. Although there have been some promising recent developments, the role of educational research as an agent of change has been, over the years, minimal in the area of deafness. In discussing the application of research findings to educational practice, one notes the lack of consistent agreement between those individuals conducting research and those educating students. Research and education in fact have usually been perceived as independent activities with little or no need of cross-fertilization. It is obvious that while the research-to-application paradigm must be considered an ideal to be pursued, it does not reflect the reality of the present.

Writing in *The First Review of Special Education,* Lilly (1973, p. 203) stated that the expectation of a linear relationship between educational research and changes in educational practice is not based in reality. He argued that the change process in education is politically based, as opposed to research-based, and draws on research findings in a random fashion at best.

Although Lilly was writing of the relationship of research to education in general, his remarks have special relevance to the present chapter. There is no area of education with a greater disjunction between research and application than that of deafness. In a review of trends of research in special education in the United States, Hurder (1973) reported that among all categories of handicaps funded by the Bureau of Education for the Handicapped over a 5-year period, hearing impairment was the only handicap in which more grants were made for demonstration projects than for research projects—a fact which suggested that service-oriented concerns exceed knowledge-oriented interests in this field.

> If this is true, it presents an unusual paradox when examined in the perspective of the potential contribution of our understanding of human behavior inherent in the resolution of such issues as the relationship of oral/aural language to cognitive development. Were a culture discovered in which all human communication took place in the complete absence of oral-aural inputs and outputs, it would surely arouse great interest within the scientific community . . . . Such individuals are interspersed throughout all oral/aural cultures; yet they seemingly provoke relatively little interest among those who seek knowledge of human cognitive development and function. (p. 194)

The present chapter explores educational implications of the effects of deafness on the individual, summarizes relevant research, and suggests areas of investigation which, in the author's opinion, are most in need of study. The reader may consider the research under review as of two types. The first is that conducted by researchers who investigate the functioning of deaf individuals so as to understand universal principles of behavior. Within this framework, deafness is essentially viewed as an "experiment of nature." The investigations of Furth (1966) on the cognitive development of deaf individuals and of Bellugi (1972) on the *American Sign Language* are the most widely known examples of this type. The second type of research has a more specific orientation to the practical problems of deafness and seeks to incorporate psychological and linguistic advances in educational programs for the deaf. Examples of this approach are the computer-assisted instruction language and math programs for the deaf developed by Suppes and associates (Charrow, 1974; Fletcher & Beard, 1973; Suppes, Fletcher, & Zanotti, 1973) and the evaluation of preschool programs for the deaf conducted by Moores and associates (Moores & McIntyre, 1971; Moores, McIntyre, & Weiss, 1972; Moores, Weiss, & Goodwin, 1973; Moores, Weiss, & Goodwin, 1974).

The author has not attempted to duplicate recent reviews or summaries treating in detail specific facets of educating the deaf. For extensive background information the reader should refer directly to such reviews concerned with educational research on manual communication (Moores, 1971, 1974; Rodda, 1972), early childhood education (Moores, 1975, in press), and psycholinguistics and deafness (Bonvillian & Charrow, 1972; O'Rourke, 1973).

EDUCATIONAL PROGRAMS

In the United States approximately 50,000 children with severe hearing loss receive some type of special educational service. The figure is consistent with estimates placing the incidence of deafness in the school-age population at 7-10 per 10,000 (Carhart, 1969). These numbers are affected by cyclical epidemics, such as the rubella epidemic which swept Western Europe and the United States from 1963 to 1965 and resulted in two to four times the numbers of deaf children that would normally be expected.

While the deaf are readily identified, the hard of hearing often are not. To estimate the number of school-age hard-of-hearing children in the United States, those whose hearing is mildly or moderately affected, is almost impossible. No accurate data exist and there are very few programs specifically designed for them. A conservative estimate of 1% of the school-age population as being hard of hearing to various degrees would place the number at approximately 500,000 children. These children typically are educated in programs for the normally hearing. They may sometimes receive special help from professional resource personnel, but until recently, most educators were unaware of their special problems. Research on this type of child is quite limited.

The annual Directory of Services for the Deaf in the United States (Craig & Craig, 1974), published by the *American Annals of the Deaf,* lists a total of 51,837 children in preschool, elementary and secondary schools, and classes for the deaf as of October 1, 1973. Program and student data are presented in Table 1. Males outnumber females 28,007 to 23,830 a 54 to 46% ratio which, according to enrollment data in previous issues of the Directory of Services, has remained relatively stable since the beginning of the 20th century.

TABLE 1
SUMMARY OF SCHOOLS AND CLASSES FOR THE DEAF IN THE UNITED STATES
OCTOBER 1973

Schools and classes	Program data				Student data					
Category	Number	Pre-schools	Accredited high schools	Multi-handicapped programs	Total enrollment	Male	Female	Residential	Day	Multi-handicapped
Public residential schools	63	40	35	37	19,420	10,775	8,645	14,900	4,500	3,609
Private residential schools	12	9	2	0	1,387	753	634	924	463	69
Public day schools	65	49	14	29	6,304	3,392	2,912	0	6,304	1,801
Private day schools	22	20	0	5	1,139	611	528	34	1,105	276
Public day classes	525	304	70	60	20,265	10,706	9,559	215	20,050	2,849
Private day classes	61	52	3	1	1,025	534	491	9	1,016	96
Multi-handicapped only	48	28	3	0	1,160	627	533	156	1,004	895
Specific handicapped facilities	31	7	1	0	1,137	609	528	1,018	119	1,137
Totals	827	509	128	132	51,837	28,007	23,830	17,276	34,561	10,732

Adapted from W. Craig and T. Craig (Eds.), Directory of Services for the Deaf, *American Annals of the Deaf*, 1974, 119, p. 159.

The number of children in programs for the deaf has increased significantly, more so than would be predicted on the basis of school-age population. For example, in 1961 a total of 28,529 children were enrolled in programs for the deaf, representing an increase from 1961 to 1973 of 23,308 students or 82% over a 12-year period. The reasons for the rising enrollment figures must remain partly conjecture. However, it is safe to assume that one reason for the increase is the recent presence in programs of large numbers of children who became deaf as a result of the rubella epidemic of the early 1960s. Hopefully the nation will never face such a large-scale epidemic again.

On the positive side there have been increasing efforts to extend services to hearing handicapped children across a broader scale. These include: (a) establishment of preschool programs under public school auspices; (b) provision of nursery school and home training services in many large school programs from the time a child has been diagnosed as deaf; (c) acceptance of responsibility for education and training of multiply handicapped children, many of whom previously had been neglected; (d) the beginnings of a commitment to provide equal educational opportunity to deaf children from minority groups; and (e) the provision of supportive services on a part-time basis to children with less severe hearing losses in integrated settings.

Programmatic provisions

Examination of Table 1 reveals that public school day classes represent the largest single program category, serving 20,265 children, approximately 40% of the total. The second biggest grouping is that of the 63 public residential schools, which enrolled 19,420 students. Counting the 1,387 children in 12 private schools, a total of 20,807 or 40% of the deaf children receiving services were being educated in residential schools. However, of this number, 4,963 or approximately 25% were day students. A complete breakdown of figures reveals that 34,561 students, representing 67% of the total, were day students. The majority of residential schools are supported by the various states. Most day programs are run by local public school systems which receive state aid. Both day and residential programs are eligible for various types of federal government funding. The trend toward public day classes and the increasing tendency toward greater numbers of day pupils in residential schools have been continuing since World War II.

Multiply handicapped deaf children

Of the 51,837 students enrolled, 10,732 or 21% have been categorized as multiply handicapped (Table 2), according to the 1974 Directory of Services for the Deaf (Craig & Craig, p. 159). The figures, of course, do not necessarily reflect the number of children requiring services but rather those identified as requiring or receiving services. There is no way of knowing how many unidentified children there are.

Changing populations

The characteristics of children served by classes for the deaf appear to be changing. In the past, large numbers of children were adventitiously deaf. For example, one study of graduates of Gallaudet College who had gone on to receive postbaccalaureate training in colleges and universities for the hearing reported that 64% of its sample became deaf after age 3 (Quigley, Jenne, & Phillips, 1969). Vernon (1969) has reported the effects of advances in medicine in the area of the hearing impaired. Twenty years ago a typical hearing-impaired child with an etiology of meningitis might have lost his hearing around the age of 4 or later. Most younger children with meningitis would have died. The probability of additional handicaps for a child who becomes deaf after the age of 4 is small, perhaps including no more than a somewhat impaired sense of balance. He also has some base of English on which to build. This means that the deaf child of earlier generations was usually easier to manage and to instruct.

Given improved medical treatment, the typical hearing-impaired child in a program today has lost his hearing before verbal functioning was adequately developed, i.e., before the age of 3. (Older children who have had their ear disorders treated with antimicrobiotics may presumably be expected to recover with no lasting aftereffects.) The preverbal deaf child, who might have died before the era of antibiotics, is now being saved and placed in a program for the deaf. His educational prognosis, in contrast to the postverbal meningitic one's, is very limited because he lacks an original language base and because the sequalae of his illness frequently involve other severe handicaps in addition to his deafness.

Postsecondary programs

Gallaudet College in Washington, D.C., the only college for the deaf in the world, has been in existence since 1864 and offers a liberal arts education to its students. The college is supported by the federal government, its enrollment is approximately 1,000, and deaf students from many parts of the world attend. It has a Graduate Department offering degrees in Education of the Deaf, Audiology, and Counseling and Guidance. Both deaf and hearing students are eligible for the graduate programs.

In 1968 the National Technical Institute for the Deaf was established in affiliation with the Rochester (New York) Institute of Technology. Projections call for a total of 600 deaf students to be enrolled in advanced vocational programs at any one time. In addition to the National Technical Institute for the Deaf, three regional vocational-technical programs for the deaf have been

TABLE 2
MULTIHANDICAPPED DEAF CHILDREN
ENROLLED IN PROGRAMS:
OCTOBER 1973

Category	Number
Deaf blind	1,068
Deaf mentally retarded	3,175
Deaf aphasic	796
Deaf and all other handicaps	5,693
Total deaf multiply handicapped	10,732

established with federal support as research and demonstration projects within the framework of already existing programs for students with normal hearing. They are based in St. Paul, New Orleans, and Seattle.

In total, Stuckless and Delgado (1973) identified 27 postsecondary programs for the deaf. Most of these programs have been established since 1969, following federal mandates for states to provide vocational training to handicapped individuals.

LANGUAGE AND DEAFNESS

The work of the linguist Noam Chomsky (1957, 1965) and his systematic presentation of a model of generative-transformational grammar has had a tremendous impact on linguists and psychologists. It has caused linguists to view grammar from a different perspective and to approach it as a potentially infinite, open-ended system. It has caused psychologists, particularly those of a behavioristic background, to reassess their positions in regard to species specificity, biological predisposition, and the relationship of reinforcement to learning (Osgood, 1968). Chomsky's work has been the basis for an explosion of original research into childhood language acquisition, among the most notable of which has been the work of Berko (1958), Brown and Bellugi (1964), Lenneberg (1967a), McNeill (1966a), Menyuk (1968) and Slobin (1966). Two of these investigators (McNeill, 1966b; Lenneberg, 1967b) have addressed themselves specifically to deafness and language.

Chomsky's work also was the impetus for an explosion of research activities which has gone far beyond his original parameters. The most important example of this has been the investigation of the semantic bases of language acquisition and functioning, such as that undertaken by Antonucci and Parisi (1973), McNamara (1972), and Schlesinger (1974). Although Chomsky has recently (1972) minimized differences between transformational grammar and "generative semantics," the

25

above-named individuals unquestionably have devoted far more attention to cognitive and semantic aspects of language than has Chomsky.

There is scant evidence, however, that transformational grammar—by itself or complemented by generative semantics—can contribute mightily to solving the problems of deafness. There is little doubt that children have innate propensities toward the learning of language and that the child is an active agent in the learning process, rather than some passive organism to be shaped completely by reinforcement contingencies. However, it hardly benefits people trying to educate deaf children to tell them that the environment merely triggers the language acquisition process. The teacher of the deaf is painfully aware of the large numbers of nonverbal deaf children for whom the trigger has not been found. Faced with this dilemma, educators of the deaf are constantly reminded of the importance of the environment and the need for a continued search for more effective ways of altering it to meet the needs of their pupils.

The majority of studies concerned with assessment of the deaf's language proficiency have concentrated on written compositions in expressive language and on performance on standardized reading tests in the receptive sphere. Comparisons of the written language of deaf and hearing children clearly indicate that the deaf are significantly inferior to their hearing peers in all aspects of English language development and facility.

Studies of expressive language

Heider and Heider (1940) compared the written language of deaf children at three residential schools (ages 11 to 17) to that of hearing students at two public schools (ages 8 to 14). A traditional grammatical analysis of 1,118 compositions describing a short motion picture shown to the subjects found that the deaf children exhibited simple, rigid, and immature patterns of written behavior. The investigators stated that the differences between the deaf and hearing were of such a nature as to prevent their description in completely quantitative terms.

Thompson (1936) analyzed 16,000 written compositions by 800 students attending 10 schools for the deaf in the United States and found an average of 104 mistakes per 1,000 words. Birch and Stuckless (1963) in an investigation of the written language of deaf children, employing basically the same techniques, reported a total of 5,044 grammatical errors from a corpus of 50,050 words, or slightly more than 100 errors per 1,000 words, a result in close agreement with the findings of Thompson.

Myklebust (1964) adapted Thompson's classifications to develop a Syntax Score to measure written language. Its categories included Word Order, Additions, Substitutions, Omissions, Punctuation, and Carrier Phrases. Myklebust compared deaf and hearing children from the ages of 7 to 17 and found significant differences at every level in favor of the hearing. He reported a mean score for the 17-year-old deaf children tested, 86.2% of which approximated the score of 86.6 achieved by the average 7-year-old hearing child. Myklebust also noted that for hearing children significant differences in achievement appeared between the 7- and 9-, and the 9- and 11-year-old levels, but these were not apparent at older age levels. From this he concluded that the structure of written language is rapidly developed because it is based upon previously developed structures in spoken language.

Wells (1942), using written samples of deaf and hearing elementary school-age subjects and performance on a completion test, attempted to trace differences in growth of abstract language forms. He concluded that the older deaf function in abstract language on a level similar to that of younger hearing children; they displayed comprehension equal to that of their hearing peers for concrete words but were retarded from 4 to 5 years in understanding abstract terms. They commonly omitted conjunctions and adverbs which resulted in the type of expression observed in the verbal utterances of young children and characterized by Brown and Fraser (1963) as "telegraphic." It should be noted, however, that the telegraphic nature of the utterances of young hearing children differs from the written expression of deaf children. While in both cases messages are shortened and words omitted, the patterns of word combinations used and the types of omissions that result vary between the two groups.

Simmons (1959) used a type-token ratio (TTR) to determine the relative flexibility or rigidity of deaf and hearing subjects in word usage. Studied were five written compositions and one spoken composition, elicited by picture sequences. The subjects were 54 students at the Central Institute for the Deaf and 112 hearing students attending public schools in the St. Louis area. The TTR, a measure of vocabulary diversity, was computed by dividing the number of different words (types) in a language sample by the total number of words (tokens). Results of Simmon's analysis emphasized the redundancy of deaf children's language. Commenting on their rigid and stereotyped expression, as contrasted to the rich language of hearing children, the investigator used the following example (p. 35) to illustrate how even relatively correct grammatical sentences of the deaf are frequently stilted and repetitive:

> A girl threw a ball to a boy. The boy bat a ball. The boy bat the ball to the window and the window was broken. The mother heard the boy broke the window. The mother saw a broke the window. She went to see the ball game.

Simmons commented that deaf children repeatedly referred to the child in a picture as a *boy*, while the hearing children would call him the *kid, boy, urchin, friend, young man, youngster, him, Tom,* etc. She also reported a lower TTR for Class II words for the deaf, owing to their tendency to repeat four verbs—*have, be, go,* and *feel.* A glance at the example presented above also illustrates the relatively low TTR found in the deaf's use of determiners. Although, like the

27

deaf, hearing children frequently used *a, an,* and *the,* they also employed other definite articles such as *these, that,* and *those,* and possessives.

Tervoort (Tervoort & Verbeck, 1967) investigated the ingroup communication of students ranging from 7 to 17 over a 6-year period in four schools for the deaf: two in the United States, one in Belgium, and one in the Netherlands. He filmed the conversations of pairs of students who were informally interacting. Tervoort reported that the deaf children conversed among themselves in a relaxed fluent manner, using their hands regularly, sometimes with and sometimes without speech. Their communication with normally hearing individuals, however, frequently showed hesitance, awkwardness, and embarrassment. Tervoort also studied the relationship between what he perceived as two separate systems and concluded that the ''private'' system is predominantly employed by younger deaf children and is the main reason for the stereotyped mistakes which characterize their attempts to use the language of adult society. The adult system influences the private even at an early age to the extent that normal vocabulary and structure penetrate into private communication.

Tervoort reported a consistent growth in grammatically correct usage by the deaf through the elementary years. American students continued to improve through adolescence in contrast to the students in the Benelux schools. American students showed the influence of the esoteric (or adult) system by their more efficient use of word order, auxiliary verbs, conjunctions and other function words, especially prepositions. Only 2% of the utterances of the American children consisted of imitative gesture sentences as compared to the 10% of the European total.

At all ages the most common mode of expression of the deaf in Tervoort's investigation was the use of signs, with finger spelling increasing with age. Speech, when used, was most frequently combined with signs and spelling. At first these results seem contradictory. The subjects continued to use esoteric means (signs and spelling) but used them increasingly within the context of an esoteric grammatical (English or Dutch) structure. Tervoort resolved the paradox to his own satisfaction by treating speech and language as functionally separate. In support of his thesis, he claimed that data showed no consistent relationship between speech and language, i.e., some children showed good articulation and poor grammatical skills, while others had poor articulation but adequate grammatical abilities. All possible combinations emerged.

Two explanations for the superiority of the American deaf students in language, but not necessarily speech, were advanced by Tervoort. He first suggested that the influence of a structured approach to teaching language is evident in the sentences of the American students and appears to be more beneficial to the development of grammar than the ''natural language'' approach in the European schools. Another possible factor, which raises the question of the effect of manual communication on the development of speech and language skills, was the exposure of deaf American students to deaf adults proficient in English. Tervoort presented his findings as a challenge to exclusively oral methods of instruction.

> The sign language of the American adult deaf is a source from above, strongly influencing the interchange of the deaf teenager, on campus too, and on the contrary the fact that no such source from above is available for their mates across the ocean with whom they are matched. Once the esotericity of at least part of the subjects' private communication is established as a fact (whether this is a fact that should have been prevented, should be corrected, or even denied, is not the issue here), it is evident that normal need for communication finds a better outlet in an adult arbitrary system, than in uncontrolled and half-grown symbolic behavior not fed from above. In educational terms: it seems clear that the choice has to be: either well controlled, monitored signing tending towards an adult level, semantically and syntactically, or no signing whatsoever; but no signing that is uncontrolled and left to find its own ways. ([*sic*], p. 148)

Studies of receptive language abilities of deaf students

Johnson (1948) reported on the ability of 253 children in the Acoustic (hard of hearing), Oral, and Manual departments of the Illinois School for the Deaf to understand various methods of communication. All children were given tests of reading, speech-hearing ability, speech-reading ability, hearing plus speech reading, finger spelling only, and signs plus finger spelling. The results favored the Acoustic group. For the three groups as a whole reasonable success was only achieved with finger spelling, (with a mean score of 74%) and reading (with a mean of 72%). Johnson recommended that finger spelling be added to the instructional method of the Oral group and that it be emphasized even more, in relation to signs, with the Manual group. Her findings were similar to those of Montgomery (1966) who studied 59 prelingually deaf Scottish students and reported that a mere 7% could produce fairly fluent intelligible speech and that only 25% could follow a normal conversation with a moderate degree of adequacy by speech reading. Even though no form of manual communication was officially allowed in the classrooms Montgomery studied, she found that 71% of the students could communicate fluently by means of the finger alphabet.

Klopping (1972) studied the language understanding of adolescent deaf students in a residential school under three conditions: (*a*) speech reading with voice, (*b*) finger spelling simultaneous with speech reading with voice (the Rochester Method), and (*c*) signs and finger spelling simultaneous with speech reading with voice (Total Communication). Consistent with Johnson's findings, he reported that scores under the Rochester Method were superior to speech reading with voice. However, he found Total Communication to be superior to the Rochester Method, a finding in opposition to Johnson's.

Moores and associates (Moores et al., 1972, 1973, 1974) investigated the relative efficiency of receiving information in young deaf children. Five different modes were studied: (a) sound alone, (b) sound plus speech reading, (c) sound and speech reading plus finger spelling, (d) sound and speech reading plus signs, and (e) the printed word. Excluding scores for the printed word, the same order of difficulty was obtained for each of the 3 years (1972-74) of the investigation; sound and speech reading plus signs were most efficient, followed by sounds and speech reading plus finger spelling, and then sound plus speech reading, and sound alone. Reception of the printed word showed great improvement from 1972, when it was superior only to sound alone, to 1974, when it ranked second only to sound and speech reading plus signs. The results essentially support Klopping's findings with older children. They are presented, in detail, in the section on preschool programs.

Results of investigations into performance on standardized tests of reading achievement suggest that deaf children are also retarded in the ability to decode linguistic signs. Wrightstone, Aronow, and Moskowitz (1963) tested 5,307 deaf students in the United States and Canada between the ages of 10-6 and 16-6 on the Metropolitan Achievement Test, Elementary Level, in Reading and found that less than 10% could read on a fourth-grade level. They estimated that 54% of all eligible children with performance IQs of 75 or above were tested. In emphasizing the linguistic deficiencies of the deaf, Furth (1966, p. 54) noted that, in comparison with hearing norms, the data published by Wrightstone et al. indicated that the mean reading score of the deaf rose between the ages of 11 and 16 from a grade equivalent of 2.6 to 3.4, i.e., there was less than 1 year of improvement in 5 years of schooling.

Myklebust (1964), using the Columbia Vocabulary Test as a measuring instrument, compared the reading vocabulary of deaf and hearing children at four age levels. The average score of 11.32 for the deaf students at age 15 was inferior not only to the score of their hearing contemporaries but also to the average score of 21.37 made by the 9-year-old hearing group. A point of interest is the large increase in mean scores achieved by the hearing subjects at each successive age level. In contrast, improvement in scores for the deaf appears to taper off between the ages of 13 and 15. Thus it appears that hearing children are consistently consolidating and increasing their relative superiority in reading vocabulary—and the deaf are not. In a similar vein, Goetzinger and Rousey (1959), in a study of 101 students at a residential school for the deaf, concluded that deaf children of average mentality tend to reach a plateau between the ages of 14 and 21 at grade 5 in Vocabulary and Paragraph Meaning as measured by the Stanford Achievement Test. And Magner (1964) reported that the 11 members of the graduating class of the Clarke School, a private residential school for the deaf, achieved reading scores at the sixth-grade level on the Stanford Achievement Test.

Pugh (1946) established reading norms for the deaf at different age levels on the Iowa Silent Reading Test based on the performance of students at 54 day and residential schools for the deaf. In her standardization, no group scored above seventh-grade level. She found that improvement in reading achievement scores was slight from the 7th to 13th year of schooling and that during this period the gap between the hearing and deaf is widened. Her work is thus in agreement with the previously mentioned studies of Goetzinger and Rousey, Myklebust, and Wrightstone et al.

Some justifiable criticism has been leveled at the use of reading achievement test scores as a measure of linguistic proficiency for deaf students. Cooper and Rosenstein (1966) have pointed out that a person may be illiterate and unable to respond to the demands of a reading test, which measures skills commonly acquired in the educational process, and yet possess a high degree of linguistic competence. This is usually the case with normally hearing children who, while typically entering school without the skills necessary for reading proficiency, nevertheless possess relatively sophisticated morphological and syntactical abilities.

To expand on this theme, the difficulty of interpreting a reading achievement score is compounded in the case of a deaf child. The tests have been standardized for hearing subjects and assume a basic competence in English. The normally hearing child already has at his disposal predictive integrations by which he is automatically capable of handling the structure of his language. Even by the age of 6 he has mastered the basic foundations of morphology. For him, performance on a standardized reading test is less an indication of linguistic proficiency, which has been established prior to the initiation of instruction in reading, than it is a measure of skills necessary for the reading process. The deaf child does not have comparable English skills built up as a function of the redundancy, frequency, and contiguity of auditory input variables. He has not internalized the structure of his language. Thus, given a relatively low score in reading achievement for a deaf child, it is difficult to ascertain the extent to which the basic weakness may be attributed to inadequate English facility or to poor development of skills basic to reading proficiency. With deaf subjects, mastery of the structure of language cannot be assumed.

There is another issue of importance in testing reading skills. Performance scores of deaf children on standardized tests of reading, despite their relative inferiority to scores for the hearing, may give a spuriously inflated estimate of their English language capabilities. Standardized reading tests require a multiple choice response; the student is instructed to select the most appropriate of four or five alternatives. His range of choices typically falls within one of the five general grammatical classes, i.e., nouns, verbs, adjectives, adverbs, or function words, and thus limits the selection procedure to a grammatically correct subset. Such a procedure, which entails selection from a set of grammatically correct words, fails to account for grammatical insufficiencies and thus might artificially raise estimates of reading ability for many deaf children. In relation to this, Fusfeld (1955) found a discrepancy between apparent command of language as measured by the Stanford Achievement Test, which reported median achievement scores of Grade 6 for Vocabulary and Grade 8 for Paragraph Meaning, and written compositions of 18- and 19-year-old deaf students entering the preparatory class at Gallaudet College. In spite of the relatively high reading achievement scores of this group, Fusfeld stated (p. 70) that the written compositions submitted by the students represented a "tangled web type of expression in which words occur in profusion but do not align themselves in orderly array."

Moores (1970b) investigated the sensitivity of Cloze procedures in differentiating between deaf and hearing students matched on reading achievement scores. The experimental group consisted of 37 students with an average age of 16 years-9 months and mean grade reading achievement of 4.77 on the Metropolitan Achievement Test. They were matched with 37 fourth-grade hearing students with an average of 9 years-10 months and a mean grade reading achievement of 4.84. Three passages of 250 words were chosen from fourth-, sixth-, and eighth-grade textbooks, with every fifth word deleted. Subjects were instructed to fill in the blanks with the most appropriate words. Responses were scored for each passage for (a) verbatim reproduction—replacing the exact word deleted from the text; (b) form class reproduction—supplying a word of the same grammatical class as the original word; and (c) verbatim-given-form class reproduction—the percentage of correct verbatim responses given correct form class responses.

Results showed the hearing group to be superior on all measures. The inferiority of the deaf on verbatim scores supported the argument that standardized reading scores overestimate the English language ability of the deaf. The form class scores suggest that at least part of the inferiority may be explained by inadequately developed English grammatical structures. By scoring subjects on the basis of verbatim given form class scores, it was possible to compare the vocabulary level of the groups while holding grammatical proficiency constant. The lower performance of the deaf group on this measure indicated that, in addition to poorly developed English grammatical skills, the deaf are further handicapped by redundant stereotyped modes of expression and limited vocabulary.

Tervoort (1970) investigated the ability of deaf Dutch children, ages 10 to 18, to understand passive sentences. On a task in which two hearing 6-year-olds and two hearing 12-year-olds obtained perfect scores, deaf children under CA 13 scored 27.5% correct (chance was 20.0%) and those over 13 scored 74% correct. The higher scores for the older children to a large extent reflected more efficient processing of nonreversible than reversible passives[1] as well as more sophisticated grammatical performance. In results consistent with those reported for deaf students taught in English, Tervoort reported that if the grammatical subject at the beginning of a sentence was the acted-upon object, the sentences were refused or acted upon randomly. He concluded that the simple active is mastered first by deaf students and used almost exclusively thereafter.

METHODS OF INSTRUCTION

The methods controversy

The methods controversy, which has been raging for over 200 years, perhaps has accounted for more confusion than any other question concerned with the hearing impaired. The issues have been distorted beyond recognition, and it is not surprising that these are misunderstood by professionals on the periphery. It is inaccurate to speak of an Oral-Manual controversy because no present-day educators of the hearing impaired advocate a "pure" or "rigid" manual position. All educators of the hearing impaired in the United States are oralists and all are concerned with developing the child's ability to speak and understand the spoken word to the highest degree possible. The difference is between Oral-alone educators, who argue that all children must be educated by purely oral methods, and the Oral-plus educators who argue that at least some children would progress more satisfactorily with simultaneous or combined Oral-Manual presentation. At present, although variations exist, four basic methods of instruction may be identified in the United States: The Oral Method, the Auditory Method, the Rochester Method, and the Simultaneous Method.

1. *Oral Method:* Also called the Oral-Aural method, this conveys input to the child through speech reading (lipreading) and amplification of sound, while the child expresses himself through speech. Gestures and signs are prohibited. In its purest form reading and writing are discouraged in the early years as a potential inhibitor to the development of oral skills.

2. *Auditory Method:* As opposed to the Oral, this method is basically unisensory. It concentrates on developing listening skills in the child who is expected to rely primarily on his hearing. Reading and writing are usually discouraged in the child, as is dependence on speech reading. Although developed for children with moderate losses, some attempts have been made to use it with profoundly impaired children.

---

[1]An example of a reversible passive is "The boy was pushed by the girl." Compare this to the nonreversible passive, "The house was painted by the girl." The understanding of the first sentence obviously requires more "grammatical" knowledge than that required for the second.

3. *Rochester Method:* This is a combination of the Oral Method plus finger spelling. The child receives information through speech reading, amplification, and finger spelling, and he expresses himself through speech and finger spelling. Reading and writing are usually given great emphasis. When practiced correctly, the teacher spells in the manual alphabet every word simultaneous with speech. A proficient teacher can present at the rate of approximately 100 words per minute. This approach is quite similar to the system of Neo-Oralism developed in the Soviet Union.

4. *Simultaneous Method:* This is a combination of the Oral Method plus signs and finger spelling. The child receives input through speech reading, amplification, signs, and finger spelling. He expresses himself in speech, signs, and finger spelling. Signs are differentiated from finger spelling in that they represent complete words or ideas. A proficient teacher will sign in coordination with the spoken word, using spelling to illustrate elements of language for which no signs exist, e.g., some function words such as *of, and, the* and indications of some verb tenses. This method has been limited to the use with children with profound losses.

Recent trends

Until quite recently, the Oral Method has been predominant. Its ascendency may be traced as far back as the International Congress on Deafness in Milan, Italy, in 1880 in which a resolution was passed that the use of manual communication of any kind would restrict or prevent the growth of speech and language skills in deaf children.

Almost without exception, programs for the deaf have followed a completely oral approach, even including the "manual" schools in which simultaneous methods of instruction typically are not introduced into the classroom below the age of 12. Thus it might be argued that the history of failure in education of the deaf is a history of failure of the completely oral method and evidence that it is more appropriate for children with moderate to severe losses than for those with severe or profound losses. A spate of articles (Bruce, 1970; Karlin, 1969; Miller, 1970) appearing in the *Volta Review,* an American journal dedicated to the advancement of oral methods, has reacted vigorously to such an interpretation.

Although one of the goals in educating the hearing impaired is to produce children proficient in speech and speech reading, the possibility must be faced that rigid adherence to learning language by means of speech and speech reading, even with the best of auditory training, might be self-defeating for some children. A straight oral approach is confined to teaching language through speech and speech reading, although research indicates (Lowell, 1959; Wright, 1917) that a primary requisite for speech reading is grammatical ability. Deaf people, after years of training in speech reading cannot speech read as well as hard of hearing people (Costello, 1957) because they lack the ability to utilize context and anticipate, integrate, and interpret in consistent grammatical patterns those sounds, words, and phrases which are difficult to distinguish from the lips. Many distinct sounds in English either look like other sounds (e.g., [p], [m], [n]), or present very limited clues (e.g., [k], [g], [h]). The less residual hearing the individual possesses, the more difficult decoding becomes. The task of a speech reader, then, is a complex one: To understand utterances he must differentiate between sounds that look similar on the speaker's lips and at the same time perform closure—i.e., fill in—on parts of the message which are not readily available to the eyes. A.G. Bell, a leading exponent for the development of oral skills in hearing-impaired children, was aware of these difficulties and was quoted (Deland, 1923) as stating:

> Spoken language I would have used by the pupil from the commencement of his education to the end of it; but spoken language I would not have as a means of communication with the pupil in the earliest stages of education, because it is not clear to the eye and requires a knowledge of language to unravel the ambiguities. In that case I would have the teacher use written language and I do not think that the manual language (fingerspelling) differs from written language except in this, that it is better and more expeditious. (p. 37)

The Auditory Method, in its unisensory form, can be traced to the success of people such as Wedenberg (1954) in Sweden and Whetnall and Fry (1964) in Great Britain with severely hard-of-hearing children. The Auditory Method in the United States and Canada, patterned after their work in western and northern Europe, has been used mostly with pre-school-aged children (Griffith, 1967; Ling, 1964; McCroskey, 1968; Stewart, Downs, and Pollock, 1964), and some attempts have been made to extend it to even the most severely hearing-impaired child (Griffith, 1967; McCroskey, 1968; Stewart et al., 1964).

The work of Gaeth, who has been studying the effects of unimodal and bimodal sensory presentation since 1957, is of great relevance to consideration of the Oral (bimodal) and Auditory (unimodal) methods. His investigations (1963, 1966) with deaf, hard-of-hearing, and normally hearing students suggest that looking and listening is never better than either listening alone or looking alone. In bimodal presentation attention is directed to the modality which is most efficient for a particular task. These results contradict the finding of Numbers and Hudgins (1948) that bimodal presentation (look and listen) was superior to visual (look) or auditory (listen) alone. It is possible that Numbers and Hudgins, in comparing groups, overlooked individual differences and interaction effects. Within any group of students with varying degrees of hearing impairment, some may be oriented toward vision and some toward audition, a factor not readily apparent when using group statistics.

Gaeth (1966) reported that hard of hearing subjects, defined as having a loss less than 60 db (decibels) in the better ear, although somewhat inferior, functioned much as normal subjects in that they attended to the modality, either visual or auditory, which was most meaningful. There was some indication that the performance of the hard-of-hearing group in the bimodal situation was affected by a confusion as to which modality was more meaningful. Deaf students, defined as those with a loss greater than 60 db in the better ear, attended to the visual modality.

As opposed to possible interference between simultaneous bimodal presentation, Gaeth (1966) reported no inhibition in the use of two stimuli presented simultaneously to the same modality. If so, this could lend support to the simultaneous use of speech and finger spelling, or of speech, signs, and finger spelling, for children with severe losses. However, at present, the relative efficacy of multisensory stimulation has not been adequately studied and the implications of Gaeth's work to the education of the deaf remains unclear. Also, research has concentrated on simultaneous auditory-visual input. There is no justification for generalizing from these data to other types of stimulation, such as auditory-kinesthetic or visual-haptic.

Whetnall and Fry have been especially effective in promoting the educational separation of deaf and hard-of-hearing children and in providing services for hard of hearing children within the regular public schools in Great Britain. The benefits for hard-of-hearing child were immediate. But separate treatment of the deaf child has served so far only to point up to the extent of his failures. In a survey of children born in 1947 who were in schools for the deaf in Great Britain in 1962-63, the two researchers reported (1964) that only 11.6% of the students could carry on a reasonably clear conversation in speech and speech reading.

The question of methodology was deemed serious enough to appoint a committee to investigate the possible use of signs and finger spelling in Great Britain. The result, commonly referred to as the Lewis Report *(The Education of Deaf Children,* 1967) concluded that more study was needed. An interesting sidelight was the enthusiastic reaction of educators sent to observe programs in the Soviet Union, which had rejected traditional oral methods in favor of Neo-Oralism, a combination of speech and finger spelling similar to the Rochester Method in the United States. The observers reported:

> The children of four, five, and six years old whom we saw in class certainly understood their teacher well, and mostly spoke freely and often with good voice, although they were regarded as being profoundly deaf and were unselected groups. We could not judge the intelligibility of the speech, but our interpreter (who had never previously seen a deaf child) said that she could understand some of them. The children were also very lively and spontaneous, and did not appear to be oppressed by the methods used, which might strike someone accustomed to English methods as unsuitable for young children.

> It appeared to us, from what we were shown, that the Russians are more successful than we are in the development of language, vocabulary and speech in deaf children once they enter the educational system. This seemed to us a strong point in favor of their method (use of fingerspelling from the very start as an instrument for the development of language, communication and speech), the investigation of which was the main object of our visit. (pp. 44-45)

Their enthusiasm matched that of Morkovin's (1960) observations after visiting the Soviet Union. The Russians claim that by starting finger spelling in the home and nursery at age 2 the child is able to develop a vocabulary of several thousand words by 6 years of age. They also report that, rather than inhibiting oral development, the use of finger spelling enhanced speech and speech reading skills. Such claims have created a renewed interest in the Rochester Method, which was first used in the United States in 1878 at the Rochester School for the Deaf in New York (Scouten, 1942). Anecdotal substantiation is provided by the case of Howard Hofsteator (1958), a deaf individual whose parents provided him with an early language environment through finger spelling all conversations. His parents would read to him from books by placing their hands close to the printed page and spelling the stories. He was thus able to read at a very early age. Several preschool programs using the Rochester Method have recently been developed in the United States, and their numbers appear to be increasing.

A reservation concerning the use of the Rochester Method with young children should be noted. The presentation of connected English by means of rapidly changing hand configurations might place too great a burden on the perceptual and cognitive abilities of a young deaf child. His ability to form letters manually may also be limited. No such difficulty was encountered by Hofsteator, but he may have been an exceptional case.

Possible use of the Simultaneous Method with very young children is also gaining support throughout the country, a support which may be traced to a number of factors: (a) evidence that deaf children with deaf parents achieve more than those with hearing parents; (b) the growing tendency to accept sign language as a legitimate mode of communication; (c) dissatisfaction with results of traditional methods with the profoundly deaf; (d) the increasing militancy of deaf adults who are only beginning to make an impact on the field, the majority of whom, despite their own rigid oral training, strongly support use of the Simultaneous Method. The *Deaf American,* a journal produced by deaf professionals, has been particularly active in this question. It is interesting that the first public school system to use the Simultaneous Method with young deaf children—Santa Ana, California in 1968—also had the only program for the hearing impaired in the United States at the time to be directed by a deaf person.

Research and opinion on methods of instruction

In view of the frequent bitterness involved in the methods controversy, it is somewhat surprising to find that until 1965 objective research on the subject was almost nonexistent. Most of the available literature still primarily consists of position papers in favor of one or another of the various methods. It is note worthy that while most educators of the hearing impaired have preferred straight oral methods, many psychologists, psychiatrists and "outside" educators who, for one reason or another, have become interested in the problems of limited hearing argue for some form of manual communication (Moores, 1970c).

In a paper presented to the International Conference on Oral Education of the Deaf, Lenneberg (1967a) stressed that the primary goal of education must be language, not its subsidiary skills. He went on to criticize educators of the deaf for not distinguishing between speech and language. Stressing that the key is to introduce as many examples of English to the child as possible, he argued that the establishment of language is not inseparably bound to phonics and, echoing Bell's position cited earlier (Deland, 1923), urged that graphics (reading and writing) be introduced in addition to oral methods at the earliest possible time. Lenneberg included finger spelling and signs within his definition of graphics. His theoretical position is consistent with Tervoort's (1967) finding that manual communication had no deleterious effects on speech. It should be emphasized that both Lenneberg and Tervoort recognize the primary importance of oral communication in our society. They adovcate balanced, as opposed to rigid manual or rigid oral, communication. Their position, of course is in direct opposition to that of the Congress of Milan.

In his study of the relationship of manual and oral skills, Montgomery (1966) came to the same conclusion as Lenneberg and Tervoort, based on findings that (a) no negative correlations existed between any measures of oral skills and manual communication ratings; (b) positive significant correlations were recorded between the manual communication rating and the Donaldson Lipreading Test. In his discussion, Montgomery states (p. 562), "There thus appears to be no statistical support for the currently popular opinion that manual communication is detrimental to or incompatible with the development of speech and lipreading."

Kohl (1967), more widely known for his work in education of urban children, produced a highly controversial study on language and education of the deaf. Largely equating the position of the deaf to that of a disadvantaged group, Kohl noted that although he was aware of no school which officially taught sign language, it was the means of communication used by most deaf children with each other, no matter what the educational policies of the particular school. Kohl argued that teachers of the deaf should master sign language and utilize it in the schools. Oral language would then be the child's second language and would occupy more of the curriculum as he grows older. Kohl's suggestions drew a storm of protest. They were dismissed by Quigley (1969) as representing "support for the use of manual communication by individuals with only a superficial knowledge of the problems of education of deaf children, who apparently believe that the use of manual communication will correct most of the inadequacies of the educational system" (p. 18). According to a follow-up report on Kohl's study (Lederer, 1968), reaction was violent to an extreme. The editor of the *Volta Review* "attempted to discredit Kohl as patently unqualified to write or speak on the subject" (p. 8). The superintendent of an exclusively oral school in New York was quoted (p. 10) as dismissing Kohl's work as an "expanded master's thesis" and as agreeing only to answer specific questions put to him by a bona fide specialist on the deaf.

In a less emotional vein, Quigley (1969) attempted in two studies to assess the effects of the Rochester Method (oral plus finger spelling) on achievement and communication. The first involved a comparison over 5 years of three residential schools where students at the high school level received instruction in the Rochester Method matched with three control schools in contiguous states. The experimental group was superior in finger spelling but no differences were found in speech reading or speech intelligibility. The experimental group scored higher on all subtests of the Stanford Achievement Test, with an overall battery median of Grade 5.88 compared to 5.04 for the contrast schools. In various analyses of written language one statistically significant difference emerged favoring the experimental group on the Grammatical Correctness Ratio. Applications of Moores' Cloze procedures revealed the experimental groups to be superior in form class (grammatical functioning) with no differences in verbatim and verbatim-given-form class performance.

Quigley reported that, in two of the three experimental schools studied, the Rochester Method was not introduced until age 12. The school that used the method with children beginning at a younger age was the one that enjoyed the greatest advantage relative to its control (p. 77). Quigley's second study involved a comparison of two preschool programs for the hearing impaired, one using the Rochester Method and one a traditional oral. After 4 years of instruction, as shown in Table 3, Quigley reported that the students taught through the Rochester Method were superior in finger spelling, in one of two measures of speech reading, in five of seven measures of reading, and in three of five measures of written language. The control group received superior scores on Grammatical Correctness Ratio, which was attributed to a function of their limited language production (p. 89). Quigley suggested that these children tended to use more correct stereotyped and restricted language. He drew the following implications from the two studies:

1. The use of finger spelling in combination with speech as practiced in the Rochester Method can lead to improved achievement in deaf students, particularly on those variables where meaningful language is involved.

2. When good oral techniques were used in conjunction with finger spelling there need be no detrimental effects on the acquisition of oral skills.

3. Finger spelling is likely to produce greater benefits when used with

younger rather than older children. It was used successfully in the experimental study with children as young as 3 ½ years of age.

4. Finger spelling is a useful tool for instructing deaf children, but it is not a panacea.

Deaf children with deaf parents

The work of such people as Tervoort, Lenneberg, Montgomery, and Kohl in recent years has caused renewed interest in combined methods to educate at lease some hearing-impaired children. Because there are relatively few programs using any form of manual communication with young children, some investigators have turned to the study of deaf children (with deaf parents) who have received manual communication in the home.

Stevenson (1964) examined the protocols of all 134 children of deaf parents enrolled at the California School for the Deaf at Berkeley between 1914 and 1961 and matched them to deaf children of hearing parents. He reported that 38% of those with deaf parents went to college, compared to 9% of those with hearing parents, and that in the 134 paired comparisons, those with deaf parents were better students and attained a higher educational level in 90% of the cases.

Stuckless and Birch (1966), in a matched pair design, compared 38 deaf students of deaf parents to 38 deaf students of hearing parents from five residential schools for the deaf. The deaf parents had used the language of signs with their children as babies. Pairs were matched on age, sex, age of entrance to school, extent of hearing impairment, and intelligence test scores. No differences between the groups were found on speech intelligibility or teachers' ratings of psychosocial adjustment. Children with deaf parents were superior on measures of speech reading, reading, and written language.

In an unplanned ramification of a study of the effects of institutionalization, Quigley and Frisina (1961) studied 16 deaf students of deaf parents from a population of 120 deaf day students. They reported that the group with deaf parents had higher scores in finger spelling and vocabulary, with no differences in educational achievement and speech reading. The group with hearing parents had better speech.

Meadow (1966) compared 59 children of deaf parents to a carefully matched-pair group of deaf children with hearing parents. She reported that children with deaf parents ranked higher in self-image tests and in academic achievement, showing an average superiority to their matched pairs of 1.25 years in arithmetic, 2.1 years in reading, and 1.28 years in overall achievement. The gap in overall achievement increased with age, reaching 2.2 years in senior high school. Ratings by teachers and counselors favored children with deaf parents on (a) maturity, responsibility, independence; (b) sociability and popularity; (c) appropriate sex-role behavior; and (d) appropriate responses to situations. In communicative functioning the group with deaf parents was rated superior in

TABLE 3
ACHIEVEMENT OF HEARING IMPAIRED CHILDREN RECEIVING
PRESCHOOL INSTRUCTION IN THE ROCHESTER AND ORAL METHODS[1]

	Students taught by Rochester Method (N = 16)		Students taught by Oral Method (N = 16)			
	Mean score	s.d.	Mean score	s.d.	t	Level of significance
Age	7.81	0.40	7.85	0.68	0.34	—
Finger spelling	33.71	21.60	2.34	3.74	8.32	.001
Speech reading						
Craig Word	44.85	16.73	39.79	14.81	1.06	—
Craig Sentence	37.73	12.02	23.21	9.78	3.42	.01
Reading						
SAT Paragraph	2.28	.53	2.10	.68	1.49	—
SAT Word Meaning	2.31	.50	2.02	.61	2.81	.01
SAT Combined Reading	2.27	.49	2.04	.57	2.19	.05
Metro. Word Knowledge	2.09	.59	1.83	.57	2.69	.02
Metro. Reading	1.96	.54	1.70	.62	3.35	.01
Gates Vocabulary	2.21	.81	1.68	.64	2.55	.02
Gates Comprehension	2.00	.61	1.74	.59	1.57	—
Written language						
Total words written	61.53	29.24	37.47	18.54	2.46	.02
Sentence length	5.79	1.60	4.49	1.44	3.45	.01
Strings analysis	3.59	1.16	4.07	1.36	1.52	—
Subordination ratio	3.23	6.41	2.22	7.61	2.94	.01
Grammatical correctness ratio	79.53	19.70	89.33	21.82	2.42	.05

Quigley, S. *The influence of fingerspelling on the development of language, communication and educational achievement in deaf children.* Urbana: University of Illinois, 1969.

written language, use of finger spelling, use of signs, absence of communicative frustration, and willingness to communicate with strangers. No differences were reported for speech or lipreading ability.

Commenting on the deaf children's reactions to their deafness, Meadow claimed (p. 306) that hearing parents viewed their deaf children's deprivation in terms of an inability to *speak* rather than an inability to *hear*. She also found that deaf children of hearing parents tend to ask questions regarding their deafness at a later age than deaf children of deaf parents.

Vernon and Koh (1970) matched 32 pairs of genetically deaf children for sex, age, and intelligence. One group had deaf parents and had been exposed to manual communication from infancy. The other group, consisting of recessively deaf children, had hearing parents and no early exposure to manual communication. On a standardized achievement test the early manual group's general achievement was higher on the average by 1.44 years. They were also superior in reading, vocabulary, and written language. No differences were found in speech, speech reading, or psychosocial adjustment.

The results reported by Stevenson, Quigley and Frisina, Stuckless and Birch, Meadow, and Vernon and Koh, while interesting in themselves, must be evaluated in relation to the richer environment to which children of hearing parents, theoretically, should be exposed. The socioeconomic status of children with hearing parents is superior; e.g., Meadow had to equate deaf fathers who were skilled craftsmen with professional, managerial, clerical and sales workers among the hearing fathers. The English language and speech limitations of deaf adults have also been documented extensively. In addition, deaf children of hearing parents are far more likely to receive preschool training and individual tutoring. Meadow reported that 60% of the children with deaf parents received no preschool training, as compared with only 18% of those with hearing parents. Half of the group with hearing parents not only attended preschool but also had additional experience either at home or at a speech clinic (p. 272). Almost 90% of the hearing families interviewed in the study had had some involvement with the Tracy Correspondence Course, offered by the John Tracy Clinic in Los Angeles, but none of the deaf families had sent for it. Given the higher socioeconomic levels, more adequate linguistic and speech skills, and higher academic attainments to be found in the hearing families (in addition to preschool educational and speech training for children with hearing parents), the educational, social, and communicative superiority of those with deaf parents takes on added significance.

PRESCHOOL PROGRAMS

Consistent with developments in other areas, educators of the hearing impaired have been turning with more and more emphasis to the development of programs for children below the age of 5. The main reasons for such a movement may be traced to increased awareness of the importance of the first 5 years of life, to dissatisfaction with results obtained with older children, and to the growing awareness and appreciation of the tremendous potential of very young children which has been documented by modern research in psycholinguistics, perception, and cognition. Perhaps more important than purely methodological considerations, which have already been discussed extensively, are what might be referred to as the two different philosophies of education developing in preschool programs for the hearing impaired.

The first philosophy has its roots in the pioneering work of educators of the hearing impaired in Western Europe, with much of the leadership coming from Great Britain. This may be labeled the Home-Centered Socialization philosophy. Attention is focused on activities around the home and a "natural-language" environment is emphasized. Parent guidance is a major aspect of such a program and physical placement contiguous to hearing peers is usually an essential component. Stress is placed on the spontaneous development of language skills and speech skills. Descriptions of such programs may be found in the writings of Pollock (1964), Reed (1963), Griffith (1967), and Knox and McConnell (1968).

The second major philosophical approach, which may be labeled Child-Centered, Cognitive-Academic, is exerting influence on many new programs. Its impetus has grown out of the failure of traditional socially oriented preschool and nursery programs to serve disadvantaged children in the United States and, to a lesser extent, Israel. Beginning in 1966, a number of research investigations have suggested that the only successful programs for the disadvantaged have been those containing a highly structured component with specific academic-cognitive training. The work of such investigators as Bereiter and Englemann (1966), DiLorenzo (1969), and Karnes, Hodgins, & Teska (1968 have had the greatest impact.

As the work of these researchers has become more widely known among educators of the hearing impaired, there has been a change in their orientation toward development of cognitive academic skills. Generalizing from the few such programs presently in existence, the focus may be expected to shift from the parent to the child; skills such as those related to reading readiness and number concepts would be trained as early as 2 years of age.

Related research

The paucity of educational research is especially marked in regard to the effectiveness of various intervention programs for the very young hearing-impaired child. Most of the literature cited as research or "proof" for the benefits of one approach or another may more properly be classified as program description. The typical article or paper describes, defends, and praises a program by the person who developed it or who in some way is closely related to it. Except for an occasional tape or audiogram, no data are presented. Position papers and descriptive works can serve an important function, but too often they have been treated as evidence.

In the few attempts at assessment, measured benefits have been negligible. Comparisons of children receiving traditional preschool training with children having no preschool training suggest a washout effect (Craig, 1964; Phillips, 1963): By 9 years of age there appear to be no differences between experimental and control groups. These results are consistent with those reported for traditionally based preschool programs for the disadvantaged. One of two conclusions may be reached. The first is that such a preschool experience is of no benefit to the children. The second is that such experience was effective but its benefits were dissipated by the failure of the schools to take advantage of them in the primary grade years.

McCroskey (1968) compared children who participated in a home-centered program with auditory emphasis to children who received no training and found few differences between the groups. What differences existed tended to favor the control group, those with no previous training. The investigator postulated that the experimental group consisted of a "basically inferior product" which had been brought to a position of equality with the control group. However, this conclusion must remain conjectural.

One study which directly compared preschool hearing impaired children receiving instruction under different methodologies has been discussed. Quigley (1969) reported that children being taught by the Rochester Method (Oral plus fingerspelling) were superior to those taught by the Oral-only method.

The lack of research studies with the preschool hearing impaired is not surprising considering that the difficulties in evaluating any type of educational intervention are multiplied when dealing with the preschool hearing impaired. Underlying the hostility and suspicion endemic to the field is the tremendous complexity of the task only hinted at by some of the following questions. How does one measure the speech, language, and communication ability of 3-, 4-, and 5-year-old children with severe hearing impairments? Are there any valid measures of parent attitudes? Are differential programatic effects transitory? Do or can children in a program who are behind in one area at age 4 close the gap by age 8? Is it possible to develop measurement techniques which will be fair to children in programs which have different goals and therefore different concepts of success?

A longitudinal evaluation

A longitudinal evaluation based on a modification of Cronbach's (1957) Characteristics by Treatment Interaction Model was conducted in cooperation with seven early education programs by Moores and associates (Moores, 1970a,

1975; Moores & McIntyre, 1971; Moores et al., 1972; Moores, McIntyre & Weiss, 1973; Moores, Weiss & Goodwin, 1973a; Moores, Weiss & Goodwin, 1973b; Moores, Weiss & Goodwin, 1974).

The evaluation was designed to avoid what had been perceived as weaknesses in previous evaluations. Among the steps taken were the following:

1. Programs were involved which provided services from time of identification.

2. Programs which served complete, not select, populations were involved.

3. Programs themselves had no formal role in the evaluation.

4. Measures of use of residual hearing were employed.

5. Decisions to include pupils in the study were made by an audiologist on a "blind" basis, i.e., data presented to the audiologist did not identify the program from which a child came.

6. Investigators were able to follow children who entered neighborhood schools, i.e., those who were "mainstreamed."

7. Measures of expressive and receptive communication abilities were developed and administered in addition to tests of articulation and receptive vocabulary.

Results

Complete results are presented in detail in the reports themselves, to which the interested reader is referred.

Academic achievement. Achievement in the sample, as measured by the Metropolitan Achievement Test, Primer Battery, is comparable to that of hearing children of the same age in reading and below hearing children in arithmetic. In each case the lowest scoring program was the same traditional Oral-Aural parent-centered program with emphasis on socialization and integration.

Illinois Test of Psycholinguistic Abilities (ITPA). The average scores of the subjects on the five visual-motor subtests of the ITPA were almost identical to norms established for children with normal hearing, suggesting normal functioning in these areas. The deaf subjects consistently have exhibited superiority on one subject, Manual Expression.

Receptive communication. Subjects were assessed in their receptive abilities across five modes: printed messages, sound alone, sound and speech reading, sound and speech reading and finger spelling, sound and speech reading and signs. Table 4 indicates that for 1972, 1973, and 1974, excluding understanding of the printed word, the least efficient mode was sound alone. Understanding increased with the addition of each element—speech reading, finger spelling, or signs. Scores on the printed word increased dramatically from 1972 to 1974 as a function of increased attention to reading in all programs.

TABLE 4
RECEPTIVE COMMUNICATION SCALE (CORE ITEMS):
PERCENTAGE SCORES OBTAINED IN
1972, 1973, AND 1974

Subtest	1972	1973	1974
Printed word	38	56	76
Sound alone	34	43	44
Sound and speech reading	56	63	68
Sound and speech reading and finger spelling	61	72	75
Sound and speech reading and signs	72	86	88
Total percent correct	50	62	69

Scores on understanding of passives, negatives, and verb tenses suggest that the deaf students tended to process all sentences as simple, active declaratives, ignoring indications of tense, mood, and negation, regardless of the mode of communication. However, their performance was better when dealing with the printed word.

Cognitive development. Tests of Classification, Conservation, and Seriation reveal no differences between programs in 1974 on any of the measures. Previous differences in favor of a ''Piagetian'' preschool (Program F) disappeared, suggesting that the activities themselves had no lasting effect on cognitive development, as measured in the above three areas.

Communication patterns. Classroom observation consistently revealed that the least communication occurred in Oral-Aural classes and the most in Total Communication classes.

Parent attitude. At the beginning of the evaluation, parents of children in Oral-Aural programs saw the goals of early intervention programs to be the development of speech and speechreading skills, while parents of children in combined Oral-Manual programs placed greater emphasis on academic skills such as reading and math. By 1974, the attitudes of parents in Oral-Aural programs had changed to essentially the same as those in combined programs.

Discussion.

Although, in general, the programs involved in the evaluation have been more successful than those in previous studies to facilitate communicative, cognitive, and academic growth, each program exhibits a unique pattern of strengths and weaknesses. The author presently is involved in the development of guidelines for early intervention programs based on the findings of the longitudinal evaluation.

CONCLUSIONS

The author believes that the future of education of the deaf may be viewed with cautious optimism. More deaf individuals are being served at the preschool and postsecondary levels. Although the present situation is still inadequate, educational provisions for deaf individuals from cultural and ethnic minorities are improving. Growing numbers of students are receiving supportive services in neighborhood schools. Multiply handicapped deaf individuals are still shamefully neglected, but there is a movement to improve this condition.

Educators of the deaf have long been isolated from general education. As a result, they have neither contributed greatly to nor benefitted from advances in other fields. Hopefully, this isolation is in the process of ending. Research in the effects of hearing loss on cognitive, linguistic, perceptual, and social functioning has caused many of the problems related to education of the deaf to be viewed in a new perspective. Some educators of the deaf are now involved in such "pure" disciplines as psycholinguistics and cognition and applied disciplines such as reading and special learning disabilities. If they can put aside the divisiveness of the past, the benefits for children will be enormous.

References

Antonucci, F., & Parisi, D. Early language acquisition: A model and some data. In C. Ferguson & D. Slobin (Eds.), *Studies of child language development*. New York: Holt, Rinehart & Winston, 1973.

Babbidge, H. *Education of the deaf in the United States*. Report of the Advisory Committee on Education of the Deaf. Washington, D.C.: United States Government Printing Office, 1965.

Bereiter, C., & Engelmann, S. *Teaching disadvantaged children in the preschool*. Englewood Cliffs, N.J.: Prentice-Hall, 1966.

Berko, J. The child's learning of English morphology. *Word*, 1958, **14**, 150-177.

Bellugi, U. Studies in sign language. In T. O'Rourke (Ed.), *Psycholinguistics and total communication*. Silver Spring, Md.: American Annals of the Deaf, 1972.

Birch, J., & Stuckless, E. *Programmed instruction as a device for the correction of written language in deaf adolescents*. Washington: U.S. Office of Education Project Report No. 1769, 1963.

Bond, G., & Dykstra, R. The cooperative research program in first-grade reading instruction. *Reading Research Quarterly*, 1967, **2**, 180-209.

Bonvillian, J., & Charrow, J. *Psycholinguistic implications of deafness*. Stanford, Calif.: Stanford University Institute for Mathematical Studies in the Social Sciences, 1972.

Broadbent, D., & Gregory, M. On the recall of stimuli presented alternately to two sense organs. *Journal of Experimental Psychology*, 1961, **13**, 103-109.

Brown, R., & Bellugi, U. Three processes in the child's acquisition of syntax. *Harvard Educational Review*, 1964, **34**, 133-151.

Brown, R., & Fraser, C. The acquisition of syntax. In N. Cofer and B. Musgrave (Eds.), *Verbal behavior and learning*. New York: McGraw-Hill, 1963.

Bruce, W. Assignment of the seventies. *Volta Review*, 1970, **72**, 78-80.

Carhart, R. *Human communication and its disorders*. Bethesda, Md.: National Institutes of Health, Public Health Service, 1969.

Charrow, V. *Deaf English*. Stanford University Institute for Mathematical Studies in the Social Sciences. Technical Report #236, September, 1974.

Chromsky, N. *Syntactic structures*. The Hague: Mouton, 1957.

Chomsky, N. *Aspects of the theory of syntax*. Cambridge, Mass.: Massachusetts Institute of Technology Press, 1965.

Chomsky, N. *Studies on semantics in generative grammar*. The Hague: Mouton, 1972.

Cooper, R., & Rosenstein, J. Language acquisition of deaf children. *Volta Review*, 1966, **68**, 58-67.

Costello, M. *A study of speech reading as a developing language process in deaf and in hard of hearing children*. Unpublished doctoral dissertation, Northwestern University, 1957.

Craig, W. Effects of preschool training on the development of reading and lipreading skills of deaf children. *American Annals of the Deaf*, 1964, **109**, 280-296.

Craig, W., & Craig, H. (Eds.). Directory of services for the deaf. *American Annals of the Deaf*, May 1974, 119.

Cronbach, L. The two disciplines of scientific psychology. *American Psychologist*, 1957, **12**, 671-684.

Deland, F. An ever-continuing memorial. *Volta Review*, 1923, **25**, 34-39.

DiLorenzo, L. *Prekindergarten programs for the disdavantaged*. Albany: New York State Office of Research and Evaluation, December 1969.

Doctor, P. Directory of services for the deaf in the United States. *American Annals of the Deaf*, May 1970, 115.

Fletcher, J., & Beard, M. *Computer-assisted instruction in language arts for hearing-impaired students*. Stanford University Institute for Mathematical Studies in the Social Sciences. Technical Report #215. October 1973.

Furth, H. Research with the deaf: Implications for language and cognition. *Volta Review*, 1966, **68**, 34-56.

Fusfeld, I. The academic program of schools for the deaf. *Volta Review,* 1955, **57**, 63-70.

Gaeth, J. *Verbal and nonverbal learning in children including those with hearing losses.* Washington: United States Office of Education Project No. 1001, 1963.

Gaeth, J. *Verbal and nonverbal learning in children including those with hearing losses: Part II.* Washington: United States Office of Education Project No. 2207, 1966.

Gallagher, J. New directions in special education. *Exceptional Children,* 1967, **33**, 441-447.

Goetzinger, C., & Rousey, E. Educational achievement of deaf children. *American Annals of the Deaf,* 1959, **104**, 221-224.

Griffith, C. *Conquering childhood deafness.* New York: Exposition Press, 1967.

Heider, F., & Heider, G. A comparison of sentence structure of deaf and hearing children. *Psychological Monographs,* 1940, **52** (1), 52-103.

Hirsh, I. Communication for the deaf. *Proceedings, 41st Convention of American Instructors of the Deaf.* Washington, 1963, 164-183.

Hofsteator, H. *An experiment in preschool education: An autobiographical case study.* Washington, D.C.: Gallaudet College, 1958.

Hurder, W. United States of America. In J. McKenna (Ed.), *The present situation and trends of research in the field of special education.* Paris: UNESCO, 1973.

Hurley, O. Perceptual integration and reading problems. *Exceptional Children,* 1968, **35**, 207-215.

Johnson, E. The ability of pupils in a school for the deaf to understand various methods of communication. *American Annals of the Deaf,* 1948, **98**, 194-213.

Karlin, S. Et tu oralist? *Volta Review,* 1969, **71**, 478e-478g.

Karnes, M., Hodgins, A., & Teska, J. An evaluation of two preschool programs for disadvantaged children: A traditional and a highly structured experimental preschool. *Exceptional Children,* 1968, **34**, 667-676.

Klopping, H. Language understanding of deaf students under three auditory-visual stimulus conditions. *American Annals of the Deaf,* 1972, **117**, 389-396.

Knox, L., & McConnell, F. Helping parents to help deaf infants. *Children,* 1968, **15**, 183-187.

Kohl, H. *Language and education of the deaf.* New York: Center for Urban Education, 1967.

Lederer, J. *A follow-up report on: Language and education of the deaf.* New York: Center for Urban Education, 1968.

Lenneberg, E. Prerequisites for language acquisition. *Proceedings, International Conference on Oral Education of the Deaf,* New York, 1967, 1302-1362. (a)

Lenneberg, E. *Biological foundations of language.* New York: Wiley and Sons, 1967. (b)

"Lewis Report": *The education of deaf children: The possible place of fingerspelling and signing.* London: Department of Education and Science, Her Majesty's Stationery Office, 1967.

Lilly, M. The impact (or lack of it) of educational research on changes in educational practice. In L. Mann & D. Sabatino (Eds.), *The First Review of Special Education.* Vol. 2. Philadelphia: JSE Press, 1973.

Ling, D. An auditory approach to the education of deaf children. *Audecibel,* 1964, **4**, 96-101.

Lowell, E. Research in speech reading: Some relationships to language development and implications for the classroom teacher. *Proceedings, 34th Convention of American Instructors of the Deaf,* 1959, 68-73.

McCroskey, R. *Final progress report of four-year home training program.* Paper read at A.G. Bell National Convention, San Francisco, July 1968.

McNamara, J. Cognitive basis of language learning in infants. *Psychological Review,* 1972, **79**, 1-13.

McNeill, D. Developmental psycholinguistics. In F. Smith and G. Miller, (Eds.), *The genesis of language.* Cambridge: Mass. Massachusetts Institute of Technology Press, 1966.

McNeill, D. The capacity for language acquisition. *Volta Review,* 1966, **68**, 17-31. (b)

Magner, M. Reading: Goals and achievement at Clarke School for the Deaf. *Volta Review,* 1964, **66**, 464-468.

Marshall, W. Contextual constraint on deaf and hearing children. *American Annals of the Deaf,* 1970, **115**, 682-689.

Meadow, K. The effect of early manual communication and family climate on the deaf child's development. Unpublished doctoral dissertation, University of California at Berkeley, 1966.

Menyuk, P. *Sentences children use.* Cambridge, Mass.: Massachusetts Institute of Technology Press, 1968.

Miller, J. Oralism. *Volta Review,* 1970, **72,** 211-217.

Montgomery, G. The relationship of oral skills to manual communication in profoundly deaf adolescents. *American Annals of the Deaf,* 1966, **111,** 557-565.

Moores, D. Evaluation of preschool programs: An interaction analysis model. *Proceedings of the International Congress in Education of the Deaf.* Stockholm: 1970, **1,** 164-168. (a)

Moores, D. An investigation of the psycholinguistic functioning of deaf adolescents. *Exceptional Children,* 1970, **36,** 645-654. (b)

Moores, D. Psycholinguistics and deafness. *American Annals of the Deaf,* 1970, **115,** 37-48. (c)

Moores, D. *Recent research on manual communication.* University of Minnesota Research, Development and Demonstration Center in Education of Handicapped Children. Occasional Paper #7. April 1971.

Moores, D. Neo-oralism and education of the deaf in the Soviet Union. *Exceptional Children,* 1972, **38,** 377-384.

Moores, D. Non-vocal systems of verbal behavior. In R. Schiefelbusch & L. Lloyd (Eds.), *Language perspectives–acquisition, retardation and intervention.* Baltimore: University Park Press, 1974.

Moores, D. Early childhood education for the hearing handicapped. In H. Spicker (Ed.), *Early childhood special education.* Minneapolis: University of Minnesota Press, 1975, in press.

Moores, D. & McIntyre, C. *Evaluation of programs for hearing impaired children: Report of 1970-71.* Univeristy of Minnesota Research, Development and Demonstration Center in Education of Handicapped Children. Research Report #27, December 1971.

Moores, D., McIntyre, C., & Weiss, K. *Evaluation of programs for hearing impaired children: Report of 1971-72.* University of Minnesota Research, Development and Demonstration Center in Education of Handicapped Children, Research Report #39, September 1972.

Moores, D., McIntyre, C., & Weiss, K. Gestures, signs and speech in the evaluation of programs for hearing impaired children. *Sign Language Studies,* 1973, **2,** 9-28.

Moores, D., Weiss, K., & Goodwin, M. *Evaluation of programs for hearing impaired children: Report of 1972-73.* University of Minnesota Research, Development and Demonstration Center in Education of Handicapped Children, Research Report #57, December 1973. (a).

Moores, D., Weiss, K., & Goodwin, M. Receptive abilities of deaf children across five modes of communication. *Exceptional Children,* 1973, **40,** 22-28. (b)

Moores, D., Weiss, K., & Goodwin, M. *Evaluation of programs for hearing impaired children: Report of 1973-74.* University of Minnesota Research, Development and Demonstration Center in Education of Handicapped Children, Research Report #81, December 1974.

Morkovin, B. Experiment in teaching deaf preschool children in the Soviet Union. *Volta Review,* 1960, **62,** 260-268.

Myklebust, H. *The psychology of deafness.* New York: Grune and Stratton, 1964.

Numbers, M., & Hudgins, C. Speech perception in present day education for deaf children. *Volta Review,* 1948, **50,** 449-456.

O'Rourke, T. (Ed.). *Psycholinguistics and total communication.* Silver Spring, Md.: American Annals of the Deaf, 1973.

Osgood, C. Toward a wedding of insufficiencies. In T. Dixon and D. Horton (Eds.), *Verbal behavior and general behavior theory.* Englewood Cliffs, N.J.: Prentice-Hall, 1968.

Phillips, W. *Influence of preschool training on achievement in language arts, arithmetic concepts, and socialization of young deaf children.* Unpublished doctoral dissertation, Teachers College, Columbia University, 1963.

Pollock, D. Acoupedics: A uni-sensory approach to auditory training. *Volta Review,* 1964, **66,** 400-409.

Pugh, G. Summaries from the appraisal of the silent reading abilities of acoustically handicapped children. *American Annals of the Deaf,* 1946, **91,** 331-349.

Quigley, S. *The influence of fingerspelling on the development of language, communication, and educational achievement in deaf children.* Urbana: University of Illinois, 1969.

Quigley, S., & Frisina, R. *Institutionalization and psycho-educational development in deaf children.* Washington, D.C.: Council for Exceptional Children, 1961.

Quigley, S., Jenne, W., & Phillips, S. *Deaf students in colleges and universities.* Washington, D.C.: Alexander Graham Bell Association, 1969.

Reed, M. Preprimary education. *Proceedings: 41st Convention of American Instructors of the Deaf.* Washington, June 1963, 543-550.

Rodda, M. *A critique of research studies on total communication.* Paper presented at Alexander G. Bell Association Annual Meeting, Chicago, July 1972.

Schlesinger, I. Relational concepts underlying language. In R. Schiefelbusch & L. Lloyd (Eds.), *Language Perspectives–acquisition, retardation and intervention.* Baltimore: University Park Press, 1974.

Schmitt, P. Deaf children's comprehension and production of sentence transformations and verb tenses. Unpublished doctoral dissertation, Urbana, University of Illinois, 1969.

Scouten, E. *A re-evaluation of the Rochester method.* Rochester, N.Y.: Rochester School for the Deaf, 1942.

Simmons, A. A comparison of the written and spoken language from deaf and hearing children at five age levels. Unpublished doctoral dissertation, Washington University, 1959.

Slobin, D. Soviet methods of investigating child language. In F. Smith and G. Miller (Eds.), *The Genesis of Language.* Cambridge, Mass.: Massachusetts Institute of Technology Press, 1966.

Stevenson, E. A study of the educational achievement of deaf children of deaf parents. *California News,* 1964, **80,** 143.

Stewart, J., Pollock, D., & Downs, M. A unisensory approach for the limited hearing child. *ASHA,* 1964, **6,** 151-154.

Stuckless, E., & Birch, J. The influence of early manual communication of the linguistic development of deaf children. *American Annals of the Deaf,* 1966, **111,** 452-460, 499-504.

Stuckless, E., & Delgado, G. *A guide to post-secondary programs for the deaf.* Rochester, New York: National Technical Institute for the Deaf and Washington, D.C.: Gallaudet College, 1973.

Suppes, P., Fletcher, J., & Zanotti, M. *Models of individual trajectories in computer-assisted instruction for deaf students.* Stanford University Institute for Mathematical Studies in the Social Sciences. Technical Report #214, October, 1973.

Survey of children born in 1947 who were in schools for the deaf in 1962-1963. The health of the school child, 1962-1963. Report of the Chief Medical Office of the Department of Education and Sciences. London: Her Majesty's Stationery Office, 1964.

Tervoort, B. The understanding of passive sentences by deaf children. In G. Flores, D. Arcais & W. Levelt (Eds.), *Advances in psycholinguistics.* Amsterdam: North Holland Publishing Company, 1970.

Thompson, W. An analysis of errors in written composition by deaf children. *American Annals of the Deaf,* 1936, **81,** 95-99.

Vernon, M. *Multiply handicapped deaf children: Medical, educational and psychological considerations.* Washington, D.C.: Council for Exceptional Children Research Monograph, 1969.

Vernon, M., & Koh, S. Early manual communication and deaf children's achievement. *American Annals of the Deaf,* 1970, **115,** 527-536.

Walter, J. A study of the written sentence construction of profoundly deaf children. *American Annals of the Deaf,* 1955, **100,** 235-252.

Walter, J. Some further observations on the written sentence construction of profoundly deaf children. *American Annals of the Deaf,* 1959, **104,** 282-285.

Wedenberg, E. Auditory training for severely hard of hearing preschool children. *Acta Oto-Laryngologica,* Supplementum 110, 1954.

Wells, C. *The development of abstract language concepts in normal and in deaf children.* Chicago: University of Chicago Libraries, 1942.

Whetnall, E., & Fry, D. *The deaf child.* Springfield, Ill.: Charles C Thomas, 1964.

Wright, J. Familiarity with language the prime factor. *Volta Review,* 1917, **19**, 222-223.

Wrightstone, J., Aronow, M., & Moskowitz, S. Developing reading test norms for deaf children. *American Annals of the Deaf,* 1963, **108**, 311, 316.

FUNCTIONAL CENTERS HYPOTHESIS: THE SOVIET VIEW OF LEARNING DYSFUNCTIONS

Ivan Z. Holowinsky

Rutgers University

Current social concern for the intellectually abnormal has brought into focus multiple, complex problems relating to information processing, its storage, and retrieval for the purpose of competitive survival. Notwithstanding a variety of efforts along multiple pathways leading in numerous directions (it is virtually impossible for anyone to have a grasp of the studies published in thousands of journals which deal with learning problems or problems related to learning), we are witnessing at the same time a scarcity of works which attempt to synthesize available knowledge into workable theoretical frameworks. For that reason, some skeptics would prefer to label the present-day knowledge explosion as an "ignorance explosion" (Lukasievich, 1972). Fortunately, however, efforts have been made, most notably by Piaget (1971) and Luria (1966), to relate information available in neurology, neurochemistry, biology, and psychology to the field of learning and learning disorders and to synthesize such information into meaningful and comprehensive theories or hypotheses.

This chapter suggests a model to interpret the Soviet view of learning disorders, the functional centers hypothesis, and reviews some relevant Soviet research in sensory-motor, perceptual, and complex cognitive disorders. Understandably, the Soviet view of learning disorders is based upon Pavlovian psychology and upon dialectical-materialistic interpretations of behavior.[1] In this respect, the Soviet view of behavior considers development of complex cortical functions both from the ontogenetic and phylogenetic points of view. From the ontogenetic point of view, Soviet psychology acknowledges the importance of training and conditioning in the development of mental abilities (Galperin, 1969;

---

[1] "(*a*) The environment (in the broad sense of the word, including education and training), which forms abilities and does not merely provide the conditions for the manifestation of genetic programming; (*b*) the individual's genetic programming, which determines not the abilities but the predisposition of those abilities" (Krutetskii, 1972).

Kohnstamm, 1966; Krutetskii, 1972; Obuchova, 1966; Vygotsky, 1956). From the phylogenetic point of view, complex cognitive abilities are viewed as mechanisms the organism uses to adapt to its environment and, as such, are influenced by sociohistorical and cultural evolution. In this respect, the Soviet view of behavior differs from 19th century orthodox materialism (Piaget, 1971).

THEORETICAL BACKGROUND

As mentioned earlier, the Soviet view of learning and learning disorders is based upon a dialectical-materialistic interpretation. This theoretical position among Soviet psychologists did not occur suddenly but developed gradually between 1920 and 1936. As described by Nikolskaya, (1974), the leading Soviet psychologist Blonsky's own views changed from an idealistic interpretation of behavior to mechanistic materialism and finally to dialectical materialism.[2] Blonsky was one of the first Soviet psychologists to maintain that scientific psychology should base itself upon Marxism. He was also one of the first to suggest that in order to understand development one has to view it simultaneously from an ontogenetic and phylogenetic point of view. Furthermore, he gave considerable attention to the influence of sociohistorical evolution.

Vygotsky formulated a theory of the sociohistorical origin of higher mental functions in man and developed new methods for investigating various mental processes. According to him, all higher human mental processes—logical memory, voluntary attention, conceptual thought—arise with the help of tools of "mental production": These tools are symbols, above all, symbols of language. These symbols originated in society, being first formed in the joint activity of people, later becoming individual psychological means of communication as well, used by the individual for thinking and voluntary direction of his behavior.

The role of words depends on their meanings, which change through the individual's social experience. The development of verbal concepts is based on the individual's acquisition of social experience accumulated by past generations. Consciousness is made up of a system of significations and a system of meanings. Meanings and words do not create the development of mental life, however. A human being, his life, his motives, and his emotions—all evolve from interaction with environment. The idea of evolution is central to all of Vygotsky's books (Brozek & Slobin, 1972).

In Soviet defectology the social context is extremely important; an organic defect should only be considered as a social abnormality of behavior (Vygotsky, 1974). From a psychological point of view, a physical defect has

---

[2]Idealistic means in this context deterministic; mechanistic means orthodox materialism; dialectical materialism is positivistic determinism.

meaning as a disturbance of the social form of behavior. For Soviet defectology the problems of educating the handicapped consequently can be resolved only as problems of social pedagogy.

Iaroshevsky (1973) agrees with Vygotsky that development of attitudes toward defect does not take place in a vacuum of pure thinking but in a real sociohistorical environment and is determined by its economical, political, and ideological considerations. In the context of this Soviet theoretical position, Anokhin, a noted Soviet neurologist, suggested that complex forms of behavior require a more complex conception of cortical functional centers (Garfunkel, 1969).

Anokhin stated that we are at the threshold of serious changes in how we perceive the conditioned reflex. He maintained that higher cortical functions are related not only to lower, or neurophysiological, functions but also to higher, or psychological, functions. In psychological terms, future behavior becomes reflected in present temporal behavior. As assessment of temporal reality, e.g., "cold" or "fear," embodies in itself a projection of the future, e.g., "to avoid cold," to escape "fear." For Anokhin (1974) the important role of psychology in the future is to develop an adequate concept of the relationship between temporal, or present, and future behavior. While studying with Pavlov, Anokhin developed his theoretical foundations of research into those physiological principles which are at the root of complex forms of organized goal-directed activity. From the beginning he suggested that complex forms of behavior cannot be reduced to elementary reflexes and that reflexes themselves should be viewed as complex functional systems which will enable us to better study the laws of behavior. Numerous studies conducted by Anokhin and his co-workers revealed that the reflex arc, although it remains an essential element of the central nervous system, cannot explain more complex forms of behavior. What is needed is the more complex concept of "functional centers."

Further understanding of functional centers is provided by Luria (1966). According to this eminent neuropsychologist, intellectual and perceptual processes should be understood as complex functional systems of socio-historical origin.

We therefore agree with the view that evolution under the influence of social conditions accomplishes the task of conversion of the cortex into an organ capable of forming *functional organs* [Leontiev, 1961, p. 38] and that the latter property is one of the more important features of the human brain. (Luria, 1966, p. 35)

And later in the same work, Luria stated, "We regard the higher cortical processes as complex, dynamically localized functional systems" (Luria, 1966, p. 468). Even a relatively uncomplicated process results from the simultaneous activity of several cortical zones, each playing an important role in these functional systems. A local brain lesion, in addition to producing a specific defect, also leads to a secondary disturbance of the total functional system. For example, according to Luria (1966), disorders of *writing* appear from lesions of the temporal, postcentral, and occipito-parietal region; disorders of *reading* from occipital, temporal, and frontal lesions. These and other complex, higher psychological functions are multireceptive and develop progressively in man throughout his life span (Leontiev & Zaporozhetz, 1945).

Soviet psychologists firmly believe that intellectual and psychological processes should be viewed toward adaptation and survival of the organism. However, they also believe that, unlike an animal's adaptive functional system, the human mind is the result of social-historical evolution (Mark & Engels, 1956; Zaporozhetz, 1970). The concepts of dynamic localization of higher (complex) psychological functions within the cerebral cortex and the consequent philosophical position which is essentially positivistic in nature became the cornerstone of Soviet defectology. Soviet defectologists are applying this theoretical position not only to the re-education of brain-injured patients (Tsvetkova, 1972) but to the whole field of special education.

This approach is described by Tonkonogki (1972) in his article on clinics and the treatment of aphasia. He stresses the importance of theoretical formulations in addition to practical applications when rehabilitating patients with impaired higher cortical functions. Further, in any rehabilitative program it is important to determine the degree and the level of damage to the dynamic functional system (Lykov, 1974). Lykov further suggested that in the case of acalculia (inability to comprehend numbers) it is helpful to distinguish between specific and nonspecific acalculia. Specific acalculia occurs in cases of complete inability to understand number concepts. Nonspecific acalculia refers to those cases where the defect is related to optical, acustic and motoic components of the disorder, but where understanding of the numbers remains essentially intact. However, in addition to the organic emphasis in retraining defective functions, Soviet defectologists also recognize the importance of being familiar with a patient's emotional and motivational traits (Oppel, 1972).

D'iachkov (1968), in discussing the development of Soviet defectology, stated that Vygotsky's division of defects into primary and secondary played a great role in studying the developmental features of abnormal children. Primary defects are those such as deafness, blindness, defects of the central nervous system, while secondary defects are those of speech, thinking, and activity, which arise under the influence of the primary defect and affect the personality of the abnormal child. Vygotsky demonstrated not only the negative influence of primary and secondary defects on a child's development, but the positive aspects of how such children adapt to social and educational conditions. This optimistic outlook has attempted to discover means and methods of overcoming, correcting, and compensating for defects in the physical and mental development of these children. Soviet investigations have suggested that mental development of abnormal children is socially conditioned, not just an unfolding of biologically defective capacities.

A suggested model of the Soviet view of development as an interaction of accommodation and adaptation is presented in Figure 1. Accommodation and adaptation should be viewed as a continuous interaction between structure and function. One may say that a structure in one way predetermines a function; however, a function also is continuously in the process of modifying a structure. In a temporal sense this process is happening during ontogenesis, although both structure and function have been influenced by phylogenetic (organic) and sociohistorical evolution. However, we should also be aware that various levels of structure are related to the complexity of function. The structure could be viewed as localized or diffused in a topological, mechanical, or molecular sense. The function obviously could also be observed at various levels of complexity. As a function increases in complexity, its relation to the cerebral cortex is increasingly diffused. Therefore, higher cortical functions have no direct structural counterpart. Furthermore, the ''higher'' or more complex the function is (e.g., reading or memory), the more it encompasses other functions (e.g., the sensory-motor or perceptual).

FIGURE 1
ACCOMMODATION AND ADAPTATION AS
INTERACTION OF STRUCTURE AND FUNCTION

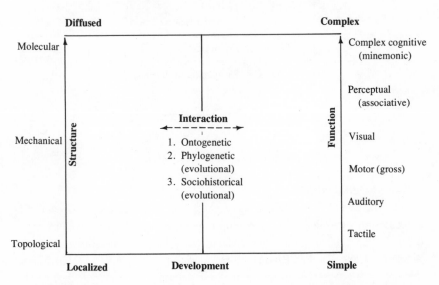

Figure 2 illustrates the Soviet view of etiopathogenesis of learning disorders and may help us understand the functional centers hypothesis. For a better overview, skills are related to the corresponding learning dysfunctions. It should be noted that in terms of etiology a defect could occur within the topological, mechanical, or molecular-neurochemical sphere of the cortex. Furthermore, it should also be remembered that the time of onset of the defect is extremely important, as are pathological conditioning and learning. Soviet research related to learning disorders reflects the above-mentioned theoretical orientation. Some relevant current research dealing with sensory functioning and defects, perceptual abilities, and complex cognitive abilities and defects will be discussed in that order.

FIGURE 2
ETIOPATHOGENESIS OF LEARNING DYSFUNCTION

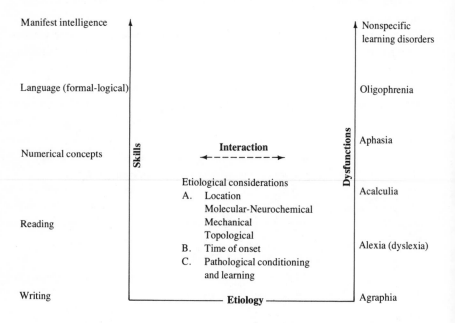

RELEVANT RESEARCH

Sensory functioning

The role of sensory elements (organs, pathways, and cortical areas) in the processes of environmental adaptability, perception, and the development of cognitive functions has been widely discussed in the professional literature (e.g., Arnheim, 1969; Kidd & Rivoire, 1966; Luria, 1966; Piaget, 1971). Although there is some interest in the educational implications of tactile modality, most of the modality literature as it relates to the cognitive development and education of handicapped children is concerned with the visual and auditory processes. In the Soviet Union the education of children with serious sensory defects is called, variously, typhlopedagogy (education of the blind), surdopedagogy (education of the deaf), and logopedagogy (education of the deaf-mute). The USSR conducts a basic research program and also attempts to develop new methods of teaching such skills as reading and arithmetic to children with serious sensory impairments. Basic research relating to sensory functioning has been conducted by Akimova (1972), Boyko (1964), Glukhova (1970), Mankovsky (1969), Peresleni (1971/72), and Zotov (1971/72)—to mention just a few examples.

Boyko (1964) conducted studies on reaction time in men. He indicated the time needed to stimulate various receptors as from 1 to 2 msec in tactile receptors and 20 msec in visual receptors. The time needed for an impulse to travel via nerve pathways is from 2 to 5 msec. For all three modalities the time needed for processing information within the central nervous system is approximately 20 msec.

Mankovsky (1969) investigated interaction between visual and auditory sensations, especially the influence of visual perception upon auditory localization of sound source.

Akimova (1972) studied the speed of habit formation as the function of individual characteristics of the strengths and weaknesses of the nervous system. The aim of this study was to ascertain the relationship between the speed of motor habit formation and the strength and liability of the nervous processes. The main conclusion of the investigation was that inaction of the nervous process is the factor impeding the quick formation and successful performance of motor habits.

Zotov (1971/1972) stated that the visual sensory system manifests specific characteristics when there is impairment of the normal functioning of the visual sense organs; the system is also an important part of higher nervous activity. Thus, as Zotov suggested, a task for research is to establish which functions of the sense organs indicate impairment of normal activity and which indicate features of the nervous system, i.e., the force of nervous processes and their dynamics and equilibrium. Zotov further suggested that experimental studies of differentiated periods of continuous visual stress should be a paramount task in the education of the blind. Knowing the cause and nature of visual fatigue can help teachers to develop effective methods of correctional work, under conditions designed to safeguard the children's vision.

Peresleni (1971/1972) investigated how deaf and normally hearing individuals identify complex tactile signals perceived through the surface of the skin. Speech signals are perceived by placing a fingertip on the speaker's larynx. It must be recognized that vibrations correspond in pitch to various sounds, while the duration of those vibrations varies from 10 to 35 msec in consonants to hundreds of milliseconds in vowels. The study raised the important question of whether difficulties in identifying speech sounds through the skin surface are related only to the frequency characteristics (pitch) of sound signals, or whether they also depend on the duration of the signals.

Soviet research on sensory impairment was reported at the 18th International Psychological Convention, and the proceedings of a symposium on sensory organ defects were reported by Meshcheriakov (1968). Several papers read at the symposium dealt with interdependence of sensory functions, auditory perception in children with speech defects, and training of blind deaf-mute children at the Institute of Defectology.

Perceptual studies and cognitive abilities

The role of social factors in the perceptual development of infants and children was first suggested by Zaporozhetz and subsequently elaborated by Venger (Kotyrlo, 1971). In one of his more recent articles, Venger (1968) revealed familiarity with theories of perceptual development as formulated by Piaget and also by Gibson. A number of articles and studies recently published in the Soviet Union reflect a major difference between the so-called Western or Piagetian interpretation of development and Soviet developmental theories as formulated by Galperin and his students (Galperin, 1969; Kohnstamm, 1966; Obuchova, 1966). Piaget's main thesis—that there is a close relationship between development of logical thinking and overall maturation—assumes that a child can learn or acquire only those skills which his level of maturation allows him to. In other words, education and training alone cannot enable a child to move, for instance, from a stage of preoperational thinking to a stage of logical operations. Galperin and his students, on the other hand, maintain that it is possible to teach logical operations even at the preoperational age (maturation) level. Krutetskii (1972), in a theoretical article, formulated what appears to be the prevailing Soviet opinion concerning the formation and development of abilities. He maintained that on the basis of extensive investigations into the formation and development of mathematical, linguistic, and technical abilities in children, two factors interact in the following way: (*a*) the environment (in the broad sense of the word, including education and training), which forms abilities and does not merely provide the conditions for the manifestation of genetic programming, and (*b*) the individual's genetic programming, which determines not the abilities but the predisposition of those abilities. Regarding this point of view, Soviet psychologists generally believe that the intellectual potential of preschool, as well as school, children is greater than had been assumed (Poddyakov, 1974).

The relationship between assimilation of knowledge and mental development of children was discussed in an article by Zhuikov (1972). He acknowledged that a certain level of mental development is a prerequisite for a child's mastery of knowledge, skills, and habits. Zhuikov maintained that, in the process of mastering such knowledge, skills, and habits, schoolchildren develop certain mental operations. The mental activity related to the assimilation of knowledge may be brought about at different developmental levels, and the assimilation of knowledge, skills, and habits can also be realized at these levels. Zhuikov suggested the following levels of mental development: (*a*) partial operations, (*b*) vaguely aware generalizations, (*c*) empirical generalizations, and

(d) theoretical generalizations. As part of their overall investigation of mental abilities, Soviet psychologists pay considerable attention to the research dealing with memory and memory processes. Leading in this effort are works of Luria's (1966) and Vuchetich and Zinchenko (1970).

Soviet psychologists suggest that memory is a complex form of activity, closely related to other higher cortical functions—first of all, to language and thinking—and is formed in the process of human social development. Soviet psychologists further believe that basic to the memory process are biochemical and physiological processes which take place at the molecular and neural levels. An example of such belief is a study by Galubeva and Rozhdestvenskaya (1969) who investigated relationships between voluntary memorization and some psychophysiological indices. The study compared efficiency of long-term (4-hour) memorization of 150 three-digit numbers with such psychophysiological indices as visual sensitivity, flicker fusion, galvanic skin response, EEG bands, etc. The study revealed that subjects with good and poor memory did not differ significantly on these psychophysiological measures. However, Malkov (1969) found positive correlation between strength or weakness of nervous processes and degree of concentration of attention.

LEARNING DYSFUNCTIONS

According to the view of Soviet defectologists, disorders in the functional centers may produce learning dysfunctions of various degrees of complexity, such as agraphia, alexia, acalculia, alalia, and oligophrenia. In the United States such disorders as agraphia, alexia (dyslexia), acalculia, and alalia are referred to as specific learning disabilities. It is not the purpose of this chapter to discuss these disorders at length. An interested reader is referred to Luria's book *Higher Cortical Function in Man* (1966) for detailed in-depth discussion of this topic. Further understanding of the Soviet position on complex learning dysfunctions is provided in Vygotsky's writings (Vygotsky, 1962).

He believed in the unity of consciousness and activity, a basic axiom of Soviet psychology today. Since, in his view, thought develops from the internalization of overt action, the internalization of external dialogue is central to his theory. Language is taken in from the environment, an external tool that must be internalized for man to become self-regulating. The very young child talks constantly, and speech is an accompaniment to his activity. By the time he starts to school he has learned to think silently, and speech has been internalized. Vygotsky found, however, that when the child faced difficult situations, when the smooth flow of activity was disrupted, he began to talk to himself. His speech took on a directive and planning function. In trying to solve a difficult problem, he would at times talk aloud, then perhaps reflect silently, then resort to talking aloud again, and repeat this procedure until the problem was solved or he gave up. Vygotsky (1962) maintained that earlier behavior is present in each of the succeeding structures at a higher level and that there is a mixture of many levels within more complex functions. Faced with difficulties at any level, the individual can regress to an earlier form of behavior which can serve more effectively in resolving the problem.

One of the more prominent learning disorders is oligophrenia (mental deficiency). Notable among the contributions in this field have been those of Pevzner (1961) and Luria (1963). Luria's theories of mediational deficit in oligophrenics received considerable attention in the USA (Balla & Zigler, 1964; Borkowski & Wanschura, 1974; Zigler & Balla, 1971; Milgram & Furth, 1963; Rieber, 1964).

In the Soviet Union and Eastern Europe the generally accepted view of mental regardation (MR) and learning disorders links them with cerebral pathology. The Soviet view of MR, known in the literature as oligophrenia (Pevzner, 1973), suggests that it is related to a diffuse maldevelopment or defect of the cortical hemispheres which leads to pathological inertia of the central nervous system. The first type is characterized by diffuse maldevelopment of the cortical hemispheres without serious neurological complications. The second involves a cortical defect with impaired perceptual abilities. The third type involves various defects of auditory and verbal perception, visual-perceptual defects, and motoric defects. The fourth is associated with psychopathological behavior. The last is related to maldevelopment of the frontal lobes, with behavior similar to that seen where there is a pathological disturbance of the personality and motor spheres.

Luria (1960) defines oligophrenia as "a profound mental underdevelopment which results from a massive cerebral lesion experienced in the intrauterine period or in early childhood, and leading to a severe disturbance of the subsequent mental development of the child" (p. 21). This view of mental deficiency thus requires diagnostic evidence of central nervous system damage, with such damage occurring early in life.

Because oligophrenia is assumed to embody "anatomical changes in brain structure" (Luria, 1963, p. 23), Soviet diagnostic procedure relies heavily on electroencephalographic (EEG) study of the child. Luria states that the degree of retardation is usually correlated with the amount of EEG abnormality. In cases of mild oligophrenia or feeblemindedness, where brain wave abnormalities may be slight, a supplementary diagnostic technique is used. In these cases, a flashing light is presented to the subject. Normal subjects reorganize or adapt their alpha-rhythms to the light frequency. In oligophrenics, however, such reorganization is either weak or absent (Luria, 1963).

Luria (1963) classifies the different types of oligophrenia according to both degree and clinical variety. Oligophrenics are labeled idiot, imbecile, or feebleminded, depending on degree of impairment. This categorization system is similar to that used in the West, except that Luria defines each type primarily according to physiological characteristics. Idiots, the most severely deficient of the retarded, have suffered damage to the brain stem and subcortical areas, as well as to the cerebral cortex; imbeciles may also suffer from subcortical as well as cerebral cortex damage, although to a somewhat lesser extent; while the feebleminded are believed to have suffered only superficial damage to the cerebral hemispheres.

Oligophrenics are also divided by Luria into five groups on the basis of behavioral aspects of central nervous system damage, such classification providing somewhat more information than description according to degree: (*a*) The basic group of oligophrenics, apparently composed primarily of the feebleminded, have suffered localized damage to the cerebral cortex, with no outstanding behavioral complications. (*b*) The excitable oligophrenics are those in whom the balance of the nervous processes is disrupted in favor of excitation. In accord with the previous discussion of this imbalance, these children are uninhibited and poorly controlled. (*c*) The inhibited oligophrenic children are also imbalanced, this time with the inhibitory processes in ascendance. Such children are listless, weak, and passive. (*d*) The fourth group is composed of oligophrenics who suffer from specific impairment in auditory or visual areas in addition to diffuse central nervous system damage. Luria states the necessity for carefully distinguishing between this group and those children who suffer from peripheral sight or hearing deficits but who are of normal intelligence. (*e*) The final group consists of those oligophrenics with ''gross underdevelopment of personality'' (1963, p. 66). These children are characterized by under-development of the frontal lobes. They are impaired in motor activity, suffer disturbances in goal-directed or purposeful activity, and are incapable of forming permanent relationships with other people. Except for the description of motor impairment, this group sounds remarkably similar to children who, in the United States and Britain, are considered to be suffering from early infantile autism.

It should be mentioned in this context that Soviet literature on atypical children makes no reference to infantile autism (Vlasova & Pevzner, 1967). This view is consistent with Pavlovian psychology, which views learning and behavioral disorders as symptomatic of a weak central nervous system. This ''weakness'' is manifested in an imbalance of excitation/inhibition properties of the central nervous system. Hence oligophrenics in whom inhibition is dominant would be unlike the typical mentally deficient in our terminology. Oligophrenics in whom excitation is dominant would be similar to autistic children. Obviously, the Soviets take a rather simplified view of a complex problem.

An equally important factor in the oligophrenic child is his inadequate verbal system. This is what Luria calls the "second signaling system" (the first is sensory-motor).

> These pathological conditions destroy the possibility of the participation of speech in the organization of mental processes, and speech is the basis of the more complex connections of the second signaling system. This involvement of complex speech connections requires particular balance and liability of the nervous processes, and each disturbance of these makes the formation of this second complex system of connections impossible. (Luria, 1963, p. 15)

Luria's thesis is that language serves two crucial functions in the child—it is a means of regulating behavior and an instrument for problem solving. In the normal child, speech serves to control behavior. At first such control is directed externally, by means of instructions or commands from the parents. As the child develops, however, speech becomes internalized and serves as the basis of the child's self-regulation of his own actions. Luria (1960) points out one of the major differences between the cerebroasthenic child and the oligophrenic: The former can utilize language to compensate for his weaknesses, while the latter cannot. The retarded youngster is characterized by a disassociation between the first and second signaling systems. Language, especially the child's own speech, serves to a much lesser extent as a controlling mechanism, and his behavior thus takes on an impulsive, unreflective character.

The second major role of language, that of a facilitator of higher mental activity, is described by Luria (1963) as follows. The basic processes in cognition are discrimination (abstraction) and generalization. The ability of the individual to discriminate relevant aspects of environmental stimuli, and to generalize or classify aspects on the basis of one or more common attributes, is the prerequisite for concept formation. According to Luria, a well-developed speech system is a necessity for these basic mental processes:

> Even during the pre-school period the verbal system is participating in the establishment of conditioned connections in healthy children, and it is because of this that the child can generalize the stimuli acting on him, refer them to defined categories, and can consequently easily discriminate those signs which are real signals. When verbal generalization is utilized, connections are formed quickly (usually in leaps and bounds) and they are stable. Most complex connections are established quickly on the basis of speech in children of school age and in adults. (p. 130)

As a result of his underdeveloped speech system, the oligophrenic child is severely limited in the processes of abstraction and generalization. He thus orients himself to the external world on an extremely concrete level.

Luria and his co-workers (1961) have devised a quite ingenious and potentially valuable technique for illustrating the poverty of the retarded child's generalization ability. Monitoring of a physiological component of the orienting reflex (OR) is done while the child is presented with a stimulus word, e.g., "cat." The subject is instructed to press a button at each presentation of this, and only this, word. In addition to "cat," words of two other categories are also presented to the child in random order. The first group consists of words semantically related to the stimulus; examples in this case would be "animal," "dog," "mouse," etc. The second group includes words which sound similar to "cat" but are not related semantically, e.g., "can," "hat," "cup."

Using the above procedures, Luria reports the following results. Normal school-age children show strong and clear orienting reflexes to all presentations of the stimulus word. In addition, physiological monitoring reveals consistent ORs to the group of words in the semantically related category, even though the child shows no button-pressing response to these words. The oligophrenic subject, on the other hand, shows the reverse results, having ORs to the stimulus word and the phonologically similar words but not to the words which are related in meaning. These findings are more pronounced as the degree of retardation increases. Luria summarizes the conclusions of this experiment as follows:

> Thus the system of connections characterizing the thinking of severe oligophrenics is sharply distinguished from the system of connections dominant in the normal child. Similarity in sense, which is normally very wide, is constricted. On the other hand similarity in sound, which plays no part in the cognition of the normal school child, and is inhibited by the real sense connections, emerges as the primary scheme. (p. 176)

Luria's technique is intriguing. It would appear to offer the opportunity to study one aspect of cognitive functioning on a basic physiological level, without depending on the often limited verbal expressive or performance abilities of the retarded youngster.

Luria's mediational deficit position provided impetus for numerous studies in the USA, providing supportive (Milgram & Furth, 1963; Rieber, 1964) or contradictory (Balla & Zigler, 1964; and Zigler & Balla, 1971) evidence. Much of the controversy seems to have arisen because samples used in Luria's and other studies are not directly comparable. Zigler and Balla themselves stated: "Furthermore, it appears probable that his [Luria's] retarded subjects were physiologically impaired." (Zigler & Balla, 1971, p. 401). This writer believes that it is not just probable but certain that Luria's subjects were physiologically impaired, otherwise they would not have been classified as oligophrenics in the Soviet Union. It would be interesting to see whether Luria's hypothesis is applicable to those who might be classified in the United States as mentally deficient.

In addition to oligophrenics, Luria (1961) acknowledges other clinical groups of children who suffer from learning dysfunctions. These are (a) the educationally backward child, who has emotional problems or who has been absent from school for prolonged periods; (b) the asthenic child, who is physically weak and easily exhausted, and (c) the child who suffers from peripheral hearing or vision defects. Although all three groups may require specialized instructional techniques, it is assumed that they are of normal intellectual potential. The child oligophrenic, on the other hand, is incapable of progressing normally:

> The narrowness of orientation, the poverty of analysis and synthesis, the backwardness of the complex mediated forms of cognitive activity, and the inability to transfer to these types of "mental" actions—all these differentiate between the mentally retarded child and his normal peer even though the latter may only be progressing with difficulty. (Luria, 1963, p. 9)

A further distinction made by Luria is between the true mentally deficient child in whom brain damage has occurred, either prenatally or in infancy, and the individual who suffers such damage after early childhood. In the latter case, the author holds that central nervous system impairment has less dire effects and that the child is often able to compensate to some extent for his disability. Thus he is not to be considered oligophrenic.

Luria's classification of children with learning dysfunctions is essentially clinical in nature. Em (1972) provides a look into pedagogical (educational) classifications of such children. The children in this study (conducted by the Institute of Defectology of the Academy of Pedagogical Sciences) were divided into three groups: (A) well-achieving, (B) moderately achieving, and (C) poorly achieving children. Group A was further subdivided into two groups. One group included children who had some difficulty with symbolic and abstract problem solving. Otherwise they were well behaved, punctual, always completing their work on time. The second subgroup consisted of impulsive and hyperkinetic children. They usually were trying to perform with speed but at the expense of accuracy. They appeared intellectually stronger than children of the first group but actually achieved less.

Group B was further subdivided into two subgroups of oligophrenics: those in whom inhibition predominated over excitation, and those in whom excitation predominated over inhibition. Group C consisted of children who were multiply handicapped with a low level of intellectual functioning. In this group impairments were noted in verbal, auditory, and motor areas, as well as in space perception and the emotional sphere.

An interesting article concerning the education of multiply handicapped children has been published by Meshcheriakov (1973). He applied behavior modification principles to the education of the blind-deaf-mute. His main thesis rests upon the premise that acquisition of human skills is the result of need satisfaction in interaction between adults and children.

CONCLUSION

Developing cognitive, as compared to concrete sensory-motor skills, is without question the most important task in adjusting to a complex, contemporary, technological, and competitive society. For that reason, perhaps, we are witnessing a general growth of interest in questions related to learning, development, education, schooling, as well as learning dysfunctions. In the United States, in part due to social pressure, we observe attempts to redefine mental retardation (as in the 1973 AAMD definition); to redefine education; and to redress social discrimination (as in *Ruiz* v. *California Board of Education*). At the same time there is increased interest in specific learning disabilities and efforts to explain cognitive malfunctioning.

In the Soviet Union, a highly centralized, totalitarian, ideologically orthodox society, the current view of learning dysfunction developed gradually. At the cornerstone of this view is Pavlovian psychology with its concepts of a "weak" and "strong" central nervous system, elaborated in the works of Blonsky, Vygotsky, Luria, Zaporozhetz, and others. Above all, this view has been formulated in the context of dialectical-materialistic philosophy, which views development of human abilities as the necessary sequence of socio-historical evolution. The Soviet view obviously acknowledges the limitation imposed by neurological or physiological defects, as in the case of oligophrenia, but it also stresses possibilities of retraining defective functions. Work performed by Soviet psychologists and defectologists certainly merits our attention. Research by Luria, Pevzner, Zaporozhetz, Zinchenko, Venger, and others contributes immensely to our understanding of learning dysfunctions. It would be a mistake, however, in the opinion of this writer, to attribute all of the successes of Soviet defectologists and psychologists to the dialectical-materialistic philosophy. The most successful special educators have been those who, in addition to their theoretical, scholarly knowledge, possessed faith in the human being and human intellect, regardless of ideological or philosophical considerations, as has been demonstrated by the life and work of Itard, Helen Keller, Maria Grzegorzewska, Fernald, and many others.

References

Akimova, M.K. Speed habit formation as a function of the individual characteristics of the strength and the liability of the nervous system. *Voprosy Psychologii,* 1972, **2**, 94-101.

Anokhin, P.V. The problem of decision-making in psychology and physiology. *Voprosy Psychologii,* 1974, **4**, 21-30.

Arnheim, R. *Visual thinking.* London: Faber & Faber, 1969.

Balla, D., & Zigler, E. Discrimination and switching learning in normal, familiar retarded and organic retarded children. *Journal of Abnormal and Social Psychology,* 1964, **69**, 664-669.

Borkowski, J. & Wanschura, P. Mediational processes in the retarded. In N. Ellis (Ed.), *International review of research in mental retardation.* Vol. 7. New York: Academic Press, 1974.

Boyko, E.I. *Reaction time in man.* Moscow: Medicine Publishing Co., 1964.

Brozek, J.A., & Slobin, D. *Psychology in the USSR: An historical perspective.* White Plains, N.Y. International Arts and Sciences Press, 1972.

D'iachkov, A.I. Teaching handicapped children. *Soviet Education,* 1968, **10** (5), 47-54.

Em, E.B. Pedagogical study of elementary grade pupils of an auxiliary school. *Defectology,* 1974, **1**, 33-40.

Galperin, P.J. On the investigation of intellectual development of children. *Voprosy Psychologii,* 1969, **1**, 15-25.

Garfunkel, P.S. At a higher level of integration. Book review of P.K. Anokhin's *Biology and neurophysiology of conditional reflex.* (Moscow: Medicine Publishing Co., 1968) in *Voprosy Psychologii,* 1969, **5**, 163-168.

Golubeva, E.A. & Rozhdestvenskaya, V.I. On the relationship between voluntary memorization and some psychophysiological indices. *Voprosy Psychologii,* 1969, **5**, 48-60.

Glukhova, N.K. An experiment in applying a bio-potential amplifier for electromyographic studies of motor-speech reactions in children. *Voprosy Psychologii,* 1970, **2**, 169-171.

Iaroshevsky, M.G. The categorical analysis of development of psychological cognition. *Voprosy Psychologii,* 1973, **3**, 15-32.

Kidd, A.H., & Rivoire, J.L. *Perceptual development in children.* New York: International Universities Press, 1966.

Kohnstamm, G.A. *Teaching Piagetian thought operations to preoperational children.* Paper presented at the 18th International Congress of Psychology, Symposium 32: Learning as a factor in mental development. Moscow, 1966, 93-97.

Kotyrlo, V.K. L.A. Venger's book on perception and learning. *Voprosy Psychologii,* 1971, **1**, 163-166.

Krutetskii, V.A. The problem of formation and development of abilities. *Voprosy Psychologii,* 1972, **2**, 3-14.

Leontiev, A.N. The social nature of human mental activity. *Voprosy Filosofii,* 1961, **1**.

Leontiev, A.N. & Zaporozhetz, O.W. *Reconstruction of hand movements after war trauma.* Moscow: Sovetskaya Nauka, 1945.

Lukasievicz, J. The ignorance explosion—a contribution to the study of confrontation of man with the complexity of science-based society and environment. *Transactions of the New York Academy of Sciences,* 1972, **34**, 373-392.

Luria, A.R. *The role of speech in the regulation of normal and abnormal behavior.* Bethesda, Md.: U.S. Department of Health, Education and Welfare, 1960.

Luria, A.R. An objective approach to the study of the abnormal child. *American Journal of Orthopsychiatry,* 1961, **31**, 1-16.

Luria, A.R. (Ed.). *The mentally retarded child.* New York: Pergamon Press, 1963.

Luria, A.R. *Higher cortical functions in man.* New York: Basic Books, 1966.

Lykov, V.M. Disturbance and recovery of counting with the local brain lesions. *Voprosy Psychologii,* 1974, **4**, 174-176.

Malkov, N.E. The strength of the nervous system and the concentration of attention. *Voprosy Psychologii*, 1969, **2**.

Mankovsky, V.S. The effect of visual perception on the auditory localization of sound source. *Voprosy Psychologii*, 1969, **4**, 57-66.

Marx, K., & Engels, F. *Early works*. Moscow, 1956.

Meshcheriakov, A.I. The disucssion of the problems of mental activity development in case of sense organs defect in man. *Voprosy Psychologii*, 1968, 157-161.

Meshcheriakov, A.I. Education of multiply handicapped children. *Defectology*, 1973, **3**, 65-70.

Milgram, N., & Furth, H. The influence of language on concept attainment in educable retarded children. *American Journal of Mental Deficiency*, 1963, **67**, 733-739.

Nikolskaya, A.A. On Blovsky's psychological views. *Voprosy Psychologii*, 1974, **3**, 3-20.

Obuchova, L.F. *Experimental formation of concepts of constancy in children 5 to 6 CA*. Paper presented at the 18th International Congress of Psychology, Symposium 24: Psychology of concept formation and mental activity. Moscow, 1966, 97-102.

Oppel, W.W. *Re-establishment of speech after damage*. Moscow: Medicine Publishing, 1972.

Peresleni, L.I. Elements in the perception of complex tactile signals by the deaf. *Soviet Education*, 1971/1972, **1-3**, 128-146.

Pevzner, M.S. *Oligophrenia, mental deficiency in children*. New York: Consultants Bureau, 1961.

Pevzner, M.S. (Ed.) *Clinical-genetic research on oligophrenia*. Moscow: Pedagogy Publishing, 1973.

Piaget, J. *Biology and knowledge*. Chicago: University of Chicago Press, 1971.

Poddyakov, N.N. The development of elementary forms of thinking in preschool children. *Soviet Psychology* (Journal of Translations) 1974, **13**, (1), 40-101.

Rieber, M. Verbal mediation in normal and retarded children. *American Journal of Mental Deficiency*, 1964, **68**, 634-641.

Tonkonogki, I.N. Clinics and treatment of aphasia. *Voprosy Psychologii*, 1972, **2**, 166-168.

Tsvetkova, L.S. Basic principles of a theory of reeducation of brain-injured patients. *Journal of Special Education*, 1972, **6**, 135-144.

Vuchetich, G.G., & Zinchenko, V.P. Scanning of successively fixed traces in short-term memory. *Voprosy Psychologii*, 1970, **1**, 39-53.

Venger, L.A. Two foreign theories of perceptual development. *Voprosy Psychologii*, 1968, **5**, 172-181.

Vlasova, T.A., & Pevzner, M.S. *For teachers about children with developmental anomalies*. Moscow: Academy of Pedagogical Sciences, 1967.

Vygotsky, L.S. *Selected psychological studies*. Moscow: Academy of Pedagogical Sciences, 1956.

Vygotsky, L.S. *Thought and language*. Cambridge, Mass. Massachusetts Institute of Technology Press, 1962.

Vygotsky, L.S. Psychology and pedagogy of children's handicapping conditions. *Defectology*, 1974, **3**, 71-76.

Zaporozhetz, O.V. Lenin's theory of reflection and problems of the child's mental development. *Voprosy Psychologii*, 1970, **2**.

Zhuikov, S.F. The psychological basis of evaluation of native language, knowledge and mental development of junior school children. *Voprosy Psychologii*, 1972, **3**, 70-80.

Zigler, E., & Balla, D. Luria's verbal deficiency theory of mental retardation and performance on sameness, symmetry, and opposition tasks: A critique. *American Journal of Mental Deficiency*, 1971, **75**, 400-413.

Zotov, A.I. Scientific research in the Department of Typhlopedagogy of the Leningrad A.I. Herzen State Pedagogical Institute. *Soviet Education*, 1971/1972, **1-3**, 103-114.

CHILDREN WITH RETARDED BEHAVIOR AND SENSORY IMPAIRMENTS: A REVIEW

S. Kenneth Thurman,
Beth Langley,
Thomas A. Wood

George Peabody College for Teachers

This chapter provides a review of the literature dealing with children displaying retarded behavior and sensory impairments. Earlier attempts to bring together this body of literature can be found in the form of both review and bibliography. Anderson (1965a; 1965b), e.g., has provided selected bibliographies concerning both visually impaired and auditorily impaired retarded children. While his efforts are commendable initial attempts to assemble this literature in an organized fashion, they provided little in the way of analysis or synthesis. Consequently, the need for synthesis and review became apparent.

Subsequently, Guess (1967) studied the literature to examine the nature of the interaction between visual impairment and retardation. While his conclusions suggested the need for more research with visually impaired retarded children, most of the literature in this area published since his review has been pointed toward program and facility description rather than toward research efforts.

The present review has as its purpose not to reiterate earlier efforts at summation and review such as those of Guess, but rather to extend them and provide some additional recommendations for the further study and programming of children with retarded behavior and sensory impairment.

The literature dealt with in this chapter has been divided into the following organizational categories: (*a*) Definition, (*b*) Prevalence, (*c*) Evaluation, (*d*) Service Delivery Systems, (*e*) Education and Habilitation, and (*f*)

Research Studies. As with any categorization, overlapping exists. Because of the paucity of literature in this area prior to 1950, we have tried to be as thorough as possible and to cover all applicable sources appearing in the last 25 years.

DEFINITION

Standard definitions of both sensory impairment and mental retardation identify continuums of severity (cf. Grossman, 1973; Jones, 1962; Myklebust, 1954) for these conditions. Thus, children may exhibit sensory impairment and retarded behavior in any combination of severity. It should be recognized that such multiple disabilities combine together to form a third continuum of total disability. Fraenkel (1964) and Hart (1969), have, for example, suggested that mental retardation and blindness combine to make a third condition which is more encompassing than either of the other two separately.

Furthermore, definition may be a function of the agency responsible for service. In the case of visual impairment, for example, the agency involved may determine whether blindness or mental retardation is viewed as the main disability. Those agencies primarily concerned with the blind will refer to these people as "retarded blind" and will view the blindness as the major disabling factor. On the other hand, mental retardation institutions will use the term "blind retarded" and will place major emphasis on the retardation (Fraenkel, 1964). Such distinctions have been important in determining the programs, planning, and placement made available for these individuals. Furthermore, the label placed on an individual by society can significantly affect his life chances (Farber, 1968). His status within society may be modified because of these labels (Mercer 1970; 1973); and self-fulfilling prophecies may result (Dexter 1958, 1964). Thus the sociological implications of which agency renders service may be greater than one would suspect at first glance.

In discussing deafness and retardation in children, Anderson and Stevens (1969) have pointed out that the conflicts implicit in classifying children with low functioning behavior and sensory deficit have led to confusing arguments over educational policies and terminology. In agreement with Anderson and Stevens, the present authors would suggest that sensory-impaired retarded children should not be classified and defined in a rigid categorical manner but should be viewed as a function of their individual physiology, their previous reinforcement histories, and the contingencies of reinforcement presently existing within their environments. Simply put, children should be dealt with according to their own individual level of behavioral functioning and sensory deficit, regardless of the administrative or sociological label attached to them. Nonetheless, children are still labeled as "blind retarded," "deaf retarded," and "multiply impaired" and through such labels are given service. How much service they receive may indeed depend on the prevalence of other individuals carrying these labels.

PREVALENCE

In a sense the significance of any problem lies in how.often it occurs. For our purposes, prevalence signifies the frequency with which children or adults are classified by some means as having both a sensory impairment and a retarded level of behavioral functioning. Such handicapping conditions are often found in combination. For example, Wishik (1964) found that two-thirds of the handicapped children in his Georgia study were multiply handicapped. On the average, the handicapped children studied manifested two handicaps per child. Graham (1967) presents similar figures from a national survey. He indicates that 63% of those children studied had one or more disability in addition to visual impairment, with the figure jumping to 86.8% for children under 6 years of age.

In addition to these studies, a number of prevalence studies have dealt with sensory impairments specifically in combination with mental retardation. Most often the populations employed in these studies have been identified from residential facilities of one type or another and may not, therefore, be representative of the prevalence of sensory-impaired mentally retarded children in the general population. Prevalence figures vary, of course, because of methodologies employed in data collection. In spite of these limitations a reasonable range of prevalence figures for both visually impaired and auditorily impaired retarded children can be found in existing literature.

Prevalence of Visually Impaired Mentally Retarded Children

Tretakoff and Farrell (1958) estimated that nationally 10 to 14% of the blind population is mentally retarded. Walsh (1963) reported that 4% of the population at Rosewood Training School (a retardation institution) was blind or near-blind at the time of the study.

In a survey by Bennett and Oellerich (1966) the percentage of blind residents in 68 mental retardation institutions reported was 8.8. Forty-two percent had mental ages of less than 2 years; 23% had mental ages ranging from 2 to 5 years; while 18% had mental ages from 6 years up.

Cawley and Spotts (1967) reported 744 as being partially sighted and 714 as being blind, out of a total resident population of 30,002 (CA=3-15) in 61 institutions responding. Standard legal definitions were employed. Of the total number reported to be visually handicapped, 1,024 fell in the IQ range 0-29.

Wolf (1967) surveyed the administrators and teachers of schools enrolling 6,696 visually handicapped children. Based on the questionnaire responses, 25% of this population was characterized as mentally retarded. Additional data indicated the average number of disabilities per child to be 3.18.

In addition to Graham's (1967) figures cited earlier, he also indicated that 80.2% of the 8,887 multiply impaired blind children he surveyed were also retarded. In light of the above figures, Graham's seen somewhat inflated. This may in part result from the definitions employed in his study.

Prevalence of auditorily impaired retarded children

Birch and Matthews (1951) employed pure tone audiometers to assess the hearing of 247 residents (CA 10-19) of Polk State School (a state mental retardation facility). Of these residents, 56.5% had significant hearling losses, and 32.7% had hearing impairments severe enough to interfere with daily activities.

Using a similar age range, Foale and Paterson (1954) tested 100 boys from a Scottish retardation facility. They concentrated on high frequency deafness and found that 13% of the population studied had hearing handicaps which impaired daily activities. Neither in this study nor in the Birch and Matthews (1951) study is it clear what level of hearing impairment is defined as "interfering with daily activities."

In two closely related studies conducted by Johnston and Farrell (1954, 1957), the authors report that 24% of the fifth-grade level children ($N=270$) at Fernald State School showed significant hearing losses. The subjects had a mean IQ of 60.9 with a mean CA of 155.5 months. The 1957 data suggest that hearing losses among retarded children at Fernald were 5 times more prevalent than they were among a similar population in Massachusetts public schools.

Kodman, Powers, Philip, and Weller (1958) identified 84 children from the Kentucky Training Home. The subjects ranged in age from 7 to 19 years and were tested with pure tone audiometers. Using a 30 dB loss as indicative of hearing impairment, 19.04% of the subjects were identified as having auditory acuity problems. Although pure tone audiometry was employed, the testing room was not sound proof; yet it was described by the authors as relatively quiet.

Schlanger and Gottsleben (1956) trained subjects to respond with hand responses to a tone. They tested 498 individuals (CA=28.9; MA=7.8) and found that 35% had demonstrable hearing losses. The training employed may not have provided reliable testing, thus making the results suspect.

Using a traditional pure tone screening test with 616 mentally retarded females of child-bearing age (CA=15-44), Siegenthaler and Krzywicki (1964) found hearing losses in 147 subjects. Hearing losses of this population were generally less than 30 dB, suggesting that they were mild in nature and did not interfere with the development of language or daily activities.

Rigrodsky, Prunty, and Glovsky (1961) performed audiological assessments of the 325 (CA=5-71) residents of Vineland Training School. Approximately 25% had hearing impairments. Of this 25%, 11% had conductive loss, 44% perceptive loss and 45% mixed loss. Rigrodsky et al. also present figures for hearing losses among different etiological groups. They indicate, for example, that 60% of Vineland's Down's syndrome population (i.e., 43 individuals) had hearing impairments. This finding is not unusual since other syndromes (e.g., de Lange's and Waardenburg) associated with mental retardation also display auditory deficits (cf. Moore, 1970; Partington, 1964). Furthermore, Fulton and Lloyd (1968) reported that 24 of 79 Down's syndrome subjects had hearing impairments. Only 7 of these, however, were sensorineural in nature. While this percentage is approximately 10% higher than that reported by Fulton and Griffin (1967), it is almost twice that reported by Glovsky (1966) in his study of hearing impairment in Down's syndrome subjects. Such differences are most reasonably accounted for by the differences in criteria for hearing loss applied by the authors of each report.

Nelson and Siblio (1962) employed speech reception, binaural free field spondee, and phonetically balanced words, in addition to pure tone testing, to assess hearing in 28 male and 15 female residents (CA=11-38 years) of the Coldwater Training Home in Michigan. Based on speech reception thresholds, 5 subjects had normal hearing, 10 mild losses, 2 severe losses, and 14 total deafness.

Audiometric data gathered in acoustically treated rooms using pure audiometry has been reported by Lloyd and Reid (1967) for all 638 residents of Parsons State Hospital and Training Center. Results indicated that 22% of this population displayed "active" hearing impairments. The authors applied a lax criterion of 15 dB or greater, thus suggesting that the prevalence of significant hearing loss in this population may not be quite so high.

The prevalence studies reported so far have employed populations selected primarily from mental retardation facilities. Fewer studies have identified mental retardation in populations drawn from programs for hearing-impaired children.

In a doctoral dissertation Frisina (1955) reported that 10 to 12% of the population of residential schools for the deaf could be classified as mentally retarded. Earlier MacPherson (1952) had reported that only 4% of the children in day schools for the deaf were also mentally retarded. MacPherson, did not, however, use actual test results but rather surveyed a number of schools.

Summary

Some apparent differences can be seen between the prevalence studies conducted with visually impaired retarded children and those completed with auditorily impaired retarded children. The former relied much more heavily on survey and questionnaire techniques while the latter more often employed direct assessment of a specified population. Accepting the fact that direct assessments are more valid, it can be concluded that the figures presented in the literature for prevalence of hearing-impaired retarded populations are more accurate.

Comparisons of the figures from various studies is difficult. Webb, Kinde, Weber, and Beedle (1966) pointed out, after surveying 10 major incidence studies carried out with mentally retarded populations, that there is a wide variation in the specification of hearing loss. Studies dealing with visual impairments can be similarly criticized. A standard definition of the diagnostic categories (e.g., the AAMD definitions and classification for mental retardation) involved could provide a much clearer basis upon which to compare incidence and prevalence figures. In addition, direct assessment of impairments in various populations seems essential since questionnaires leave the definition of each impairment to the discretion of the individual respondent.

Advancements in assessment of retarded children's sensory impairments is another factor which may allow for better identification of multiply-impaired populations and, as a result, provide better prevalence figures. Perhaps the most promising of these efforts has been the work in operant audiometry (cf. La Crosse & Bidlake, 1964; Lloyd & Fulton, 1972; Lloyd, Spradlin, & Reid, 1968). This paradigm employs the principle of stimulus generalization through requiring subjects to respond to a tone with a button press followed by reinforcement. Tones are systematically varied in frequency and loudness. Thus, a subject will respond only to those tones which are audible to him. Although such operant audiometry is reliable and particularly useful with severely and profoundly retarded children, it may be more involved than is necessary with mildly and moderately retarded subjects. Kopatic (1963) has indicated that pure tone audiometry using traditional methods can be used reliably with a moderately retarded population (CA=43.3 years and C=63.5). Bradley, Evans, and Worthington (1955), however, did demonstrate significant relationships between time involved in administering audiometric tests and MA and IQ. This result suggests that operant audiometry may be just as time efficient as more traditional audiometric techniques.

Macht (1971) has reported success in using operant technology to assess the visual acuity of retarded children. In this case a lever press was used to signify a response to the Snellen "E" Chart. His results indicated that reliable assessments could be obtained using this procedure even in subjects who were non-verbal; this study meets some of Sherdian's (1960) earlier criticisms of the Snellen "E" Chart.

Certainly, more definitive research is required in the assessment of sensory acuity (especially vision) in retarded children. It seems important, too, to conduct prevalence studies which act to identify, independently, sensory-impaired retarded children. Rather than selecting a population of children who are already judged to be retarded, visually impaired, or auditorily impaired, it seems more logical to identify children from the general population and then assess them to determine which grouping of handicaps exists. Better determination of primary and secondary handicapping conditions could then be arrived at.

Any prevalence data are dependent upon the researchers' ability to identify and evaluate the particular populations being studied. The problems posed here certainly hold for children with sensory impairments and mental retardation. For this reason the issues in the evaluation of sensory-impaired mentally retarded children require more detailed study.

EVALUATION

The existence of more than one handicapping condition creates a problem for the educational or psychological evaluator. It is often difficult to determine which condition creates the more serious handicap. It is obvious, too, that a single sensory impairment may itself bring about delays in other areas of function. Furthermore, as Regler (1960) pointed out, it is difficult to tell why a child with a sensory impairment (blindness in the present case) is developing slowly. His slow development could be the result of such things as brain damage, mental retardation, emotional disturbance, parental expectations, a multitude of other disturbances—or as a result of the sensory impairment itself.

Donlon (1964) suggested that the way to circumvent this problem is through an interdisciplinary approach to evaluation. He used the term evaluation rather than diagnosis, because he felt the former term "implies assessment of functional level, which includes a prediction about the maximum level to be reached and the means for reaching it" (p. 76). The interdisciplinary team should include a social worker, a physician, a psychologist, and an educator—each of whom should give a complete examination in his own area of speciality. Rabinowitz (1968) has made a similar point using illustrative case studies of rubella children. She suggested that comprehensive evaluation could go a long way toward improving the programming of multiply handicapped children.

Curtis (1966) discussed the interdisciplinary team in operation at the Syracuse University Center for the Development of Blind Children. The team specialists represented the fields of pediatrics, neurology, opthamology, psychology, speech pathology, audiology, social work, and special education. Four major recommendations were presented which, if followed, could potentially improve the evaluation procedure of any sensory impaired-retarded child. These recommendations stated that the child should (*a*) be seen on more than one occasion; (*b*) be examined prior to exploring his case records and to interviewing his parents; and (*c*) be probed for capabilities and assets as well as liabilities. In addition, it was recommended that the examiner should remain aware of the difference between isolated and multiple disabilities.

Rapaport (1961) recommended that such an evaluation should be ongoing and should consist of three phases. The initial phase should remain tentative in nature and result from the first evaluation of the interdisciplinary team. The second phase delineated by Rapaport involves program and placement planning which should have its basis in the need hierarchy of the particular child. She suggested that a third feature of the evaluation should be follow-up and reevaluation.

Intellectual assessment •

Intellectual evaluation of multiply handicapped retarded children may, on the surface, seem routine; and perhaps it would be, if it were not dealing with the sensory impairment. Sensory impairment presents many problems to traditional testing and evaluative techniques. Many tests are not applicable for blind or deaf subjects, owing not only to their reliance on sensory abilities but also to their lack of standardization for these subjects. Using blind children as an example, Lowenfeld (1964) has stated the problem in the following terms:

> The intelligence tests presently used with the blind were originally designed for the seeing and are, therefore, somewhat less reliable (and valid) for blind children. This is particularly true for those without any sight because they do not necessarily experience the world around them in the same way as seeing children do. (p. 217)

Certainly similar statements could be made for children with auditory impairments.

Still, the need for special tests for blind children was seen long before Lowenfeld's statement. Hayes devised a revision of the 1937 Stanford-Binet which was published in 1942 as the Interim Hayes-Binet Test of Intelligence for the Blind (Davis, 1962). This test was developed from the verbal items on Form L of the Stanford-Binet.

The development of the Wechsler Scales has helped in testing blind children's intelligence. The verbal scales of the Wechsler Pre-School and Primary Scale of Intelligence, the Wechsler Intelligence Scale for Children, 'and the Wechsler Adult Intelligence Scale have been employed quite effectively in evaluation of the blind. Parker (1969) has discussed the types of essential information which can be gleaned from the Wechsler Scales.

Davis (1962), however, has pointed out that the drawbacks of such tests lie in the fact that they are strictly verbal, provide no measure of tactile perception and organization (of great importance to blind children), and make no provision for residual vision. Two studies (Ashcroft, Holliday, and Barraga, 1965; Barraga, 1964) presented empirical evidence which lends support to Davis' opinion regarding residual vision. These studies demonstrated how training procedures can be used to increase visual efficiency and, in turn, increase educational advancement.

The Perkins-Binet (Coveny, 1972) presents two forms, one for Braille readers and another for print readers. Reliability coefficients for both forms reached significance at the .01 level. Results also indicate that this test corrects some of the drawbacks pointed out by Davis (1962). The Perkins-Binet gives valuable information both about degree and quality of vision. It has not, however, proven to be a particularly valuable tool for predicting academic success since research data are not yet available.

It should be obvious that the intellectual assessment of multiply handicapped hearing-impaired children presents problems similar to those experienced with multiply handicapped visually impaired children. As with blind retarded children, the Wechsler Scales are useful in assessing the intelligence of deaf retarded children. In their case it is the performance rather than the verbal sections of the Wechsler test which are particularly useful. It is interesting to note that one dissertation study (Luszki, 1964) employing an institutionalized mentally retarded population found no differences of WISC and WAIS Performance Scale scores between subjects with and without hearing impairments. Results such as this add to the construct validity of the Wechsler procedure for assessing intellectual functioning in hearing-impaired retarded children and adults.

The dilemma of assessing the intelligence of deaf children manifests itself when one considers the number of deaf children admitted to retardation institutions, as well as deaf children refused entrance to schools for the deaf on the basis of their low nonverbal scores.

Although numerous assessment instruments have been used to determine the functioning level of deaf children, only two—the Hiskey-Nebraska Test of Learning Aptitude and the Ontario School Ability Examination—have been standardized for this population. The Grace Arthur Point Scale of Performance Tests, the Leiter International Performance Scale (LIPS), the Goodenough Draw-A-Man, the Pitner Patterson, Cornell Cox Performance Scale, the Ravens Progressive Matrices, and performance subtests of the Wechsler are among those most frequently administered to deaf children.

Kirk and Perry (1948) criticized the Pitner Patterson, Cornell Cox, and the Grace Arthur not only on the basis that they had not been standardized on deaf children and that, therefore, pantomiming the instructions affected the results; but also because these tests were heavily loaded with formboard items and thus assessed an uneven sample of abilities. We also find Doehring (1965) asserting that nonverbal tests are very poor predictors of almost any aspect of scholastic or linguistic achievement. Stating that although nonverbal tests appeared useful in educational placement, he cautioned against the validity of such procedures in predicting verbal learning ability.

Conversely, Birch and Birch (1956) found a .71 correlation between scores of 35 children (CA=3-11 to 8-6 years) on the LIPS and ratings of school achievement by their supervising teachers and a .86 correlation between Leiter scores and teacher evaluation of intelligence. The results obtained by Birch, Stuckless, and Birch (1963) also disagreed with Doehring's admonitions; comparing children's scores on the Leiter with those on the Stanford Achievement Test, a .63 correlation was obtained.

Kirk and Perry (1948) administered the Hiskey-Nebraska and the Ontario to 49 deaf children and to 49 hearing children who had received the Binet.

Subjects were matched for age and race, and their performance on the tests was compared. The hearing-impaired children obtained a mean IQ of 102.9 on the Ontario, as opposed to a mean learning quotient of 95.8 on the Hiskey. The non-hearing-impaired children achieved a mean IQ of 102.9 on the Ontario, 107.3 on the Binet, and a mean learning quotient of 95.7 on the Hiskey. Kirk and Perry concluded in favor of the Ontario on the basis of the higher scores derived from it in comparison with the Hiskey. The authors found that the Ontario cost less than the Hiskey, besides taking less time to administer, score, and handle.

Mira (1962) favored the Hiskey-Nebraska over the Arthur Adaptation of the Leiter in a study comparing the scores of 60 children. Higher scores were obtained on the Hiskey, and only a .36 test-retest reliability was obtained on the Leiter adaptation.

On a battery of tests given to 120 hearing-impaired and 120 normal hearing children of average intelligence, Oleron (1950) and Farrant (1964) found that hearing-impaired children were deficient in abstract thinking, digit symbols, reading, number processes, and verbal comprehension. Farrant (1964) and Hiskey (1956) found that deaf children were superior to the normal hearing in visual perception. Farrant (1964) stated that deafness distorts and hampers the integration of mental abilities.

Hiskey (1956) discovered a population of deaf children to be 6 months behind their normal hearing peers in their performance on all items of the Hiskey-Nebraska except visual perception. He hypothesized that the deaf children score lower because of communication difficulties and an inability to use their potential effectively in situations where verbalization may be needed to aid retention and analysis.

Personality and social competency assessment

It is often as necessary to assess personality variables in sensory-impaired retarded children as it is intelligence. However, attempts to assess personality in these children have not been reported to any extent in the literature. Talkington and Reed (1969) compared Rorschach response patterns of hearing-impaired retarded children with normally hearing children. Their results indicated that the normally hearing subjects gave a greater number of responses than the hearing-impaired subjects.

While not reporting data, other authors have addressed themselves to personality assessment in visually impaired retarded children. For example, Dishart (1959) and Hepfinger (1962) both suggested how a series of tests measuring different aspects of the blind person's personality can be presented in profile form to make clarity of evaluation easier. Hepfinger, in addition to recommending the intelligence scales mentioned above, also suggested the following psychometric devices as being useful in the personality testing of blind children: (a) the Merrill Palmer Scale of Mental Tests, (b) the Guess-Why Game (a projective personality test), (c) the Vineland Social Maturity Scale— modifications of this scale have been used also (cf. Regler, 1960), and (d) the Maxfield-Buchholz Scale of Social Competence for Use with Blind Pre-School Children. Ashcroft (1967) reported the use of many of these same instruments with multiply handicapped children.

Functional assessment

More often than not the factor of sensory impairment has made the testing of the multiply impaired retarded child difficult. However, other behavioral factors such as hyperactivity and/or short attention span can also create problems. In addition, the question of whether the low IQs found in these children are caused by sensory-impairment or actual retardation still remains moot. There is no psychometric tool available today which can adequately answer this question, nor may there ever be. Moreover recent arguments against the use of standardized intelligence tests have suggested that more emphasis be placed on assessment of individual competence rather than on "intelligence" per se (McClelland, 1973; Neiseworth, 1969).

It seems imperative that assessment of sensory-impaired retarded children be made with devices other than psychometric tools based on often elusive hypothetical constructs. The alternative which the present authors suggest is based on establishing relevant educational goals for individual children developed from functional assessment. These goals must be established in accordance with those behaviors deemed necessary to operate adequately and competently within an individual's environment.

Anderson and Stevens (1969) have suggested that such functional assessments be made in the areas of mobility, communication, self-concept, and social interaction. We would suggest, in addition, that self-help and motor skills also be assessed in a functional manner. Anderson and Stevens (1969) postulate that through such assessments "a reduction or absences of performance in one or more of these factors [is identified and] provides a basis for quantifying in more precise terms the effect of loss of body function or impairment on school adjustment" (p. 20). In addition, specific instructional objectives can be formulated which will facilitate the educational processes required to remediate identified functional deficits.

Recently, several researchers have developed functionally based evaluation tools which provide extremely useful information for educational programming. Hart and Dubose (1971) developed an easily administered check sheet based on a comprehensive task analysis of a number of self-help skills. These include eating, toileting, dressing, and the like. A similar scale devised by Folio and Dubose (1974) follows the same format to assess motor function in multiply impaired children. Both scales provide an indication of the amount of shaping still necessary to teach a child a particular skill.

Langley (1974) has presented data on the use of a language board to assess cerebral palsied children using the Peabody Picture Vocabulary Test (PPVT). The PPVT provides a functional measure of receptive language. Pictures from the PPVT were placed on blocks which were pushed by the subject into a hole on the language board. It seems likely that with some modifications a similar procedure could be used with other multiply impaired children.

Kephart, Kephart, and Schwarz (1974) have reported on a functional scale to measure personal and environmental awareness in young blind children. Their results indicated that blind children tend to be misinformed, develop fragmented concepts, and are limited in their use of differential information. This scale appears to have potential for assessing these factors in individual visually impaired retarded children.

Summary

It appears that traditional psychometric devices are somethat limited in their usefulness with sensory-impaired retarded children. First, their reliability and validity with these populations can be questioned and, second, they seem for the most part, to provide little in the way of functional, educationally relevant information. Recent trends in the assessment of multiply impaired children seem to be geared more toward a functional-interdisciplinary approach which presumably leads to more effective ongoing programming for these children. The present authors would certainly advocate continued research activity in this direction. In particular, research is needed to develop functional assessment tools so that relevant behaviors and curricula can be established which will lead to the implementation of improved educational programs for sensory-impaired retarded children. Interdisciplinary evaluation approaches should also be examined with particular attention to follow-up processes and team monitoring of individual children.

SERVICE DELIVERY SYSTEMS

The earlier section on prevalence of sensory-impaired retarded children would tend to indicate that their numbers in any given population are likely to be quite small. This is not a new point; it was previously made by Root (1963) and Roos (1969). The existence of these small populations creates difficulty in establishing justification for adequate programming in many areas. Local programs, therefore, give way to regional or state facilities. It still remains to be seen what effect the mandatory special education legislation being passed in many states will have on this situation. Presently it seems that agencies tend pass these children back and forth to each other without rendering any substantial level of service.

Service delivery trends

Fraenkel (1964) pointed out that blind retarded children are in a no man's land with respect to agency services. The agencies for the blind clients refer them to the agencies for the retarded clients, and the agencies for retarded clients refer them to the agencies for the blind clients. Programs for blind retarded children tend to be geared toward the educable level child and few can be found which provide any services to those children who function at lower behavioral levels. Fraenkel also pointed out that the main facilities for the blind retarded children are classes in retardation institutions, private schools, public school special education classes, EMR classes in schools for the blind, and foster homes. DeLeo and Boly (1956) pointed out that blind retarded children are most often found in retardation institutions.

Other authors have lent support for the fact that a similar phenomenon exists with auditorily impaired retarded children. Costello (1966) makes a somewhat analogous point to Fraenkel's (1964). He suggests that the status of mentally retarded deaf children is confused since, typically, institutions for the deaf will not accept them. On the other hand, mental retardation institutions will accept such children but will tend not to understand them or be sensitive to their needs. An early survey by Schunhoff and MacPherson (1951) supports this statement. They reported that retardation institutions are much more likely to accept auditorily impaired retarded children than are institutions for the deaf. Twenty years later (Hall & Talkington, 1972) the same point was made. Hall and Talkington suggest that if an individual has a combined handicap of deafness and retardation, chances are 10 to 1 that he will end up being serviced in a mental retardation facility.

Several surveys have been conducted in respect to the types and extent of facilities available for retarded children with auditory and visual impairments. Anderson and Stevens (1970) surveyed 80 residential schools for the deaf with a total of 17,381 students. While IQ scores were not a specific criterion for admittance to such schools, children with multiple disabilities had not typically been admitted. Administrators indicated that they believed a minimal IQ of 80 was prerequisite for success in their programs. Such results raise the question of whether even a moderately retarded hearing-impaired child could be successful at a school for the deaf, even if he were admitted.

In a survey of residential retardation institutions Mitra (1969, 1970) reported that of the institutions responding, 25% had established programs for auditorily impaired retarded children. Of these pupils, 80% had mild levels of retardation but profound and severe hearing losses. Most of the programs in these institutions stressed prevocational training and development of communication skills, employing combinations of manual and oral-aural methods.

A survey reported by Rodden (1970) indicated that 68 retardation institutions had large enough visually handicapped populations to justify responding in the survey. The results indicated that 11 of these institutions had separate living facilities for their visually impaired residents.

Paraskeva (1959) surveyed 46 schools for the blind. He received 29 replies. Of the schools replying 90% reported that they accepted children in the educable range (i.e., IQ 50-80). Of the 29, 45% had no special classes for educable level children, but almost all the schools recognized the need for such a program. One, the Royer Greaves School, accepted only blind retarded children, 75% of whom were on the educable level.

Bennett and Oellerich (1966) conducted a survey of 165 retardation institutions. They received 68 completed questionnaires: 11 reported having special units for the blind residents; 36 had at least one blind retarded child in a structured school program; 22 had blind retarded clients considered as vocational rehabilitation candidates; and 22 had at least one such resident in job training.

Boly and DeLeo (1956) sent questionnaires to 104 state retardation institutions and received 52 replies. Of the 52, 47 reported having blind residents and 33 had blind residents attending school programs. Only 8, however, had special classes for their blind clients. The existence of these special classes for blind residents had no relationship to the actual number of blind residents within an institution. The following recreational and educational activities were most commonly reported in these classes: dusting, making beds, Braille reading, hand weaving, musical activities (choir, glee club, etc.), and dancing.

A more recent survey by Cawley and Spotts (1964) reported data based upon 61 responding retardation institutions. Of these institutions 49 reported that blind residents were integrated with sighted residents in living quarters and 3 reported they were not. Educational training programs in 41 of the institutions responding reported having blind and sighted residents in the same program; whereas 9 did not. Of 967 teachers employed by these institutions, 25 were assigned specifically to visually impaired residents. Only 5 of these teachers met state certification requirements for teaching visually impaired children. Blind residents were reported as starting educational programs at a mean CA of 5.68. Retarded residents started at a mean CA of 5.67. Sighted residents remained in these programs almost 5 years less on the average but spent on the average 100 minutes more a day than the blind engaged in educational and/or training programs.

Elonen, Polzien, and Zworensteyn (1967) have presented some minimal empirical evidence based on six children moved from mental retardation institutions to schools for the blind. They reported that educational gains and IQ increases obtained in the latter situation.[1]

Although a number of the programs reported seem to be providing at least adequate levels of service to sensory-impaired retarded children, very few have undergone intensive empirically based program evaluation. Thus, many conclusions drawn from these reports may or may not be generalizable to other similar populations.

Service delivery programs

As might be easily concluded from the survey data reported above, a large preponderance of actual service programs reported for sensory-impaired retarded children are housed in residential institutions. Most of the institutions are state operated and are designed primarily to provide services to retarded clients.

One of the earliest programs for auditorily impaired retarded children is reported by Glovsky and Rigrodsky (1963). This program was designed to serve eight children ranging in CA from 11-17 years and in MA from 6.6 to 7.6 years. Stress was placed on activities to promote and develop greater awareness of auditory and visual communication. Of the eight children, only one learned to lip-read all 250 words that had been taught during the course of the program. Other children made less spectacular gains in communication skills.

Schaeffer (1968) described a comprehensive program at the Pennhurst State School and Hospital, a retardation institution. The program included 251 visually handicapped retarded residents who were screened and evaluated. The institution also has a 74-bed vision unit.

One of the few programs for sensory-impaired retarded children which has been established outside of a residential institution is reported by Mattis (1967) and Thomas (1969). These authors describe the Day Treatment Program established through the Jewish Guild for the Blind to serve severely retarded blind children. The program places emphasis on concept formation and other functional skills, relying heavily on operant techniques for training. Thomas remarks that data are being collected routinely to monitor progress of the children; however, he did not include any specific data in his report.

Blanchard, Bowling, and Roberts (1968) described an educational program carried out at Pacific State Hospital and School in the summer of 1966.

---

[1]None of the surveys reported how long any of these programs for blind retarded individuals had been in existence, nor did they give any indication of whether or not separate facilities had been built solely for them. Farrell (1955) reported on the first state facility built solely for blind retarded residents at the Walter E. Fernald State School in Massachusetts.

Basic activities were used to teach blind retarded children self-help and communication skills. Progress of individual children was assessed through subjective observation rather than an empirically based system; thus, the actual success of the program is difficult to assess.

A three-phase program for multiply handicapped blind residents at Clover Bottom Hospital and School (Donelson, Tennessee) was described by Wood (1969). The three phases consisted of self-help skills, formal classroom programs, and adult vocational training. Wood contends that the educational needs of the multiply handicapped blind can best be met by segregated units for their education. The present authors would suggest that such a statement represents an empirical question for further study rather than a validated conclusion. Wood goes on to outline a number of procedures for teaching self-help skills which, again, are not empirically validated.

Leverett and Bergman (1970) described the staffing pattern of the Sunrise Project for blind residents at the Austin (Texas) State School. The project served 20 children (CA=7-17 years) and employed 22 full-time and 1 part-time supportive therapist, 3 degree-level teachers, a registered nurse, a research assistant, a psychologist, a part-time pediatrician, a part-time social worker, a secretary, and a director. These authors would have done well to report data on the effectiveness of this program in improving behavior; and, in addition, some data on program cost would have been helpful. On the surface, it appears that this program should have been successful in changing behavior, probably at a high cost; however, in the absence of data it is impossible to make such a statement definitely.

What appears to be a program similar to that reported by Leverett and Bergman (1970) is discussed by Iverson and Hartong (1971). The program at the Illinois Braille and Sight Saving School, was designed to teach many of the basic skills suggested by Wood (1969). The age range was 4½ to 14 years. Again, while some attention is devoted to the staffing pattern, no data on cost or program effectiveness are reported. The philosophical goal, i.e., to place children in the regular school program, is certainly commendable.

Johnston (1971) reported a program for visually impaired retarded clients at Orange Grove Center, a private multiphasic retardation facility in Chattanooga, Tennessee. The program takes a "total life" approach and is perhaps more normalized in character than other programs reported in the literature. Blind and sighted clients are integrated, and intensive evaluation is carried out. During the first 18 months, four trainees were placed in competitive employment and two in semiskilled employment. No discussion of staffing, pattern, costs, or number of clients served is provided.

Talkington (1972) reported a program for blind retarded residents at Boulder River School (Montana), a public retardation institution. Twelve residents were included in the program which stressed sensory stimulation, communication, mobility, and socialization. Pre- and postevaluation with the

Verbal Language Development and the Vineland Social Maturity Scale indicated that the program recipients benefited from the program. A more vigorous approach to evaluation might have lent better support to claims for the program's effectiveness. Nonetheless, Talkington is one of a few authors who presents any empirical support for program effectiveness.

A Rubella Unit at Fernald State School (Massachusetts) has been reported by Dolan (1972). The unit's objectives were (a) to improve the child's life style, (b) to help the child reach his maximum potential, and (c) to determine the techniques which are most effective for teaching these children. The 10 children in the program were served by 9 staff members who stressed self help, socialization, basic mobility, and communication skills. While all the children showed gains, the author still concluded that the program should be modified to include more structure and content.

Summary

Several conclusions are apparent from the literature dealing with service delivery systems for sensory-impaired retarded children: (a) Most programs for sensory-impaired retarded children are housed in state retardation institutions. (b) Fewer schools for the visually and auditorily impaired accept retarded children or have provisions for them. (c) The scope and quality of the program provided for the multiply handicapped seem to vary greatly from institution to institution. The overwhelming lack of empirical validation of these programs makes a definitive statement on program quality impossible. (d) If the literature presented is indicative of the service system present in the country as a whole, we can conclude that many more programs exist to serve visually impaired retarded children than auditorily impaired ones.

Some have recommended that communities establish mechanisms by which local or regional services can be provided to sensory-impaired retarded children. Thus, Smith and Arkans (1974) have recently pointed out the need for continued support to special education classes for severely and profoundly handicapped children returning from institutions. Others, notably Leshin and Stahlecker (1962), have advocated the establishment of institutional programs to provide the primary service systems for sensory-impaired retarded children. Although strong empirical support is lacking for either position, the present trends toward deinstitutionalization and community programming should cause local authorities to consider the possibilities of meeting the educational needs of even the most severely handicapped children within their own locales.

While the programs presently reported in the literature might provide some models for local programmers to follow, their quality and relative merits are difficult to assess. More often than not they fail to report on staffing patterns and program cost. Goals are nebulously stated and little—in most cases, no—data are presented to indicate either the overall effectiveness of the various programs or their effectiveness for specific children. Thus it seems imperative that program reports in the future include at least the following types of data in order to properly assess their merits and deficiencies:

1. Number of children served and nature of their handicaps

2. General staffing pattern of the program (i.e., numbers and types of personnel)

3. Cost of the program

4. Specifically stated goals and the procedures implemented to attain those goals

5. Some empirical statements as to the effectiveness of their procedures in attaining those goals and, in addition, data concerning the actual educational benefits (i.e., behavior changes) of the individual children involved.

If authors in the future would incorporate these suggestions into their program reports, much needed information could be gleaned. In their present form, most program reports provide very weak approximations of what is necessary.

EDUCATION AND HABILITATION

In general, the educational goals for sensory-impaired retarded children are no different from those for other severely handicapped groups. Goals of the educational program for blind retarded children should be to improve social behavior and, by so doing, allow the blind retarded child to take more functional roles in society (Davidow, 1962). Farrell (1955) concurred that social adjustment is the greatest need of the blind retarded child.

Budds (1960) suggested that the goals for the blind retarded child should consist of self-realization, human relationships, economic efficiency, and home responsibility—just as they do for the retarded child without a visual handicap. These goals, Budds felt, could be accomplished through the same curriculum one would use with the nonblind retarded child, the only modification being the introduction of Braille. Somewhat later, Thomas (1972) made a similar point relative to mobility training.

Addressing the educational problems of institutionalized deaf retarded children, Mitra (1971) suggested some similar guidelines. These guidelines included the following specific objectives:

1. Developing skills according to capability of the individual

2. Developing interpersonal relationships for harmonious living

3. Developing academic skills according to capability

4. Developing habits conducive to the child's physical, mental, and emotional health

5. Developing habits of safety for living and moving about the community

6. Developing effective work habits and occupational skills

7. Developing aptitude to make worthwhile use of leisure time.

Tretakoff and Farrell (1958) contended that the mildly retarded blind child should be prepared educationally to work in a sheltered workshop. Those with a more severe mental handicap should be taught to make an adjustment to custodial care (a position the present authors would question). The child, in order to accomplish these goals, should be allowed to progress at his own rate through an open-ended curriculum. The basis of the curricula proposed by Tretakoff and Farrell is play therapy and sense training in the early years, followed by music, recreational, vocational, and occupational training later on.

Regler (1960) suggested that the education of these children should begin with a preschool program dealing with development of skills in locomotion, activities of daily living, communication, constructive play activities, and socialization. Such a program would help combat the problem of meaningless verbalism as well as teaching the child how he appears to others. These aspects of the program were also emphasized by DeLeo and Boly (1956).

Albrecht (1957) suggested that, above all, the curriculum for multiply handicapped children should be flexible but at the same time routinized. To accomplish this, she saw the curriculum for the blind retarded child as based on a series of sequences, not just a set course of study. There should be 10 sequences, each one of which represents a major curricular area for the blind retarded child. Albrecht's sequences follow:

I. Social studies (family, houses, furniture, food, transportation, animals)

II. Handicrafts (beadwork, peg board, pop beads, wooden puzzles, frames [as in Montessori]—for discrimination of shapes, size, use, type, and texture)

III. Crafts (clay modeling, paper folding and pasting, cutting, painting [finger, spatter, block], papier maché modeling, sewing, weaving)

IV. Arithmetic (vocabulary study with games, meaning of numbers and counting, combinations, reading and writing numbers [Braille], time, money, amounts, and measurements)

V. Reading (Braille)

VI. Physical education (daily gym, stationary fundamental rhythms, ball skills, mat and floor stunts)

VII. Writing

VIII. Music

IX. Speech and phonics

X. Literature.

McLennen (1969) suggested similar curricular areas for institutionalized blind retarded children. He, however, differed from Albrecht in that he did not feel Braille instruction was usually worthwhile. Neither author, however, presented data in support of his position.

In a now classic study, Stuckless and Birch (1966) pointed out the importance of early manual communication for deaf children. They stated:

> The deaf child with early manual communication may have an increased awareness of the significance of language, concepts contingent upon language, and increased resource of knowledge and experiences facilitated by communication. (p. 452)

Certainly their argument can be extended to include deaf retarded children, and perhaps, it becomes even more potent when applied to them. In general, early intervention, whether along language dimensions or those of various other skills, seems to be an important factor in the education of severely handicapped children (e.g., Cooke & Parsons, 1968). In an effort to survey the effectiveness of the language training program for deaf children at Rosewood State Hospital School in Maryland, Mitra (1974) employed subtests from the TMR Performance Profile as a pre- and posttest measure of communication skills. Eight mildly retarded, severely to profoundly deaf children (CA = 12-19 years) with various nonverbal communication modes, were administered a 50-minute language lesson 5 days a week. The sessions were divided into 20-minute sentence structure, 15-minute vocabulary, and 15-minute reading comprehension periods. Subjects were taught sentence structure through using whole sentences without regard for grammatical rules. Shown pictures from magazines or workbooks, the students were asked to describe what they saw in any communication style (gestures, fingerspelling, signs).

Sentences about each picture were written on the board and discussed. The sentences were broken down to subject and verb phrases, and the students placed them together to form the sentences; words were treated similarly. The subjects were given mimeographed sheets containing the training pictures and were required to (a) match sentences to the pictures, (b) combine subject and verb phrases to match to the pictures, and (c) write the sentences next to the pictures. Vocabulary words were taught through pictures and actions, while pictures were also used for reading comprehension. At the end of the 5 months, every subject had achieved significant gains in all areas. Mitra attributed this to the concreteness of the learning situation. "The generic approach to language training for retarded deaf should have major emphasis on use of visual modality and active involvement in concrete things and events to develop a level of comprehension with verbal and/or a gestural response" (p. 47). Other authors (e.g., Hart, 1969; Henriella, 1961), have pointed out the necessity of assuming that educational interventions with multiply impaired children are both individualized as well as properly supervised and structured.

Techniques and procedures

Several general sources have been presented which discuss procedures and techniques for educating multiply handicapped and sensory-impaired retarded children. In addition, Tretakoff (1969) has addressed himself to the variables which should be taken into account in the education of the multiply handicapped blind child: the cognitive, sensory, affective, motor, and remediation (e.g., discrimination and socialization) areas.

The American Foundation for the Blind (1966) has also suggested some guidelines for establishing and developing curricula for the blind retarded. Unfortunately, only educable mentally retarded visually handicapped adolescents were dealt with. Be this as it may, some helpful suggestions were provided.

A book by Bluhm (1968) provided many helpful and practical suggestions for teaching blind retarded children. Bluhm is an experienced teacher who had made use of many of these ideas in her own classroom. Empirical testing of some of these methods and materials would greatly increase knowledge about their efficacy.

At least four other sources have been identified which provide some general considerations for the education of the sensory-impaired retarded child. The first is a monograph by Swartz and Cleland (1973), *Multihandicapped Mentally Retarded: Training and Enrichment Strategies*. The second is a book by Wolf and Anderson (1969) entitled, *The Multiply Handicapped Child*. Third is a recent book by Hart (1974), *Beginning with the Handicapped*. Last is a chapter by Hatlen (1973) which appears in *The Visually Handicapped Child in School* (Lowenfeld, 1973).

Mobility

In a recent literature review of mobility for multiply handicapped visually impaired, Wood and Berger (1972) found a distinct lack of services in this area. They attributed this to inappropriate educational placement and an insufficient number of trained professionals to meet the demand for services. Several programs, however, have been reported which do address themselves to these services. For example, Murphy (1964) described a case of a low functioning EMR boy with 20/200 vision who was taught mobility through special techniques. Seelye and Thomas (1966) reported accomplishing similar results with several other low-functioning blind children.

McDade (1969) has commented that orientation and mobility training for visually impaired retarded children should not vary in technique from that employed with nonretarded children. His data indicated that 43.6% of the blind retarded residents at Fernald State School (Mass.) could benefit from mobility instruction. Thus, he concludes that orientation and mobility training should be part of any curriculum for blind retarded children. Harley, Merbler, and Wood

(1975) reported the development of a scale to measure the mobility performance of multiply handicapped blind children. A pilot study by the same authors (Harley, Wood, & Merbler, 1974) demonstrated that low-functioning blind children could derive benefit from a program in orientation and mobility tailored to their individual needs.

Although they did not deal exclusively with mobility training, several authors have reported on various techniques for improving motor skills, environmental exploration, and awareness. "Touch and Tell" and the Wonder Texture Book were used in training blind retarded residents at Sunland Training School (Williams, 1964). The program emphasized development of sensory perception, social skills, and neuromuscular skills—all of which contribute to facilitating mobility.

Stephens (1973) reported on a "running cable" which allowed low-functioning blind retarded adolescents to explore their environments. The cables were stretched between two telephone poles so that the child could be guided from pole to pole. Presumably, this activity helped to develop adequate pace and gait while facilitating personality development by drawing the child into the environment. Such conclusions are subjective, however, since the author presents no data in support of her position.

Bongers and Doudlak (1972) suggested techniques for initiating visual-motor behavior in visually impaired retarded children. They used light to reinforce motor behavior, yet they present no data that indicate this technique's effectiveness. They also recommended restricting visual environment and directing attention to objects. Bongers and Doudlak would have been well advised to provide data supporting the efficacy of these techniques, which appear to be rather sound but require support.

Obviously mobility training is a necessity for any visually-impaired retarded child, and the techniques reported in the literature should be considered by anyone attempting mobility training with these children. If incorporated in programs, it is obvious that additional data are necessary to establish their ultimate usefulness.

Operant technology

Ashcroft's (1967) statement regarding an operant approach cannot be discounted. "We are intrigued by the Skinnerian approach—the experimental analysis of behavior modification and shaping techniques for lower order types of behavior." (p. 59). Specific training in these techniques would provide teachers with powerful tools for the implementation and evaluation of educational programs. The effectiveness of these techniques with other low functioning individuals has been well enough demonstrated (e.g., by Ferster & DeMyer, 1962; Kerr, Meyerson & Michael, 1965; Lovaas, Berberich, Perloff &

Schaeffer, 1966; Sailor, Guess, Rutherford, & Baer, 1968; Wolf, Birnbrauer, Williams, & Lawler, 1965; and Wolf, Risley, & Mees, 1964) that they should be attempted with sensory-impaired retarded children. Larsen (1970) has suggested a number of considerations for applying operant techniques in the training of multiply handicapped children. In addition, he suggests some methods for measuring whether or not teachers are employing these techniques in their classrooms.

Sklar and Rampulla (1972) used an operant approach to reduce inappropriate classroom behavior of a multiply handicapped blind student. A token system was implemented which reduced both inappropriate and rocking behavior. A procedure employing differential reinforcement of other behavior (DRO) was used.

Brown (1968) reported the use of operant procedures for increasing attending behavior and speech sound repertoires of deaf children with retarded behavior. The four subjects employed were generally deficient in both of these skills. Through the use of tokens, correct speech imitations were reinforced. Behaviors which competed with attending were ignored. Brown's results suggest that such techniques may be useful with other auditorily impaired retarded children.

Thomas' (1969) description of the day training program discussed earlier presents a definitive case for the use of operant procedures to intensively train severely retarded blind children. Unfortunately he presents no data supporting his position, though reporting that, during the course of the program, positive data were available.

Certainly, additional empirical data are necessary to demonstrate the effectiveness of operant techniques with sensory-impaired retarded children. Special attention should be paid to the various operant paradigms that may be used, as well as to the establishment of reinforcement hierarchies for these children. It is time for study in this area to address itself more to those operant procedures and reinforcers which are most effective than to prove for the "umpteenth" time that operant technology has a place in the programming of sensory-impaired retarded children.

Other ways to bring operant procedures to bear on assessment of multiply handicapped children should also be explored. The work in operant audiometric and visual assessment should provide some direction for the further use of operant procedures in evaluating sensory-impaired retarded children.

Techniques for personality improvement

A report by Avery (1968) has discussed the use of para-analytic group therapy with multiply handicapped blind adolescents, after decrying the lack of literature dealing with group therapeutic techniques for multiply handicapped children. Separate groups were established for girls and boys at the Connecticut Institute for the Blind. The groups, led by qualified leaders, gave the participants an opportunity to discuss feelings about such topics as sex, dating, reproduction, death, blindness, and relations with sighted people. As is often the case with reports on psychotherapy, no real conclusions are presented, nor is data reported. Landau (1968) reported the use of similar group therapy techniques with deaf retarded adults. The purpose was to improve social responsiveness, and the author states that all participants underwent a positive therapeutic experience. Categorical acceptance of such statements is difficult when more empirical, supporting data are lacking.

Knight (1971) has relied on the use of a tape recorded "radio show" in class to improve the self-confidence of multiply handicapped blind children. Although lacking data, the author concluded that the self-confidence gained from the experience helped the children develop more positive attitudes toward attempting new learning experiences.

Because of this lack of any empirical data, techniques discussed in the literature for improving personality variables in sensory-impaired retarded clients are, at best, suspect. While the present authors realize the difficulty of assessing personality variables in multiply handicapped children, it is abundantly clear that unless such variables can be successfully operationalized, it will continue to be difficult to assess the techniques of personality change.

Teacher training

Regardless of the curriculum used, the techniques employed, or the goals sought, it is the teacher who provides the critical variables in any educational system. Misbach (1953) suggested that in order to do the job competently, the teacher of blind retarded children should have knowledge of mental retardation, normal development of the blind child, his expectations, and his psychology. Furthermore, the teacher should have full background on all the children she teaches so that a child's capabilities can be established before teaching is begun.

Hart (1969) has described what is perhaps the most definitive training program to prepare teachers of multiply handicapped children. She contended that teacher training must not follow the categorical model or patchwork quilt design. This practicum-based program emphasized the use of prescription programming in order to individualize the learning situation. Certainly, the teacher training institutions in this country must respond with similar programs to the challenge put forth by mandatory special education legislation and court decisions which demand the right of education for all children regardless of handicapping condition. Simultaneously, programs must be implemented which provide continued inservice training for teachers of multiply impaired children by local education institutions.

Summary

While a number of authors have made suggestions about curriculum, techniques, and procedures to use with sensory-impaired retarded children, few, if any, present data to support their conclusions and recommendations. The present authors are not questioning the potential usefulness of these suggestions for successful education of multiply handicapped children. We must, however, point out that as the literature in this area now stands it represents little more than a mass of subjective opinion which may or may not be empirically sound. Educational programmers employing present-day techniques and procedures should therefore make every effort to empirically verify their effectiveness.

RESEARCH STUDIES

While we have already made several recommendations for further research, there remain to be examined empirical studies of psychological and behavioral variables affecting sensory-impaired children. While some of these studies resemble basic research paradigms, others are of a more applied nature. We hope that examination of these studies will stimulate further research by providing models for additional research efforts. In some cases these models most certainly can be improved upon.

Basic research studies

Several empirical studies appear in the literature which deal with the stereotyped behavior ("blindisms") of blind retarded individuals. Berkson and Davenport (1962) conducted a survey of institutionalized retarded residents. They found more autoerotic behaviors in their blind sample than they did in a matched group of sighted residents.

Guess (1966) studied the relationship between visual and ambulation restrictions on stereotyped behaviors in retarded subjects. He employed eight ambulatory and eight nonambulatory subjects with "less than travel vision" as well as sighted controls for each of these groups. His finding that the blind subjects displayed significantly more stereotyped behaviors than the sighted subjects (p .01), agrees with the findings of Berkson and Davenport (1962). Guess's study has weaknesses in its generalizability since it employed a small number of subjects from one institution and a rather subjective operational definition of visual restrictions.

Using 13 ambulatory blind retarded subjects, Guess and Rutherford (1967) attempted experimentally to reduce a stereotyped behavior consisting of body movements and repetitive manipulation of clothing or other objects. The subjects were observed under experimental, ward, and control conditions. The experimental groups heard miscellaneous sounds, objects, or were exposed to unique sounds produced by a sound generating apparatus. Introduction of objects and sound generating apparatus significantly reduced the stereotyping rates for subjects below those rates found for ward, control, and sound conditions. The authors also reported an inverse relationship ($r=.61$; $p<.05$) between object manipulation and stereotyping rates.

Stone (1964) studied what he defined as ''alerting'' and ''withdrawal'' blindisms in blind retarded subjects. He reported finding a different EEG pattern associated with each. He concluded from these patterns that blindisms are responsible for altered levels of consciousness in blind retarded subjects.

Lane and Curran (1963) used three retarded subjects to demonstrate gradients of auditory generalization which are similar to those for normal adults. Hartlage (1965) studied the listening comprehension in blind retarded subjects, and a year later (Hartlage, 1966) did a replication incorporating the variables of social maturity and intelligence.

Friedlander and Knight (1973) studied brightness sensitivity and preference in post-rubella deaf-blind retarded children. Each of the 16 subjects employed was to operate a two-choice lever switch which regulated two separate projectors. The investigators found that all subjects would make a response down to 5 foot-candles (ft-c) of intensity. In comparing intensities, they found that 13 children demonstrated preference at 300 ft-c rather than 10; 11 at 150 ft-c rather than 10; and 9 at 75 ft-c rather than 10. These results would, in part, lend credence to the earlier suggestion of Bongers and Doudlak (1972) that light is potentially a reinforcer for visually limited low functioning children. The authors suggested that a similar approach might be useful in assessing boundary conditions of visual competence for low functioning children.

A descriptive study by Talkington and Hall (1969) reports results indicating the prevalence of hearing-impaired retarded children. Two groups were matched on age, sex, date of institutional admission, and level of retardation, and compared on 10 variables as measured by the WICHE Population Census Standard Form.

Applied research studies

Talkington and Hall (1970) assessed an educational program for institutionalized deaf retarded residents at a state retardation facility. Their purpose was to determine the success of a manual approach to programming. A pretest-posttest design used as its primary measures the subject's manual language skill and score on the Verbal Language Development Scale. Manual language skill was assessed as the subjects were shown 100 overhead transparencies and asked to fingerspell or sign the labels corresponding to the noun-object pictures. The hearing-impaired residents showed significant gains in both manual sign language and Verbal Language Development. After computing a Fisher t test between the groups using pre- and posttesting differences in scores, the authors concluded that:

> The manual system offers the dual advantage of providing an initial communication system which is both flexible and simple for the student and one which aides and peers can easily learn and use in daily living activities outside the classroom. (p. 380)

This study has relevance not only because it demonstrated the usefulness of an important educational technique but also because it represents the best example of empirical verification of program success. Hopefully, it will provide an impetus to other programmers to follow a more delineated effort of program evaluation.

In another study, Candland and Conklyn (1962) demonstrated the use of the oddity problem in teaching reading to deaf retarded subjects. They employed four subjects but report data for only one. Although they suggested the usefulness of the oddity problem in teaching reading to deaf retarded subjects, additional data are necessary to support their claims for its utility.

Another study with possibilities of application is that of Templar and Hartlage (1965) who attempted to determine the reliability of the hand-face test with blind retarded subjects. Results indicated no differences in tactile discrimination between 12 blind and 12 sighted retarded subjects matched on CA, MA, and sex. The test-retest reliabilities reported by the authors were .83, .77, and .85 for the blind, sighted, and pooled samples respectively. All were significant at the .01 level. Somewhat lower rank order correlations were reported between mental age and hand-face test scores.

CONCLUSION

This chapter has reviewed the literature relating to sensory-impaired retarded children in terms of Definition, Prevalence, Evaluation, Service Delivery Systems, Education and Habilitation, and Research Studies. While somewhat more literature has been made available in recent years, there is still a great lack of empirical, data-based reports on variables affecting sensory-impaired retarded children and their programs.

In addition, identification and evaluation in this area are made difficult because of the multiple handicapping situation. Sensory impairment causes special problems to psychometrists. Some of these problems have been dealt with by modification of existing testing materials. The suggestion has been made that the individual multiply handicapped child be evaluated in terms of the individual behaviors which they require to make them competent to function in their own environments. Research is necessary to assist toward these goals.

Few local facilities are available for sensory-impaired retarded children. Most available facilities tend to be in institutional settings, typically in retardation institutions. There remains a pressing need to develop more facilities equipped to meet the educational and training needs of sensory-impaired retarded children. Research is also needed to provide methods to evaluate the types of facilities most effective in bringing about behavioral change in these children. Particular attention should be paid to the number of children served and the nature of their handicaps, the staffing patterns, program costs, specific goals and procedures, and program effectiveness in terms of behavior outcomes in the children served.

Early education and intervention seems mandatory for sensory-impaired retarded children, predicated on facilitating the maximum level of behavioral functioning for each individual child. Educational programs reported thus far have suffered from their nonvalidated approaches. Many of these programs have incorporated methods, procedures, and materials which have high face validity. Unfortunately, nothing has been done to give these programs or their individual components any empirical validation.

The scientist interested in sensory processes certainly would gain pertinent information from sensory-impaired retarded populations. Longitudinal and cross-sectional studies could provide much relevant information on sensory development in the presence of a multiple handicapping condition. Those interested in the experimental analysis of behavior might do well to follow the example of Lane and Curran (1963) and demonstrate the generalizability of their analyses to other behaviorally inadequate populations.

In fact, with the present dearth of empirically based literature dealing with sensory-impaired retarded children, almost any well-designed research studies would be appreciated. Such children provide a challenge to both basic and applied researchers as well as to educational programmers. How this challenge is met depends only upon the initative and creativity of educational, psychological, and medical professionals. Surely there are enough unanswered questions about sensory-impairments and retardation in combination to insure fruitful research efforts for many years to come.

References

Albrecht, M. A curriculum for a class of mentally retarded blind children. *The International Journal for the Education of the Blind,* 1957, **7**, 33-42.

American Foundation for the Blind. *An introduction to development of curriculum for educable mentally retarded visually handicapped adolescents.* New York: American Foundation for the Blind, 1968.

Anderson, R.M. Hearing impaired and mentally retarded: A selected bibliography. *Volta Review,* 1965, **67**, 425-432. (a)

Anderson, R.M. The visually impaired, mentally retarded: A selected bibliography. *New Outlook for the Blind,* 1965, **59**, 357-360. (b)

Anderson, R., & Stevens, G.D. Deafness and mental retardation in children: The problem. *American Annals of the Deaf,* 1969, **114**, 15-22.

Anderson, R.M., & Stevens, G.D. Policies and procedures for admission of mentally retarded deaf children to residential schools for deaf. *American Annals of the Deaf,* 1970, **115**, 30-36.

Ashcroft, S.C. The multiple handicapped child with a visual disability. In J.F. Cawley & N.D. Matkin (Eds.), *Visual and auditory defects accompanying mental retardation.* Hartford: University of Connecticut, 1967.

Ashcroft, S.C., Holliday, C.C., & Barraga, N.C. *Study II: Effects of experimental teaching on the visual behavior of children educated as though they had no vision.* Nashville, Tenn.: George Peabody College for Teachers, 1965.

Avery, C. Para-analytic group therapy with adolescent multihandicapped blind. *New Outlook for the Blind,* 1968, **62**, 65-72.

Barraga, N. *Increased visual behavior in low vision children.* New York: American Foundation for the Blind, 1964.

Bennett, F., & Oellerich, D.W. Institutional facilities for the visually handicapped, mentally retarded. *New Outlook for the Blind,* 1966, **60**, 233-235.

Berkson, G., & Davenport, R.K. Stereotyped movements of mental defectives: I, Initial survey. *American Journal of Mental Deficiency,* 1962, **66**, 849-852.

Birch, J.R., & Birch, J.W. Predicting school achievement in young deaf children. *American Annals of the Deaf,* 1956, **101**, 348-352.

Birch, J., & Matthews, J. The hearing of mental defectives: Its measurement and characteristics. *American Journal of Mental Deficiency,* 1951, **55**, 384-393.

Birch, J.R., Stuckless, E.R., & Birch, J.W. An eleven-year study predicting school achievement in young deaf children. *American Annals of the Deaf,* 1963, **108**, 236-240.

Blanchard, I., Bowling, D., & Roberts, R.L. Evaluation of an educational testing program for retarded blind children. *New Outlook for the Blind,* 1968, **62**, 131-133.

Bluhm, D.L. *Teaching the retarded visually handicapped: Indeed they are children.* Philadelphia: W.B. Saunders, 1968.

Boly, L.F., & DeLeo, G.M. A survey of educational provisions for the institutionalized mentally sub-normal blind. *American Journal of Mental Deficiency,* 1956, **60**, 744-749.

Bongers, K.H., & Doudlak, A.M. Techniques for initiating visuomotor behavior in visually impaired retarded children. *Education of the Visually Handicapped,* 1972, **4**, 80-82.

Bradley, E., Evans, W.E., & Worthington, A.M. The relationship between administration time for audiometric testing and the mental ability of mentally deficient children. *American Journal of Mental Deficiency,* 1955, **60**, 346-53.

Brown, D.W. Operant conditioning of attending and verbal imitation of deaf children with deviant behaviors. *Dissertation Abstracts,* 1968, **28**, 4904-4905.

Budds, F.C. Some initial experiences with mentally handicapped children who are attending schools for the blind. *The International Journal for the Education of the Blind,* 1960, **10**, 16-23.

Candland, D.K., & Conklyn, D.H. Use of oddity problems in teaching mentally retarded deaf-mutes to read: A pilot project. *Training School Bulletin,* 1962, **59**, 38-41.

Cawley, J.F., & Spotts, J.V. Mental retardation and accompanying sensory defects: Some implications of a survey. In J.F. Cawley & N.D. Matkin (Eds.), *Visual and auditory defects accompanying mental retardation*. Hartford: University of Connecticut, 1967.

Cooke, R.M., & Parsons, P. A program in basic communication development for retarded blind children. *Journal of Special Education*, 1968, **2**, 329-336.

Costello, P.M. Dead-end kid: Schools for deaf-retardates. *Volta Review*, 1966, **68**, 639-43.

Coveny, T.E. A new test for the visually handicapped: Preliminary analysis of the reliability and validity of the Perkins-Binet. *Education of the Visually Handicapped*, 1972, **4**, 97-100.

Curtis, W.S. The evaluation of verbal performance in multiply handicapped blind children. *Exceptional Children*, 1966, **32**, 367-374.

Davidow, M.E. A study of instructional techniques for the development of social skills of retarded blind children. *The International Journal for the Education of the Blind*, 1962, **12**, 61-62.

Davis, C.J. The assessment of intelligence of visually handicapped children. *The International Journal for the Education of the Blind*, 1962, **12**, 48-51.

DeLeo, G.M., & Boly, L.F. Some considerations in establishing an educational program for the institutionalized blind and partially sighted mentally subnormal. *American Journal of Mental Deficiency*, 1956, **61**, 134-140.

Dexter, L.A. A social theory of mental deficiency, *American Journal of Mental Deficiency* 1958, **62**, 920-928.

Dexter, L.A. On the politics and sociology of stupidity in our society. In H.S. Becker (Ed.), *The other side: Perspectives on deviance*. New York: Free Press, 1964.

Dishart, M. Testing the blind for rehabilitation: Using a psychological profile. *New Outlook for the Blind*, 1959, **53**, 1-4.

Doehring, D.G. The validity of intelligence tests for evaluating deaf children. *The Journal of Speech and Hearing Disorders*, 1965, **30**, 299-300.

Dolan, W.S. The first ten months of the rubella living-unit. *New Outlook for the Blind*, 1972, **66**, 9-14.

Donlon, E.T. An evaluation center for the blind child with multiple handicaps. *The International Journal for the Education of the Blind*, 1964, **13**, 75-78.

Elonen, A.S., Polzien, M., & Zwarensteyn. The "uncommitted" blind child: Results of intensive training of children formerly committed to institutions for the retarded. *Exceptional Children*, 1967, **33**, 301-307.

Farber, B. *Mental retardation: Its social context and social consequences*. Boston: Houghton Mifflin, 1968.

Farrant, R.H. The intellective abilities of deaf and hearing children compared by factor analysis. *American Annals of the Deaf*, 1964, **109**, 306-325.

Farrell, M.J. A state facility for the blind retarded. *New Outlook for the Blind*, 1955, **49**, 166-168.

Ferster, C.B., & DeMyer, M.K. A method for the experimental analysis of the behavior of autistic children. *The American Journal of Orthopsychiatry*, 1962, **32**, 89-98.

Foale, M., & Paterson, J.W. The hearing of mental defectives. *American Journal of Mental Deficiency*, 1954, **59**, 254-258.

Folio, M.R., & Dubose, R.F. *Peabody Developmental Motor Scale* (Experimental ed.). Imrid Behavioral Sciences Monograph #25. Nashville, Tenn. IMRID Publications, 1974.

Fraenkel, W.A. Blind retarded—or retarded blind? *New Outlook for the Blind*, 1964, **58**, 165-169.

Friedlander, B.Z., & Knight, M.S. Brightness sensitivity and preference in deaf blind retarded children. *American Journal of Mental Deficiency*, 1973, **78**.

Frisnia, D.R. A psychological study of the mentally retarded deaf child. *Dissertation Abstracts*, 1955, **15**, 2287-2288.

Fulton, R.T., & Giffin, C.S. Audiological-otological considerations with the mentally retarded. *Mental Retardation* 1967, **5**, 26-31.

Fulton, R.F., & Lloyd, L.L. Hearing impairment in a population of children with Down's syndrome. *American Journal of Mental Deficiency*, 1968, **73**, 298-302.

Glovsky, L. Audiological assessment of a mongoloid population. *Training School Bulletin*, 1966, **63**, 27-36.

Glovsky, L., & Rigrodsky, S. A classroom program for auditorally handicapped mentally deficient children. *Training School Bulletin,* 1963, **60,** 56-69.

Graham, M.D. Multiply-impaired blind children: A national problem. New York: American Foundation for the Blind, 1967.

Grossman, H.J. (Ed.). *Manual on terminology and classification in mental retardation.* Washington, D.C.: American Association on Mental Deficiency, 1973.

Guess, D. The influence of visual and ambulation restrictions on a stereotyped behaviors. *American Journal of Mental Deficiency,* 1966, **70,** 542-547.

Guess, D. Mental retardation and blindness: A complex and relatively unexplored dyad. *Exceptional Children,* 1967, **33,** 471-479.

Guess, D., & Rutherford, G. Experimental attempts to reduce stereotyping in blind retardates. *American Journal of Mental Deficiency,* 1967, **71,** 984-986.

Hall, S.M., & Talkington, L.W. Trends in programming for deaf mentally retarded in public residential facilities. *Mental Retardation,* 1972, **10,** 2, 50-52.

Harley, R.K., Merbler, J.B., & Wood, T.A. The development of a scale in orientation and mobility for multiply impaired blind children. *Education of the Visually Handicapped,* 1975, **7,** 1-5.

Harley, R.K., Wood, T.A., & Merbler, J.B. A pilot study in orientation and mobility for multiply impaired blind children. Unpublished paper. George Peabody College, Nashville, Tennessee, 1974.

Hart, V. The blind child who functions on a retarded level: The challenge for teacher preparation. *New Outlook for the Blind,* 1969, **63,** 318-321.

Hart, V. *Beginning with the handicapped.* Springfield, Ill.: Charles C Thomas, 1974.

Hart, V., & DuBose, R.F. A manual for the development of self-help skills in multiple handicapped children (Experimental ed.). Mimeographed paper, George Peabody College, Nashville, Tennessee, 1971.

Hartlage, L.C. Listening comprehension in the retarded blind. *Perceptual and Motor Skills,* 1965, **20,** 763-764.

Hartlage, L.C. Social maturity, listening comprehension and intelligence in retarded blind. *Psychology,* 1966, **3,** 12-15.

Hatlen, P.H. Visually handicapped children with additional problems. In B. Lowenfield (Ed.), *The visually handicapped child in school.* New York: John Day, 1973.

Hepfinger, L.M. Psychological evaluation of young blind children. *Outlook for the Blind,* 1962, **56,** 309-315.

Hevriella, S.M. The slow learning deaf child. *Volta Review,* 1961, **63,** 300-384.

Hiskey, M.S. A study of intelligence of deaf and hearing children. *American Annals of the Deaf,* 1956, **51,** 331-343.

Iverson, L.A., & Hartong, J.R. Expanded opportunities for multiply handicapped children. *New Outlook for the Blind,* 1971, **65,** 117-119.

Johnston, B.C. "Total life" rehabilitation for the mentally retarded blind person. *New Outlook for the Blind,* 1971, **65,** 331-333.

Johnston, P.W., & Farrell, M.J. Auditory impairments at W.E. Fernald State School. *American Journal of Mental Deficiency,* 1954, **58,** 640-643.

Johnston, P.W., & Farrell, M.J. Auditory impairments among resident school children at the Walter Fernald State School. *American Journal of Mental Deficiency,* 1957, **62,** 230-237.

Jones, J.W. Problems in defining and classifying blindness. *New Outlook for the Blind,* 1962, **56,** 115-121.

Kephart, J.G., Kephart, C.P., & Schwarz, G.C. A journey into the world of the blind child. *Exceptional Children,* 1974, **40,** 421-427.

Kerr, N., Meyerson, L., & Michael, J. A procedure for shaping vocalization in a mute child. In L.P. Ullmann & L. Krasner (Eds.), *Case studies in behavior modification.* New York: Holt, Rinehart, & Winston, 1965.

Kirk, S.A., & Perry, J.A. A comparative study of the Ontario and Nebraska. *American Annals of the Deaf,* 1948, **93,** 315-323.

Knight, J.J. Building self-confidence in the multiply handicapped blind child. *New Outlook for the Blind*. 1971, **65**, 152-154.

Kodman, F., Powers, T.R., Philip, P.P., & Weller, G.M. An investigation of hearing loss in mentally retarded children and adults. *American Journal of Mental Deficiency*, 1958, **63**, 460-463.

Kopatic, N.J. The reliability of pure tone audiometry with the mentally retarded: Some practical and theoretical considerations. *Training School Bulletin*, 1963, **60**, 130-137.

La Crosse, E.L., & Bidlake, H. A method to test the hearing of mentally retarded children. *Volta Review*, 1964, **66**, 27-30.

Landau, M.E. Group psychotherapy with deaf retardates. *International Journal of Group Psychotherapy*, 1968, **18**, 345-351.

Lane, H., & Curran, C. Gradients of auditory generalization for blind retarded children. *Journal of the Experimental Analysis of Behavior*, 1963, **6**, 585-588.

Langley, M.B. An experimental use of a language board for administration of the Peabody Picture Vocabulary Test. Unpublished paper. George Peabody College, Nashville, Tennessee, 1973.

Larsen, L.A. Behavior modification with the multi-handicapped. *New Outlook for the Blind*, 1970, **64**, 6-14.

Leshin, G., & Stahlecker, L. Academic expectancies of slow-learning deaf children. *Volta Review*, 1962, **64**, 599-602.

Leverett, J., & Bergman, A.I. Sunrise project for the blind. *New Outlook for the Blind*, 1970, **64**, 38-40.

Lloyd, L.L., & Fulton, R.F. Audiology's contributions: Programming with the retarded. In J.E. McLean & D. Yoder (Eds.), *Language intervention with the retarded: Developing strategies.* Baltimore: University Park Press, 1972.

Lloyd, L.L., & Reid, M.J. Incidence of hearing impairment in an institutionalized mentally retarded population. *American Journal of Mental Deficiency*, 1967, **71**, 746-63.

Lloyd, L.L., Spradlin, J.E., & Reid, M.J. An operant audiometric procedure for difficult to test patients. *Journal of Speech and Hearing Disorders*, 1968, **33**, 236-245.

Lovaas, O.I., Berberich, J.P., Perloff, B.F., & Schaeffer, B. Acquisition of imitative speech by schizophrenic children. *Science*, 1966, **151**, 705-707.

Lowenfeld, B. *Our blind children: Growing up and learning with them* (2nd ed.). Springfield, Ill: Charles C Thomas, 1964.

Lowenfeld, B. (Ed.). *The visually handicapped child in school*. New York: John Day, 1973.

Luszki, W.A. Degree of learning loss related to intelligence as measured by the WAIS and WISC. *Dissertation Abstracts*, 1964, **25** (5), 3113-3114.

Macht, J. Operant measurement of subjective visual acuity in non-verbal children. *Journal of Applied Behavior Analysis*, 1971, **4**, 23-35.

MacPherson, J.R. The status of the deaf and/or hard of hearing mentally defective in the United States. *American Annals of the Deaf* 1952, **97**, 375-386, 448-469.

Mattis, S. An experimental approach to treatment of visually impaired multi-handicapped children. *New Outlook for the Blind*, 1967, **61**, 1-5.

McClelland, D.C. Testing for competence rather than for "intelligence." *American Psychologist*, 1973, **28**, 1-14.

McDade, P.R. The importance of motor development and mobility skills for the institutionalized blind mentally retarded. *New Outlook for the Blind*, 1969, **63**, 312-317.

McLennen, S. Teaching techniques for institutionalized blind retarded children. *New Outlook for the Blind*, 1969, **63**, 322-325.

Mercer, J.R. Sociological perspectives on mild mental retardation. In H.C. Haywood (Ed.) *Social-cultural aspects of mental retardation*. New York: Appleton-Century-Crofts, 1970.

Mercer, J.R. *Labeling the mentally retarded*. Berkely: University of California Press, 1973.

Mira, M.P. Use of the Arthur Adaptation of the Leiter International Performance Scale and Nebraska Test of Learning Aptitude with pre-school deaf children. *American Annals of the Deaf*, 1962, **107**, 224-228.

Misbach, D.L. Happy gracious living for the mentally-retarded blind child. *New Outlook for the Blind*, 1953, **47**, 61-66.

Mitra, S.B. A descriptive study of institutional educational programs for the mentally retarded deaf. *Dissertation Abstracts* 1969, **30**, (5-A), 1784.

Mitra, S.B. Educational provisions for mentally retarded deaf students in residential institutions for the retarded. *Volta Review* 1970, **72**, 225-236.

Mitra, S.B. Guidelines for hospitalized retarded deaf children. *American Annals of the Deaf*, 1971, **116**, 385-388.

Mitra, S.B. Language training for retarded-deaf children in a state institution. *The Training School Bulletin*, 1974, **71**, 41-49.

Moore, M.V. Speech, hearing, and language in deLange syndrome. *Journal of Speech and Hearing Disorders*, 1970, **35**, 66-69.

Murphy, T.J. Teaching orientation and mobility to mentally retarded blind persons. *New Outlook for the Blind*, 1964, **58**, 285-287.

Myklebust, H.R. *Auditory disorders in children.* New York: Grune & Stratton, 1954.

Neisworth, J.T. The educational irrelevance of intelligence. In R.M. Smith (Ed.), *Teacher diagnosis of educational difficulties.* Columbus, Ohio: Charles E. Merrill, 1969.

Nelson, M., & Siblis, J.P. Audiologic aspects of a deaf retarded population. *Volta Review*, 1962, **64**, 426-427.

Oleron, P. A study of the intelligence of the deaf. *American Annals of the Deaf*, 1950, **95**, 179-195.

Paraskeva, P.C. A survey of the facilities for the mentally retarded blind in the United States. *The International Journal for the Education of the Blind*, 1959, **8**, 139-143.

Parker, J. Adapting school psychological evaluation to the blind child. *New Outlook for the Blind*, 1969, **63**, 305-308.

Partington, M.W. Waardenburg syndrome and heterochromia iridum in a deaf school population. *Canadian Medical Association Journal*, 1964, **90**, 1008-1011.

Rabinowitz, M. Rubella: Case histories. *National Hearing and Speech Journal*, 1968, **22**, 4.

Rapaport, I. Mental handicap—diagnosis and placement. *New Outlook for the Blind*, 1961, **55**, 291-293.

Regler, J. An experimental program for slowly developing blind children. *The International Journal for the Education of the Blind*, 1960, **9**, 89-92.

Rigrodsky, S., Prunty, F., & Glovsky, L. A study of the incidence, types and associated etiologies of hearing loss in an institutionalized mentally retarded population. *Training School Bulletin* 1961, **58**, 30-44.

Rodden, H. Teaching techniques for institutionalized blind retarded children. *New Outlook for the Blind*, 1970, **64**, 5-8.

Roos, P. The challenge: *The blind child who functions on the retarded level: Selected papers.* New York: American Foundation for the Blind, 1969.

Root, F.K. Evaluation of services for multiply-handicapped blind children. *The International Journal for the Education of the Blind*, 1963, **13**, 33-38.

Sailor, W., Guess, D., Rutherford, G., & Baer, D.M. Control of tantrum behavior by operant techniques during experimental verbal training. *Journal of Applied Behavior Analysis*, 1968, **1**, 237-243.

Schaeffer, M.H. Meeting the needs of the blind-mentally retarded at the Pennhurst State School and Hospital. *New Outlook for the Blind*, 1968, **62**, 254-258.

Schlanger, B.B., & Gottsleben, R.H. Testing the hearing of the mentally retarded. *Journal of Speech and Hearing Disorders*, 1956, **21**, 487-493.

Schunhoff, H., & MacPherson, J. What about the deaf or hard of hearing mentally deficient? *Training School Bulletin*, 1951, **48**, 71-75.

Seelye, W., & Thomas, J.E. Is mobility feasible with: A blind girl with leg braces and crutches? A deaf-blind girl with a test IQ of 50? A blind boy with an IQ of 51? *New Outlook for the Blind*, 1966, **60**.

Sheridan, M.D. Vision screening of young and handicapped children. *British Medical Journal*, 1960, **5196**, 453-463.

Siegenthaler, B.M., & Krzywicki, D.F. Incidence and patterns of hearing loss among an adult mentally retarded population. *American Journal of Mental Deficiency*, 1964, **68**, 444, 449-59.

Sklar, M.J., & Rampulla, J. Decreasing inappropriate classroom behavior of a multiply handicapped blind student. *Education of the Visually Handicapped,* 1972, **5**, 71-74.

Smith, J.O., & Arkans, J.R. Now more than ever: A case for the special class. *Exceptional Children,* 1974, **40**, 497-502.

Stephens, R. Running free: The use of a "running cable" with blind adolescents who function on a retarded level. *New Outlook for the Blind,* 1973, **67**, 454-456.

Stone, A.A. Consciousness: Altered level in blind retarded children. *Psychosomatic Medicine,* 1964, **26**, 14-19.

Stuckless, E.R., & Birch, J.W. The influence of early manual communication on linguistic development of deaf children. *American Annals of the Deaf,* 1966, **111**, 452-460.

Swartz, J.D., & Cleland, C.C. *Multihandicapped mentally retarded: Training and enrichment strategies.* Austin Texas: The Hogg Foundation for Mental Health, 1973.

Talkington, L.W. An exploratory program for blind retarded. *Education of the Visually Handicapped.* 1972, **4**, 33-35.

Talkington, L., & Hall, S.M. Hearing impairment and aggressiveness in the MR. *Perceptual Motor Skills,* 1969, **28**, 303-306.

Talkington, L.W., & Hall, S.M. Evaluation of manual approach to programming for deaf retarded. *American Journal of Mental Deficiency,* 1970, **75**, 378-80.

Talkington, L., & Reed, K. Rorschach response patterns of hearing impaired retardation. *Perceptual Motor Skills,* 1969, **29**, 546-549.

Templar, D., & Hartlage, L. The reliability and utilization of the hand-face test with the retarded blind. *American Journal of Mental Deficiency* 1965, **70**, 139-141.

Thomas, E.J.B. Services and training methods in a day care center for severely retarded, blind children. New York: Jewish Guild for the Blind, 1969.

Thomas, J.E. Mobility education for multiply handicapped blind children in day schools: What it encompasses. *New Outlook for the Blind,* 1972, **66**, 307-313.

Tretakoff, M. Teaching the multiply handicapped blind child. In *The blind child who functions on a retarded level: Selected papers.* New York: American Foundation for the Blind, 1969.

Tretakoff, M.I., & Farrell, M.J. Developing a curriculum for the blind retarded. *American Journal of Mental Deficiency,* 1958, **62**, 610-615.

Walsh, F.B. Blindness in an institution for the feeble-minded. *Archives of Ophthalmology,* 1963, **69**, 1965.

Webb, C., Kinde, S., Weber, B., & Beedle, R. Incidence of hearing loss in institutionalized mental retardates. *American Journal of Mental Deficiency* 1966, **70**, 563-568.

Williams, D. Sunland's program for the blind. *Mental Retardation,* 1964, **2**, 244-245.

Wishik, S.M. *Georgia study of handicapped children.* Atlanta: Georgia Department of Public Health, 1964.

Wolf, J.M. The blind child with concomitant disabilities. *American Foundation for the Blind, Research Series Number 16.* New York: American Foundation for the Blind, 1967.

Wolf, J.M., & Anderson, R.M. (Eds.). *The multiply handicapped child.* Springfield, Ill.: Charles C Thomas, 1969.

Wolf, M.M., Birnbrauer, J.S., Williams, T., & Lawler, W. A note on apparent extinction of the vomiting behavior of a retarded child. In L.P. Ullmann & L. Krasner (Eds.), *Case studies in behavior modification.* New York: Holt, Rinehart & Winston, 1965.

Wolf, M.M., Risley, T., & Mees, H. Application of operant conditioning procedures to the behavior problems of an autistic child. *Behaviour Research and Therapy,* 1964, **1**, 305-312.

Wood, T.A., & Berger, H. Review of the literature: Orientation and mobility for multiply handicapped visually impaired. Unpublished Paper, George Peabody College, Nashville, Tennessee, 1972.

Wood, W.J. Educational and psychological management. In *The blind child who functions on a retarded level: Selected papers.* New York: American Foundation for the Blind, 1969.

TAXONOMIES IN SPECIAL EDUCATION

Jenny R. Armstrong

University of Wisconsin

Taxonomies have been developed for many years in a variety of disciplines to classify phenomena. They provide a way of simplifying complicated universes to make them easier to deal with—both conceptually and practically. Comprehensive and unambiguous classificatory systems can greatly enhance scientific advances. Historically, taxonomies were first developed in biology in the mid-1700s (Frederiksen, 1971). The approach taken was inductive: Biologists observed and identified hundreds of plants and established criteria based on a specific purpose to group the plants. Their purpose was to classify plants so as to reflect their evolutionary development. Therefore, the purpose of the problem defined the criteria. Once set, criteria established the guidelines for the classification system which resulted. This same approach has also characterized the establishment of taxonomies in special education.

Taxonomies have been developed to clarify and solve particular problems in special education. In most cases, such taxonomies have been very reflective of the way the problems have been viewed philosophically. Thus, taxonomies which have been developed to address the treatment and education of handicapped children have changed as the attitudes toward these children have changed.

Any classification system is to some degree arbitrary and biased. Taxonomies may be purely descriptive, or they make take on a theoretical orientation, depending upon their purpose or intent. Taxonomies may be exhaustive or not, and their categories may be mutually exclusive or overlapping. In some cases, relationships among elements or categories will be provided; in other cases, they will not. In special education, there are few well-established taxonomies except in the domain of individual differences. A similar state of affairs greets us in the fields of psychology and education.

The issue in special education has been whether the objects of the classification were individuals, their behaviors or attributes, or an interaction of the two. In the diagnostic labeling of handicapped children, it is important to note that the child's behavior or demonstrated attributes are being classified, not the child. (As behaviors or attributes change, so do the groupings which place certain children together for various taxonomic purposes.) The object is to classify the child's expected or actual behavior, as compared to an ideal or standard for behavior, at a particular stage of development.

Determining what classification systems are relevant to special education might itself be considered a taxonomy. The problem is one of defining those elements which comprise special education and determining how they might be categorized or labeled to best express, clarify, and simplify this universe of activity. At a general level, special education is only distinguished from regular education by the children involved in the educational programs. Consequently, given a taxonomy of educational processes which provides for individual differences in learners, some of the same taxonomies developed in general psychology and education would be applicable to special education.

One of the earlier taxonomies of such "teaching-learning" processes proposed by Macdonald (1965) included four major elements: (a) teaching, (b) learning, (c) curriculum, and (d) instruction. Drawing on this taxonomy, Armstrong (1970) proposed an enlarged version involving input, output, and process components. This enlarged taxonomy included as elements in the input mode: (a) teachers, (b) learners, (c) curriculum, (d) instructional methods, (e) instructional materials and media, and (f) instructional environments. Included as elements in the output mode were (a) cognitive learning, (b) affective learning, and (c) psychomotor learning. The process mode within this classificatory scheme was teaching (Armstrong, 1969).

Such taxonomies of the educational process are very global and thus provide a useful working outline for all other taxonomies which might be established to clarify the educational process as it relates to the education of handicapped children. This general taxonomy will also be used to provide the organization for this review; it will provide the "classes" for examining taxonomies which have been developed to further clarify each of the main areas: learners, curriculum, instructional materials and media, instructional environments, instructional methods, teachers, and teaching. Unfortunately, in a majority of these areas very little work relevant to the education of handicapped children has been completed. Such a lack points to the need for additional taxonomic work.

LEARNER TAXONOMIES

The definition of the children to be served by special education has in essence not only defined the field, but also determined, to a certain extent, the way in which taxonomies in all other areas have been developed. As indicated previously, taxonomies of individual differences involve the classifications of behaviors and attributes, not individuals. Consequently, the focus of the review is on the *attributes and behaviors* of handicapped children which have been used to devise such taxonomies.

Project on the classification of exceptional children

One of the most comprehensive efforts undertaken to review and examine taxonomies for classifying exceptional children is that of the Project on Classification of Exceptional Children (Hobbs, 1975a, 1975b). This project not only examined the taxonomies which have been used for classifying exceptional children but also discussed many of the issues surrounding the diagnosis and labeling of exceptional children. The project systematically reviewed systems for classifying and labeling children with handicaps and assessed the consequences of such classification and labeling (Hobbs, 1975a). One group of project participants, the National Advisory Committee, was composed of professionals and laymen who had been involved for extended periods of time with exceptional children. The second group, the Inter-Agency Task Force, was comprised of professionals representing the nine federal agencies which sponsored the 18-month study. Those agencies were (*a*) the Office of Child Development, (*b*) the Bureau of Education for the Handicapped, (*c*) the National Institute of Mental Health, (*d*) the National Institute of Child Health and Human Development, (*e*) the Division of Developmental Disabilities of the Social and Rehabilitation Service, (*f*) the Bureau of Community Health Services in the Health Services Administration, (*g*) the President's Committee on Mental Retardation Coordination, (*h*) the Office of Civil Rights in the Office of the Secretary of Health, Education, and Welfare, and (*i*) the Council on Juvenile Delinquency of the Department of Justice. The project was conducted at Vanderbilt University under the direction of Nicholas Hobbs.

As results of this study, seven major general conclusions were drawn about classification:

(1) Classification of exceptional children is essential to get services for them, to plan and organize helping programs, and to determine the outcomes of intervention efforts; (2) Public and private policies and practices must manifest respect for the individuality of children and appreciation of the respect for the individuality of children and appreciation of the positive values of their individual talents and diverse cultural background; classification procedures must not be used to violate this fundamental social value; (3) There is growing public concern over the uses and abuses of categories and labels as applied to children, and there is widespread dissatisfaction with inadequate, uncoordinated, and even hurtful services for children; we assume that all citizens share responsibility for these unsatisfactory circumstances as well as for their repair; (4) Special programs for handicapped children should be designed to encourage fullest possible participation in the usual experiences of childhood, in regular schooling and recreational activities, and in family and community life. When a child must be removed from normal activities, he or she should be removed the least possible distance in time, in geographical space, and in the psychological texture of the experience provided; (5) Categories and labels are powerful instruments for social regulation

and control, and they are often employed for obscure, covert or hurtful purposes—to degrade people, to deny them access to opportunity, to exclude "undesirables" whose presence in some way offends, disturbs familiar custom, or demands extraordinary effort; (6) Categories and labels may open up opportunities for exceptional children, facilitate the passage of legislation in their interest, supply all rallying points for volunteer organizations, and provide a rational structure for the administration of governmental programs; and (7) Our nation provides inadequately for exceptional children for reasons linked to their being different; it also provides inadequately for exceptional children because it provides inadequately for all children. There is urgent need for a quickened national conscience and a new national policy with this as a goal: to nurture well all of our children, in body, mind, and spirit, that we as a people may grow in widsom, strength, and humane concerns. (Hobbs, 1975a, pp. 5-14)

As illustrated by the diversity of the conclusions drawn from this study on the classification of exceptional children, the issues involved and the solutions to appropriate design and use of taxonomies are a long way from being resolved. Taxonomies can be helpful and hurtful, depending on how they are used, by whom, and for what purposes. Let us reiterate: Taxonomies are not value-free. They are developed to serve particular purposes, and those used with handicapped children are based to a considerable degree on the way in which treatment and education of the handicapped is viewed by the classifiers or definers.

Problems leading to the creation of learner taxonomies

It is informative to examine some of the early problems which led to the classification of handicapped children as being distinct from "normal" children. Such problems and their solutions were very much part of the social tenor of the times. Some have identified the Compulsory Attendance Act, and its associated legislation between 1852 and 1918, as one of the critical factors influencing the establishment of the first learner classification systems (Rhodes & Sagor, 1975). This law required that all children in the United States attend school.

The law was to provide opportunities for all children to learn, irrespective of their parents' financial or social position. The social phenomenon which encouraged this law's establishment was the large influx of impoverished aliens with different cultures, values, and languages. The threat that these posed to the dominant core of social mores encouraged the development of an institution designed to "socialize" the alien elements (Hoffman, 1972).

Their influx into the schools created problems. The view during this period (i.e., roughly 1852-1918) is best reflected by the attitudes toward alien children expressed in a statement taken from the Harper Report prepared in 1898 by the educational commission of the city of Chicago:

The Compulsory Attendance Act has for its purpose the reformation of these vicious children. They cannot be received or continued in the regularly organized schools; they were admitted into these schools; they were reproved; they were punished for misconduct; they have been suspended from further attendance in their classes; their parents cannot or will not control them; teachers and committees fail to correct their evil tendencies and vicious conduct. What shall be done with them? The Compulsory Attendance Act commands that they shall be placed in schools; if not in regular schools, then in other schools to be provided for them. (Hoffman, 1972, p. 14)

In yet another citation:

There are also a large number of children who are constantly dropping out of our schools because of insubordination to discipline and want of cooperation between the parents and the teachers and they are becoming vagrants upon the streets and a menace to good society. The welfare of the city demands that such children be put under restraint. . . . I, therefore, call attention again to the necessity of the establishment of a parental school for the benefit of such children. (Hoffman, 1972, p. 14)

Such attitudes toward deviance in children and its relationship to their education led to one of the first taxonomies of individual differences: "deviance" and "nondeviance." New schools were established in the 1800s to provide for the special education of deviants, with the rationale of deviance being the basis of exclusion from regular schools. The problems surrounding the issues of such classification were viewed in part within the context of the Compulsory Attendance law, which ruled that all children must be in school, and in part from the inability of regular schools of that time to cope with these so-called deviant children. Subsequently, in 1871 in New Haven, Connecticut, the first ungraded school for "mischievous and disruptive children" was established. This school was said to be a place where "unreasonably disobedient and insubordinate" youths, considered to be a detriment to "good order and instruction," could be separated from the children in the regular school, taught, and controlled without disturbing others (Rhodes & Sagor, 1975).

Society's attitudes towards deviancy during the 19th century put the stability of the community and society ahead of concern for the poor, criminal, and insane. The almshouse, orphanage, penitentiary, reformatory, and insane asylum all represented an effort to guard and insure the stability of the community from the thread of deviance. The growth and development of these institutions in the early 1800s only briefly antedated the compulsory attendance laws and correctional programs for juveniles. In addition, the threat created by large masses of immigrant children crowded into the slums of urban areas led to other specialized confinement environments for such children. Orphanages, institutions for the retarded, refuges for delinquents, and special schools for all types of deviance saw great growth during this period (Mercer, 1973; Rhodes & Sagor, 1975). They were designed to provide "ideal parent" and beneficial "social-environmental" surrogates.

As such institutions were established, the taxonomy of handicapped learners was expanded from deviance-nondeviance to include such descriptive categories as "poor," "orphan," "retarded," "delinquent," and "insane." Other descriptors in use at the same time were: "diseased minds," "weak minds," and "evil and pernicious children."

As early as 1844, the first professional organization of administrators of the new institutions and asylums was formed, the Association of Medical Superintendents of American Institutions for the Insane (Rhodes & Sagor, 1975). This organization later became the American Psychiatric Association.

Professional organizations dealing with deviants were soon faced with a typical dilemma. Although originally formed to eliminate deviancy or delinquency, they soon became creators of it (Rothman, 1971). These agencies placed people with vastly different needs into the same facilities. Some were there only because they were poor. This development, in turn, necessitated new views concerning the treatment and education of these individuals. Thus, taxonomies of individual traits, attributes, and behaviors were expanded to accommodate the changing views and attitudes toward deviancy and its classification.

In the early 1900s, many organizations devoted to preventive medicine came into being. Led by such professionals as William James and Adolf Meyer, they created a new term, "mental hygiene" and, at the same time, a new philosophy of deviance and the deviants (Rhodes & Sagor, 1975). Classifications such as "weak minds," "diseased minds," and "evil and pernicious children" gave way to such terms as "mental deficiency," "emotional disturbance," and "delinquency."

With the advent of these more expanded classification schemes, professionals began to focus their attention on more narrowly defined groups of handicapped. This focus then led to separate description systems for each of the more narrowly defined categories: "mental deficiency," "emotional disturbance," and "delinquency."

Mental deficiency

One of the first definitions of mental deficiency was that of Esquirol (1845) as reported by Blanton (1975). Esquirol stated that "idiocy" was not a disease, but rather a condition wherein the intellectual faculties were either never manifested or failed to develop ways to enable the "idiot" to acquire the same amount of knowledge as persons of his own age in similar circumstances (Esquirol, 1845). Esquirol created a taxonomy which grouped the retarded into two classes, "idiots" and "imbeciles," on the basis of speech development. This taxonomy was very much a reflection of Esquirol's (1845) view of mental deficiency which was much the same as that of Séguin (1866). Both felt that except in cases of identifiable brain injury, mental deficiency was caused by sensory isolation or deprivation. Thus they felt that mental deficiency could be eliminated by strong programs of sensory stimulation. Esquirol's (1845) taxonomy based on speech development stayed in force until the early 1900s. After this time developments in neurology and brain pathology led to more medically oriented classifications of mental retardation. One classification scheme under the medical egis was "congenital" and "noncongenital" (Duncan & Millard, 1866). The congenital cases were classified functionally into: (a) profound idiots, (b) those able to walk and stand, (c) those able to use hands for easy mechanical work and to feed themselves, and (d) feebleminded cases who require supervision for their own protection and that of others. Noncongenital cases were divided into: (a) those with disease or injury to the brain after birth, (b) those with epilepsy, (c) hydrocephalics, and (d) those debased during early youth from vice (Blanton, 1975).

In contrast, Ireland (1898), offered a classification system based on etiological considerations. The categories were (a) genetous, (b) microcephalic, (c) eclampsic, (d) epileptic, (e) hydrocephalic, (f) paralytic, (g) cretinism, (h) traumatic, (i) inflammatory, and (j) idiocy by deprivation (Blanton, 1975). Genetic defects were placed first in the listing, undoubtedly reflecting the theories and evidence being developed during this time by such individuals as Morel (1857), Lombroso (1876), and Down (1866). Deprivation, as viewed during this time, signified sensory deprivation in the physiological sense rather than the socio-economic-cultural deprivation which later became part of classification schemas.

Another development which had a profound effect on the establishment of taxonomies for mental retardation was mental testing. The first intellectual function to be measured in the retarded was memory span (Galton, 1887; Jacobs, 1887). In general, the results showed that "feebleminded" children fell far below normals in memory span, although there were exceptional cases who had better memory span than the averages among the normals (Blanton, 1975).

In 1895, Binet began publication of his work on mental tests. He viewed the tests as a means to compare individuals on various tasks rather than to estimate or get an absolute measure of ability (Binet, 1898). In 1900, Binet (1900) published a study on reaction time, perception, immediate memory, and several other tasks in two groups of children who differed greatly in ability as judged by their teachers. In 1904, Binet and Simon began to collect materials and develop new tasks which they might use in classifying children by intellectual development. The first Binet-Simon scales were published in 1905, the authors revising them in 1908 to include the mental age concept with tasks so classified (Binet & Simon, 1905; 1908).

In 1910, after giving the Binet-Simon scales to over 400 children at the

Vineland Training School in New Jersey, Goddard (1910) suggested a classification of children based on mental age. Children with a mental age of less than 2 were designated as "idiots," those from 3 to 7 as "imbeciles," and those from 8 to 12 as "morons." Children with a mental age above 12 were to be classified as "normal."

Along with the widespread use and testing of the Binet-Simon scales came the controversies of what exactly these tests measured. Since discrepancies in mental age were found to be a function of racial and/or cultural backgrounds, the need for separate norming of the test on diverse populations was seen to be imperative for any use on a wide scale. It was further argued that the responses to the tasks and the questions on the tests were both a function of sociocultural (i.e., racial-cultural) background and past educational experiences. Thus, intelligence should be defined in a more functional sense, reflecting the capacity of the individual to adapt to social situations, rather than as the speed with which some of the basic perceptual-memory functions operate (Treves & Saffiotti, 1910). The same points about intelligence tests are still being made today (Mercer, 1971, 1973, 1974, 1975).

Cronbach (1975) has provided a good recent review of the issues surrounding the use of intelligence tests. He addressed the rationale for the early development of the tests, beginning with Terman's (1919) work, as well as the pros and cons for using such tests to classify individuals on intelligence. He made several points: (a) Public controversy over intelligence testing has in general dealt with the generalities, not the specifics, of testing. As such, it has not provided avenues for the improvement of tests. (b) In general, sound policy has not been for tests or against tests, but rather related to how tests and their results are used. (c) Tests should not be used to determine an individual's future. Unfortunately, they have been used to estimate how much education an individual could use or what careers an individual might thrive in. (d) Educational goals must be distinguished, e.g., to prepare an individual for service to society, to prepare him to get more out of living, or to educate him in the means of certifying social status. Each goal provides different implications for the use of tests. Consequently, developers of taxonomies which utilize intelligence tests as their basis for scaling must consider the issues surrounding the use of such tests.

Three major classification systems of mental retardation currently in use in the United States are based in part on measured intelligence. They are the U.S. Department of Health, Education and Welfare's (1967) *International Classification of Diseases Adapted for Use in the United States, Eighth Edition* (ICDA-8); the American Psychiatric Association's (1968) *Diagnositc and Statistical Manual of Mental Disorders, Second Edition* (DSM-II) and the

American Association on Mental Deficiency's (AAMD) fifth revision of the *Manual on Terminology and Classification in Mental Retardation* (Heber, 1959, 1961), which has recently been replaced by a sixth revision (Grossman, 1973). The ICDA-8 and the DSM-II are adaptations of the World Health Organization's (1967) *International Classification of Diseases,* which is currently undergoing revision (Filler, Robinson, Smith, Vincent-Smith, Bricker, & Bricker, 1975).

The most recent revisions of the AAMD classification system (Grossman, 1973) are characterized by the following changes: (*a*) The diagnosis level has been lowered to two standard deviations below the mean as the upper limit for the classification of mental retardation according to measured intelligence. (*b*) The category "borderline mental retardation" is no longer included. (*c*) The major categories of the medical classification scheme have been changed to conform to those of the ICDA-8 and DSM-II systems. (I.e., the number of major medical categories have been expanded from eight to ten [coded 0-IX], and the specific disorders within each major classification have been reorganized; additionally, the numerical coding system has been changed to conform to one employed by the ICDA-8 system.) (*d*) Although the adaptive behavior levels (I through IV) have been maintained, Level I has been set at two standard deviations below the population mean, rather than one standard deviation as in the Heber (1961) manual. The four levels of retardation provided in the 1973 AAMD revision with standard deviation ranges based on measured intelligence are: (*a*) -2.01 to -3.00 (mild); (*b*) -3.01 to -4.00 (moderate); (*c*) -4.01 to -5.00 (severe); and (*d*) -5.01 and below (profound). These correspond to IQ ranges on the Binet (B) and Wechsler (W) as follows: (*a*) B: 68-52, W: 69-55 (mild); (*b*) B: 51-36, W: 54-40 (moderate); (*c*) B: 35-20, W: 39-25 (severe); and (*d*) B: 19 and below, W: 24 and below (profound) (Grossman, 1973). Clinical opinion, however, remains the major factor in determining levels of adaptive behavior. The glossary of terms has also been revised. Phrases such as "labor induced," which have no special meaning within the context of mental retardation, have been dropped and terms such as "positive reinforcement," "shaping," and "contingency management" have been added (Filler et al., 1975).

The AAMD classification system is similar to the ICDA-8 and DSM-II systems in that all three require multiple criteria for the diagnosis of retardation and employ the same terminology to describe the different degrees of severity (Grossman, 1973; Filler et al., 1975). Two major differences do exist, however. First, ICDA-8 and DSM-II include the category of borderline mental retardation. Second, ICDA-8 and DSM-II combine indices of measured intelligence and adaptive behavior into a single composite score, whereas the AAMD system encourages separate recording. Thus, intelligence scores have different meanings in the two systems. In the AAMD, it reflects only the patient's measured intelligence; in DSM-II and ICDA-3, it presumably reflects the general level of functioning (Wilson & Spitzer, 1969).

Emotional disturbance

The identification of emotional disturbance has been traced back to the Stone Age (Hewett & Forness, 1974). The earliest descriptions were of individuals who suffered severe headaches and convulsive disorders. The next historical period, during Greek and Roman times (i.e., 500 B.C. to A.D. 400), dealt with emotional disturbance described as "madness" or "insanity" and rejected all references to the "gods" as a causative factor in mental disease. Based on his beliefs, Hippocrates (460-375 B.C.) developed a classification system of mental disorders which included, "mania," "melancholia," and "phrenites." This system and its description indicated that Hippocrates had an awareness of epilepsy, hysteria, and postpartum psychosis and saw the relationship between acute brain disorders and infectious diseases and hemorrhage (Kolb, 1973). Even so, the major philosophical orientation toward mental disorders during this period was religious. It was suggested that the deviant behavior of such individuals be kept under cover of the home (Hewett & Forness, 1974). The term "maniac" was also used during this period to describe the mentally ill. Attitudes toward their condition ranged from fear and awe (i.e., dealing with the exorcism of the evil spirit) to compassion and understanding (Zilboorg & Henry, 1941). During the Middle Ages (400 to 1500), supernatural beliefs continued to dominate views toward the mentally ill. They were viewed as being "possessed by the devil" (Zilboorg & Henry, 1941). Even so, within both Arabic and Christian contexts more compassionate views toward the mentally ill often emerged during this period (Browne, 1921).

During the 16th and 17th centuries, religious views which incorporated spiritualism, sorcery, and mythology still continued to affect the view of the mentally ill. The medical profession of this period hypothesized that mental illness was related to the "great Motion of the Liquid of the Brain, which throws the Patient into a wild Fury or Madness" (Zilboorg & Henry, 1941, p. 298). Treatments for this "Madness" included such enlightened approaches as holding a patient under water until his attack was stifled or spinning him into unconsciousness on a special twirling stool. No real hospitals for the mentally ill in Western Europe were established until late in the 18th century. Often, these hospitals were linked to or supported by religious institutions.

The French Revolution was a critical event in the care and treatment of the mentally ill. The philosophy of this period encouraged individual social responsibility and, more important, responsibility of the community for its members. French physicians, most specifically Philippe Pinel who served as physician-in-chief of two major hospitals for the mentally ill during this critical period of social upheaval encouraged a more humanistic view toward the mentally ill than had previously been held (Hewett & Forness, 1974). Pinel's work in France was paralleled by work by Chiaruggi (1759-1820) in Italy, Tuke (1827-1895) in England, and Rush (1745-1813) and Dix (1802-1887) in the United States.

Through the work of these leaders, the chains on patients were removed and the surroundings within hospitals changed to better provide for the care of mental patients from a humanitarian perspective. Classification systems reflected more of an understanding of mental disorders as disease or illness (Colman, 1972; Hewett & Forness, 1974; Kolb, 1973; Zilboorg & Henry, 1941). Pinel, for example, on the basis of his case studies classified mental diseases in a manner similar to Hippocrates as: "mania," "melancholia," "dementia," and "idiocy."

In England and in the United States, during this same period, more humane treatment was instituted for the mentally ill. The first comprehensive volume on psychiatry was written in the United States by Benjamin Rush who directed the Pennsylvania Hospital for the mentally ill. His word reflected the more humanistic trend toward both the view and treatment of mental illness in the United States (Coleman, 1972).

Dorthea Dix was a leader in the fight to improve conditions for treatment of the mentally ill. Her presentation to Congress in 1848 was very descriptive of the state of treatment during that time:

> More than 9,000 idiots, epileptics, and insane in the United States destitute of appropriate care and protection . . . [are] bound with galling chains, bowed beneath fetters and heavy iron balls attached to drag chains, lacerated with ropes, scourged by rods and terrified beneath storms of curel blows; now subject to jibes and scorn and torturing tricks; now abandoned to the most outrageous violations. (Zilboorg & Henry, 1941, pp. 583-584)

Between 1841 and 1881, Dorthea Dix established 32 modern mental hospitals (Hewett & Forness, 1974). In the early 1900s the work of Sigmund Freud had a great impact on the efforts undertaken in these mental hospitals and in the way subsequent classification systems were derived. Some of Freud's significant contributions to the field have been summarized by Coleman (1972, p. 56):

> 1. Development of techniques for becoming acquainted with conscious and unconscious aspects of the mental life of the patient;
>
> 2. Demonstration that abnormal mental phenomena were simply exaggerations of normal phenomena; and
>
> 3. Development of a therapeutic technique—psychoanalysis—for the psychological treatment of the mentally ill.

Freud also encouraged viewing the child as a unique individual rather than as a miniature adult, an extremely important contribution to the understanding and treatment of childhood emotional disturbance. The work of Freud influenced the development of classification schemes in the following ways: (*a*) development was taken into account in describing a disturbance; (*b*) abnormal behaviors were considered and defined in terms of normal behavioral repretoires; and (*c*) the causes or reasons for the abnormal behavior were considered in describing or classifying a disturbance.

Around 1900, several publications began to describe psychiatric phenomena occurring in childhood, in contrast to earlier work which considered mental illness only as a condition of postchildhood years (Kanner, 1962). It was not until the early 1930s, however, that systematic studies of children with severe emotional disturbance were reported. Reports at this time began to incorporate diagnosis, etiology, therapy, and prognosis (Kanner, 1962). From 1936 to 1959, the approaches taken to describe emotionally disturbed children were varied and highly clinical in rature (Anthony, 1970).

Anthony (1970) has provided a summary of the clinically based taxonomies which were developed and reported during this period (Ackerman & Neubauer, 1958; Cameron, 1955; Chess, 1959; Gerard, 1953; Louttit, 1947; and Miller, 1936). Such classifications were quite diverse and eluded systematic synthesis into a single taxonomy. Even so, a certain degree of consensus did exist despite the differing times, locations, and theoretical positions of the clinicians. There was rough agreement that the behavior disorders manifested themselves in bodily disturbances, in inhibited, anxious, neurotic reactions, and in active, outgoing, aggressive conduct.

Anthony (1970), in summarizing the work of others, constructed a taxonomy of behavior disorders based on some of the main facets of normal behavior. This classification system included as major categories: (*a*) functional behavior (i.e., eating, eliminating, sleeping, moving, speaking); (*b*) cognitive behavior (i.e., thinking, remembering, learning, orienting, evaluating; (*c*) affective behavior (i.e., fearfulness, anxiety, depression-elation, shame-guilt, disgust); (*d*) social behavior (i.e., attacking, avoiding, oppositional, dominance-submission, abnormal sexual); and (*e*) integrative behavior (i.e., poor impulse control, low frustration tolerance, rigid-stereotyped, inadequate coping, disorganized). This approach to classification has distinct advantages when one is concerned with the emotional disturbance of children. First, it makes allowances for those variations in the child's behavior disorders which are a function of development. Second, it provides separate classifications for the different types of development which are expected to occur.

Other classification schemes for emotional disturbance have been developed primarily for research purposes. Again, these approaches to classification have been summarized by Anthony (1970). One research classification scheme, based on physiological and psychological measurements, included four major categories: (*a*) autistic-disjunctive (i.e., predominantly psychotic); (*b*) immature-labile (i.e., predominantly borderline); (*c*) sociopathic-paranoid (i.e., primarily children manifesting antisocial behavior); and (*d*) anxious-neurotic (i.e., predominantly neurotic) (Fish & Shapiro, 1964).

The need has been identified for a classification scheme to facilitate research, clinical practice, and communication by providing for diverse theoretical positions and views on emotional disturbance. Needed are explicit and clearly defined categories that researchers, clinicians, and other professionals can directly relate to and use (Group for Advancement of Psychiatry, 1966). Morse has suggested (1973) the criteria for such a classification system including the requirement that the scheme deal with such fundamental issues as: (*a*) the child's current status (clinical profile); (*b*) the genesis of the child's problems (etiology) in relation to a developmental framework, family experiences, and other factors; and (*c*) the implications of intervention in regard to choice of treatment method and prognosis.

Still another set of criteria for the establishment of taxonomies for emotional disturbance have been recommended by Rutter (1965). They address the following principles:

1. If the classification is to be acceptable, it must be based on facts, not concepts, and it must be defined in operational terms.

2. If it is to be useful, it must convey information relevant to the clinical situation and it must have predictive value.

3. The aim is to classify disorders, not to classify children.

Using these guidelines, Rutter proposed a specific taxonomy with 11 major categories:

(*1*) Neurotic disorders, (*2*) antisocial or conduct disorders, (*3*) mixed group in which neither neurotic nor antisocial symptoms predominate, (*4*) developmental disorders, (*5*) hyperkinetic syndrome, (*6*) child psychosis, (*7*) psychosis developing at or after puberty, (*8*) mental subnormality, (*9*) educational retardation, (*10*) depression, and (*11*) adult-type neurotic illnesses. (Rutter, 1965, pp. 79-80)

The classification systems proposed to date to define emotional disturbance have failed to gain widespread agreement or adoption. Classification systems which have been developed to describe children's behavior disorders on the basis of etiology have failed because of the difficulties in adequately accounting for all the multiple interrelated causative factors of emotional disturbance (Prugh, Engel, & Morse, 1975). Other proposed classification systems have failed because of difficulties in adequately accounting for all the different theoretical positions currently held by practicing clinicians (Group for Advancement of Psychiatry, 1966; Prugh, 1969; Rhodes and Tracy, 1972). It appears, therefore, that in the area of emotional disturbance, in order for a classification scheme to be developed which will gain widespread acceptance and adoption it must be multidimensional to account adequately for the variety of theoretical positions currently held and it must be descriptive rather than explanatory (Group for the Advancement of Psychiatry, 1966; Engel, 1969; Rutter, Lebovici, Eisenberg, Sneznevshy, Sadoun, Brooke, & Lin, 1969).

The 1961 revision of the *Standard Nomenclature of Diseases and Operations* (American Medical Association, 1961) provided a classification scheme based upon the concepts of dynamic psychology in the psychobiologic unit prepared by the American Psychiatric Association in its *Diagnostic and Statistical Manual,* First Edition, (DSM-I). This classification system offered descriptive-dynamic definitions for the categories, but failed to include many of the developmental features of emotional disturbance in children and young adolescents. However, in the most recent revision of the *Diagnostic and Statistical Manual,* Second Edition (DSM-II), the American Psychiatric Association (1968) added a category for ''Behavioral Disorders of Childhood and Adolescence.'' Still, even with this new revision which included many of the developmental aspects of emotional disturbance, criticism has been substantial (Prugh, Engel, & Morse, 1975). One criticism was based on the taxonomy's mixture of phenomenological and theoretical assumptions (Rutter, 1965). Another criticism was based on contradictive descriptors within categories (Rutter, 1965). The system has also been criticized for its lack of correspondence to factor analytic studies of behavioral disorders (Jenkins & Cole, 1964; Shaw & Lucas, 1970; Finch, 1969; Fish, 1969; Silver, 1969). The *International Classification of Diseases* (World Health Organization, 1967), which used much the same approach to devising a taxonomy of behavior disorders, has received similar amounts of criticism (Prugh et al., 1975).

The Group for Advancement of Psychiatry's (GAP) Committee on Child Psychiatry has formulated a classification system for dealing with mental and emotional disorders in children (GAP, 1966). This classification system provides operational definitions of clinical categories, which are in turn based on such theoretical concepts as stress conflict, crisis, and vulnerability (Anthony, 1970). The system further pioneered the category of ''healthy reaction'' in order to confront clinicians with an obvious, but often overlooked, phenomenon, ''the presenting normal'' (Anthony, 1970). The Committee's reference to recent findings linking mental illness and symptoms tolerance with social and ethnic factors represents an important forward look.

One of the favorable aspects of the GAP classification scheme is its provision for more complex categorizations. These encourage comprehensive descriptions of the emotional disturbance by allowing more of the elements of the typical ''case record'' to be represented (Anthony, 1970). The richness that this adds to the diagnostic profile may facilitate the planning of treatment, education, and prognosis. The GAP system has done the best job to date of including and integrating diverse theoretical positions and points of view. Included were psychosomatic, developmental, and psychosocial points of view, with contributions from such fields as psychoanalytic theory, learning theory, neurophysiology, child development, social science, and ethology (Prugh et al., 1975). In general, the GAP classification system has been favorably received by professionals working with emotionally disturbed children. Even so, criticisms have been cited (Ashburner, 1968; Bemporad, Pfeiffer, & Bloom, 1970; Fish, 1969; Kessler, 1971; Santostefano, 1971). Among the most cogent criticisms has been the failure to employ criteria for disorders in psychosocial functioning (Prugh et al., 1975). To meet this criticism and to permit usage of the GAP classification by professionals other than those in mental health, Prugh (1969) offered to the Joint Commission on Mental Health of Children a classification scheme based on levels of psychosocial functioning that involves a developmental framework and correlates well with the GAP nomenclature.

One other approach to the classification of children's disorders has been recommended by the Third Seminar on Psychiatric Disorders, Classification and Statistics sponsored by the World Health Organization (WHO) (Rutter et al., 1969). The participants included individuals of different disciplines, backgrounds, and theoretical positions but who were all involved in psychology, psychiatry, and related professions. This group offered a "triaxial" classification scheme for behavior disorders which included a "clinical psychiatric syndrome," a "level of intellectual functioning," and "any associated or etiological factors" (Rutter et al., 1969). It was suggested that items be coded by sex, age, referral agency, current parental situation, duration of symptoms, level of social adjustment, follow-up, and amended diagnosis.

The clinical categories offered by the WHO group have been compared to those in the earlier GAP classification scheme, and considerable similarity can be noted (Prugh et al., 1975). The 11 comparative terms for WHO and GAP, respectively, follow:

1. Normal Variations—Healthy Responses
2. Adaptive Reactions—Reactive Disorders
3. Specific Developmental Disorders—Developmental Deviations
4. Neurotic Disorders—Psychoneurotic Disorders
5. Personality Disorders—Personality Disorders
6. Mental Subnormality—Mental Retardation
7. Psychosomatic Disorders—Psychophysiological Disorders
8. Psychosis—Psychotic Disorders
9. Neurological Disorders—Brain Syndromes
10. Conduct Disorders—Tension-Discharge Disorders
11. Other Clinical Syndromes—Other Disorders. (p. 273)

The current status of the various classification systems has been reviewed and summarized by Prugh et al. (1975) and specific recommendations have been made: (*a*) Although the DSM-II and ICD classification schemes are the only ones which have any official recognition, the GAP classification is preferable and, thus, recommended for widespread adoption and use. (*b*) The GAP classification scheme should be integrated, as proposed by Ashburner (1968), into the ICD system and into the WHO "triaxial" structure (Rutter et al., 1969). (*c*) Some classification on the basis of psycho-social functioning like, for example, that developed by Prugh (1969) should be integrated into the GAP system so that it can more readily be used by professionals other than mental health clinicians. (*d*) The definitions of psycho-social functioning should be translated into a listing of the fundamental needs of children, healthy and disordered, at different levels of development. These would include dependency needs, cognitive needs, as well as the needs for limits, peer interaction, and figures of identification. These needs could then be correlated with such environmental factors as parent loss or poverty, thus providing guidelines to define support systems inside and outside the home (Prugh, 1969) and within the context of the school (Michigan Association for Emotionally Disturbed Children, 1973) for appropriate educational and treatment programs (Prugh et al., 1975).

Classification systems to describe emotional disturbance have, naturally, changed throughout the course of history as understanding of mental disorders has grown. The systems, in general, have reflected social attitudes, pressures and concerns to better facilitate the care, treatment, and education of individuals with various types of behavioral disorders.

Those systems proposed by GAP, ICD, and WHO are currently recommended for use and expansion. The major area of their work which currently needs attention, as is true in other areas of classification as well, is the translation of descriptions of disorders into listings of the fundamental mental and emotional needs of healthy and disordered children at various stages of development within different environmental contexts (i.e., home, school, community).

Specific learning disabled

The category of specific learning disabled (SLD) is a relatively new addition to the general learner taxonomy in special education. Disorders currently so classified were first identified and described in conjunction with brain injury and/or minimal cerebral dysfunction (Lehtinen & Strauss, 1944; Strauss & Lehtinen, 1947). The term used to describe such children was "perceptually handicapped child."

The medical profession's early interest in studying localization of function within the brain led to a series of studies of brain-injured adults and the difficulties they exhibited in writing, speaking, problem solving, and dealing with differential stimulus presentations (Bogen, 1969a, 1969b; Clemens, 1966; Cohn, 1961; Gazzaniga & Sperry, 1967; Lashley, 1951; Rudel & Denckla, 1974; Rudel & Teuber, 1971; Saul & Sperry, 1968; Sperry, 1966; Sperry, 1968; Sperry & Gazzaniga, 1967). Some of these early studies identified two types of syndromes which were frequently presented: "congenital auditory imperception" and "congenital word blindness" (Lashley, 1929).

The World War I epidemic of encephalitis directed attention to additional behavior disorders resulting from brain damage caused by this disease. Studies of cerebral-palsied individuals resulted in the identification of still other descriptions of disability among the brain injured—"clumsy child syndrome" and "minor cerebral palsies"—and also established the relationship between cerebral palsy and a host of perceptual and learning disorders (Pasamanick & Knobloch, 1966). Among the terms identified in the medical literature to categorize the learning disabled were: "minimal brain damage," "clumsy child syndrome," "minimal cerebral dysfunction," "hyperactive child," "hyperkinetic behavior disorder," and "minimal brain dysfunction" (Wepman, Cruikshank, Deutsch, Morency, & Strother, 1975).

Speech pathology has also contributed a series of categories for describing the SLD, including such terms as "congenital auditory imperception," "congenital aphasia" and "developmental language disability" (Wepman et al., 1975). Language development disorders associated with reading have been designated by such terms as: "dyslexia," "specific reading disability," "primary reading retardation," and "strephosymbolia" (Haring & Miller, 1969).

The general term "learning disabilities" was first suggested by Kirk in 1962 (Kirk & Bateman, 1962), then was adopted by the Association for Children with Learning Disabilities and the United States Office of Education, and has now come into general use in educational circles. The most widely accepted definition of SLD has been provided by the National Advisory Committee on Handicapped Children:

> Children with special learning disabilities exhibit a disorder in one or more of the basic psychological processes involved in understanding or using spoken or written languages. These may be manifested in disorders of listening, thinking, talking, reading, writing, spelling or arithmetic. They include conditions which have been referred to as perceptual handicaps, brain injury, minimal brain dysfunction, dyslexia, developmental aphasia, etc. They do not include learning problems which are due primarily to visual, hearing or motor handicaps, to mental retardation, emotional disturbance, or to environmental disadvantage (U.S. Department of Health, Education, and Welfare, 1973, p. 7411).

Perceptual deficits constitute one of the central factors in SLD which has been identified consistently by the medical, psychological, and educational professions, since these deficits can lead to problems in normal development.

121

The specific types of perceptual deficits which, in turn, define specific learning disabilities have been summarized by Wepman et al. (1975):

(*1*) recognizing fine differences between auditory and visual discriminating features underlying the sounds used in speech and the orthographic forms used in reading, (*2*) retaining and recalling those discriminated sounds and forms in both short term and long term memory, (*3*) ordering the sounds and forms sequentially both in sensory and motor acts, (*4*) distinguishing figure-ground relationships, (*5*) recognizing spatial and temporal organizations, (*6*) obtaining closure, (*7*) integrating intersensory information, and (*8*) relating what is perceived to specific motor functions. (p. 306)

Barsch (1975) focused on some of the same perceptual avenues when describing an approach for working with SLD pupils, but stressed the importance of both development and experience in developing processing modes. When describing the strengths and weaknesses of various processing modes, he suggested that both the order of development of the sensory modes—that is, the sequence of gustatory, olfactory, tactile, kinesthetic, auditory, and visual—and the experiences of the child which lead to a "processing mode of favor" should be considered. In general, he suggested that the major modes to be focused upon are the tactile, kinesthetic, visual, and auditory. For each individual the "significance," "meaning," and "value" of the events processed through these modes is varied and unique. Therefore, in describing profiles of disabilities to develop subcategories of SLD, these factors should also be considered. In essence, then, the current classification scheme for SLD by definition includes perceptual-motor deficiencies. The subcategories within SLD are based upon various profiles of these types of deficits which provide groupings for instructional purposes. The main processing modes used for subcategories are the auditory, visual, kinesthetic, and tactual. Focus is on the preferred or best mode for processing information.

Physically handicapped and other health-impaired

This category includes those individuals who have been termed: "crippled," "health impaired," "neurologically impaired," "blind," "partially sighted," or "visually handicapped," "deaf," "hard of hearing," or "hearing impaired." Since this is a most diverse group of disabilities and anomalies, general descriptions by subgroups seem appropriate. As in other areas, the development of taxonomies has been primarily within the medical profession. Consequently, many of the extant taxonomies in this area are more helpful in medical treatment than in education. Even so, the categories can still assist in communication about more homogeneous subgroups of individuals.

Blindness and visual impairment, for example, is a descriptive and helpful category for focus in educational planning. The label "legally blind" has been reasonably well-defined for many years. As stated by the House of Delegates of the American Medical Association in 1934, a person shall be considered blind whose central visual acuity does not exceed 20/200 in the better eye with correcting lenses or whose visual acuity, if better than 20/200, has a limit of the central field of vision to such a degree that its widest diameter subtends an angle of no greater than twenty degrees. (Connor, Hoover, Harton, Sands, Sternfeld, & Wolinsky, 1975, p. 240)

This "legal" definition usually accompanies two dictionary definitions as well: (a) the blind are those who have no sense of vision; and (b) the cecutients are those who have an impaired sense of vision. Since the general definition for blind specifies no levels of disability, the implication is that all "blind" have the same visual needs (Connor et al., 1975). This, of course, is not the case. Cecutients are faced with a myriad of visual problems, and these disabilities are often difficult to evaluate. But without such evaluation, no clear description of educational needs can be formulated. Sensory deficits of this type need to be better described to more adequately discriminate between the educational needs of the cecutient and the totally blind. As with other taxonomies, this one too calls for additional subclasses with associated descriptions and definitions.

Some work along these latter lines is currently being undertaken by the Society for the Prevention of Blindness. The categories which have been proposed are: (a) partial impairment of vision, (b) social blindness, (c) virtual blindness, (d) total blindness, and (e) unspecified or undetermined blindness. Each of these categories is defined on the basis of visual acuity in the better eye after correction and in terms of visual field in the better eye (Connor et al., 1975).

Several categorizations of partial blindness have also been offered for educational purposes. Thse include: (a) 20/250 to 20/70 (attendance in regular classes); (b) light perception to 1/200 (braille instruction if possible); (c) 2/200 to 4/200 (use of one's eyes if possible); (d) 5/200 to 20/300 (use of one's eyes with the possible aid of low-vision devices and large-print materials. (Fonda, 1960).

These classification systems offer a start toward further definitions and refinements of the taxonomies for the partially sighted. Certainly, more needs to be done to increase the capabilities of individuals to use other sensory modalities to supplement their lack of vision. For example, a type of classification scheme based both upon modality of preference as well as degree of blindness would provide further refinement in description and thus, hopefully, further sophistication in the design of educational programs. Too often, in work with handicapped such as the blind where the primary deficit is so apparent, it has been assumed that all other sensory channels are intact and highly functional. This has not always been the case. For example, some blind individuals cannot learn to read Braille because of deficits present in the tactile processing mode. This same observation is true for other sensory handicapps, e.g., the deaf. Even though the auditory mode is deficient it cannot be assumed that each of the other major processing modes—visual, kinesthetic, and tactile—are equally as effective for all deaf individuals as processing modes.

Unlike blindness which has been defined primarily in terms of existing visual function, the definition for deafness and hearing impairment has included both etiology and description of current auditory function. The deaf and hearing impaired are defined as "those individuals whose hearing loss is so severe at birth or during the prelingual period that is precludes the normal acquisition of language comprehension and expression" (Connor et al., 1975, p. 242). The partially hearing or hearing impaired are defined as "persons whose hearing loss, although significant in degree, was either acquired after the critical period for language acquisition, thus enabling the individual to develop some communicative skills, or does not totally impair oral language development" (Connor et al., 1975, p. 242).

Classification systems which have been devised to describe hearing loss are multifaceted. They include: (*a*) the description of the loss in terms of decibel levels, (*b*) the effects of the loss on ability to hear and understand speech sounds, (*c*) the site of lesion or other etiological factors associated with the anomaly, (*d*) hearing sensitivity at a variety of (dB) levels and frequency cycles, and (*e*) response to a variety of stimuli conditions in the sound-field situation (e.g., music, live voice presentations of a name, animal sounds, pulsed pure tones, etc.).

Currently, one of the difficulties with diagnosis and description of hearing loss is the amount of time required (Connors et al., 1975). Also, the descriptions derived from such evaluations have not been systematically organized by classificatory categories to facilitate communication from one diagnostician to another. Further, current taxonomies for description do not adequately delineate age of onset and its implications for retardation in speech, language, or other areas of development which are crucial in the specification of appropriate educational programs (Committee on Nomenclature of Executives of American Schools for the Deaf, 1937).

Not only are the categories of "deaf" and "partially hearing" inadequate in any descriptive sense but so are some of the other categories which have been suggested. For example, using "mild," "moderate," "severe," and "profound" to describe hearing impairment implies homogeneity within groupings when in fact there is very little. The terms "educational," "social," or "occupational" deafness are equally heterogeneous. Consequently, what is needed in the taxonomy of deafness and hearing impairment is a multidimensional classification scheme which describes specific etiology, symptomology, performance capability in a variety of situations (including educational, social, and occupational), and deficits in all areas relative to normal development. Even so, taxonomies for blindness and deafness are far more refined from an educational standpoint than are taxonomies for "crippled," "health-impaired," or "neurologically impaired." Many attempts have been made by a number of different groups to isolate, define, and describe these handicapping conditions.

The physically handicapped and other health-impaired individuals, as defined in Public Law (PL) 91-230 of the Elementary and Secondary Act, have been considred by three national study institutes (Connor et al., 1975). For educational purposes, the category has been considered as multiply handicapped and, for classification purposes, has been described according to several factors: age, stability or outcome of difficulty, and required educational or treatment setting for optimal programming.

Physicians have been the primary agents in the refinement of systems to classify physical impairments. In this regard, the American Medical Association has produced a series of guides for evaluating permanent mental and physical impairments. The separate guides deal with extremities and back (1958); visual system (1958); cardiovascular system (1960); ear, nose and throat (1961); central nervous system (1964); peripheral spinal nerves (1964); digestive system (1964); respiratory system (1965); endocrine system (1966); and mental illness (1966) (Connor et al., 1975). These publications were designed to provide for more precise diagnosis and treatment of the handicaps identified.

Definitions of these handicapping conditions have also been provided by private health agencies. Such agencies have been established to serve in advocate capacities for various categories of physically handicapped and health-impaired individuals. Some of the subcategories which have been established by them are: (a) cerebral palsy-athetoid, spastic, ataxic, rigid, tremor, or a combination of these; (b) cardiac involvement—with no limitation of physical activity, some limitation of physical activity, or major limitations on physical activity and an inability ot carry on any physical activity without discomfort; (c) epilepsy—with grand mal seizures, petit mal seizures, psychomotor involvement, or other (Connor et al., 1975). The difficulty with these categorical descriptors is that they focus on only one dimension: the physical. An examination of that is important but it must be considered relative to its effect on potential learning strategies. Similarly, the effect of the physical disability on visual, auditory, kinesthetic, and tactile processing modes should be considered. As in deafness and blindness, the single sensory mode of deficit (auditory, visual) must not be the only focus for diagnosis and description. The state of the other channels must also be described and considered so that an appropriate educational system can be designed. Some work on other multidimensional classification systems has been initiated.

For example, one classification scheme was developed by the Canadian Army (1943) and called PULHEMS (Connor et al., 1975). This scheme defined categories on the basis of physique (P), upper extremities (U), lower extremities

(L), hearing and ears (H), eyes and vision (E), mental capacity (M), and stability (S). Ratings were assigned using a Likert-type scale with ranged from one (normal) to five (totally unfit). The United States Army (1956) devised a taxonomy which was comparable, except that stability was described in terms of both mental capacity and stability.

Ehrle (1972), approaching the problem of classification from the point of view of rehabilitation, developed a multidimensional classification system which included physical, psychological, social, and vocational parameters. The categories of functional disabilities which he proposed were: (*a*) instrumental dysfunctions—limited mobility, ineffective communication, problems in activities of daily living, use of prosthesis and the resultant learning and economic consequences; (*b*) psychological dysfunctions—related to the individual's tolerance for frustration and ambiguity, response to limited choice, acceptance of changed status, limited ego strength, personal identity, internal controls over behavior, and learning to defer gratification; and (*c*) role dysfunction—suggesting failure to learn to carry out behaviors society expects, such as competitive, interpersonal relations in shcool, family, and community (Ehrle, 1972). This system deals with all major areas of functioning and thus provides a good outline for the types of behaviors which might be identified in each category. Unfortunately, the major behavioral subclassifications have not yet been itemized or specific approaches to their assessment outlined.

Specific checklists have, however, been devised to assist in both describing and observing behavior in these major functional areas. These behaviors seem, at least upon limited inspection, to be related to the disabled individual's successful performance of many of the common tasks involved in daily living, such as eating, dressing, socializing, finding, and keeping a job. One checklist developed in the 1940s is still widely used in rehabilitation centers, hospitals, and school settings with interdisciplinary staff (Scranton, Fogel, & Erdman, 1970). A second system which parallels the Ehrle (1972) taxonomy is a 79-item checklist describing capabilities in the physical, emotional, social, and vocational areas (Sokolow, Taylor, & Rusk, 1970).

A series of reasonably detailed classification systems have also been provided by the National Institute of Neurological Diseases and Stroke (Riviere, 1970). Their Rehabilitation Codes Classification System includes four major areas:

(*1*) voice disorders (i.e., pitch, loudness, control, intonation, quality associated with resonance); (*2*) hearing-function disorders, including impairment due to reduction of sensitivity to hearing speech (decibles for hearing), speed reduction of intelligibility for speech (percentage of correct responses), estimated reduction of hearing in the speech range (decibels based on thresholds for pure tones in speech-hearing range), estimated reduction of auditory sensitivity based on procedures not otherwise covered or specified, distortion of hearing function, and apparent disturbance of hearing function; (*3*) speech-function disorders (impairments of articulation, inappropriate disfluencies, inappropriate rate, impairments in patterning, impairments of concomitant audible behavior, and impairments of concomitant visible behavior); and (4) disorders of language comprehension and use (limitations of language comprehension, of ability to formulate language, of ability in spontaneous expression, of ability to imitate linguistic patterns, and of ability to imitate nonlinguistic patterns). (Connor et al., 1975, pp. 254-255)

Many different classification systems have been devised to describe the physically handicapped, sensory handicapped, and other health impaired. The first classification systems, developed by the medical profession, were oriented toward definition of physical disability diagnosis and treatment. Later systems of classifications have been developed with the participation of a wider spectrum of professionals. The current systems are consequently more multidimensional in character. But again, in this category, as in other categories of the handicapped learner taxonomy, a more detailed development of sub-classes is needed to provide for fine-level descriptions of behavior attributes. Such descriptions might be amenable to translation into learner needs and specifications for educational programming.

The first level, then, of the handicapped learner taxonomy has gradually expanded from two major categories, "deviants" and "non-deviants," to four major categories: (a) mentally retarded, (b) emotionally disturbed, (c) specific learning disabled, and (d) physically handicapped, sensorially handicapped and other health impaired. The large category "physically handicapped, sensorially handicapped, and other health impaired" is often treated as five separate categories: (a) crippled and/or orthopedically handicapped, (b) deaf or hearing impaired, (c) blind or partially sighted, (d) speech impaired, and (e) other health impaired (U.S. Department of Health, Education, and Welfare, 1973). Using this latter breakdown, there are then seven major categories in the first level of the handicapped learner taxonomy which are most frequently used. Additional levels of subclassification are then provided within each of the first level categories. A summary of the leveled taxonomies used to describe handicapped learners is provided in Table 1. The global levels for these taxonomies have been reasonably well developed and defined. Additional taxonomic development, refinement and definition now needs to occur at the major, minor, and operational levels of the hierarchy. Only when descriptions at the operational levels are refined can good translations be made to define quality educational programs.

CURRICULUM TAXONOMIES

Curriculum has been defined as "plans for action" and the process of curriculum development has been defined as "producing plans for further action." Curriculum can more specifically be defined as a course of study, a

TABLE 1
HIERARCHICAL TAXONOMIES DESCRIBING LEARNERS

Hierarchical level	Class descriptors
I	Learners
I-A	Mentally retarded
B	Emotionally disturbed
C	Specific learning disabled
D	Physically handicapped
E	Health impaired
F	Speech impaired
G	Blind and partially sighted
H	Deaf and hearing impaired
I-A-1	Mildly mentally retarded
2	Moderately mentally retarded
3	Severely mentally retarded
4	Profoundly mentally retarded
I-A-1-a	Early childhood CA/MA (0-2)
b	Preschool CA/MA (3-4)
c	Kindergarten CA/MA (5)
d	Primary CA/MA (6, 7, 8)
e	Intermediate CA/MA (9, 10, 11)
f	Junior high CA/MA (12, 13, 14)
g	Secondary CA/MA (15, 16, 17)
h	Vocational/college CA/MA (18, 19, 20, 21)
I-A-1-a-(1)	Reading skill level
[Cognitive]	Mathematics skill level
	Social skill level
I-A-1-a-(2)	Visual perception
[Psychomotor]	Auditory perception
	Motor coordination
I-A-1-a-(3)	Interests
[Affective]	Attitudes
	Values
	Achievement motivation
I-A-1-a-(1)-(a)	Word attack
[Cognitive]	Study skills
I-A-1-a-(1)-(b)	Figure-ground perception
[Psychomotor]	Spatial-temporal perception
I-A-1-a-(1)-(c)	Sports
[Affective]	Aviation
	Astrology
I-A-1-a-(1)-(a)-(1)	Consonant discrimination
[Cognitive]	
I-A-1-a-(1)-(b)-(1)	Simple line
[Psychomotor]	Background-foreground in black and white
	Color background-foreground
I-A-1-a-(1)-(c)-(1)	Baseball
[Affective]	Hockey

curriculum guide, or a specific textbook or program series which has been adopted by a nation, region, state, district, or single school (Macdonald, 1965). To view curriculum in a taxonomic context, one must first view it as a statement of educational goals and objectives which, in turn, define programs. Goals and objectives will differ as a function of the values of their creators who, hopefully, are influenced by the character of the learners for whom the curriculum is being developed (Armstrong, 1975).

As in the learner taxonomies, most of the development and refinement of curriculum taxonomies has also taken place at the global rather than operational levels. For example, the most comprehensive work in learner taxonomies has been to define and describe distinctions between the mentally retarded and the emotionally disturbed. In contrast, very little effort has been exerted on forming a description of the processing modes of favor for the mildly mentally retarded who operate at the primary level instructionally and who have interests comparable to intermediate level normals (see Table 1). Likewise in the area of curriculum taxonomies, the most comprehensive work has been done at the global level, specifying overall goals of the school. These goals are specified by identifying major content and process areas. Globally, then, the specification of the major areas has been well defined, but at the operational level very little has been done to specify exactly what will be taught within each of the major subject areas.

Educational objectives for handicapped children, when stated, are usually stated in global terms which cannot be readily converted into the specific kinds of objectives which the teacher needs (Gorelick, 1963). Typical global educational objectives might be: "to develop civic responsiblity," "to learn to get along with others," "to learn to use leisure time effectively and constructively," "to learn to adjust to the forces of nature" (Stevens, 1961). What needs to be provided is a taxonomic structure which breaks down complex concepts, attitudes, and skills into single definable objectives (Gorelick, 1963). This structure would consist of a hierarchy of content or process objectives which proceed from single global (complex) levels to operational (simple) ones which are definable behaviorally for the particular learner.

Unfortunately, the task which needed to be done has only been outlined, not completed (Gorelick, 1963). Even so, good examples in at least two areas of how the task might be approached are available. If these examples are followed in all areas of the curriculum, one of the more urgently needed hierarchical taxonomies for special education would become available for widespread use. These two sample taxonomies are shown in Table 2.

As can be seen, hierarchical taxonomies in the curriculum area could greatly facilitate educational planning and implementation by more precisely defining curricula and linking global levels to operational levels, that is, linking

129

TABLE 2
HIERARCHICAL TAXONOMIES DESCRIBING
CURRICULUM—CONTENT AND PROCESS

Hierarchical level	Class descriptors
I	Content or process areas
I-A	Affective development
I-A-1	Development of positive interpersonal relationships
I-A-1-a	Learning to take turns
I-A-1-a-i	Waiting in line for a drink without crowding or pushing ahead of others
I-B	Reading skill development
I-B-1	Word attack skills
I-B-1-a	Discriminating initial consonants
I-B-1-a-i	Discriminating between the consosants "b" and "s"

plans to action. Hierarchical taxonomies provide a systematic, descriptive approach to the achievement of long-range objectives which is carefully worked out in an operational sequence. Taxonomies which do not get to the operational level are not particularly helpful in defining, implementing, or evaluating instruction for handicapped children.

In describing hierarchical curriculum taxonomies, the relationship among values, objectives, procedures, and evaluation has been discussed, with examples, by Hartman (1975). A particular hierarchy follows: (a) Value position: social humanism, worth of the individual. (b) Objectives: positive self-concept, positive interpersonal relations, self-direction and responsibility, environmental awareness, location of information, and communication skills. (c) Procedures: setting an emotional climate within the classroom which fosters the development of positive self-concepts by encouraging pupils to feel good about themselves; achieving positive interpersonal relations by encouraging pupils to recognize both themselves and others as individuals with their own needs, wants, and desires, and encouraging good working relationships in group settings; encouraging sensitivity to one's environment through reading of cues both verbal and nonverbal; and encouraging the development of "learning how to learn" by teaching children how to locate needed information from a wide variety of resources and to communicate information clearly and correctly using a wide variety of media. (d) Evaluation: describing specific learner behaviors which indicate development in each of the desired areas of growth (Hartman, 1975).

Hierarchical taxonomy development in the curriculum area is at the beginning stages of growth. The need for this growth has been identified and guidelines for approaching the problem have been provided by example. As in learner taxonomies, the higher order levels have been more adequately described and defined than the lower, or more specific, levels. Even so, a review of some of the more recent curriculum guides which define programs for the handicapped in several different states indicates that more and more refinement of these taxonomies at the lower levels is beginning to occur (Alabama Department of Education, n.d. a, b; Michigan Department of Education, 1972, 1973a, b; Mississippi State Department of Education, n.d.; Nevada State Department of Education, n.d.; New Mexico State Department of Education, 1970; North Carolina State Department of Public Instruction, 1972, 1974; North Dakota Department of Public Instruction, 1974a, b; Sough Dakota Department of Education and Cultural Affairs, 1973-74, n.d.; Southwest Georgia Cooperative Educational Service Agency, 1973; Staff of Riverview School, 1973; Virginia State Department of Education, 1973; Wisconsin Department of Public Instruction, 1969, n.d.).

INSTRUCTIONAL MATERIALS AND MEDIA TAXONOMIES

Instructional materials and media are the objects, programs, or devices which are used to instruct learners. Thousands of instructional materials are currently produced and available from large numbers of publishers and commercial producers. Consequently, systems for describing the characteristics of these materials are needed to provide the information a teacher requires to select the most appropriate materials for the defined curriculum and for the handicapped learners to be taught.

Two major taxonomic systems have been developed for describing instructional materials. One system, the Media Analysis and Retrieval System (MARS), was developed from an empirical approach (Rude, 1973), while the other system was developed from a theoretical base (Brown, 1974). The major categories of the MARS taxonomy are (a) major area, (b) major skill, (c) instructional level, (d) interest level, (e) format, (f) input mode, (g) output mode, and (h) teacher-learner interaction (Rude, 1973). The major area and major skill categories refer to the content, concepts, and skills which the material is designed to teach if used in the prescribed manner. The major skills and their associated descriptors are subsets of the major areas. An example of a major cognitive area descriptive category would be "reading." An example of the major skills descriptive category is "phonics" and then, at the next level, "initial blends."

The instructional level descriptors correspond to mental age ranges, and the interest level descriptors refer to chronological age ranges. Format refers to the form of the material, for example, film, tape, book, etc. Input mode describes the sensory channels which are involved when the child uses the material. The descriptors in this area are: visual, auditory, kinesthetic, tactile, etc. Output mode refers to the expressive channel through which the learner responds to information or stimuli presented by the material. The descriptors in

131

this category are: verbal (spoken response) and nonverbal (manipulative, marking, writing, etc.). Teacher-learner interaction refers to the amount of teacher direction required in using the material and the size of the instructional group which is more appropriate to the material's use. Examples of two of the subcategories in this area are: independent large group (more than six learners) and teacher-directed individual (one learner working with one teacher).

The MARS taxonomy is probably one of the most complete systems currently available for describing instructional materials. Even so, it needs much refinement to make all areas of the taxonomy more complete and logically consistent.

The other system which has been developed is based on Guilford's (1967) Structure of the Intellect (SI) Model (Brown, 1974). After establishing a rationale for the development of such a materials taxonomy, the essential components of the system were outlined in accordance with the SI model. The major materials categories identified were (a) stimulus properties—figural, symbolic, semantic, or behavioral in content; (b) stimulus flexibility—rate of stimulus presentation control available to the teacher, changeability of stimulus properties; (c) input mode—visual, auditory, tactile, kinesthetic, olfactory, or gesticulatory; (d) operations the material is designed to help the child develop—cognition, memory, convergent production, divergent production, or evaluation; (e) the organizational form information takes in the learner's processing of it—units, classes, relations, systems, implications, and transformations; (f) response mode—the exact response the learner is required to make in utilizing a given instructional material; (g) difficulty level; (h) time requirements; (i) independence of pupil use—teacher involvement; (j) whether the material is reusable or consumed in a single use; (k) other identification and descriptive information (Brown, 1974).

Now that we have the two taxonomies proposed for analyzing and describing instructional materials, a logical next step would be an integration of the positive elements of the separate systems to form a refined single system. The theoretically based taxonomy lacks specific subcategories of descriptors, while the MARS system has these features but lacks the broader theoretical framework for use in identifying missing categories and logical consistency. A combination of the two systems would provide a good beginning instructional materials taxonomy which could be refined with use.

INSTRUCTIONAL ENVIRONMENT TAXONOMIES

The physical and social environments created in the schools have been demonstrated to be important determinants of the handicapped learner's educational growth (Bednar & Haviland, 1969; Cruikshank, 1966; Phillips &

Haring, 1959; Strauss & Lehtinen, 1947). Although both physical environments (Abeson & Blaklow, 1971; Blatt, 1970, 1973; Cornell, 1960; Hewett & Forness, 1974; Larson, 1965) and social environments (Wiseman, 1964) have been defined and described within the literature, no systematic efforts have been undertaken to organize and classify the critical elements.

The negative effects of unfavorable environments on the educational growth of handicapped children have been demonstrated (Blatt, 1970, 1973). Therefore, it is important for special educators to develop taxonomies which will isolate the important factors in the educational environment and provide for their description. In this way, the important elements within the educational environment can be specifically provided, evaluated and improved.

INSTRUCTIONAL METHOD TAXONOMIES

Instruction has been defined as "putting plans into action." Instruction also involves teacher-learner interactions, i.e., the total stimulus setting within which systematic stimuli are presented to the pupil and desired responses occur and are given feedback (Macdonald, 1965). Although there has been considerable research on instruction and instructional methods, there are very few good description systems for instruction. The critical elements have not been systematically identified and organized into any descriptive hierarchy.

Since the character of instruction within the special education classroom is an important determinant of the quality of instruction provided, systems should be designed to better define and describe this process. A major start has been provided by the proponents of applied behavioral analysis. By developing procedures for systematically observing and describing antecedents and consequents as they operate to influence behavior, these proponents have provided a set of procedures for building an instructional taxonomy. Although this approach does provide a start, any good taxonomy of instruction should also include other theoretical and philosophical positions.

TEACHER TAXONOMIES

Teachers are, of course, a critical component in the educational system, and the role of the teacher in the classroom is central to the quality of instruction provided. Therefore, those factors which make a person effective or ineffective in his or her role as teacher need to be identified and described. The concern is for those skills, characteristics, experiences, values and attitudes which make an individual a "good" teacher.

Although extensive taxonomies have not been developed to describe the important teacher characteristics which affect and influence teaching behaviors, there are studies which point to the importance of teacher variables in the learning process of the handicapped (Jones, 1966). Rarely, however, have these teacher characteristics been sufficiently described so as to relate them to any of the specific aspects of cognitive or noncognitive achievement of the handicapped (Jones, 1973). There are, however, studies regarding competencies for special education teachers which may provide a starting point for more detailed taxonomy development. One study, for example, offers a detailed listing of competencies that a special education teacher should have in the vocational and career education areas (Brolin, 1973). Once such competencies are established, it may be possible to better delineate the important teacher characteristics which lead to these competencies.

Another approach to isolating and describing teachers' characteristics has been provided by applied behavioral analysis procedures. One taxonomy using this approach specified both positive and negative teacher characteristics (Berman, 1973). The positive characteristics were listed as:

> (1) sensitivity to subtleties of response, (2) potential for warmth in interactions with instructees, (3) ability to deal with less objective features of instructees' response and of instructions themselves, (4) ability to monitor certain behaviors with which a machine would have difficulties, (5) generally more flexible than a machine or text, (6) ability to easily dispense consequences for following instructions, especially if number of instructees is small; also ability to be more sensitive to the need for changes in consequences. (Berman, 1973, pp. 646-647)

In this taxonomy the teacher is compared with a machine, rather than focusing on personal attributes and how they might affect learning. Still, the study does provide a first look at the teacher of handicapped children within a behaviorally oriented context.

A more dynamic approach to identifying critical teacher attributes has taken place in general education, for example in the classic study by Travers, Rabinowitz, Page, Nemovicher and Ventur (1953). Certainly, more research needs to be completed on the relationships between teacher attributes and handicapped learning. Hopefully, taxonomies of the important teacher attributes and characteristics could then be identified. Using this information, taxonomies could subsequently be developed to more adequately describe special education teachers.

TEACHING TAXONOMIES

Neither general education nor special education have produced taxonomies of teaching, although some descriptions of the teaching process are beginning to be formulated and have appeared in the literature. One of the more comprehensive descriptions of teaching has been provided by Hunter (Resnik, 1974). Her description postulated that teaching is based upon specific skills: Teachers were viewed as highly trained professionals, and teaching was viewed as the process of applying these identified skills in the instructional situation. Eleven skills were identified:

(*1*) Deliberate separation of genuine educational constraints (illness, hunger) from the ethnic, financial, intellectual or emotional variations that constitute fashionable (and unfortunately, acceptable) excuses for learning failure; (*2*) Determination of what the child has already achieved and what he is ready to learn next, and the degree of complexity of that learning in terms of its feeling, thinking and psychomotor requirements; (*3*) Identification of the productive learning behavior for achievement of the learning task, and for particular learners; (*4*) Determination of an instructional objective that is specific in content and perceivable in terms of learner behavior; (*5*) Identification of the principles of learning that are relevant to the accomplishment of that instructional objective; (*6*) Adaptation of those principles to the particular situation and to each learner; (*7*) Incorporation of a teacher's own personality attributes and competence in the specific learning area in order to enhance the learner's probability of success; (*8*) Synthesis of decisions one through seven into a deliberate design or blueprint for a teaching-learning episode; (*9*) During the actual teaching-learning episode, from the first second, the teacher's observations are used to augment or correct the decision-making process; (*10*) Evaluation is an integral and continuous aspect of the teaching-learning process, not merely a terminal function; and (*11*) On the basis of the evaluative data collected during the teaching-learning process, the teacher must finally decide what the next episode will be: reteaching, practice and extending, moving on to new learning or abandoning ship if it turns out the objective isn't appropriate for the learner at this time. (Resnik, 1974, pp. 25-26)

This analysis of the teaching process is quite comprehensive and could provide a start toward the development of a taxonomy of teaching.

Another description of the teaching process which may offer a start toward taxonomy construction has been provided in the form of a flowchart (Armstrong, 1969). Six basic components are identified: (*a*) pupil assessment, (*b*) selection of behavioral objectives, (*c*) selection of methods and materials, (*d*) classification and generalization, (*e*) application, and (*f*) reassessment. Supplemental activities include: (*a*) the analysis of instructional materials, (*b*) materials development, (*c*) analysis of instructional procedures, and (*d*) procedures development. This construction of the teaching process was based upon research with trainable mentally retarded pupils in a summer laboratory school program.

Currently, there are no comprehensive taxonomies of the teaching process. The need for such taxonomies, however, has been recognized as projects and teacher training institutions have begun to develop competency-based training programs in special education.

SUMMARY AND CONCLUSIONS

The purpose of this chapter has been to review taxonomies in special education. A general model was used to organize the review of the multiple taxonomies which are involved in the process of educating handicapped children.

This general model included the following taxonomies of: learners, curriculum, instructional materials, environments, instruction, teachers, and teaching.

The identified purposes of taxonomies in special education were: (*a*) to facilitate communication, (*b*) to solve problems, (*c*) to simplify complex universes of phenomena to make them easier to deal with, both conceptually and practically, and (*d*) to assist in the improvement of the quality of education for handicapped learners by providing better descriptions of the critical elements involved in the educational process. These purposes can be met only to the degree that these taxonomies are complete. The most complete and comprehensive taxonomies discussed are those developed to describe handicapped learners. Taxonomies of instructional materials have also been reasonably well developed. Those relating to curriculum, teachers, instruction, environments, and teaching have been less well developed.

In all areas, the taxonomies need to have additional subclasses formulated to deal with the more specific descriptions which are most helpful in specifying appropriate educational programs. If this work is completed, great progress can be made in improving the quality of instruction in educating the handicapped.

References

Abeson, A., & Blacklow, J. *Environmental design: New relevance for special education.* Arlington, Va.: Council for Exceptional Children, 1971.

Ackerman, N.W., & Neubauer, P.B. Failures in the psychotherapy of children. In P. Hoch (Ed.), *Failures in psychiatric treatment.* New York: Grune & Stratton, 1958.

Alabama Department of Education. *Serving trainables through educational management.* Montgomery, Ala.: State Department of Education, n.d. (a)

Alabama Department of Education. *Special education experiential development.* Montgomery, Ala.: State Department of Education, n.d. (b)

American Medical Association. *Standard nomenclature of diseases and operations.* Chicago: American Medical Association, 1961.

American Medical Association. Guides to the evaluation of permanent mental and physical impairments. *Journal of the American Medical Association,* 1958-1966.

American Psychiatric Association. Committee on Nomenclature and Statistics. *Diagnostic and statistical manual of mental disorders (DSM-II).* Washington, D.C.: American Psychiatric Association, 1968.

Anthony, E.J. The behavior disorders of childhood. In P.H. Mussen (Ed.), *Carmichael's manual of child psychology.* Vol. 2. New York: Wiley, 1970.

Armstrong, J.R. Teaching: An ongoing process of assessing, selecting, developing, generalizing, applying and reassessing. *Education and Training of the Mentally Retarded,* 1969, **4**(4), 168-176.

Armstrong, J.R. An educational process model for use in research. *Journal of Experimental Education,* 1970, **39**(1), 2-7.

Armstrong, J.R. The evaluation of instructional materials for the handicapped: The relative effects of contrived structures in a dynamic system. In *Proceedings of the 1974 Big Ten Body of Knowledge Symposium.* Iowa City: University of Iowa, 1975.

Ashburner, M.V. Some problems of classification with particular reference to child psychiatry. *Australian and New Zealand Journal of Psychiatry,* 1968, **2**, 244.

Barsch, R.H. The dynamic perceptual composite—GOTKAV. Paper presented at the International Federation of Learning Disabilities, Brussels, Belgium, January 1975.

Bednar, M.J., & Haviland, D.S. *The role of physical environments in the education of children with learning disabilities.* Troy, N.Y.: Center for Architectural Research, Rensselaer Polytechnic Institute, 1969.

Bemporad, J.R., Pfeiffer, C.M., & Bloom, W. Twelve months' experience with the GAP classification of childhood disorders. *American Journal of Psychiatry,* 1970, **127**, 658-665.

Berman, M.L. Instructional and behavioral change: A taxonomy. *Exceptional Children,* 1973, **8**, 644-650.

Binet, A. La mésure en psychologie individuelle. *Révue Philosophique,* 1898, **46**(2), 113-123.

Binet, A. *L'étude experimentelle de l'intelligence.* Paris: Schleicher Frères, 1900.

Binet, A., & Simon, T. Sur la nécessité d'établir un diagnostic scientifique des états inférieurs de l'intelligence. [Upon the necessity of establishing a scientific diagnosis of inferior states of intelligence.] *L'Année Psychologique,* 1905, **11**, 1-28.

Binet, A., & Simon, T. Le développement de l'intelligence chez les enfants. *L'Année Psychologique,* 1908, **14**, 1-94.

Blanton, R.L. Historical perspectives on classification of mental retardation. In N. Hobbs (Ed.), *Issues in the classification of children.* Vol. 1. San Francisco: Jossey-Bass, 1975.

Blatt, B. *Exodus from pandemonium.* Boston: Allyn & Bacon, 1970.

Blatt, B. *Souls in extremis: An anthology on victims and victimizers.* Boston: Allyn & Bacon, 1973.

Bogen, J.E. The other side of the brain, I: Dysgraphia and dyscopia following cerebral commissurotomy. *Bulletin of the Los Angeles Neurological Societies,* 1969, **34**(2) 73-105. (a)

Bogen, J.E. The other side of the brain, II: An appositional mind. *Bulletin of the Los Angeles Neurological Societies,* 1969, **34**(3), 135-162. (b)

Brolin, D. Career education needs of secondary educable students. *Exceptional Children*, 1973, **39**(8) 619-624.

Brown, L.F. The analysis of instructional materials. *Mental Retardation*, 1974, **12**(5), 21-25.

Browne, E.G. *Arabian medicine*. New York: Macmillian, 1921.

Cameron, K. Diagnostic categories in child psychiatry. *British Journal of Medical Psychology*, 1955, **28**(1), 67-71.

Canadian Army. *Physical standards and instructions for medical examination of serving soldiers and recruits*. Ottawa: Canadian Army, 1943.

Chess, S. *An introduction to child psychiatry*. New York: Grune & Stratton, 1959.

Clemens, S.D. (Ed.). *Minimal brain dysfunction in children*. Washington, D.C.: U.S. Department of Health, Education, and Welfare, 1966.

Cohn, R. Dyscalculia. *Archives of Neurology*, 1961, **4**, 301-307.

Coleman, J.C. *Abnormal psychology and modern life* (4th ed.). Glenview, Ill.: Scott, Foresman, 1972.

Committee on Nomenclature of Executives of American Schools for the Deaf, 1937. In National Advisory Council on Neurological Diseases and Stroke, *Human communication and its disorders*. Bethesda, Md.: National Institute on Neurological Diseases and Stroke, 1969.

Connor, F.P., Hoover, R., Horton, K., Sands, H., Sternfeld, L., & Wolinsky, G.F. Physical and sensory handicaps. In N. Hobbs (Ed.), *Issues in the classification of children*. Vol. 1. San Francisco: Jossey-Bass, 1975.

Cornell, F.G. Plant and equipment. In C.W. Harris (Ed.), *Encyclopedia of educational research*. New York: Macmillan, 1960.

Cronbach, L.J. Five decades of public controversy over mental testing. *American Psychologist*, 1975, **30**(1), 1-14.

Cruickshank. W.M. (Ed.). *The teacher of brain-injured children*. Syracuse, N.Y.: Syracuse University Press, 1966.

Down, J.L. Observations on the ethnic classification of idiots. *London Hospital Clinical Lectures Reports*, 1866, **3**, 229-262.

Duncan, P.M., & Millard, W. *Manual for the classification, training, and education of the feebleminded, imbecile, and idiotic*. London: Churchill, 1866.

Ehrle, R.A. Diminishing functional disability: Complementary rehabilitation efforts. *Rehabilitation Psychology*, 1972, **19**(4), 174-179.

Engel, M. Dilemmas of classification and diagnosis. *Journal of Special Education*, 1969, **3**(3), 231-239.

Esquirol, J. *Mental maladies*. Trans. E.K. Hunt, Philadelphia: Lea and Blanchard, 1845.

Filler, J.W., Jr., Robinson, C.C., Smith, R.A., Vincent-Smith, L.J., Bricker, D.D., & Bricker, W.A. Mental retardation. In N. Hobbs (Ed.), *Issues in the classification of children*. Vol. 1. San Francisco: Jossey-Bass, 1975.

Finch, S. Nomenclature for children's mental disorders needs improvement. *International Journal of Psychiatry*, 1969, **7**, 414.

Fish, B. Limitations of the new nomenclature for children's disorders. *International Journal of Psychiatry*, 1969, **7**, 393-398.

Fish, B., & Shapiro. T. A descriptive typology of children's psychiatric disorders: II: A behavioral classification. In R.L. Jenkins & J.O. Cole (Eds.), *American Psychiatric Association Psychiatric Research Reports* (No. 18), 1965.

Fonda, G. Definition and classification of blindness with respect to ability to use residual vision. In *Blindness, 1960 AAWB Annual*. Washington, D.C.: American Association of Workers for the Blind, 1960.

Frederiksen, N. *Toward a taxonomy of situations*. Paper presented at the 79th annual convention of the American Psychological Association, Washington, D.C., September, 1971.

Galton, F. Supplementary notes on 'prehension' in idiots. *Mind*, 1887, **12**, 79-82.

Gazzaniga, M.S., & Sperry, R.W. Language after section of the cerebral commissures. *Brain*, 1967, **90**, 131-148.

Gerard, M.W. Genesis of psychosomatic symptoms in infancy. In F. Deutsch (Ed.), *The psychosomatic concept in psychoanalysis*. New York: International Universities Press, 1953.

Goddard, H.H. Four hundred feebleminded children classified by the Binet method. *Journal of Psycho-Asthenics*, 1910, **15**, 17-30.

Gorelick, M.C. A typology of curriculum objectives for the mentally retarded: From ambiguity to precision. *Mental Retardation*, August 1963, **1**(4), 213-215.

Grossman, H.J. (Ed.), *Manual on terminology and classification in mental retardation*. Washington, D.C.: American Association on Mental Deficiency, 1973.

Group for the Advancement of Psychiatry. *Psychopathological disorders in childhood: Theoretical considerations and a proposed classification* (G.A.P. Report No. 62). New York: Group for Advancement of Psychiatry, 1966.

Guilford, J.P. *The nature of human intelligence*. New York: McGraw-Hill, 1967.

Haring, N., & Miller, C.A. (Eds.). *Minimal brain dysfunction in children*. Proceedings of National Project on Learning Disabilities in Children. Washington, D.C.: U.S. Public Health Service, 1969.

Hartman, C.L. Describing behavior: Search for an alternative to grading. *Educational Leadership*, 1975, **32**(4), 274-277.

Heber, R.F. A manual on terminology and classification in mental retardation. *American Journal of Mental Deficiency*, 1959. Monograph supplement.

Heber, R. Modifications in the manual on terminology and classification in mental retardation. *American Journal of Mental Deficiency*, 1961, **65**, 499-500.

Hewett, F.M., & Forness, S.R. *Education of exceptional learners*. Bostom: Allyn & Bacon, 1974.

Hobbs, N. *The futures of children*. San Francisco: Jossey-Bass, 1975. (a)

Hobbs, N. (Ed.) *Issues in the classification of children*. Vols. 1 and 2. San Francisco: Jossey-Bass, 1975. (b)

Hoffman, E. *The treatment of deviance in the education system*. Ann Arbor, Mich.: Institute for the Study of Mental Retardation and Related Disabilities, 1972.

Ireland, W.W. *The mental affections of children: Idiocy, imbecility, and insanity*. London: J. Churchill, 1898.

Jacobs, J. Experiments in 'prehension.' *Mind*, 1887, **12**, 75-79.

Jenkins, R.L., & Cole, J.O. (Eds.). *Diagnostic classification in child psychiatry*. Washington, D.C.: American Psychiatric Association, 1964.

Jones, R.L. Research on special education and special education teaching. *Exceptional Children*, 1966, **33**, 251-257.

Jones, R.L. Accountability in special education: Some problems. *Exceptional Children*, 1973, **39**(8), 631-643.

Kanner, L. Emotionally disturbed children: A historical review. *Child Development*, 1962, **33**, 97-102.

Kessler, J.W. Nosology in child psychopathology, In H.R. Rie (ED.), *Perspectives in child psychopathology*. Chicago: Aldine & Atherton, 1971.

Kirk, S.A., & Bateman, B. Diagnosis and remediation of learning disabilities. *Exceptional Children*, 1962, **29**(2), 73-78.

Kolb, L.C. *Modern clinical psychiatry* (8th ed.). Philadelphia: Saunders, 1973.

Larson, C.T. *Environmental analysis* (Research Publication No. 3). Ann Arbor, Mich.: University of Mighican, School Environments Research Publications, 1965.

Lashley, K.S. *Brain mechanisms and intelligence*. Chicago: University of Chicago Press, 1929.

Lashley, K.S. The problem of serial order in behvaior. In L.A. Jeffers (Ed.), *Central mechanisms in behavior*. New York: Wiley, 1951.

Lehtinen, L.E. & Strauss, A.A. A new approach in educational methods for brain-crippled deficient children. *American Journal of Mental Deficiency*, 1944, **48**, 283-288.

Lombroso, C. *L'uomo delinquent in rapporto antropologia giurisprudenza, e alle discipline carcerie*. Torino: Hoepli, 1876.

Louttit, C.M. *Clinical psychology of children's behavior problems*, New York: Harper, 1947.

Macdonald, J.B. Educational models for instruction—Introduction. In *Theories of Instruction*. Washington, D.C.: Association for Supervision and Curriculum Development, 1965.

Mercer, J. Sociocultural factors in labeling mental retardates. *Peabody Journal of Education*, 1971, **48**(1), 188-203.

Mercer, J. *Labeling the mentally retarded*. Berkeley: University of California Press, 1973.

Mercer, J.R. *The who, why and how of mainstreaming*. Paper presented at the national convention of the American Association on Mental Deficiency, June 1974.

Mercer, J.R. Psychological assessment and the rights of children. In N. Hobbs (Ed.), *Issues in the classification of children*. Vol. 1. San Francisco: Jossey-Bass, 1975.

Michigan Association for Emotionally Disturbed Children. *Educating emotionally disturbed children*. Detroit: MAEDC, 1973.

Michigan Department of Education. *A handbook of suggestions for developmental learning*. Lansing, Mich.: Michigan Department of Education, 1972.

Michigan Department of Education. *Creating learning-aids*. Lansing, Mich.: Michigan Department of Education, Division of Special Education, 1973. (a)

Michigan Department of Education. *Techniques and technology: Handbook for curriculum resource consultants*. Lansing, Mich.: Michigan Department of Education, Bureau of Educational Services, 1973. (b)

Miller, W.R. Psychogenic factors in the polyuria of schizophrenia. *Journal of Nervous Mental Disorders*, 1936, **84**, 418-426.

Mississippi State Department of Education. *Resource guide: Specific learning disabilities–A guide for teachers and administrators*. Jackson, Miss.: State Department of Education, Special Education Office, n.d.

Morel, B.A. *Traité des dégénérescences physiques, intellectuelles et morales de l'espèce humaine et des causes qui produisent ces variétés maladives*. Paris: Ballière, 1857.

Morse, W.C. *Working paper for task force on classification of emotionally disturbed children*. Nashville: Project on Classification of Exceptional Children, 1973.

Nevada State Department of Education. *A curriculum guide for exceptional pupil education*. Carson City: Nevada State Department of Education, n.d.

New Mexico State Department of Education. *A guide for the teacher of the trainable mentally handicapped*. Santa Fe: New Mexico State Department of Education, Division of Special Education, 1970.

North Carolina State Department of Public Instruction. *Curriculum guide for teachers of trainable mentally retarded children*. Raleigh, N.C.: State Department of Public Instruction, Division for Exceptional Children, August 1972.

North Carolina State Department of Public Instruction. *Educating for the future: 21st century teaching*. Raleigh, N.C.: Department of Public Instruction, Division for Exceptional Children, 1974.

North Dakota Department of Public Instruction. *Guide IV–A curriculum system for classes for trainable mentally handicapped students*. Bismarck, N.D.: Department of Public Instruction, August 1974. (a)

North Dakota Department of Public Instruction. *Guide II–A curriculum system for classes for educable mentally handicapped students*. Bismarck, N.D.: Department of Public Instruction, 1974. (b)

Pasamanick, B., & Knobloch, H. Retrospective studies on the epidemiology of reproductive casualty: Old and new. *Merrill-Palmer Quarterly*, 1966, **12**(1), 7-26.

Phillips, E.L., & Haring, N.G. Results from special techniques for teaching emotionally disturbed children. *Exceptional Children*, 1959, **26**, 64-67.

Prugh. D.G. Psychosocial disorders in childhood and adolescence: Theoretical considerations and an attempt at classification. In Joint Commission on Mental Health of Children, *The mental health of children: Services, research, and manpower*. New York: Harper and Row, 1969.

Prugh, D.G., Engel, M., & Morse, W.C. Emotional disturbance in children. In N. Hobbs (Ed.), *Issues in the classification of children*. Vol. 1. San Francisco: Jossey-Bass, 1975.

Resnik, H.S. Madeline Hunter: Eleven crucial teaching decisions. *Learning,* 1974, 3(4), 24-29.

Rhodes, W.C., & Sagor, M. Community perspectives. In N. Hobbs (Ed.), *Issues in the classification of children.* Vol. 1. San Francisco: Jossey-Bass, 1975.

Rhodes, W.C., & Tracy, M.L. *A study of child variance: Conceptual project on emotional disturbance.* Ann Arbor: University of Michigan Press, 1972.

Rivière, M. *Rehabilitation codes: Classification of impairment of visual functions.* Bethesda, Md.: National Institute of Neurological Diseases and Stroke, 1970.

Rothman, D.J. *The discovery of the asylum.* Boston: Little, Brown, 1971.

Rude, C.R. The media analysis and retrieval system (MARS): A specific procedure for classification of information on instructional materials and media. In J.R. Armstrong (Ed.), *A source-book for the evaluation of instructional materials and media.* Madison, Wisc.: University of Wisconsin, Special Education Instructional Materials Centers, 1973.

Rudel, R.G., & Denckla, M.B. Relation of forward and backward digit repetition to neurological impairment in children with learning disabilities. *Neuropsychologia,* 1974, **12**, 109-118.

Rudel, R.G., & Teuber, H.L. Pattern recognition within and across sensory modalities in normal and brain-injured children. *Neuropsychologia,* 1971, **9**, 389-399.

Rutter, M. Classification and categorization in child psychiatry. *Journal of Child Psychology and Psychiatry,* 1965, **6**, 71-83.

Rutter, M., Lebovici, S., Eisenberg, L., Sneznevskij, A.V., Sadoun, R., Brooke, E., & Lin, T. A tri-axial classification of mental disorders in childhood. *Journal of Child Psychology and Psychiatry,* 1969, **10**, 41-61.

Santostefano. S. Beyond nosology: Diagnosis from the viewpoint of development. In H.E. Rie (Ed.), *Perspectives in child psychopathology.* Chicago: Aldine & Atherton, 1971.

Saul, R., & Sperry, R.W. Absence of commissurotomy symptoms with agenesis of the corpus callosum. *Neurology,* 1968, **17**, in press.

Scranton, J.A., Fogel, M.L., & Erdman, W.J. Evaluation of functional levels of patients during and following rehabilitation. *Archives of Physical Medicine and Rehabilitation,* 1970, **51**, 1-21.

Shaw, C.R., & Lucas, A.R. *The psychiatric disorders of childhood.* New York: Appleton-Crofts, 1970.

Silver, L.B. DSM-II and child and adolescent psychopathology. *American Journal of Psychiatry,* 1969, **125**, 1267-1269.

Sokolow, J., Taylor, E.J., & Rusk, H.A. *Development and standardization, validation, and field trial of a method of clarifying the physical, emotional, social, and vocational capacities of the disabled individual function.* Washington, D.C.: U.S. Government Printing Office, 1970.

South Dakota Department of Education and Cultural Affairs. *Curriculum guide for trainable mentally retarded children.* Pierre, S.D.: Department of Education and Cultural Affairs, Section for Exceptional Children, 1973-1974.

South Dakota Department of Education and Cultural Affairs. *K-12 curriculum resource book: Creative speech communication for South Dakota.* Pierre, S.D.: Department of Education and Cultural Affairs, Division of Elementary and Secondary Education, n.d.

Southwest Georgia Cooperative Educational Service Agency. *Clues for teaching the EMR child.* Leary, Ga.: Southwest Georgia Cooperative Educational Service Agency, 1973.

Sperry, R.W. Brain bisection and mechanisms of consciousness. In J.S. Eccles (Ed.), *Brain and conscious experience.* New York: Springer-Verlag, 1966.

Sperry, R.W. Hemisphere deconnection and unity in conscious awareness. *American Psychologist,* 1968, **23**, 723-733.

Sperry, R.W., & Gazzaniga, M.S. Language following surgical disconnection of the hemispheres. In C.H. Milikan (Ed.), *Brain mechanisms underlying speech and language.* New York: Grune & Stratton, 1967.

Staff of Riverview School. *A science program for children with exceptional needs.* Manitowoc County, Wisc.: Manitowoc County Handicapped Children's Education Board, September 1973.

Stevens, G. An analysis of the objectives for the education of children with retarded mental development. In J. Rothstein (Ed.), *Mental retardation*. New York: Holt, Rinehart & Winston, 1961.

Strauss, A.A., & Lehtinen, L.E. *Psychopathology and education of the brain-injured child.* New York: Grune & Stratton, 1947.

Terman, L.M. *The intelligence of school children.* Boston: Houghton-Mifflin, 1919.

Travers, R.M., Rabinowitz, W., Page, M.H., Nemovicher, E., & Ventur, P. *Exploratory studies in teacher personality.* New York: City College, Division of Teacher Education, 1953.

Treves, Z., & Saffiotti, F.U. *La scala intelligenza di Binet e Simon: Espositione critica.* Part I. Milan: Civelli, 1910.

U.S. Army. Physical standards and physical profiling for enlisting and induction. *U.S. Army Regulations,* 1956, **40**, 503.

U.S. Department of Health, Education, and Welfare. Programs for the education of the handicapped: Proposed guidelines and requirements. *Federal Register,* 1973, **38**(196).

U.S. Department of Health, Education, and Welfare. *International classification of diseases, adapted for use in the United States* (8th Edition) Public Health Publication No. 1693). Washington, D.C.: U.S. Government Printing Office, 1967.

Virginia State Department of Education. *Guide for curriculum development for teachers of trainable mentally retarded children.* Richmond, Va.: State Department of Education, Division of Special Education, January 1973.

Wepman, J.M., Cruickshank, W.M., Deutsch, C.P., Morency, A., & Strother, C.R. Learning disabilities. In N. Hobbs (Ed.), *Issues in the classification of children.* Vol. 1. San Francisco: Jossey-Bass, 1975.

Wilson, P.T., & Spitzer, R.L. A comparison of three current classification systems for mental retardation. *American Journal of Mental Deficiency,* 1969, **74**, 428-435.

Wisconsin Department of Public Instruction. A needs approach to curriculum development involving prescriptive teaching. *Bureau Memorandum,* 1969, **11**(2), 3-15.

Wisconsin Department of Public Instruction. *A persisting life needs approach to a curriculum for the educable mentally retarded.* Madison, Wisc.: Wisconsin Department of Public Instruction, Division for Handicapped Children. n.d.

Wiseman, S. *Education and environment.* Manchester, England: Manchester University Press, 1964.

World Health Organization. *Manual of the international statistical classification of diseases, injuries, and causes of death.* Geneva: World Health Organization, 1967. (a)

World Health Organization. *International classification of diseases* (8th ed.). Geneva: World Health Organization, 1967. (b)

Zilboorg, G., & Henry, G.W. *A history of medical psychology.* New York: W.W. Norton, 1941.

READING AND THE MILDLY RETARDED: REVIEW OF RESEARCH AND IMPLICATIONS[1]

Linda P. Blanton

Appalachian State University

Merrill C. Sitko

Indiana University

Patricia H. Gillespie

Indiana University

Teaching reading to mildly retarded children (i.e., those with IQs of approximately 60-80/5) is probably one of the most difficult academic tasks. Not only is the teacher dealing with a group of children who exhibit a wide range of reading problems but he also must deal with research literature which offers him few definitive conclusions regarding the superiority of one method of teaching reading over the other (Cawley, Goodstein, & Burrow, 1972; Cegelka & Cegelka, 1970; Gillespie & Johnson, 1974; Kirk, 1964; Spicker & Bartel, 1968). Although many programs have been developed for nonretarded groups, educators in the fields of special education and reading have offered teachers relatively few complete curricula designed to meet the specific reading needs of the retarded. Yet, those educators would hardly take issue with the importance of effective reading instruction for retarded children. In fact, many would argue that the success of a particular program of instruction depends on the maximum development of reading skill in its pupils.

Teachers themselves report that they feel inadequate in teaching reading to the retarded (Meyen & Carr, 1970; Windell, 1974). More specifically, they often express concern over finding an effective reading methodology and selecting instructional materials and seatwork activities in reading. Because of the lack of knowledge regarding effective reading instruction with retarded children, the present chapter was completed to present:

1. A review of reading studies which have been conducted using mentally retarded children as subjects.

2. A comprehensive look at recent work in psycholinguistics and cognitive psychology, particularly information processing, as these fields relate to the investigation of reading problems of retarded children. Although many studies have investigated possible correlates of reading, e.g., perception, the present review will emphasize a language approach to teaching reading.

3. Implications of past and proposed research for instructional practice and teacher training in reading with retarded children.

AN INTRODUCTION TO READING RESEARCH
WITH RETARDED CHILDREN

Reviews of the research literature have been undertaken primarily in the areas of reading characteristics of the educable retarded and the efficacy of reading methods used in teaching the retarded. The research on reading characteristics of the retarded has indicated that many educable retarded (EMR) children do possess problems that have been typically associated with reading deficiency. According to Cawley, et al. (1972), EMR children are comparatively inferior in specific reading skills related to linguistic development. Moreover, they possess deficits in word function skills and in using complex rules and principles of structural analysis. In addition, associative and synthesis abilities in phonics are comparative deficits for EMR children.

Spicker and Bartel (1968) concluded that there is no evidence to support any one characteristic as the basis of all reading problems in the EMR. Similar conclusions were drawn more recently by Gillespie and Johnson (1974). They emphasized that there are no causal relationships between problems more often possessed by EMR children (e.g., poor home background, perceptual motor differences, language deficiencies), as compared to average learners, and reading retardation. Moreover, Gillespie and Johnson (1974) stressed that intraindividual differences in four reading characteristics, e.g., modality preferences and processing skills, should be considered in future research.

Orlando (1973), after summarizing selected research with the retarded in reading skills, concluded that "much of the research on sight-word recognition and paired-associate learning should be abandoned in favor of investigations which will yield evidence about the nature of the relationships of language-reading abilities within EMR and TMR groups" (p. 267). Orlando also stressed that research efforts could be directed to language training and hence individual reading programs which would be based on language constructions that a child has learned.

Review of the effectiveness of specific reading methods with EMR children generally concur in their conclusions. Kirk (1964), in his extensive review, summarized early findings as follows:

> Studies on methods of teaching reading have been made largely on remedial cases, those who have become educationally retarded below their mental age. In general, remedial reading has been quite successful. The phonic method appears to have its advocates, but some also stress an eclectic approach. Unfortunately, only one controlled experiment on the kinesthetic method was reported. It is likely that this approach may be more beneficial than the sight or phonic method with some retarded children (p. 75).

Hence, the early research reveals no superiority of one reading method over another. Moreover, early studies concentrated on comparing phonic to sight-word approaches, with other reading methods seldom investigated.

In their review of various reading approaches used with retarded children, Cegelka and Cegelka (1970) concluded that "some reading methods may be more efficacious for specific learning constellations" (p. 198); however, the emphasis in teaching reading to the retarded should be on individual differences, matching reading methods to individual profiles, rather than on group instructional procedures. Gillespie and Johnson (1974) agreed with an approach based on the individual child's needs. Cawley, et al. (1972) summarized their findings as follows:

> Thus, the selection of an approach to reading represents only the best thinking at the local level in relation to considerations such as teacher style and training, the characteristics of the learners, the goals of the reading program, and the ultimate merger of any beginning technique with the overall program in the local system (p. 50).

In summary, reviewers of past reading research with the retarded have concluded that although retarded children may possess specific problems related to reading achievement, no one characteristic or set of characteristics can be assigned the cause of all their difficulties. Although an extensive amount of research has been conducted in order to determine the efficacy of specific reading methods, at the present time no conclusive results have been reported to support the superiority of one reading method over another.

Specific research studies on reading and the retarded

Basically, research on the achievement of the EMR child seems to fall primarily into the following areas: (a) studies comparing mentally retarded Ss with nonretarded Ss, (b) studies attempting to identify within-group differences among retarded Ss, (c) studies investigating reading methodology with retarded Ss and (d) studies exploring information processing models in reading comprehension with retarded Ss. Selected studies in each of the above areas were reviewed.

Studies comparing mentally retarded *S*s with nonretarded *S*s

The results of studies comparing retarded and nonretarded *S*s have generally shown that nonretarded *S*s perform significantly higher on measures of reading ability than retarded *S*s (Blake, Aaron, & Westbrook, 1967; Bleismier, 1954; Dunn, 1954; Klausmeier, Feldhusen, & Check, 1959; Shotick, 1960). In one of the most extensive investigations, Dunn (1954) compared specific reading processes and selected related factors in MR and nonretarded boys. The nonretarded group was superior to the retarded group on (*a*) all measures of silent and oral reading ability, (*b*) patterns of reading errors for faulty vowels, omission of sounds, refusals, and words aided, (*c*) ability to use context clues, and (*d*) measures of visual efficiency and auditory acuity. There were no significant differences between the groups on (*a*) patterns of reading errors for omission of words, substitution of words, addition of sounds, reversals, and faulty consonants, nor on (*b*) tests of sound-blending ability, eye movements, and recognition of tachistoscopically presented phrases and words.

Blake, et al. (1967) conducted a comprehensive study of achievement in basal reading skills by intellectually retarded, normal, and superior pupils. Fifty basal reading skills, organized into six categories, were studied. These categories included: (*a*) identifying words at sight, (*b*) phonetic analysis skills, (*c*) structural analysis skills, (*d*) dictionary skills, (*e*) word function skills, and (*f*) comprehension skills. Reported data focused upon developmental comparisons between retarded and normal children at different reading instructional levels and upon the acquisition of reading skills by retarded children during 7 months of public school instruction.

When retarded *S*s were compared with normal *S*s, either the normal group was found to exceed the retarded group in level of skill acquisition, or the two groups were found to have similar levels of acquisition. Another trend revealed that the two groups were more often similar in levels of skill acquisition at the primary level than at the intermediate level. In other words, the reading skill acquisition of the groups became more discrepant as the subjects advanced in instructional level.

The results of the above study showed a significant positive trend in the acquisition of a majority of the reading skills studied. Consequently, it may be inferred that the retarded children in this study learned the reading skills taught via the vehicle of the particular basal reading series used. Other approaches, of course, might have been equally successful.

Another approach in comparing the reading characteristics of normal and retarded children was taken by Cawley, Goodstein, and Burrow (1968). These investigators compared the reading and psychomotor characteristics of children who were indeed adequate and inadequate readers. Results showed that (*a*) good readers, retarded and average, demonstrated reading levels equivalent to their mental ages, (*b*) poor readers performed at levels that were 2½ years below their mental ages, (c) good and poor readers were often differentiated on measures of reading, (d) good and poor readers were infrequently differentiated on measures of psychomotor characteristics, and (e) the poor-reading retarded group was inferior to all of the other groups on measures of reading skills.

Still another approach was attempted in a study by Levitt (1972). Rather than using data gathered on the reading errors of retarded and nonretarded Ss to profile the characteristics of the groups, Levitt (1972) investigated the children's reading responses as they might imply underlying mediational responses. More specifically, she hypothesized that the reading processes of a group of retarded children, as inferred from their reading responses, would be qualitatively inferior to those of a group of nonretarded children. Reading response categories, which included 10 error categories, were classified as either higher-order (complex, problem-solving) responses or lower-order (relatively simple or inferior) responses.

The Levitt study revealed conflicting findings. Some supported predictions that the retarded group would use fewer higher-order reading processes than the nonretarded group: The nonretarded group made more Search for Closure responses and fewer Simple or Inferior responses than the retarded group. On the other hand, the investigation's predictions were contradicted by findings which revealed that the retarded group made more Multiple Cue responses than the nonretarded group.

Other studies which have compared retarded and nonretarded Ss have, in general, shown that nonretarded Ss perform significantly higher on measures of reading ability than retarded Ss (Blake, et al. 1967; Bleismier, 1954; Dunn, 1954; Klausmeier et al., 1959; Shotick, 1960).

Studies identifying within-group differences among mildly mentally retarded subjects

A review of the literature in this area indicates that most researchers have attempted to discriminate differences between endogenous and exogenous retarded subjects or to examine the effectiveness of methods of instruction for exogenous groups (Capobianco, 1956; Capobianco & Miller, 1958; Cruick-shank, 1961; Frey, 1960; Gallagher, 1960).

These studies, attempting to identify within-group differences among mildly retarded children, have shown no significant differences between brain-injured and non-brain-injured children in academic achievement. Additionally, special methods or programs with brain-injured groups have produced nonsignificant results (Cruickshank, 1961; Frey, 1960; Gallagher, 1960).

Several studies have compared adequate MR readers (reading to MA expectancy) with inadequate ones (not reading to MA expectancy). The research in this area, however, appears to be restricted to descriptive comparisons of these two groups among EMRs. Two such studies (Merlin & Tseng, 1972; Sheperd, 1967), investigating differences in reading ability and associated factors between groups of adequate-reading EMR children and inadequate-reading EMR children, have revealed that differences between the groups on such measures of reading and psycholinguistic abilities as silent and oral reading, word recognition, auditory association, visual communication, and the like) were either in favor of the adequate group or the differences were not significant.

Studies investigating reading methodology with retarded *S*s

A number of studies have compared the effectiveness of specific approaches to teaching reading with mildly retarded children (e.g., Dunn & Mueller, 1966; Dunn, Neville, Bailey, Pochanart, & Pfost, 1967; Dunn, Pochanart, & Pfost, 1967; Kaplan, 1971; Neville & Vandever, 1973; Woodcock & Dunn, 1967). Results have provided little evidence in support of one method over another.

The Woodcock and Dunn study was one of the more elaborate (1967). It compared six experimental approaches of teaching reading to EMR children: a language experience, basal reader, and programmed text approaches—all using traditional orthography; programmed text and language experience approaches—using the initial teaching alphabet *(i t a);* and a basal reader approach—using rebus symbols. The EMRs employed in this study were at the earliest stages of beginning reading or had not yet learned to read. Volunteer teachers were randomly assigned to one of the six reading approaches. Results of the Woodcock and Dunn study after 2 years indicated no significant differences between the groups on seven measures of reading ability.

Dunn and Mueller (1966) compared different reading approaches with mildly retarded children. These researchers investigated the efficacy of (*a*) *i t a* in teaching beginning reading, and (*b*) the Peabody Language Development Kit in stimulating oral language and verbal intelligence. Results after one year, relating only to the use of *i t a,* showed that groups of children receiving *i t a* performed significantly better on a reading achievement measure than groups using a basal reader approach. The results from the second year of the study (Dunn, et al., 1967) were similar. The teachers involved with the experimental groups were, however, provided with incentives (extra pay, etc.) not provided to control teachers. From this it can be concluded that results may have been biased. In order to control for this effect, Dunn, Neville, et al. (1967) later attempted to determine if *i t a*-instructed groups of disadvantaged children would perform significantly better than control groups if all the teachers were provided with extra support and incentives. In addition to *i t a,* the effectiveness of two other reading approaches was examined—Words in Color (WIC) and a Supplemented Conventional Reading Program (SCRP). The results after 1 year revealed no differences between the total experimental reading groups and the control group on a measure of school achievement. However, the SCRP treatment group tended to score higher than the other two groups.

A study by Neville and Vandever (1973) sought to determine whether either synthetic or analytic reading instruction would facilitate learning and transfer for either normal or MR children. Synthetic programs begin reading instruction with phonic components and then blend the parts into words, while analytic programs begin instruction with words and subsequently present phonic components. This investigation appears to be the first to examine the differential effects of the two methods on transfer using retarded Ss. The results revealed that: (a) both retarded and nonretarded children recognized significantly more words when the synthetic method was used; (b) both groups performed significantly better when the synthetic method was used for words taught and for transfer words; and (c) no differences were found in the learning and transfer of MA-matched retarded and nonretarded groups. These findings suggest that the synthetic method, by emphasizing letters and the way they can be combined to form words, encouraged the children to develop strategies useful in decoding new words.

A more recent study by Vandever and Neville (1974) sought to determine whether letter cues or shape cues should be emphasized in reading instruction for mildly retarded and nonretarded groups of children. The results suggest that the mildly retarded group learned more words when letter cues were emphasized than when configuration cues were stressed. The nonretarded groups performed equally well under both conditions.

Another approach in the examination of reading methodology with retarded Ss was taken in a study by Belch (1974). Belch investigated the effect of different questioning strategies in reading comprehension on the thought processes of three groups of secondary-level EMR students. One group responded to higher-order questions (which require the reader to apply, analyze, synthesize, and evaluate what is read) after reading paragraphs or passages, the other responded to lower-order levels of questions, and the third group responded to no questions. Results indicated that high order questioning strategies by teachers of EMR students had a significant effect on subsequent reading comprehension scores. More specifically, the group receiving the high-order questions had significantly higher posttest comprehension scores than the group receiving low-level questions or the group receiving no questions. There were no significant differences between the scores of the low level question and no question groups. These results suggest that mildly retarded students are capable of responding positively to questioning strategies which require higher cognitive processes.

Other approaches which have received attention for teaching reading to the mentally retarded are programmed instruction and teaching machine techniques. Numerous studies (e.g., Blackman & Capobianco, 1965; Haring, 1971; Hofmeister, 1971; Kaplan, 1971; Price, 1963) have compared programmed instruction to traditional classroom methods with EMR children. Greene's (1966) comprehensive review of the effectiveness of such techniques indicated essentially no achievement differences between the two methods in the majority of studies. His conclusion seems to hold true for more recent studies, e.g., those listed above.

One particular method which has revealed intriguing results with mildly retarded and disadvantaged children is Programmed Tutoring (Ellson, 1971). This technique provides detailed prescriptions for the individual teaching of reading and is designed to be used by nonprofessionals. Studies investigating Programmed Tutoring have shown that when the tutoring is a supplement to the regular reading program, pupils show significant increments in scores on reading achievement tests. The most recent data from studies on Programmed Tutoring also have indicated that the tutoring program has had a significant effect on the number of children assigned to special education classes. That is, fewer children receiving Programmed Tutoring were assigned to special education classes than control children (Ellson, 1971).

To sum up: Our review of the literature comparing different methods and approaches for teaching reading to retarded children has provided relatively little definitive evidence in support of one method over another. Perhaps many of these studies have placed too much emphasis on the search for a methodological panacea without sufficient consideration for individual learner abilities and characteristics. Probably the most extensive reading research program to focus on such a goal, i.e., the emphasis on individual learner abilities and characteristics, is the *Special Reading Instructional Procedures for Mentally Retarded and Learning Disabled Children* (Blake, 1973; Williams & Blake, 1974). This current project is attempting to produce special reading instruction techniques adapted to retarded and learning disabled children's learning and language characteristics.

A final note: From the review presented above, it can be seen that most methodological studies with retarded Ss have made comparisons among methods which place emphasis on the word as the basic unit of reading. The present authors suggest that perhaps shifting the focus from words to the comprehension strategies of the reader might be a more viable area for study. The work of Goodman (1965, 1968, 1969, 1972) in relation to nonretarded groups, for example, might have direct application for work with retarded and learning-disabled groups. Further discussion of this area is presented later in this chapter.

INFORMATION PROCESSING APPROACHES TO READING

One promising approach to investigating reading problems of retarded children is based on recent work in psycholinguistics and cognitive psychology, particularly information theory. Researchers in these fields are specifically concerned with the learner's selecting, storing, processing, and retrieving of information. They have frequently stressed not only the limited capacity of the human information-processing system, but also the importance of subjective organization to recode stimulus inputs so as to maximize the amounts of relevant information that can be received, processed, and remembered (Ausubel, 1968; Broadbent, 1958; Bruner, Goodnow, & Austin, 1956; Bruner, Olver, & Greenfield, 1966; Hunt, 1966; Mandler, 1967; Miller, 1956; Miller, Gallanter, & Pribram, 1960; Neisser, 1967; Olson, 1970; Taba, 1966; Tulving, 1962, 1966). Human memory, in this approach, is viewed as an active process of organization imposed by the learner on the stimulus input (Bruner et al., 1966; Mandler, 1967; Tulving, 1962). It appears a given that school learning, and social adaptation in general, are greatly dependent upon one's ability to accurately decode, interpret, and encode stimulus input. The school child is viewed as an active learner who possesses a repertory of organizational processes from which he must select those appropriate to the particular learning situation.

A particularly important application of information-processing is in teaching reading and constructing reading materials for mildly retarded children and adolescents. In fact, there is evidence that the ability to process and organize linguistic information may be strongly related to the nature of the reading process and to reading difficulties of poor or retarded readers (Bower, 1970; Goodman, 1965, 1968, 1969, 1972; Kolers, 1969; Lefevre, 1964; Neisser, 1967; Ryan & Semmel, 1969; Sitko & Semmel, 1973; Smith, 1971). However, despite the importance of active and efficient information processing in learning and memory, reading researchers in mental retardation have paid relatively little attention to the possible relationship between information processing in learning, memory, and reading behavior. Much of the reading instruction and research with MR children and adolescents has not been based upon language structure and language processing but rather upon graphic features and perceptual features of language (Sitko, Semmel, Wilcove, & Semmel, 1972).

In a comprehensive review of the literature concerning the language and language behavior of the MR, Sitko and Semmel (1973) noted that the language research reflected little concern with the fields of psycholinguistics and cognitive psychology, including information theory. As an example, the authors pointed out that little attention had been given to the cognitive or organizational strategies employed by MR children in processing linguistic information in academic learning situations. Moreover, researchers in language and reading had devoted relatively little attention to studying the grammatical or generative aspects of the language system of retarded children. Yet, considering the importance of efficient information processing in learning and memory, it is possible that these language deficits or differences, including reading, attributed to mildly retarded children may be due in part to faulty or inefficient processing and organization of stimulus input.

Theoretical models related to information processing and reading

Information processing has been related directly to reading. In summarizing the various models for reading based on the active information processing strategies of the reader, Ryan and Semmel (1969) have emphasized the importance of efficient and hierarchical language-processing strategies in beginning and mature reading. They contended that reading can be viewed as a ''constructive active process in which the reader uses his cognitive and linguistic knowledge to reproduce a probable utterance from a careful sampling of cues and then matches that prediction for appropriateness'' (p. 81). These authors suggest that the beginning reader should be encouraged to develop appropriate higher-order language strategies—strategies already available from oral language usage. ''Conceptual'' aspects of reading, rather than units or single words, should be stressed. They concluded that children's reading material should be written to maximize the child's opportunity to develop efficient habits of forming and testing hypotheses. Hence, beginning reading materials should include ''controlled syntactic patterns, highly associated words, and strong continuity among sentences'' (p. 81).

One of the earliest expositions of a language-based approach to reading instruction was by Lefevre (1964). He emphasized the importance of the sentence as a bearer of meaning and suggested that in teaching reading, words should be regarded as a minor linguistic unit, while intonation and stress patterns, clauses, and sentences should be emphasized. Using a cognitive framework, Neisser (1967) described reading as externally guided thought in which the stimulus, rather than determining perception, serves as a prompter or a cue for an ongoing language process.

Goodman's (1969) hypothesis-testing view of the reading process assumes that the ultimate goal of reading is direct passage from print to meaning, without going through surface speech processes in between. He calls for a shifting of the focus from words to the comprehension strategies of the reader. Words, Goodman has contended, should always be viewed as elements of larger, meaningful units. This approach, therefore, focuses the learner's attention on segmental units, e.g., clauses, which are based on the semantic and associative features of language. According to Goodman (1972), reading is a psycholinguistic guessing game which uses language cues selected from perceptual input. The child can engage in the reading process only by possessing language information that is encoded in graphic symbols (Goodman, 1968). Moreover, Goodman (1965, 1968, 1969, 1972) has designated ''cue systems'' that must be used by the reader in obtaining meaning from written language. He considers ''miscues'' in oral reading to be very important to the teacher because they provide information about the child's language skills. Cues may be based upon (*a*) clues within words; (*b*) the flow of the language in terms of such operations as function order, inflection or inflectional agreement, intonation or reference to what comes prior to or after the word in question; and (*c*) cues external to the language and the reader such as his dialect, experience and family background (Goodman, 1968). Qualitative analysis of a child's reading miscues will help the teacher use oral reading as a means to assess the language strategies a child employs. The Reading Miscue Inventory developed by Burke and Y. Goodman (1972) is one source for a qualitative analysis of a child's miscues and could serve as a framework for the study of a retarded child's cueing systems. Other reading researchers who have addressed the relationship of information processing and reading include Van Meel, Vlek, and Bruijil (1970), Venezky and Calfee (1970) and Smith (1971).

Exploring information processing models in reading with retarded children

The views of Ryan and Semmel (1969) mentioned previously were incorporated into the rationale of a study conducted by Sitko, Semmel, Wilcove and Semmel (1972) which sought to lay the groundwork for a psycho-linguistically based reading program. Specifically, the study attempted to (*a*) establish word-association (W-A) norms for a group of EMR children, and (*b*) empirically examine the effects of the children's word associations on reading performance. Such a study, it was expected, would lead to the development of a practical utilization of norms in creating reading materials for EMR children. Results indicated that a free W-A task with a group of young EMR children did reveal commonality of associational responses to sequentially constrained stimuli within a sentence; but this commonality did not exist for EMR pupils' sequential responses to stimulus sentences. No support was found for the efficacy of using high-association word pairs in sight vocabulary lessons for primary EMR children.

It was noted that all the teachers in the study used some variation of a basic phonic analysis approach to teaching reading. This approach takes the word as the basic unit of reading and does not attend to the relevance of linguistic context (semantic and syntactic relationships in determining word perception and comprehension. The authors concluded that in order for the associative proclivities of handicapped learners to be useful in enhancing their acquisition of reading skills, the learners must develop a set or be taught to attend to the associative (semantic) properties or features of word pairs and the associative constraints implicit in high-association sentences. The authors stressed the need to develop various activities and games that encourage retarded readers to attend to and use relevant linguistic organizational strategies which take advantage of the familiar structure of reading materials. Much of the reading instruction with retarded children has not been based upon *language structure* but rather upon graphic features of the language.

Three recent investigations by Bilsky and Evans (1970), Evans (1970), and Blanton (1974) have explored the possibility that retarded children and adolescents may have difficulty in reading comprehension because of a basic inability to organize verbal input for storage and retrieval during the act of reading. Bilsky and Evans (1970) sought to determine whether the ability to organize verbal material is central to the attainment of such reading skills as comprehension in institutionalized retarded subjects. All Ss were divided into good and poor reading groups on the basis of reading comprehension scores on the Metropolitan Achievement Test. Each subject was presented with four conceptual categories. The results indicated that organized, or blocked, presentation of words on the first two trials increased category clustering on subsequent random or nonorganized trials. Analysis of data further showed that subjects in the good-reading comprehension group revealed significantly more category clustering during free recall than subjects in the poor-reading comprehension group.

Evans' (1970) similar study investigated the effects of reading level and mode of presentation on category clustering and recall performance of public school retarded adolescent subjects. The Ss were randomly assigned to one of three experimental conditions, that is, mode of stimulus presentation. There were two unimodal (a visual and an auditory) presentation conditions and a bimodal (visual plus auditory) stimulus presentation. Each subject was shown a 20-word free recall list composed of words from four conceptual categories. Following the completion of the free recall task, all Ss were divided into above- and below-median subgroups on the basis of overall reading grade level scores. In contrast to the results of Bilsky and Evans (1970), the Evans study revealed that both clustering and recall performance were not significantly related to reading grade level. The bimodal presentation was found to have a significantly greater facilitating effect on recall than the other two presentations. It did not have, however, a significant effect on clustering performance. The overall correlation coefficient between performance and clustering was found to be statistically significant.

In order to help explain the discrepant findings between the two previous studies, Bilsky and Evans reported one major difference between the two studies. Both the reading scores and category clustering scores in the Evans study were higher than those obtained in the Bilsky and Evans study. This finding suggested that ''a certain level of organizational ability may be required for the development of reading comprehension ability. However, once this level has been attained, it is possible that other processes begin to play a more important role in determining reading comprehension'' (p. 775). The authors reported that in their study the correlation between reading comprehension and category clustering was significantly higher when clustering was "spontaneous" than when clustering was increased by the presentation of clustered lists. They suggested that in order to significantly improve reading comprehension performance, it would probably be necessary to establish "somewhat stable tendencies for individuals to organize incoming verbal materials" (p. 775). The fact that blocked presentation increased clustering on subsequent random trials suggested to Bilsky and Evans that it may be possible to increase the "effectiveness" of organizational skills in MR individuals. From the total findings they concluded that one may be able to facilitate MR educational performance on such tasks as reading comprehension by remediating specific deficiencies in input organization.

An extensive investigation by Blanton (1974) studied the relationship of organizational abilities to the comprehension of written and oral connected discourse in EMR and nonretarded children. In order to obtain a measure of subjective organization (SO), each S was individually administered 12 successive free recall learning trials on a 12-word stimulus list. Upon completion of the free recall task, Ss were administered as randomized the following reading and listening comprehension measures: (a) a traditional, standardized measure of reading comprehension, (b) a traditional reading comprehension measure with reading reinforced by listening, (c) a cloze test, and (d) two measures of listening comprehension as measured by verbatim recall across three paragraph conditions. The three paragraph, or treatment, conditions differed as to the chunking or organizational patterns provided: (a) no cueing within the text of the passage, (b) distinctive pausal cueing at phrase boundaries within the text of the passage, and (c) distorted pausal cueing at inappropriate phrase boundaries within the text of the passage.

The results supported six of the seven predictions made in the investigation. Nonretarded Ss scored significantly higher than EMR Ss on the five measures of reading and listening comprehension. As predicted, EMR children obtained significantly higher recall scores on a distinctive phrasal cueing (i.e., pauses at phrase boundaries within the text of the passage) condition than on either a no-cueing or a distorted phrasal cueing condition. Nonretarded Ss achieved significantly higher scores on a no-cueing condition than on a distorted phrasal cueing condition; they also scored higher on a distinctive phrasal cueing than on a distorted phrasal cueing condition. Results revealed that the differences obtained for EMR Ss and nonretarded Ss on a distinctive phrasal cueing paragraph compared to the differences obtained for EMR Ss and nonretarded Ss on a no-cueing paragraph were significant for one recall measure, but not for the other recall measure.

One of the major conclusions of the Blanton (1974) investigation was that EMR children do possess the competence necessary for recoding certain types of information when environmental cues are provided which facilitate the use of higher-order organizational abilities. It was also concluded that the difficulty experienced by retarded children in reading comprehension may be due to a basic inability to efficiently organize, recode, and retrieve verbal materials. A recent study by one of the present authors (Sitko & Semmel, 1972) provided additional evidence which indicates that distinctive cueing of organizational or recoding strategies may result in the use of such strategies by retarded children and improve their processing of verbal stimuli. Previous work had revealed that retarded children use primarily sequential-associative strategies in processing linguistic and cognitive information (Agard, 1971; Semmel, 1967; Semmel & Bennett, 1970; Sitko, 1970). They do not, however, tend to make use of more advanced hierarchical or rule-governed strategies *naturally,* as do nonretarded children. In the Sitko & Semmel (1972) study, making phrase boundaries distinctive through pausal cueing improved recoding and increased recall of nine-word declarative sentences by EMR children. EMR children revealed their best recall performance relative to nonretarded children when pausal cues (.5 sec pauses) were provided at phrase boundaries within sentences containing standard syntax. It was inferred from the findings the storage and retrieval abilities of retarded children in academic learning situations including reading may possibly be improved through development of specific pedogogical cueing systems and a well-organized structure and presentation of learning and reading materials.

In summary, considerable evidence amassed from the studies above has indicated that EMR children do possess the competence to recode linguistic units into hierarchical components when prompted. Considering the important role of organizational abilities in learning and memory, it seems logical to suggest the modification of relatively inefficient language processing strategies in EMR children to the more efficient hierarchical or rule-governed strategies. Such a modification would probably result in greater academic success, particularly reading comprehension, for EMR children. If EMR children store information inefficiently, then the relationships between words in storage are primitive relationships. As a result, it would be difficult for EMR children to retrieve the information. By teaching retarded children to impose organization on linguistic input, their dependence on rote memory and associative cues might be eliminated. We might thereby extend their memory capacity and hence linguistic comprehension.

IMPLICATIONS FOR TEACHING READING
TO THE RETARDED

As stated previously, researchers have not been able to identify specific characteristics that contribute to reading failure in all mildly retarded children. Neither have they been successful in isolating one reading method as more efficacious than another in teaching retarded children to read efficiently. Although there is evidence of differences between nonretarded and retarded children regarding organizational abilities in memory and in learning which may affect reading comprehension, one must be cautious in assuming homogeneity in reading problems among children categorized as mildly retarded.

It seems probable that the difficulty experienced by retarded children in reading comprehension and other areas of reading may be due to a basic weakness in their ability to efficiently process and organize reading materials. We stated above that retarded children should be taught to impose organization on linguistic information but did not indicate just how these teaching activities might be carried out. One way might be to present written and oral materials so as to cue the use of organizational strategies (e.g., Blanton, 1974; Sitko and Semmel, 1972). Using highly associated words in the construction of reading materials for retarded children should also be considered (Sitko et al., 1972).

In addition to providing cues in the text of written or oral materials, e.g., pausal cueing and/or the inclusion of highly associated words, it seems appropriate to actually train retarded children in how to learn to employ more advanced organizational abilities. Such training would facilitate skills in: (a) classification or categorization, (b) labeling, (c) matching, as well as (d) subjective organization. In fact, numerous studies have revealed that retarded children can be trained or cued to use specific linguistic and/or cognitive strategies to facilitate both acquisition and retention (Agard, 1971; Bean, 1968; Bryant, 1965; Clarke, Clarke, & Cooper, 1970; Gerjuoy & Alvarez, 1969; Hamilton, 1966; Katz, 1962; Martin, 1967; McIvor, 1970; Osler & Scholnick, 1968; Rowher, 1967; Ross & Ross, 1973; Ross, Ross, & Downing, 1973; Semmel, Lifson, & Sitko, 1967; Sitko and Semmel, 1972, 1973; Vitello, 1973; Whitely & Taylor, 1973).

It is particularly relevant for practical implications to provide knowledge for preservice and inservice teachers in special and regular education of children's organizational or recoding abilities. More specifically, teachers should be taught to develop new materials or organize extant materials for children who employ inefficient chunking strategies. In addition, teacher trainess should also be guided in structuring oral instructions or presentations to facilitate children's use of higher level organizational strategies (Gillespie & Johnson, 1974).

Further, teachers should be trained either to determine or make use of diagnostic information regarding children's organizational abilities. In essence, it seems necessary to train teachers to be both *effective organizers* of instruction and child-oriented decision makers in order to maximize children's use of efficient organizational abilities.

In conclusion, if educators are to consider the individual reading needs of handicapped children, a reorientation in research methodology, programming, and teacher training must occur. Rather than attempting to isolate or ameliorate various deficits using genetic intervention programs, it would seem more feasible (as the review in this chapter has tried to show) to conduct task analyses of children's behaviors in learning to read.

References

Agard, J.A. *Training conceptual organization in retarded children.* Unpublished doctoral dissertation, University of Michigan, 1971.

Ausubel, D.P. *Educational psychology: A cognitive view.* New York: Holt, Rinehart & Winston, 1968.

Bean, F.X. *The effect of classroom instruction upon the class inclusion behavior of the educable mentally retarded.* Unpublished doctoral dissertation, Teachers College, Columbia University, 1968.

Belch, P.J. *An investigation on the effect of different questioning strategies on the reading comprehension scores of secondary level educable mentally retarded students.* Unpublished doctoral dissertation. West Virginia University, 1974.

Bilsky, L., & Evans, R.A. Use of associative clustering technique in the study of reading disability: Effects of list organization. *American Journal of Mental Deficiency,* 1970, **74,** 771-776.

Blackman, L.S., & Capobianco, R.J. An evaluation of programmed instruction with the mentally retarded utilizing teaching machines. *American Journal of Mental Deficiency,* 1965, **70,** 262-269.

Blake, K.A. Overview of the research program activities. *Journal of Research and Development in Education,* 1973, **6,** 4-10.

Blake, K.A., Aaron, I.E., & Westbrook, H.R. Learning of basal reading skills by mentally handicapped and non-mentally handicapped pupils (BEH Project No. 5-0391). Washington, D.C.: U.S. Office of Education, 1967.

Blanton, L.P. *The relationship of organizational abilities to the comprehension of connected discourse in educable mentally retarded and nonretarded children.* Unpublished doctoral dissertation. Indiana University, 1974.

Bliesmer, E.P. Reading abilities of bright and dull children of comparable mental ages. *Journal of Educational Psychology,* 1954, **45,** 321-331.

Bower, T.G.R. Reading by eye. In H. Levin & J.P. Williams (Eds.), *Basic studies on reading.* New York: Basic Books, 1970.

Broadbent, D.E. *Perception and communication.* London: Paragon, 1958.

Bruner, J.S., Goodnow, J.J., & Austin, G.A. *A study of thinking.* New York: Wiley, 1956.

Bruner, J.S., Oliver, R.R., & Greenfield, P.M. *Studies in cognitive growth.* New York: Wiley, 1966.

Bryant, P.E. The transfer of sorting concepts by moderately retarded children. *American Journal of Mental Deficiency,* 165, **70,** 291-300.

Burke, C.L., & Goodman, Y.M. *Reading Miscue Inventory: Manual procedure for diagnosis and evaluation.* London: Macmillan, 1972.

Capobianco, R.J. Studies of reading and arithmetic in mentally retarded boys: II. Quantitative and qualitative analysis of endogenous and exogenous boys on arithmetic achievement. *Monographs of the Society for Research in Child Development, Inc.,* 1956, **19** (Whole No. 58).

Capobianco, R.J., & Miller, D.Y. *Quantitative and qualitative analyses of exogenous and endogenous children in some reading processes.* Syracuse, N.Y.: Syracuse University Research and Institute, 1958. (ED 002 747)

Cawley, J.F., Goodstein, H.A., & Burrow, W.H. *Reading and psychomotor disability among mentally retarded and average children.* Storrs, Conn.: University of Connecticut, 1968.

Cawley, J.G., Goodstein, H.A., & Burrow, W.H. *The slow learner and the reading problem.* Springfield, Ill.: Charles C Thomas, 1972.

Cegelka, P.A., & Cegelka, W.J. A review of research: Reading and the educable mentally handicapped. *Exceptional Children,* 1970, **37,** 187-200.

Clarke, A.M., Clarke, A.D.B., & Cooper, G.M. The development of a set to perceive categorical relations. In H.C. Haywood (Ed.), *Social-cultural aspects of mental retardation.* New York: Appleton-Century-Crofts, 1970.

Cruickshank, W.M. et al. *A teaching method for brain-injured and hyperactive children.* Syracuse, N.Y.: Syracuse University Press, 1961.

Dunn, L.M. A comparison of the reading processes of mentally retarded boys of the same mental age. In L.M. Dunn & R.J. Capobianco (Eds.), *Studies of reading and arithmetic in mentally retarded boys.* Monograph of the Society for Research and Child Development, 1954, **19**, 7-99.

Dunn, L.M., & Mueller, M.W. *The efficacy of the i t a and the PLDK with grade-one disadvantaged children: After one year* (IMRID papers and reports). Nashville: George Peabody College for Teachers, 1966.

Dunn, L.M., Neville, D., Bailey, C.F., Pochanart, P., & Pfost, P. *The effectiveness of three reading approaches and an oral language stimulation program with disadvantaged children in the primary grades: An interim report after one year of the cooperative reading project* (IMRID Behavioral Science Monograph No. 7). Nashville: George Peabody College for Teachers, 1967.

Dunn, L.M., Pochanart, P. & Pfost, P. *The efficacy of the i t a and the PLDK with disadvantaged children in the primary grades: An interim report after 2 years* (IMRID papers and reports). Nashville: George Peabody College for Teachers, 1967.

Ellson, D.G. The effect of programed tutoring in reading on assignment to special education classes: A follow-up of four years of tutoring in the first grade. Programed Tutoring Project, Department of Psychology, Indiana University, July, 1971.

Evans, R.A. Use of associative clustering technique in the study of reading disability: Effects of presentation mode. *American Journal of Mental Deficiency,* 1970, **74**, 765-770.

Frey, R.M. *Reading behavior of brain-injured and non-brain-injured children of average and retarded mental development.* Unpublished doctoral dissertation, University of Illinois, 1960.

Gallagher, J. *The tutoring of brain-injured mentally retarded children.* Springfield, Ill.: Charles C Thomas, 1960

Gerjuoy, I.R., & Alvarez, J.M. Transfer of learning in associative clustering of retardates and normals. *American Journal of Mental Deficiency,* 1969, **73**, 733-738.

Gillespie, P.H., & Johnson, L. *Teaching reading to the mildly retarded child.* Columbus, Ohio: Charles E. Merrill, 1974.

Goodman, K.S. A linguistic study of cues and miscues in reading. *Elementary English Review,* 1965, **42**, 639-43.

Goodman, K.S. (Ed.). *The psycholinguistic nature of the reading process.* Detroit: Wayne State University, 1968.

Goodman, K.S. Words and morphemes in reading. In K.S. Goodman, & J.T. Fleming (Eds.), *Psycholinguistics and the teaching of reading.* Newark, Del. International Reading Association, 1969.

Greene, F.M. Programmed instruction techniques for the mentally retarded. In N.R. Ellis (Ed.), *International Review of Research in Mental Retardation.* New York: Academic Press, 1966.

Hamilton, J. Learning of a generalized response class in mentally retarded children. *American Journal of Mental Deficiency,* 1966, **71**, 100-108.

Haring, N.G. Investigation of systematic instructional procedures to facilitate academic achievement in mentally retarded disadvantaged children. Final Report. Seattle: University of Washington, Child Development and Health Retardation Center, September 1971.

Hofmeister, A. Programmed instruction: Revisited implications for educating the retarded. *Education and Training of the Mentally Retarded,* 1971, **6**, 172-176.

Hunt, E.B. *Concept learning: An information processing problem.* New York: Wiley, 1966.

Kaplan, M. *An evaluation of the effectiveness of programmed instruction in elementary reading with mentally retarded adolescents in junior high school.* Dissertation Abstracts, 1971, 32-5671-A.

Katz, P.J. *Transfer of principles as a function of a course of study incorporating scientific method for the educable mentally retarded.* Unpublished doctoral dissertation, Teachers College, Columbia University, 1962.

Kirk, S. Research in education. In H. Stevens and R. Heber (Eds.), *Mental Retardation.* Chicago: University of Chicago Press, 1964.

Klausmeier, H.J., Feldhusen, J., & Check, J. An analysis of learning efficiency in arithmetic of mentally retarded children in comparison with children of average and high intelligence (Project No. 153). Washington: U.S. Office of Education, 1959.

Kolers, P.A. Reading is only incidentally visual. In K.S. Goodman & J.T. Fleming (Eds.), *Psycholinguistics and the teaching of reading*. Newark, Del.: International Reading Assoc., 1969.

Lefevre, C.A. *Linguistics and the teaching of reading*. New York: McGraw-Hill, 1964.

Levitt, E. Higher-order and lower-order reading responses of mentally retarded and nonretarded children at the first-grade level. *American Journal of Mental Deficiency*, 1972, **77**, 13-20.

Mandler, G. Organization and memory. In K.W. Spence & J.T. Spence (Eds.), *The psychology of learning and motivation*. New York: Academic Press, 1967.

Martin, C. Associative learning strategies employed by deaf, blind, retarded and normal children. Final report of U.S. Office of Education, Bureau of Research, Project Number R-069, Contract Number 5-0405-4-11-3, June 1967.

McIvor, W.B. Evaluation of a strategy oriented training program on the verbal abstraction performance of educable retardates (Interim Report — USOE). Teachers College, Columbia University. August 1970.

Merlin, S.B., & Tseng, M.S. Psycholinguistic and reading abilities of educable mentally retarded readers. Paper presented at American Educational Research Association Annual Meeting, Chicago, April 1972.

Meyen, E.L., & Carr, D.L. Teacher-perceived instructional problems: Indicators of training needs of the educable mentally retarded. *The Journal of Special Education*, 1970, **4** (1), 105-114.

Miller, G.A. The magical number seven, plus or minus two: Some limits on our capacity for processing information. *Psychological Review*, 1956, **63**, 81-97.

Miller, G.A., Gallanter, E., & Pribram, K.H. *Plans and the structure of behavior*. New York: Holt, Rinehart, & Winston, 1960.

Neisser, U. *Cognitive psychology*. New York: Appleton-Century-Crofts, 1967.

Neville, D., & Vandever, T.R. Decoding as a result of synthetic and analytic presentation for retarded and nonretarded children. *American Journal of Mental Deficiency*, 1973, **77**, 533-537.

Olson, D.R. Language acquisition and cognitive development. In H.C. Haywood (Ed.), *Social-cultural aspects of mental retardation*. New York: Appleton-Century-Crofts, 1970.

Orlando, C.P. Review of the reading research in special education. In L. Mann & D.A. Sabatino (Eds.), *The first review of special education*. Philadelphia: JSE Press, 1973.

Osler, S.F., & Scholnick, E.K. The effect of stimulus differentiation and inferential experience on concept attainment in disadvantaged children. *Journal of Experimental Child Psychology*, 1968, **6**, 658-666.

Price, J.E. Automated teaching programs with mentally retarded students. *American Journal of Mental Deficiency*, 1963, **68**, 69-72.

Rohwer, Jr., W.D. Social class differences in the role of linguistic structures in paired-associate learning: Elaboration and learning proficiency. Final Report of U.S. Office of Education, Bureau of Research, Project Number 5-0605, Contract number OE-6-10-273, November 1967.

Ross, D., & Ross, S. Cognitive training for the EMR child: Situational problem solving and planning. *American Journal of Mental Deficiency*, 1973, **78**, 20-26.

Ross, D., Ross, S., & Downing, M. Intentional training vs. observational learning of mediational strategies in EMR children. *American Journal of Mental Deficiency*, 1973, **78**, 292-299.

Ryan, E.B., & Semmel, M.I. Reading as a constructive language process. *Reading Research Quarterly*, 1969, **5**(1), 59-83.

Semmel, M.I. Language behavior of mentally retarded and culturally disadvantaged children. In J.F. Magory & R.B. McIntyre (Eds.), *Fifth annual distinguished lectures in special education*. Los Angeles: University of Southern California Press, 1967.

Semmel, M.I., & Bennett, S.W. Effects of linguistic structure and delay on memory span of EMR children. *American Journal of Mental Deficiency*, 1970, **74**, 674-680.

Semmel, M.I., Lifson, M.W., & Sitko, M.C. Learning and transfer of paradigmatic word associations by educable mentally retarded children: A preliminary study. *Studies in language and language behavior,* September 1, 1967. Center for Research on Language and Language Behavior, University of Michigan, Contract No. OEC-3-6-061784-0508, U.S. Office of Education.

Sheperd, G. Selected factors in the reading ability of educable mentally retarded boys. *American Journal of Mental Deficiency,* 1967, **71**, 563-570.

Shotick, A. *A comparative investigation of the performance of mentally retarded and normal boys on selected reading comprehension and performance tasks.* Unpublished doctoral dissertation, Syracuse University, 1960.

Sitko, M.C. Input organizational strategies of educable mentally retarded and normal boys in free recall verbal learning. Unpublished doctoral dissertation, University of Michigan, 1970.

Sitko, M.C., & Semmel, M.I. The effect of phrasal cueing on free recall of EMR and non-retarded children. *American Educational Research Journal,* 1972, **9**, 217-229.

Sitko, M.C., & Semmel, M.I. Language and language behavior of the mentally retarded. In L. Mann & D.A. Sabatino (Eds.), *The first review of special education.* Vol. 1. Philadelphia: JSE Press, 1973.

Sitko, M.C., Semmel, D.S., Wilcove, G., & Semmel, M.I. The relationship of word—and sentence—associations of EMR children to reading performance. Center for Innovation in Teaching the Handicapped, Indiana University, June 1972.

Smith, F. *Understanding reading: A psycholinguistic analysis of reading and learning to read.* New York: Holt, Rinehart, & Winston, 1971.

Spicker, H.H. & Bartel, N.R. The mentally retarded. In G.O. Johnson & H.D. Blank (Eds.), *Exceptional children research review.* Washington, D.C.: Council for Exceptional Children, 1968.

Taba, H. *Teaching strategies and cognitive functioning in elementary school children.* Cooperative Research Project No. 2404, San Francisco State College, February 1966.

Tulving, E. Subjective organization in free recall of unrelated words. *Psychological Review,* 1962, **69**, 344-354.

Tulving, E. Subjective organization and effects of repetition in multitrial free-recall learning. *Journal of Verbal Learning and Verbal Behavior,* 1966, **5**, 193-197.

Vandever, T.R., & Neville, D.D. Letter cues vs. configuration cues as aids to word recognition in retarded and nonretarded children. *American Journal of Mental Deficiency,* 1974, **79**, 210-213.

Van Meel, J.M., Vlek, C.A.J., & Bruijil, R.M. Some characteristics of visual information— processing in children with learning disabilities. In D.J. Gakker & P. Satz (Eds.), *Specific reading disability: Advances in theory and method.* Rotterdam: Rotterdam University Press, 1970.

Venezky, R.L., & Calfee, R.C. The reading competency model. In H. Singer & R.B. Ruddell (Eds.), *Theoretical models and processes of reading.* Newark, Del. International Reading Association, 1970.

Vitello, S.J. Facilitation of class inclusion among mentally retarded children. *American Journal of Mental Deficiency,* 1973, **78**, 158-162.

Whitley, S., & Taylor, A. Overt verbalization and the continued production of effective elaborations by EMR children. *American Journal of Mental Deficiency,* 1973, **78**, 193-198.

Williams, C., & Blake, K. Educational materials: Special reading instructional procedures for mentally retarded and learning disabled children: Overview of research program activities. *Education and Training of the Mentally Retarded,* 1974, **9**, 143-149.

Windell, I. *Development and evaluation of a module to train special education teacher trainees to determine a pupil's instructional reading level.* Unpublished doctoral dissertation, Indiana University, Augut, 1974.

Woodcock, R.W., & Dunn, L.M. *Efficacy of several approaches for teaching reading to the educable mentally retarded.* U.S. Office of Education Project. Nashville: George Peabody College for Teachers, 1967.

A REVIEW OF PROGRAMS FOR THE SEVERELY AND PROFOUNDLY RETARDED

Beth Stephens

University of Texas at Dallas

It is appropriate to preface a discussion of programs for the severely and profoundly retarded by a definition of these persons. There is a general dissatisfaction with a classification based solely on intelligence test scores. Yet as Tarjan, (1972) concedes, ". . . given care and attention to detail, an IQ test remains the best way of making comparative judgment of intellectual ability within a given culture" (p. 35). If intelligence is used as the criterion, severely and profoundly retarded persons are those with IQs below 35. In attending to the broader classification of severely and profoundly impaired (of which severely and profoundly retarded is a subcategory), Thompson (1974) states:

Efforts to define severely and profoundly retarded citizens in terms of etiology or level of functioning have promoted realization that these are highly heterogeneous persons, persons who present varying degrees and combinations of impairment and persons who display inconsistent development and behavior. These differences exist in mental, physical and communicative functioning, as well as in the social and emotional aspects of behavior. A definition which provides a realistic basis for program formulation recognizes the extremity of their needs.

A severely [and profoundly] handicapped child [citizen] is one who, because of the intensity of his physical, mental, or emotional problems, or a combination of such problems, needs educational, social, psychological, and medical services beyond those which have been offered by traditional regular and special education programs, in order to maximize his full potential for useful and meaningful participation in society, and for self-fulfillment.

. . . What we are looking for under this definition, this umbrella statement, is children [citizens] who have multiple learning problems. . . . Such children include those classified as seriously emotionally disturbed, schizophrenic and autistic, profoundly and severely mentally retarded, and those with two or more serious handicapping conditions, such as the mentally retarded deaf and the mentally retarded blind. . . . Such children may possess severe language and/or cognitive deprivation, and evidence a number of abnormal behaviors, including a failure to attend to even the most pronounced social stimuli, self-mutilation, self-stimulation, durable and intense temper tantrums, the absence of even the most rudimentary forms of verbal control, and may also have an extremely fragile physiological condition. (p. 73)

Proceeding from definition to provision of programs, one realizes that services for the severely and profoundly retarded not only must be an integral part of a well-coordinated statewide system, but must attend to the specific needs of this population. As yet a model operational plan has not emerged; instead, the model probably will evolve through a selective process, through review and evaluation of past and present attempts to provide effective training services.

In his historical survey of the management of mental retardation, Doll (1972) noted that severe mental retardation was first defined in 1534. Over the ensuing centuries programs generally emphasized sensory training which, in most instances, was designed and supervised by medically trained persons rather than educators (Assessment of Selected Resources, 1974).

One of the first recorded attempts to devise a training program for a low functioning person is found in Itard's 1801 biographical training record of Victor, *The Wild Boy of Aveyron* (Itard, 1932). Prior to being placed in Itard's care, this 11- or 12-year-old boy had lived completely isolated in the woods. Itard's training program for him was "planned, intensive, personalized, and therapeutically oriented" (Sarason, 1953). Moreover, Itard was assisted by a governess whose role was similiar to that of a present-day aide. Although their efforts did not result in normalization, the sensory training did promote limited improvement. Itard's statement as he reviewed the final results of efforts to train Victor stands as a hallmark for those attempting to measure progress in the severely and profoundly retarded.

> To be judged fairly this young man must only be compared with himself. Put beside another adolescent of the same age, he is only an ill-favored creature, an outcast of nature as he was of society. But if one limits oneself to the two terms of comparison offered by the past and present status of young Victor, one is astonished at the immense space which separates them, and one can question whether Victor is more unlike other individuals of his same age and species. (Quoted from Sarason, p. 329)

During the mid-19th century Séguin (as a result of his interest in lower functioning children) implemented Itard's theoretical ideas through a method which he termed "physiological." Thorough observation and diagnosis supplied positive knowledge of an individual's existing ability. Normal developmental sequences served as teaching guides for the physiological training, training which "presumed the existence of a mind which could be taught to attend to, compare, and make judgments about sensory learnings; [Séguin] reached [the mind] by activating hands, eyes, ears, nose, tongue, and body" (Talbot & Séguin, 1964, p. 65). Normal developmental sequences served as teaching guides. In this training, ongoing evaluation resulted in continuous revision and improvement of teaching techniques. The Séguin model which evolved during the last half of the 19th century was adapted by institutions for the mentally retarded in the United States.

Unfortunately, turn-of-the-century efforts to educate the retarded were diminished by the tendency, which arose from the sociological studies of the Jukes and Kallikaks, to associate mental retardation with undesirable character types and degenerate behavior (Assessment of Selected Resources, 1974, I, p. 2). The prevailing attitude resulted in an expansion of residential facilities for the mentally retarded, but the objective was segregation, not training, and the general approach was warehouse storage rather than individual training.

However, as the 20th century proceeded, public school programs for handicapped children grew in number. By midcentury, and with the formation of the National Association for Retarded Citizens, public school programs for severely retarded pupils began to appear in metropolitan areas, and by 1960 most states provided public education for their severely or trainable retarded pupils. And, although many states provided for the public school education of the *profoundly* retarded, there was general failure in implementation. Because of this neglect, the "Pennsylvania Association for Retarded Children, 14 named retarded children who were denied appropriate public education, and all other children similarly situated" filed suit against the Commonwealth of Pennsylvania in 1971. The resulting decision established that all persons "are entitled to an education regardless of the severity of their handicap" (Assessment of Selected Resources, 1974, I, p. 122, 3).

Since this decision, other states have moved either through litigation or legislation to assure their handicapped citizens the right to education, the right to treatment, and the right to protection from harm (Assessment of Selected Resources, 1974). Consequently, the support evolving during the present decade for programs for the severely and profoundly retarded is without parallel in any period of United States history. Accompanying this support is the professional obligation to develop programs which assure optimum benefit; this is the charge for the ensuing decade.

Organizations concerned with services and programs for severely and profoundly retarded persons include: the American Association for Mental Deficiency, International League of Societies for the Mentally Handicapped, International Society for the Scientific Study of Mental Retardation, National Association for Retarded Citizens, and the President's Committee on Mental Retardation. In addition, the American Association for the Education of the Severely/Profoundly Handicapped was formed in 1974. Its goals are to function as an advocate organization to develop and implement (*a*) educational services, (*b*) teacher training programs, (*c*) to develop, refine and disseminate training programs, and (*d*) to facilitate parent involvement (American Association for the Education of the Severely/Profoundly Handicapped, 1975).

Programs for the severely and profoundly retarded may be classified as those that provide services on a day basis only, those that are solely residential, and those that offer combinations of day and residential services. Add to these those which are home based, and it becomes possible to categorize programs in terms of setting. Regardless of setting, however, there are certain functional areas upon which training efforts center, and these are the basis of this review. They include (physical and motor development, cognitive processes, language, self-help and practical skills, social and emotional development, recreation, and vocational habilitation.) To provide individually appropriate programs requires knowledge of a person's present level of functioning; therefore, appraisal techniques are here considered an integral part of methodology and are included in the present review of programmatic efforts.

A comprehensive overview of resources (including programs) for severely handicapped children and youth is the subject of a five-volume study recently completed by Abt and Associates (Assessment of Selected Resources, 1974) for the United States Office of Education. Readers who desire detailed and current information on resources for the severely and profoundly retarded should peruse these reports. The present review is restricted to program efforts and centers on activity of the past decade. Before presenting programs which focus on specific training areas, we review five programs which had as their goal the total training of severely and profoundly retarded persons. These five provide examples, not an exhaustive listing, of comprehensive efforts.

1. During the 1960s the Southern Regional Educational Board prepared a handbook for ward personnel entitled *Teaching the Mentally Retarded* (Bensberg, 1965), which has enjoyed wide usage in residential facilities. The publication presented "principles and methods for teaching the retarded the various skills and information required for them to be as independent as possible. Topics . . . included . . . those things a parent might teach his own child" (p. vii).

The training program, designed for residents of varying ages, included evaluative techniques and activities for the severely and profoundly retarded in language development, self-care (with detailed suggestions for self-feeding, toileting, dressing, cleanliness, and grooming), motor development, social maturity, and occupational maturity. Positive reinforcements served as the foundation for teaching, which employed the principles of behavior modification. In an attempt to improve the self-help behavior of 6 severely retarded residents, behavior-shaping techniques were inaugurated; at the end of 7 months, each subject showed substantial improvement. When treatment was extended to 28 cottage residents, improvement reached a plateau after approximately 4 months, and improvement also was noted for the control subjects. The experimenters concluded that self-motivation, which evolved from the project, resulted in improved conditions for the control group. Detailed data analysis and follow-up procedures might serve to determine whether the plateau in improvement for the experimental subjects represented achievement of an unchangeable optimum level.

2. An instructional guide, entitled *A Manual for Parents and Teachers of Severely and Moderately Retarded Children*, has been prepared by Larsen and Bricker (1968). The manual consists of two parts: One sets forth the principles and techniques of behavior modification; the other presents 23 activities which provide opportunities to apply these methods. Included in these are:

Sitting quietly in a chair
Building puzzles
Coloring
Playing with a ball
Playing with a wagon
Toilet training
Eating correctly
Putting on a pullover shirt
Putting on pants
Putting on socks
Buttoning buttons
Tying shoelaces
Brushing teeth

Each activity is described under the headings "Task Definition Pretest," "Suggested Education Program," and "Measuring Progress." While the principles of behavior modification are capably handled, developmental appraisal to determine the child's readiness for the task is neglected; an example of such neglect is found in the Task Definition for Activity #13, Tying Shoelaces.

Tying shoelaces is one of the more difficult tasks for many children. The child must be able to use his hands and fingers very well before it will be possible for him to tie his own laces. It is good training for him though, and it is good to try to teach any child this kind of activity, even though they are not very good with their hands. (p. 56)

Apparently the emphasis on operant techniques overshadows the need, in the authors' minds, to analyze each activity in terms of level of motor and cognitive functioning required for its mastery. Nonetheless, the activities can be used successfully by persons sufficiently skilled to match the developmental levels which the activities entail with those attained by the pupil.

3. The specific goals of *Program Development for Severely Retarded Institutionalized Children* are, as listed by McCarthy, Stevens, and Billingsley (1969), to:

i. evolve a treatment program for severely retarded, institutionalized infants and young children aimed at optimizing motor, adaptive, social and language functions; ii. assess the effects of the program so that useful procedures could be incorporated into an ongoing institution-wide routine for infants and children at the project side; and iii. disseminate the procedures and results of the project to those interested in undertaking similar efforts. (p. 3)

Sequential treatment card decks were developed for Gesell's four major developmental areas: motor, social, adaptive, and language. Each card listed developmental area, a description of the task, normative age for task (in months), test for task, and treatment.

To assess the effectiveness of the treatment, two groups of 15 severely retarded, institutionalized infants (CA=0-3 years) were compared. One group, TCT, received project treatment the first and third year, and baseline care the second. The second group, CTT, received baseline care during the first year and project treatment during the second and third. No true control group was included. The cross-over design was employed to avoid treatment penalty. During the project, developmental assessment of each subject's deficits was followed by training activities designed to remediate these deficits. Activities were provided 30 minutes per day, 5 days per week, 8 months of the year. Gesell gains scores were used as pre- and posttraining measures.

At the end of the first year the TCT group surpassed the CTT group; but the two groups did not differ significantly at the end of the second year. These findings serve to indicate that the year of treatment was successful for both groups. Both groups made progress during the third year; and differences between the two groups were not significant at the end of the third year—a desired result. Three other subjects received treatment throughout the 3 years of the project; their gains were continuous and resembled those of the CTT group who received continuous treatment for 2 years. Findings indicated that continued and extensive treatment does promote development in the severely retarded.

4. As the Commonwealth of Pennsylvania observed a court mandate and prepared to open public school classes for severely and profoundly retarded pupils in 1972, an attempt was made to devise a "continuous system for delivering instructional services . . . consisting of identification, evaluation, prescription, and programming" (COMPET [Commonwealth Plan for Education and Training], 1972, p. iv). COMPILE, the Commonwealth Plan to Identify, Locate and Evaluate Mentally Retarded Children (1972), provided an evaluation form as an index of the pupil's current functioning level. The appraisal was presented in terms that could coordinate with educational and training strategies. A data instrument, the Referral/Placement Master (RPM) served to join COMPILE with COMPET. Through use of the RPM a pupil's performance in 26 areas of behavioral development served as the basis for recommended program content; thus the link was made, through referral, from evaluation to programming. In turn, COMPET, a behavioristically oriented document, contained training modules corresponding to the program categories specified on the RPM. These are:

Gross Motor Development
Fine Motor Development
Visual Motor Training
Auditory
Tactile/Kinesthetic
Self-concept
Communication
Conceptual
Math
Toileting
Feeding/Eating/Drinking
Grooming
Oral Hygiene
Nasal Hygiene
Clothing Care
Personal Safety
Self-help and Independence
Social Interaction
Prevocational
Vocational

The modules do not constitute a comprehensive curriculum; rather, their purpose is to provide a general program resource. Possibly some areas are overemphasized to the neglect of others, e.g., a minor area, nasal hygiene, and a major area, vocational training, are both topics for a module. Yet there are no modules which cover social-emotional development, recreation, leisure, or sex education. Effort has been made to arrange the behavioral objectives contained in the modules in developmental sequences; however, they frequently do not extend far enough downward to provide a framework for earliest development or upward to provide a basis for adult programming. The immediate need for the COMPET document precluded field testing, evaluation, and revision. A current project will provide a revised, amended, and extended version.

5. A *Training Program for Citizens with Severely or Profoundly Retarded Behavior* has been created by an interdisciplinary group at Pennhurst State School. The "APT Package" contains an assessment scale, a set of training programs, and a resident progress form (Brody & Smilovitz, 1974). The scale is comprised of 36 statements that describe specific actions and skills in 6 areas: motor, communication, self-help, socio recreation, discrimination, and social instruction.

This global approach to assessment apparently does not provide the developmental appraisal that is basic for appropriate programs. For example, the three statements contained in the motor area occur under the headings (*a*) sitting, (*b*) walking, and (*c*) hopping. Much finer delineation of development is needed. However, training procedures which are derived from a task analysis of the desired skill do set forth behavioral objectives plus suggested material and procedures, e.g. the behavioral objectives included in training procedures for sitting include head lifting, rolling, control of head lag, pull to sitting position, and sitting upright. The training employs a one-to-one behavior modification approach and uses techniques of backward chaining or shaping and fading.

A pilot study which involved 40 female and 40 male severely or profoundly retarded, randomly selected residents (mean age: 28 years, 2 months) served to establish the reliability of the APT scale; 2 randomly selected aides served as raters. The unique contribution of the training package, which was designed for use by aides trained in behavior modification techniques, may lie in the attempt to include such activities as shaving and towel folding which are at an adult interest level but within the performance range of the severely and profoundly retarded citizen.

PHYSICAL AND MOTOR DEVELOPMENT

In discussing the contribution of motor activity to learning, Thompson (1969) notes that Kephart (1960) identifies four motor patterns (i.e., motor acts which . . . possess extensive variations which are significant to education): (1) balance and maintenance of posture, (2) locomotion—walking jumping, etc., (3) contact—motor activities with which the child manipulates objects, and (4) receipt and propulsion—skills with which the child investigates movements in space. Many children require additional help and additional learning experiences to continue their motor learning until a level is reached which permits the use of movement, not for specific purposes, but for the more generalized purpose of information gathering. Therefore, it becomes the responsibility of the school . . . to help the child expand his motor learning.

Improvement in gross and fine motor skills increases the young retardate's ability to interact with, and therefore gain additional information from, his environment . . . and also increases his ability to participate successfully in daily activities which surround him . . . [However,] repeated demonstrations, opportunities, and training are required for him to master that which is acquired incidentally by normals. (Stephens, 1971, pp. 156-157)

As the behavioral patterns of pupils previously excluded from school are reviewed, irregularities in motor development emerge as a common characteristic. Cerebral palsy or other physical handicaps may have impaired the child's motor development; or minimal activity levels, caused perhaps by lowered vitality, poor motiviation, or inadequate receptivity to stimuli, may have resulted in little motor action or interaction on the part of the child. To get the child to act motorically and to interact with the people and things around him may be one of the primary aims of the training program for pupils previously excluded from school. Efforts to achieve this must be commensurate with the child's present level of functioning as determined by motor development scales.

Assessment

Currently a variety of scales are available which outline motor development as it proceeds from birth through the 6th or 7th year (Bayley, 1935; Gesell, 1940; Ilg & Ames, 1960). Since these are based on observable behavior they are appropriately used to measure development in the severely and profoundly retarded. Review of these assessments reveals a necessary sameness of items because they are all scaling the same process. Fokes' Developmental Scale of Motor Abilities (Stephens, 1971) is probably the most comprehensive; items for it have been selected from reliable valid scales and arranged in longitudinal sequence. The resulting measure is a continuous description of development, i.e., it contains a variety of items attained by the average child at each of the age levels listed. As with most motor scales, 7 years is the upper age limit (Stephens, Manfredini, & Malcotti, 1972, p. 13).

When Smeets (Stephens, 1971) desired a quick, concise appraisal of motor development in the severely and profoundly retarded, he followed Fokes' method of selecting items from existing valid scales and arranging them developmentally. The result, Smeets' Motor Development Scale, is an instrument which measures development from 12 to 48 months in the areas of gross motor skills, balance, eye-hand coordination, and manual dexterity. Gross and fine motor skills are measured by the Denver Developmental Survey, a widely accepted test devised by Frankenburg and Dodds (1969) which requires little training to administer.

The Teaching Research Motor Development Scale for Moderately and Severely Retarded Children (Fredericks, Baldwin, Doughty, & Walter, 1972) is designed to assess this group's motor abilities from the preschool through late adolescent years. Included in the measured abilities are imitation of movement, walking forward, standing heel to toe, and alternate opening and closing of hands.

To evaluate the sensory motor basis of behavior in the profoundly retarded the Glenwood Awareness Manipulation and Posture Index was devised (Webb, 1972). Recognition, interaction, and mobility are used as criteria to the development of awareness, movement, manipulation and posture. The spontaneous exploration of objects is measured on the manipulation scale. Although data on the validity of the instrument is not available, it continues to be used to assess alertness in motor-impaired persons.

Recognizing the need for useful procedures to assess the sensory motor performance of young, severely handicapped children, Friedlander developed an automated operant behavior play device which could be used to examine attention, purposefulness, response selectivity, and adaptive behavior. As the subjects interact with the automated toy, which has audiovisual feedback, responses demonstrate their ability to discriminate, to adapt, and to manipulate objects. Results have indicated that this "Playtest" method can be used advantageously to assess sensory motor performance in young severely and profoundly retarded persons (Friedlander, McCarthy, & Soforenko, 1967).

Additionally, (Sloan, 1948), adapted the Oseretsky Test for use with the mentally retarded. Although the resulting Lincoln-Oseretsky Motor Development Scale is not exclusively for the severely and profoundly retarded, in some instances it may be profitably applied to this population.

Because a positive relationship has been found to exist between mental age and motor skills (Distefano, Ellis, & Sloan, 1958), one would expect mentally retarded persons to exhibit impaired or delayed motor functioning. Work by Malpass (1960) and Tredgold (1937) provided data to confirm the assumption. Also, lower functioning persons tend to have a high incidence of multiple handicaps; often one of these is motor (Stephens et al. 1972).

Programming

A motor training program which sought to reduce the limitations and to meet the needs of nonambulatory profoundly retarded persons was described by Auxter (1971). His objectives included extending the range of movement for contracted joints and promoting their purposeful integrative functioning. Social and material rewards and adverse consequences were used to elicit desired responses. Each of the 12 students (CA=12 to 30, MA=6-18 months) made gains in one or more areas covered by the activities.

Webb (1969) described a project supplying sensory-motor training to 32 profoundly retarded institutionalized children for from 5 to 10 months. To raise the subjects' level of awareness, various therapy activities stimulated the senses, i.e., tactile, kinesthetic, visual, auditory, taste, olfactory, and temperature. For example, the kinesthetic sense was stimulated by rolling, bouncing, swinging, and reaching activities; sensory-motor integration was promoted by activities which involved skills of grasping, holding, throwing, sitting, crawling, standing, and stair climbing. Clinical analysis measured behavioral dysfunctions before and after treatment. Webb's review of the results of the project advanced a tentative theory that "defective sensory motor integration underlies the four syndromes [awareness, movement, manipulation of environment, posture and locomotion]" (p. 284).

Attempts to develop perceptual motor skills in a profoundly retarded child through use of operant behavioral techniques are reported by Hollis (1967). In his approach, classical conditioning was used in stimulus building, and manipulation by the trainer was employed to build responses; reinforcement was used for shaping. Through these techniques patterns of reach, contact, grasp, extension, and bilateral transfer were established. Later performance was not reduced by changes in contingency and consequence.

172

After level of motor performance was determined in four areas (gross motor skills, balance, eye-hand coordination and manual dexterity) through use of the Fokes Developmental Scale of Motor Abilities and the Smeets Motor Development Scale, individually appropriate motor programs were planned for 24 severely and profoundly retarded residential students by Stephens, Smeets, Baumgartner and Wolfinger (1970). Some members of the experimental group were preoccupied with self-stimulating behavior, and others evidenced little or no concern for the manipulative value of objects. Techniques which were devised to elicit their interest and attention employed Bruner's (1966) three levels of representation: (a) inactive—the child is physically guided through motor activity, (b) iconic—precise demonstration precedes the subject's attempt to perform an activity, and (c) symbolic—verbal instructions and explanations precede the subject's attempts (Stephens, 1971, p. 164).

Daily 1-hour training sessions were provided by a teacher and three aides. In some instances a two-tutors-to-one-pupil ratio was required; such concentrated effort was justified if it lead to self-initiated activity. The program resulted in superior performance by the experimental group in comparison to the control group.

The infant-level home development guidance program outlined by Denhoff (1967) included instructional guides in basic exercises for home use. Areas covered were gross motor skills, fine motor skills, and speech-hearing-language skills. The sequential charts focused on: (a) expected development from birth to 6 years, (b) indications of delayed or deviant development, and (c) suggested remedial activities.

An instructional program model labeled I CAN, developed by Wessel and Associates (1973), was designed as a diagnostic/prescriptive teaching and program model which sought to promote growth and development through motor activities. Primary skills curriculum materials and instructional procedures were provided in the form of instructional resource modules representing four performance areas: (a) aquatics (self-rescue skills, strokes, adjustment to water), (b) body management (body awareness, awareness of environment, controlling the body, daily living postures), (c) fundamental skills (locomotor skills, object control skills, rhythmic skills), and (d) health/fitness (physical fitness, moving and growing).

The materials design for the modules encompassed teaching-learning activities containing performance objectives, enabling objectives, and focal points for activity. The teaching cues, which set forth general as well as specific directions, were followed by teaching-assessing activities, and play and practice activities. Instructional strategies focused on "skill development, skill assessment, and prescription based upon the student's standing in the hierarchical sequence of skill learning development" (Wessel, 1975, p. 10). A unique aspect of the I CAN program was its emphasis on the coordination of physical activity with other curriculum areas, e.g. art, music, math.

Evaluation of I CAN was in two phases. The first phase was comprised of small-sample, cyclical investigations which promoted user-developer interaction and material modification. In the second phase the modified materials were field tested by 31 teachers. An inservice teacher training model was devised as an integral part of the instructional package.

COGNITIVE PROCESSES

As one works with severely and profoundly retarded persons and notes their responses to people and things—and they do respond, although the response may be only a slight fleeting smile or frown, a flicker of the eyelid, a brief visual tracking of an object, or intensification of already apparent withdrawal—one realizes that some thought processes are in action. In most instances their cognitive development surpasses that of a neonate, yet because it is difficult to elicit their responses to standard test items, they frequently are regarded as untestable and are treated as though they operate from an intellectual vacuum. However, if one observes their behavior and locates the level and type of observed activity on a scale of cognitive development, an individually appropriate basis is supplied for interaction with objects and people.

Assessment

Using traditional measures of intelligence with severely and profoundly retarded persons has been generally unsatisfactory. In a study conducted by Halpern and Equinozzi (1969) verbalization and intelligence were not found to be closely related in persons in the 29 to 78 IQ range. In order to assess learning abilities in severely retarded children Grace (1959) constructed a battery of short nonverbal tests for persons with physical handicaps and language deficits.

Comparison of the reliability of the ratio IQ and the deviation IQ with Fisher's and Zeaman's K (Silverstein, 1971) provided evidence that K was a "relatively constant indicator of the intellectual capacity of institutional mentally retarded subjects over test-retest intervals of six to seven years" (Assessment of Selected Resources, 1974, I, p. 52). When candy was used as a reinforcer with 40 severely retarded children the test-retest reliability of alternate forms of the Cattell Infant Intelligence Scale was significantly greater for them than for the control subjects (Husted, Wallin, & Wooden, 1971).

Instruments commonly employed to assess the cognitive capacity of persons with intellectual deficits have been reviewed by Allen and Allen (1967); their work provides a comprehensive overview of various approaches to testing. In his discussion of cognitive appraisal of mentally retarded persons, Parker held that the difference between cognitive capacity and empirical problem-solving ability must be recognized if valid appraisal is to be achieved; and that culture fair items should be devised (Parker, 1971). Yet when studies which involved the reliability and usefulness of IQ scores for persons with IQs below 30 were analyzed, the conclusion advanced by Ross and Boroskin (1972) was that a below-30 IQ can be meaningful; however, their conclusions have not been generally accepted (Assessment of Selected Resources, 1974, I).

Acknowledgment is given to Woodward (1959) for initially demonstrating that the level of intellectual development attained by the severely and profoundly retarded could be determined by appraising their behavior in terms of Piaget's stages of cognitive development. She holds that through use of Piaget's hierarchical scale, individuals who previously have been viewed as an undifferentiated group, and whose performance is more than 3 SDs from the mean, can be differentiated. Uzgiris' and Hunt's measure, an Instrument for Assessing Infant Psychological Development (Uzgiris and Hunt, 1966), can be adapted for use with older severely retarded subjects who appear to be functioning at a sensory-motor level (a stage which generally represents the birth-to-2-year period in normals). For criteria Uzgiris and Hunt selected situations which are easily elicitable and measurable, which are described by Piaget in his writings on the sensory-motor period, and which can be reliably observed by different people (Stephens et al., p. 32).

An assessment analogous to Uzgiris' and Hunt's sensory motor measure is not available to assess thought at the preoperational stage, a stage which normally covers the period of approximately 2 to 7 years. Need for a Piagetian-based instrument to measure thought at this level is emphasized because severely and profoundly retarded persons generally do not develop beyond this period. One measure, Cognitive Growth in Pre-school Children (Melton, Charlesworth, Tanaka, Rothenberg, Busis, Pike, & Gollin, 1968), has been devised to assess areas previously identified by Genevan research as major components in the intellectual development of the preoperational child; however, there has been no reported effort to extend use of the instrument to lower functioning children.

For children who perform at levels achieved by average children between the years 2 to 6 an instrument is available, designed by Haeussermann (1958) for use with handicapped children and later revised by Jedrysek, Klapper, Pope, and Wortis (1972). Their goal was to circumvent the child's impairment and determine his basic potential for development. To this end, alternate forms are offered for various test items, e.g., there are specific adaptations which may be employed for motor-impaired persons. Because the moderately retarded frequently are multiply handicapped, Haeussermann's techniques are particularly appropriate in their assessments.

To meet the demand for measures which identify motor, perceptual, or cognitive deficits, and which can be quickly and easily administered—preferably by the classroom teacher—Vallet selected items from a number of valid reliable scales and arranged them in a developmental sequence. The resulting Valett Developmental Survey of Basic Learning Abilities (Valett, 1966) affords a measure of development between the years of 2 to 7 in seven developmental areas.

Programming

One of the most challenging tasks in the entire field of mental retardation is programming to promote cognitive development in persons who are severely and profoundly impaired. Past decades have been characterized either by no effort or by unsuccessful effort. Now, however, we are entering an era of positive results owing largely to: (a) realization that the remedial activity must be congruent with the individual's current level of functioning, and (b) the availability of cognitive scales which measure lower levels of functioning, i.e., development from birth onward. Provided with this information, one seeks an activity which will serve to promote development from one level to the next. However, in embarking on programming attempts, one should be reminded that the programmer cannot *make* another person develop cognitively, but can provide him with a variety of developmentally appropriate opportunities to interact with people and things; in turn, if neurological functioning and other contributing factors are sufficiently present, this interaction should foster cognitive development.

During its initial stages cognition is inextricably linked with sensory-motor activity. For this reason the beginning stage of intellectual development is termed the sensory-motor stage, and programs which promote interaction with objects and people can be viewed as both cognitive and motor in orientation. Early intervention activities are appropriately used with older severely and profoundly retarded persons who function at this level.

The *Portage Guide to Early Education* (Shearer & Shearer, 1972), designed for use with children between the mental ages of birth and 5 years, is divided into five developmental areas: cognitive, self-help, motor, language, and socialization (with acknowledgment that the divisions are arbitrary). Accompanying the developmentally sequenced behavioral checklists for each of the five areas are correspondingly sequenced activity cards. When a specific behavior is defined as a curriculum goal, the accompanying activity card provides a behavioral description of the item, the criteria for success, and suggested materials and activities for teaching the behavior. Initial activities in the cognitive area are designed to promote awareness of self and the surrounding environment. Succeeding activities involve such areas as initiation of number concepts, awareness of likenesses and differences, and memory for and verbalization of stories.

Admittedly an exhaustive review of early intervention is beyond the scope of the present writing; the Portage Project is offered as an illustration of one which can be adapted for use with the severely and profoundly retarded. Studies by Bricker, Heal, Bricker, Hayes, and Larsen (1969), and Larsen and Bricker (1968) establish the feasibility of discrimination learning procedures and preacademic training activities for lower functioning children. A "remotivation technique"—a structured small group program designed to promote interaction between institutionalized mentally retarded youngsters and adults, peers, and environment—was initiated for 24 retarded children (IQ 6-30) and three aides by Sternlicht (1971). A variety of materials was used to stimulate activity; results have indicated significant improvement in sociability, alertness, and responsiveness.

Recognition of the contributions to learning which derive from play prompted Corrado and Reed (1969) to design a play activities program which utilized such objects as sensory training boards, manipulative materials, blocks, water and musical instruments. Improved characteristics and habits accrued from the 5-year project, conducted in an institution for custodial and trainable persons.

As a child moves from the sensory-motor to the preconceptual stage, scales which set forth sequential development again may be used to suggest appropriate activities. Haeussermann's *Developmental Potential of Pre-School Children* (1958) provides an excellent framework. Appropriate test tasks are listed for mental age intervals between the years 2 to 6; with adaptation and extension these may become sequentially arranged program activities. The sequentially listed items which provide activities in cognitive areas are arranged under the following headings: (*a*) Memory, (*b*) Discrimination, (*c*) Spatial Orientation, (*d*) Amount Concepts, (*e*) Relationships, and (*f*) Language. Haeussermann devised ways to permit presentation of the tasks to children with various types of handicaps.

Discussion by Painter (1967) of a program designed to promote conceptual development in the preconceptual child includes activities devised to establish skill in space, time, number, and body image concepts, as well as in categorical sorting. Connor and Talbot's *An Experimental Curriculum for Young Mentally Retarded Children* (1966) also lists activities designed to promote intellectual development in the preoperational child. In addition, Lavatelli (1970) has provided an early childhood curriculum which is termed a Piaget program, i.e., it evolves from activities and processes characteristic of the preconceptual period. It is appropriate for any child functioning at this level, whether he be mentally retarded or normal.

Cognitive activities and preacademic or academic training tend to be presented jointly in programs for the school-age severely retarded pupil (IQ less than 50). In the educational section of their diagnostic approach to teaching moderately and severely retarded children, Bradley, Hundziak, & Patterson, (1971) discuss specific teaching methods and evaluate over 450 classroom materials and techniques.

The curriculum for severely retarded children designed by D'Amelio (1971) derives from the assumption that trainable mentally retarded pupils can master the fundamentals of reading, writing, and arithmetic through special teaching methods which organize learning experiences into sequences of small units. Objectives, teaching techniques, and pupil activities are discussed for the three "Rs".

Teaching methods which derive from a developmental approach to education are described by Stevens in *The Educational Needs of Severely Subnormal Children* (1971); emphasis is on planned systematic teaching which is continuous over an extended period of time. Malloy's *Trainable Children: Curriculum and Procedures* (1972) includes a section on intellectual growth containing science, social study, number, reading, and art activities for pupils who range in age from preschool to young adults.

Realistic arithmetic goals for the severely retarded have been outlined by Kolburne (1965). After the concept of oneness, twoness, etc. is established through experience with concrete objects, effort centers on reading and writing these numbers. Following this the pupil is introduced stepwise to increasingly advanced concepts.

The relationship between cognitive development and academic skills has long been established. Yet academic programs for the severely retarded frequently presuppose skills that are not present in persons functioning at the preoperational level of reasoning. It is not by chance that academic skills which require concrete reasoning generally are acquired by normals who are beyond the age of 6. Their acquisition occurs after a period of rapid perceptual development and after the flexibility of the operational process required in grouping and categorization, as well as the reversibility required for arithmetical subtraction, are achieved. Realistic academic aims for the severely retarded have as their goals the acquisition of those skills usually realized by persons who function at the preoperational level. These include reading readiness or beginning reading, number concepts which involve 20, 10, or fewer objects, and functional writing which includes the pupil's name and address. Basic to each of these is language development; therefore, training efforts should include improvement of underlying language difficulties. Because suggestions for speech and language training are presented under separate headings, present consideration is addressed to the development of reading, handwriting, and arithmetic skills.

LANGUAGE

There is wide variance in the language capability of the severely and profoundly retarded population. Although language requires a minimum level of intelligence, it is a unique ability. In some persons delay in language development is accompanied by commensurate delays in other areas; in others, specific language deficits provoke extreme frustration because intellectual compentence exceeds language level.

Generally, programs for severely and profoundly retarded persons are initially charged with the training of nonverbal children or children with exceedingly limited language. However, the long-range training goal is to promote optimal living skills, and the ability to communicate is a prerequisite to increased independence.

Assessment

Numerous studies have traced the normal acquisition of language from birth through the 6th or 7th year. As a result a variety of language development scales are available to determine a person's present level of functioning and indicate succeeding levels of expected development.

Fokes' Developmental Scale of Language Acquisition (Stephens, 1971) is a companion instrument to her Developmental Scale of Motor Abilities. Again, she has combined items from a variety of reliable and valid scales (e.g., Berry & Eisenson, 1956; Fairbanks, 1942; Irwin, 1948; Lewis, 1963; McCarthy, 1954; Shirley, 1933; Templin, 1957; Van Riper, 1963; and Weir, 1966) in order to present a detailed, descriptive scaling of emerging ability. An additional scale which has enjoyed wide usage in the appraisal of language of mentally retarded children is Mecham's Oral-Aural Language Schedule (1963).

Abbreviated scales of language development are found in the *Portage Project Checklist* (Shearer & Shearer, 1972); the Valett Developmental Survey of Basic Learning Abilities (Valett, 1966); the Denver Developmental Screening Survey (Frankenburg, Dodds, & Fandal, 1969); and the Developmental Profile (Alpern & Boll, 1972). Developmental scales are appropriately used with severely and profoundly retarded persons because appraisal generally is based on observed behavior, rather than elicited responses. For persons who are proceeding through the early childhood stages of language acquisition and can respond to test items, the Illinois Test of Psycholinguistic Abilities (Kirk, McCarthy, & Kirk, 1968) can be used to obtain a profile of psycholinguistic abilities and disabilities.

Frequently, the ability of severely and profoundly retarded persons to receive and assign meaning to the spoken words exceeds their ability to produce meaningful speech. Therefore, appraisal of language development gains in accuracy when separate assessment is provided for its two parts, receptive and expressive. Two scales which provide separate indexes of receptive and expressive language are: Hedrick and Prather's *Behavioral System for Assessing Language Development* (Schiefelbusch, Copeland, & Smith, 1967), and Bzoch's and League's Receptive-Expressive Emergent Language Scale (1970). The latter provides a three-item assessment for expressive and for receptive language at monthly intervals from birth to 1-year levels; from 1 to 2 years assessment is based on 2-month intervals, and from 2 to 3 years on 3-month intervals.

Programming

The teacher of severely and profoundly mentally retarded pupils will be less concerned with speech therapy than with speech development. He will also realize that the speech patterns of these children generally differ from those of normally developing children. As Blanchard (1971) noted, the average child uses 23 consonants and 13 or more vowels; by contrast, the severely or profoundly retarded child may be mute or may use a vocabularly comprised of 4 or fewer consonants and 2 or fewer vowels.

Until the period of cooing and babbling blends via the process of lalling into intentional repetition of his own sounds, deaf, retarded, and normal children behave in much the same way. From this point on, verbalization requires a high degree of intelligence. The retarded child is somewhat slower to begin and stays longer at each step. It is the intent in intention that limits the retardate's learning. The lower the potential to intend to change habitual vegetative behavior (sucking) to conscious behavior (speaking), the slower and more abnormal the pattern of communication. Echoing, if perseverated beyond the emergence of meaningful words, becomes a pathologic sign of aborted development, usually signifying limitation of intention and intellectual stability.

By the time a mentally retarded child comes to a special classroom, his senses, if his sensory equipment is working, have been stimulated for over five years. At least he has seen, heard, touched, and tasted, and it is likely that he has developed preferences of things he wants to see, hear, feel, and taste. His experience with a variety of stimuli has been defined by the conditions of his retardation, by limitations of nurturance, limitations within his culture and family economy. If he has felt hunger and thirst, pain and visceral discomfort, and has not known what he felt, he will be a problem not only to his teacher but to himself. . . . Consider that the untrained youngster may not be able to recognize these sensations.

. . . Due to the nature of child development, one uses as the basis for initiating training the child's native provision, his capacity for taking in information, and the equipment with which he organizes meaning and expresses it.

The child who will learn to talk needs four basic foundations: intelligence, hearing, social interaction, and organized structures. Upon these foundation blocks, he organizes meanings and then expresses them initially with his whole body, breath, and voice, then later with articulate syllables in words, and finally in language. (Blanchard, 1971, pp. 212-13)

The approach to speech which Blanchard outlined has gained recognition because it evolved from research and training which centered on lower functioning persons. Verbal stimulation is one of the first requisites for oral language; to hear language spoken is a necessity, but the verbalization must be at a level the child can understand and possibly imitate. In her description of a language training program which uses behavior modification techniques, Kluppel (1971) notes:

> The teacher is to be a model for producing short and simple phrases and sentences used as directions and instructions. She also is the model for the imitation and learning of the names of things, for concepts such as time, relations, size, and shape, and for the learning of the underlying structure (grammar) of language. Reinforcement, or reward for desired response, is seen as a vital consequence of the verbal behavior of the child. Its use is as an attitude modifier as well as a source of feedback. Initially it follows any attempts at vocalization and subsequently occurs after phonemes, words, and combinations of words in correct grammatical order. The training program is developed after careful assessment of the level of performance of each child in the group. The central focus of the program revolves around all activities being seen as situations in which oral language is the appropriate response. (Kluppel, 1971, pp. 244-245)

Language activities which are appropriate for severely retarded children and which are developmentally sequenced from birth onward, are provided by McCarthy et al. (1969), by Shearer and Shearer (1972), and by Koontz (Blea, 1972). The technique of behavior modification is frequently and successfully employed in programs which attempt to establish communication in mentally retarded persons.

A study which sought to develop an integrated program in three training areas (language, self-care skills, and motor development) was devised for children with Down's syndrome (Chalfant & Silikowitz, 1970). The method for language instruction involved task analysis, behavior modification, systematic language instruction, and errorless learning. Results served to indicate that effective implementation of the system could be achieved by teachers with no previous experience in systematic language instruction, provided supervision was supplied; also, the language concepts of the retarded group children who received the training was superior to a group who had not.

The curriculum for trainable children devised by Malloy (1972) includes language theory. Emphasis is on a structured developmental program based on a detailed assessment of impairment and occurring in a social situation. Additional description is accorded a communication shaping program devised for use by cottage aides in the training of the severely and profoundly retarded (Malloy, 1970). This approach, involving operant conditioning, considered the nature of communication, the importance of attending skills, total body activity, facial exercises designed to strengthen speech musculatures, and the development of receptive and expressive language.

Realizing that receptive language frequently surpasses expressive language, Baer and Guess (1971) designed receptive language training activities that involved identification of comparative and superlative adjectives through pointing. Differential reinforcement was related to a high number of correct responses by each of the three severely retarded subjects. Guess (1969) designed

181

a language program for severely retarded pupils which could be implemented by nonprofessional personnel. This approach trained "language developmentalists" through reading, classroom experiences, informal discussions, and supervised use of language development materials in a token reinforcement system. Over an 18-month period, gains scores on the Illinois Test of Psycholinguistic Abilities for the experimental mentally retarded group were significantly greater than those for the control group. The study concluded that nonprofessional personnel can be used effectively in programs for mentally retarded pupils.

Lower functioning retarded persons who are nonverbal may learn to respond through the use of manual signs or motor movements. To facilitate the acquisition of a gesture language, Topper (1975) selected gestures closely related to natural action that could be easily understood and produced by persons with physical handicaps. To ensure a total communication approach, the spoken word and the gesture were simultaneously presented. Gestures were based either on the sign language of the deaf or on the Indian sign language, and correct responses were rewarded. The ability of a nonverbal, severely retarded male subject to imitate and initiate appropriate gestures tended to suggest the presence of a nonvocal language potential.

In their attempt to establish communication through gesture in severely and profoundly retarded adults, Brody and Smilovitz (1974) had initial sessions during which the trainer imitated the movements of the retarded adult. When this person realized his movements were being imitated, the trainer then proceeded to make gestures for the retarded adult to imitate (clapping, pounding, etc.); if imitation was not immediate, the trainer guided the retarded adult's hands through the motions. In succeeding sessions gestures were used to introduce specific objects or activities; reinforcement, appropriate for the sign being taught, was provided (e.g., the sign for "eat" was reinforced with food). Work by O'Rourke (1970) and Riekehof (1963) supplied the gesture vocabulary.

In his review of the language of the more severely retarded, Blount (1968) asks that these persons be regarded as individuals with a specific linguistic problem, rather than principally as mentally retarded persons. Projects conducted by Lyle (1960) and Harvey, Yep, and Sellin (1966) indicate gains are made when severely retarded subjects are afforded individually planned therapy programs. The therapy program should be oriented toward the individual's specific linguistic problem and should encompass his total environment (Blount, 1968).

SOCIAL AND EMOTIONAL DEVELOPMENT

Review of a random sample of mentally retarded pupils, previously excluded from the public schools of Pennsylvania, revealed that approximately 50% of the group had behavior problems sufficient in severity to pose a problem in classroom management. Many also had motor or sensory impairment, some were seizure-prone, and others exhibited "autisticlike" behavior (Hingtgen & Bryson, 1972). Because they had formerly been excluded from training, their social and self-help skills were emphasized in curriculums derived from their needs. Initial emphasis would serve to change problem areas into growth areas.

Assessment

In the normal (or mentally retarded) child, there are several observable [behavioral] dimensions: the autistic or self-focused, the impulsive, the ridden, the anxious, the curious, the integrated. Each of these dimensions may be translated into a variety of terms, depending on the developmental theory adhered to; each encompasses many behavioral facets. None of these is discrete, and a child may exhibit responses which incorporate or cross dimensions. The assessor, therefore, must ascertain the predominant patterns, with an eye to developmental movement.

A device, such as the Fairview Problem Behavior Record (Ross, undated), provides a means of focusing on a child's typical pattern of responses. . . . [Obtaining a score or social age] is not the prime objective; rather, it is shifting out or highlighting how a child habitually acts or reacts.

In looking at response patterns, the negative or inappropriate are often the most discernible. However, what a child does *not* do, as well as what he *does* do *appropriately,* are of equal importance. What you are looking for, primarily, then, are clues that suggest which responses constitute impediments to further learning, and which responses can be used as training tools or building blocks for further development. Once these are pinpointed, a specific program can be devised. It should be remembered, however, that emotional development is not something which can be taught. The total classroom climate, the opportunities built into the total program for the appropriate expression of emotion, the consistency and visibility of structure and attitude—these are the props which allow a child to venture forward.

Social development, while intricately related to emotional development, encompasses both general and specific skills. Usually, social development refers to a child's ability to relate himself to his environment and the people with whom he comes into contact. We expect this ability to manifest itself in myriad situations. Looking at it more concretely, however, social development can be broken down into such categories as toileting, feeding, dressing, personal hygiene, interpersonal relationships, language, cognitive development, and behavior. Each of these areas can in turn be broken down into specific sequential skill levels. Tools such as the Trainable Mentally Retarded Profile (Dinola, Kaminsky, & Sternfeld, 1963), the Vineland Social Maturity Scale (Doll, 1965), the Balthazar Scales of Adaptive Behavior for the Profoundly and Severely Mentally Retarded (Balthazar, 1971), the Program Assessment Chart (Gunzburg, 1973), and the Learning Accomplishment Profile (Sanford, 1971) permit the charting of a child's level of competency within each skill area, and serve as a guide in formulating a sequential, developmentally-based training program. As stated in previous sessions, such a program must be success-based: i.e., it must grow from those skills a child has mastered, and move in small, carefully structured steps, toward the acquisition of the new skill.

In summary, while these are some standardized guidelines, the assessment of a child's emotional and social development must be, primarily, an analysis of observations drawn from many situations. What the child does (or does not do), and under what circumstances, furnishes the base-line data necessary to begin programming. Although programming may be task- or skill-oriented, it may also involve the creation of a specific type of environment, the presenting of opportunities, or the subtle intrusion of alternate stimuli which will maximize the probability of appropriate responses. (Manfredini, 1972, p. 37-38)

Programming

Diminution of undesirable or aberrant behavior is frequently and necessarily the first objective of a training program for the severely and profoundly retarded pupil. The common approach is through operant conditioning; numerous studies can be cited to demonstrate the effectiveness of the technique (Baker & Ward, 1971; Mulhern & Baumeister, 1969; Paul & Miller, 1971; Roos & Oliver, 1969).

In an attempt to reduce self-aggression and aggression towards others, Husted, Hall, and Agin (1971) instituted a therapy program which used time-out from positive reinforcement as the basic technique; although the frequency of undesirable behavior did diminish in the controlled environment, it did not generalize to other situations. Operant conditioning also was used by Edwards and Lilly (1966) to improve the mealtime behavior of persons whose IQ's ranged from 5 to 25; again, although significant improvement did occur in this specific setting, it did not generalize to other situations.

Reduction of stereotyped behavior, i.e. highly repetitive responses, was the goal of a program conducted by Mulhern and Baumeister (1969); time spent sitting still—the positive behavior which received reinforcement—was significantly increased. In a later study by Forehand and Baumeister (1971) frustration of goal-directed behavior of severely retarded subjects resulted in an increased rate of stereotyping.

General attitudinal and behavioral changes were reported by Musick and Luckey (1970) when a system of token economy was provided a group of severely and moderately retarded state school residents. Their improvement extended from personal grooming to less frequent reports of sickness and undesirable behavior.

To answer the question "what does punishment do to the behavior of the severely and profoundly retarded?" Gardner (1969) reviewed studies which involve the use of adversive procedures (time-out, physical restraint, electric shock, hair pulling, cayenne pepper, slaps, etc.) with the severely retarded. He concluded that although most of the studies lacked methodological sophistication, their findings generally lent some support to the use of punishment techniques. Concurrently he emphasized that extensive future research must be accomplished if punishment is to be generally accepted as a method for controlling undesirable behavior.

A comprehensive review of operant techniques to modify the behavior of the severely and profoundly retarded is provided by Nawas and Braun (1970a, 1970b, 1970c). Their discussion centers on initiation of a program, methods for increasing the frequency of appropriate behavior and for decreasing the frequency of maladaptive behavior, and the maintenance of specifically desired behavior.

Yet if one posits that all behavior is caused, then an approach more penetrating than the surface control of behavior supplied by operant conditioning (which includes adversive stimuli) will be sought. If the causes of the behavior lie in the environment, then effort should be made to manipulate that environment and eliminate the causative conditions. If the causes are internal, then medical diagnosis and assistance is indicated. The fearfulness, unresponsiveness, and unawareness which frequently characterize the behavior of the profoundly retarded were diminished in an intensive play technique designed by Bradtke, Kirkpatrick, and Rosenblatt (1972) which used close body contact and physical stimulation to promote positive responses to adults and later to peers.

After Warren and Burns (1970) observed stereotyped and object manipulation behaviors in severely and profoundly retarded ambulatory children during in-crib and out-of-crib periods, they concluded that the higher frequency of in-crib repetitive behaviors might have been influenced by the confinement and the nonstimulating environment; headbanging might have been strengthened by the reinforcement (attention) it was given by staff. Man's capacity to be bored should be taken into account when programming for lower as well as higher functioning persons. If the environment is peculiarly barren of stimuli, then man seeks to provide them from his own body. Hopefully, present and future early intervention programs will provide interesting environments and establish outward-directed behavior. In doing so they will diminish the probability of self-stimulating behavior.

SOCIAL AND SELF-HELP SKILLS

Skills that promote independence in living are highly interrelated. Successful motor and perceptual functioning are basic to self-help skills. Interaction with others, first through facial expressions, gestures, and intonations, and finally through language, furnishes experiences from which social skills emerge. While basic self-help skills generally are achieved during early childhood, their attainment frequently is the focal point of curriculums for the severely and profoundly retarded. Procedures for instilling these abilities are presented by Rosenzweig and Long (1960) and cover: (a) feeding, (b) dressing, (c) toileting, (d) washing and grooming, (e) brushing teeth, (f) using handkerchief, (g) controlling self initially, (h) following instructions, (i) completing tasks, (j) employing self, (k) holding temper.

Connor and Talbot (1966) to establish self-help skills in young retarded children, devised a five-point scale for each task, a scale which ranged from inappropriate and/or ineffective activity to successful accomplishment. Teaching

185

procedures were presented for each of the five points, techniques which could be used to establish readiness for the next level. Self-help items were listed for the areas of dressing, hand washing, toileting, feeding, grooming, care of clothing, housekeeping, safety, and independent travel. The techniques which they employed for task analysis can be extended to other training areas.

Numerous studies can be cited of behavior shaping techniques used to establish self-help skills (Berkowitz, 1971; Colwell, Richards, McCarver, & Ellis, 1973; Fisher & Harris, 1966; Hollis & Gorton, 1967; Lemke & Mitchell, 1972; Martin, 1971a, 1971b). Data from a 3-year follow-up on an intensive habit training program (Leath & Flournay, 1970) served to substantiate the maintenance of gains in social maturation, as measured by the Vineland Social Maturity Scale (Doll, 1965), in a group of severely and profoundly retarded institutionalized girls.

Groves and Carroccio (1971) implemented a self-feeding program based on operant conditioning techniques and found that appropriate use of spoons increased while hand feeding and food stealing decreased in severely and profoundly retarded subjects. Operant conditioning was also used by Edwards and Lilly (1966) to promote improvement in mealtime behavior; however, the improved behavior did not transfer to other situations. A study by O'Brien, Bugle, and Azrin (1972) served to indicate that continued motivational procedures are needed to maintain operant established proper eating skills in a profoundly retarded child. Likewise, a continuing limited motivational program was used by Azrin and Armstrong (1973) to maintain proper eating habits established in profoundly retarded adults through application of reinforcement principles.

Treffry, Martin, Samels, and Watson (1970) subdivided hand and face washing skills into 12 steps; positive reinforcement, fading, and time-out punishment were used to promote the skills in severely retarded girls. At the end of 9 weeks, 7 of the 11 subjects could accomplish the task without physical prompting.

Because of the social stigma which accompanies incontinence, toilet training generally is one of the initial goals in programs for the severely and profoundly retarded. Training can be facilitated through application of behavior modification techniques. Detailed presentation of behavioral objectives for toileting and methods and materials for use in their attempt are presented in COMPET (1972). Suggestions by Bensberg (1965) for the arrangement of a schedule of toileting accompany a discussion of techniques found to be useful in the training. A 10-hour course in the use of operant conditioning devised by Levine and Elliott (1970) was provided to staff members prior to the initiation of a 10-week program of toilet training for 103 profoundly retarded residents; at the end of the ten weeks there was a marked reduction in accidental defecations. In addition, a rapid method of toilet training for the institutionalized retarded has been devised by Azrin and Foxx (1971). The method, also based on operant conditioning, emphasizes positive reinforcement, use of an electromechanical aid to indicate occurring elimination, shaping procedures, and staff reinforcement. Obtained data indicate the method reduces incontinence to near-zero.

Discrimination training was used by Abramson and Wunderlich (1972) to teach mentally retarded boys to distinguish between their toothbrush and toothpaste boxes. Following this, modeling and successive approximations taught application of toothpaste to the toothbrush and the techniques of brushing. It was suggested that similar techniques could be used to aid mentally retarded persons in the achievement of other personal hygiene habits.

Because self-help skills are the building blocks to independence and because they provide the severely and profoundly retarded opportunities for positive participation in the ongoing events of daily living, they should receive major emphasis in programming. Yet to isolate training for these skills to school hours is not desirable; normal children acquire them through modeling provided by parents and siblings in everyday home situations. Therefore, it is logical that parents or parent figures should be involved in the skills acquisition. With minimal training parents, group home workers, or ward aides can employ the techniques of behavior modification and discrimination learning that are useful in instilling these habits.

The importance of after-school training has been demonstrated by Barrett (1971). Unexpected behavioral variances, e.g., disruptive behavior and responsiveness, between two groups of children from two different buildings were attributed to differences in attitudes and practices of building employees. These practices, in turn, were influenced by staff-child ratio, behavioral requirements, inservice training, habilitative procedures for residents, and administrative support. Because of these findings Barrett held that training should be extended to after-school hours. The feasibility of using technicians to teach self-help skills to profoundly retarded persons was demonstrated by Minge and Ball (1967) in a step-by-step program which presented component parts of a specific task. Daily training (two 15-minute sessions) resulted in the display of significantly superior skills by the group trained. Using cassette tapes, Scoggins (1972) devised a method for training paraprofessionals to carry out programs for institutionalized severely and profoundly retarded persons. Audio instructions supply techniques which may be employed to modify behavior, instill self-help and language skills, and provide recreational activities. Additionally, a handbook for substitute parents of the multiply handicapped profoundly retarded person has been prepared by Penny (1967). In it she considers goals and methods, schedules, and techniques of reward within a framework devised to provide training to prospective foster parents. Thus methods are available for staff training; to implement that training probably will require the revision of job descriptions for residential aides—something which should become a high priority goal.

VOCATIONAL TRAINING

Goals of ongoing programs for more severely handicapped children should take into account the expected adult status of the pupil (Rosenkranz, 1973). Realistically, opportunity centers providing extended training in self-help skills and in supervised activities for tasks which require basic perceptual motor ability may be the appropriate adult assignment for the profoundly retarded. However, numerous projects which have attempted to train severely retarded adults on selected workshop tasks have achieved significant gains in vocational skills. Task analysis was used in a project by Crosson and DeJung (1967) which sought to train severely and profoundly retarded persons in the performance of selected workshop tasks. The program was based on the behavioristic principles of shaping, operant discrimination, and chaining of responses; it resulted in the acquisition of complex chains of 100 or more discrete behaviors by the group which received training. Subsequently a similar study compared the benefits of low but constant levels of social reward to scheduled token reinforcement; findings indicated that scheduled extrinsic reinforcement resulted in higher and more stable rates of work-oriented behavior than did social reward. Application of the postulates of discrimination learning by Gold to the workshop training of severely retarded persons has resulted in "a systematic plan for programming the acquisition of relevant tasks in terms of specific training as an alternate to planning a broad and vague program aimed at perceptual-motor abilities" (Gold and Scott, 1971, p. 443). The study reported in 1971 involving the training of 64 moderately and severely retarded adolescents (mean IQ = 47) in the assembly of 15- and 24-piece bicycle brakes. Criterion performance (6 correct assemblages out of 8 attempts) was reached by 63 of the subjects. Gold's systematic approach to training is generalizable to other workshop tasks. Future expectations for the vocational productivity of severely and profoundly retarded persons exceeds present accomplishments (Gold, 1973). When these persons are afforded individually appropriate training from birth onward, their receptivity to work training should greatly exceed that of the present generation, which has experienced far too many barren, vacant days of backward assignment.

RECREATION

Although there is indication that severely and profoundly retarded persons enjoy play activities, there is a paucity of information on recreational programming for these persons. Guidelines, however, are available for therapeutic recreation (Therapeutic Recreation Service and Mental Retardation, 1969) which can be initiated in cottage-type settings. Likewise, physical education activities which may be viewed as recreational are provided by Fait (1969) and by Wessel and Associates (1973). Plans for including multiply handicapped totally dependent children in church activities are supplied in a monograph by Martin and Travis (1968), which contains objectives, preparation of teachers and aides, curriculum resources, and procedures for enrollment. Receptivity to music has been noted by numerous persons who work with lower functioning persons, and the effective use of music as a reinforcer has been documented by Jorgenson (1971).

Support for habilitative recreation for the severely retarded was evident in the responses recreation personnel supplied to a questionnaire which asked them to list justifications for their program.

The three primary justifications which evolved are:

1. Recreation is fun and it gives the residents a break from the monotomy of the day-to-day schedule.

2. Recreation gives the cottage personnel a daily break from the responsibility of caring for the residents.

3. When the resident is kept busy and given the opportunity to participate in varied activities, he presents fewer behavior problems. (Freeman & Mundy, 1971, p. 283)

The respondents viewed their services as suplementary rather than necessary and, in doing so, failed to emphasize the gains which can accrue from habilitative recreation. That is, recreation which is goal-oriented is based on evaluation, is sequential in nature, and provides opportunity to progress toward greater "social independence, physical well-being, emotional stability, and intellectual advancement" (p. 295).

Socio-recreative activities as defined by Avedon and Arje (1964) are appropriate for all ages and for all degrees of retardation. Anderson and Stephens (1971) noted:

The concept of socio-recreative programming is built upon the use of recreation as a means for promoting the process of socialization. Such a program provides a continuum of structured experiences which gradually introduce the retardate to various levels of activity. . . . Thus it is argued that recreation education not only promotes the process of socialization but also helps prepare the individual for participation in vocational activities.

The aim of socio-recreative programming for the younger retardate is prevention—that is, prevention of social isolation. For the teenager or adult retardate the aim is primarily supportive or remedial—either an extension of the experiences begun earlier or an attempt to overcome social handicaps which may have been caused by isolation and/or rejection. The experiences provided the individual are divided into three phases: "(1) learning social and prevocational skills in a sheltered situation, (2) practicing these skills in realistic social situations, and (3) learning to make independent and appropriate use of as many as possible of the community's resources for recreation." (Avedon & Arje, 1964, p. 2)

Most recreational activities can be adapted to the level of the [severely retarded person.] Activities should be analyzed in terms of the basic skills they require. These skills are then taught separately but sequentially as children proceed from mastery of one step to mastery of the next higher one. In this way, the child learns to integrate and coordinate skills and achieves success all along the way. Following such training, even spectator sports will become more meaningful because the retardate will be more capable of following the sequential events in the game. To list the activities which can be taught is unnecessary because of the availability of activities guides (e.g., Avedon & Arje, 1964; American Association for Health, Physical Education and Recreation, 1966; Katz, 1968). However, activities would generally fall under the headings of games and sports, performing arts, fine arts and crafts, hobbies, social activities, and religious activities. More recently, camping and outdoor education have proved valuable in promoting language development, physical development, social experiences, and in stimulating creative activities (Baer & Stanley, 1969; Morlock & Mason, 1969).

Certainly a program designed to meet the recreational and leisure-time needs of the mentally retarded cannot be the total responsibility of the schools. The integration, coordination, and cooperation of all the available services in the community is needed. The community should plan a comprehensive network of services and facilities to promote the highest level of social usefulness and self-fulfillment in the mentally retarded and their families (Begab, 1967). Indeed, the community itself remains the key to successful socio-recreative programming (Avedon & Arje, 1964).

In summary, recreational activities can play a major role in successful training; they also can provide opportunities for lower functioning persons to achieve desired and rewarding companionship.

PARENT COUNSELING AND TRAINING

The initial need of parents of retarded infants for explanation and concrete information was noted by Zook and Unkovic (1968), as they presented techniques for defining developmental levels and for advising parents on childrearing practices. Generally the target populations of early intervention efforts are severely and profoundly impaired persons, because their deficits are apparent during the early stages of development, and generally parents assist in implementing these intervention activities.

Systematic training should begin early in the lives of profoundly retarded children. . . . There is particular need to ensure that physical problems do not result from abnormal positions assumed during prolonged periods in bed. Such conditions can be minimized by providing opportunities for weight bearing each day, and by placing shoes on the children's feet while they are in bed. Problems such as scissoring of the legs can be prevented by proper positioning exercises and the proper use of splints or leg restraints. Other common deformities of the head, rib cage, and spine may also be prevented by correct body positioning and physical therapy (Finnie, 1970; Pearson & Williams, 1972; Robinault, 1973). (Luckey & Addison, 1974, p. 124)

Specific training suggestions are given to parents of the mongoloid baby by Coriat (1970); these include activities which promote sitting, crawling, and self-feeding. Parents' participation also should include involvement in the planning and administration of agencies and institutions that exist to service their child's needs (Posternak, 1971; Rybak & Todd, 1968). It is beyond the scope of the present writing to review the plethora of parent training programs that have evolved during the past half decade. Nonetheless, parental involvement means realizing that severely and profoundly retarded pupils spend generally fewer hours in school than any other group of students. Therefore effective programming for school age persons must include both home and school environments. It frequently focuses on the application of behavior modification techniques (Galloway & Galloway, 1970; Hirsch & Walder, 1969).

As the right of every child to a public education becomes assured during the last half of the decade, private, parent-sponsored, agency programs probably will decline; thus, parent organizations are expected to assume a more active role in the monitoring of programs, i.e., in assuring quality control. To do this effectively will require training. Therefore, an increasing number of parents of retarded children are expected to enroll in courses which provide knowledge of assessment and programming. Benefits to be derived from their involvement do not center exclusively on the monitoring of services. These parents might also assume another role, that of professionally trained volunteer workers. In so doing they could provide the one-to-one ratio which frequently is required for the severely and profoundly retarded to achieve developmental gains.

CONCLUSIONS AND IMPLICATIONS

The current federal commitment to the education of the severely and profoundly handicapped marks a progression from token acts of charity to rcognition of this group's legal rights to public education. Presently this is the only disability area that has separate priority status within the Bureau for the Education of the Handicapped. Concomitant support should enable us to approach issues which to date are unanalyzed and unanswered. Still to be determined are optimal instructional settings: Are these found in the public school, in the home, in activity centers, or where? Still to be determined are valid instructional goals: Should self-care and socialization be viewed as terminal points, or can goals be extended upward as training methods are perfected? Still to be determined are the most fruitful combinations of interagency and intergroup collaboration in establishing programs: Should there be a triumvirate composed of representatives from schools, community agencies, and families? Still to be determined are the necessary teacher competencies: Can present teacher-training models be revised to assure adequate preparation, or are innovative approaches required to meet the needs of this highly heterogeneous lower functioning population? What are the merits of the occupational and physical therapist as training instructor versus special education teacher? Still to be determined are the most effective transition strategies to move the pupil from prevocational programs to community agencies: What organizational structure is required to assure successful relocation? Still to be determined are the most efficient systems for delivery of community services (of which education is one): Should there be national effort to devise a comprehensive delivery system, or should individual communities seek to evolve one specific to their local needs (Vayda, 1974).

Additionally research which is specific to the needs of the severely and profoundly handicapped is required. For example:

1. Appropriate vision and auditory screening devices should be available for persons who do not respond to traditional approaches.

2. Suitable instructional materials should be constructed or adapted and evaluated.

3. National support is needed to formulate a comprehensive remedial system, providing sequentially arranged activities for development in motor, language, cognitive, social, and emotional areas.

4. Technical research on prosthetic devices should supply equipment to circumvent handicaps and channel intact functioning.

5. Methods should be sought which increase the educational receptivity of tri-handicapped individuals, e.g., the deaf-blind-retarded person.

6. Possible contributions from a variety of theoretical approaches to programming should be explored (including findings concerned with the physiological basis of behavior).

Since development is promoted by the day-long action and interaction of the individual with objects and people, the need for parent or substitute parent participation is clear if training is to be extended rather than stifled in the home environment. Job descriptions for substitute parents should be revised from those which are largely custodial to those which are developmentally oriented.

If such progress in programming as envisioned for the next decade is realized, our present evidence of the advantages to accrue from individually appropriate programming will be remembered as the first faint rays to penetrate the decades of dark, back ward maintenance. Could it be that the 1970s will be remembered as the renaissance of Itard's and Séguin's convictions?

References

Abramson, E.E., & Wunderlich, R.A. Dental hygiene training for retardates. *Mental Retardation,* 1972, **10** (3), 6-8.

Allen, R.M., & Allen, S.P. *WPS Professional handbook series number 3: Intellectual evaluation of the mentally retarded child.* Beverly Hills, Calif.: Western Psychological Services, 1967.

Alpern, G.D., & Boll, T.J. *Developmental profile.* Indianapolis: Psychological Development Publications, 1972.

American Association for the Education of the Severely/Profoundly Handicapped, Association Goals, 1975, **1** (5), 4.

American Association for Health, Physical Education and Recreation. *Recreation and physical activity for the mentally retarded.* Washington, D.C.: AAHPER, 1966.

Anderson, D.W., & Stephens, B. Recreation and leisure time. In B. Stephens (Ed.), *Training the developmentally young.* New York: Thomas J. Crowell, 1971.

Assessment of selected resources for severely handicapped children and youth. Vol. I: A state of the art paper. Cambridge, Mass.: Abt Associates, Inc., 1974.

Avedon, R.M., & Arje, F.B. *Socio-recreative programming for the retarded.* New York: Columbia University, 1964.

Auxter D. Motor skill development in the profoundly retarded. *Training School Bulletin,* 1971, **68** (1), 5-9.

Azrin, N.H., & Armstrong, P.B. The mini-meal: A method for teaching eating skills to the profoundly retarded. *Mental Retardation,* 1973, **11** (1), 9-13.

Azrin, N.H., & Foxx, R.M. A rapid method of toilet training the institutionalized retarded. *Journal of Applied Behavioral Analysis,* 1971, **4** (2), 89-99.

Baer, D., & Guess, D. Receptive training of adjectival inflections in mental retardates. *Journal of Applied Behavior Analysis,* 1971, **4** (2), 129-139.

Baer, L., & Stanley, P. A camping program for the trainable retarded. *Education and Training of the Mentally Retarded,* 1969, **4,** 81-84.

Baker, B.L., & Ward, M.H. Reinforcement therapy for behavior problems in severely retarded children. *American Journal of Orthopsychiatry,* 1971, **41** (1), 124-135.

Balthazar, E.E. *Balthazar Scales of Adaptive Behavior for the Profoundly and Severely Mentally Retarded* (Section 1, Parts 1-4). Champaign: Research Press, 1971.

Barrett, H. Behavioral differences among an institution's backward residents. *Mental Retardation,* 1971, **9** (1), 4-9.

Bayley, N. The development of motor abilities during the first three years. *Monograph of the Society for Research in Child Development,* 1935, pp. 1-26.

Bensberg, G.J. (Ed.). *Teaching the mentally retarded: A handbook for ward personnel.* Atlanta, Ga.: Southern Regional Education Board, 1965.

Begab, M.J. Community planning. In E.L. Meyen (Ed.), *Planning community services for the mentally retarded.* Scranton, Pa.: International Textbook Company, 1967.

Berkowitz, S. Teaching self-feeding skills to profound retardates using reinforcement and fading procedures. *Behavior Therapy,* 1971, **2** (1), 62-67.

Berry, M., & Eisenson, J. *Speech disorders.* New York: Appleton-Century-Crofts, 1956.

Blanchard, I. Establishment of speech patterns. In B. Stephens (Ed.), *Training the developmentally young.* New York: Thomas J. Crowell, 1971.

Blea, William A. (Ed.). *Proceedings of the Special Institute for Teachers of Deaf-Blind Multi-Handicapped.* Washington, D.C.: Bureau for Education of the Handicapped, 1972.

Blount, W.R. Language and the more severely retarded: A review. *American Journal of Mental Deficiency,* 1968, **73** (1), 21-29.

Bradley, B.H., Hundziak, M., & Patterson, R. *Teaching moderately and severely retarded children: A diagnostic approach.* Springfield, Ill.: Charles C Thomas, 1971.

Bradtke, L., Kirkpatrick, W., & Rosenblatt, K. Intensive play: A technique for building affective behaviors in profoundly mentally retarded young children. *Education and Training of the Mentally Retarded*, 1972, **7** (1), 8-13.

Bricker, W.A., Heal, L.W., Bricker, D.D., Hayes, W.A., & Larsen, L.A. Discrimination learning and learning set with institutionalized retarded children. *American Journal of Mental Deficiency*, 1969, **74** (2), 242-248.

Brody, J.F., & Smilovitz, R. (Eds.). *APT, A training program for citizens with severely or profoundly retarded behavior*. Spring City, Pa.: Pennhurst State School, 1974.

Bruner, J.S. *Toward a theory of instruction*. Cambridge, Mass.: Harvard University Press, 1966.

Bzoch, K.R., & League, R. *Receptive-expressive emergent language scale*. Gainsville, Fla.: Tree of Life Press, 1970.

Chalfant, J., & Silikowitz, R. *Systematic instruction for retarded children: The Illinois program experimental edition*. Final Report. Urbana, Illinois: Institute for Research on Exceptional Children, 1970.

Colwell, C.N., Richards, E., McCarver, R.B., & Ellis, N.R. Evaluation of self-help habit training for the profoundly retarded. *Mental Retardation*, 1973, **11** (3), 14-18.

COMPET, Commonwealth plan for education and training of mentally retarded children. Harrisburg: Pennsylvania Department of Education and Welfare, 1972.

COMPILE, Commonwealth plan to identify, locate and evaluate mentally retarded children. Harrisburg: Pennsylvania Department of Education and Welfare, 1972.

Connor, F.P., & Talbot, M. *An experimental curriculum for young mentally retarded children*. New York: Teachers College Press, 1966.

Coriat, L. El problema de la infancia (The problems of infancy). *Deficiencia Mental: Cuestion Urgent*, Madrid, Spain, 1970, pp. 269-291.

Corrado, J., & Reed, J. *Play with a difference*. New York: Play School Associations, 1969.

Crosson, J.E., & DeJung, J.E. *The experimental analysis of vocational behavior in severely retarded males*. Final Report (Office of Education Grant #32-47-0230-6024). Eugene: University of Oregon, 1967.

D'Amelio, D. *Severely retarded children: Wider horizons*. Columbus: C.E. Merrill, 1971.

Denhoff, E. *Cerebral palsy: The preschool years*. Springfield: Charles C Thomas, 1967.

Dinola, A.J.., Kaminsky, B.P., & Sternfeld, A.E. *TMR performance profile for the severely and moderately retarded*. Ridgefield, N.J.: Reporting Service for Exceptional Children, 1963.

Distefano, M.K., Jr., Ellis, N.R., & Sloan, W. Motor proficiency in mental defectives. *Perceptual and Motor Skills*, 1958, **8**, 231-234.

Doll, E.A. *Vineland Social Maturity Scale*. Philadelphia: Educational Publishers, 1965.

Doll, E.A. A historical survey of research and management of mental retardation in the United States. In E.P. Trapp & P. Himelstein (Eds.), *Readings on the exceptional child* (2nd ed.). New York: Appleton-Century-Crofts, 1972.

Edwards, M., & Lilly, R.T. Operant conditioning: An application to behavioral problems in groups. *Mental Retardation*, 1966, **4** (4), 18-20.

Fairbanks, G. An acoustical study of the pitch of infant hunger wails. *Child Development*, 1942, **13**, 227-232.

Fait, Hollis F. (Ed.). *Curriculum guide for teaching physical education to the profoundly and severely retarded*. Mansfield, Conn.: Mansfield Training School, 1969.

Finnie, N.R. *Handling the young cerebral palsied child at home*. New York: E.P. Dutton, 1970.

Fisher, J., & Harris, R.E. (Eds.). *Reinforcement theory in psychological treatment*. Eacramento: California State Department of Mental Hygiene, 1966.

Fokes, J. Developmental scale of language acquisition. In B. Stephens (Ed.), *Training the developmentally young*. New York: Thomas J. Crowell, 1971.

Forehand, R., & Baumeister, A.A. Rate of stereotyped body rocking as a function of frustration of goal-directed behavior. *Journal of Abnormal Psychology*, 1971, **78**(1), 35-42.

Frankenburg, W.K. & Dodds, J.B. *Denver developmental survey*. Denver: University of Colorado Medical Center, 1969.

Fredericks, H.D., Baldwin, V.L., Doughty, P., & Walter, L.J. *The teaching research* motor-development scale for moderately and severely retarded children. Springfield, Ill.: Charles C Thomas, 1972.

Freeman, B.L., & Mundy, J. Habilitative recreation. In B. Stephens (Ed.), *Training the developmentally young*. New York: Thomas J. Crowell, 1971, 281-296.

Friedlander, B.Z., McCarthy, J.J., & Soforenko A.Z. Automated psychological evaluation with severely retarded institutionalized infants. *American Journal of Mental Deficiency*, 1967, **71** (6), 909-919.

Galloway, C., & Galloway, K.C. Parents groups with a focus on precise behavior management. Ann Arbor: *Institute on Mental Retardation and Intellectual Development: Papers and reports*, 1970, **7** (1), 1-38.

Gardner, W. Use of punishment procedures with the severely retarded: A review. *American Journal of Mental Deficiency*, 1969, **74** (1), 85-103.

Gesell, A. *The first five years of life*. New York: Harper & Brothers, 1940.

Gold, M.W. Research on the vocational habilitation of the retarded. In N.R. Ellis (Ed.), *International review of research in mental retardation*. New York: Academic Press, 1973.

Gold, M.W., & Scott, K.G. Discrimination learning. In B. Stephens (Ed.), *Training the developmentally young*. New York: Thomas J. Crowell, 1971.

Grace, A. *Measurement of the educability of severely mentally retarded children*. New York: New York University, School of Education, 1959.

Groves, I.D., & Carroccio, D.F. A self-feeding program for the severely and profoundly retarded. *Mental Retardation*, 1971, **9** (3), 10-12.

Guess, D. *A language development program for mentally retarded children*. Final Report. Lawrence: Kansas University, 1969.

Gunzburg, H.C. Progress assessment chart. London: National Association for Mental Health, 1973.

Haeussermann, E. *The developmental potential of preschool children*. New York: Grune & Stratton, 1958.

Halpern, A.S., & Equinozzi, A.M. Verbal expressivity as an index of adaptive behavior. *American Journal of Mental Deficiency*, 1969, **74** (2), 180-186.

Harvey, A., Yep, B., & Sellin, D. Developmental achievement of trainable mentally retarded children. *Training School Bulletin*, 1966, **63**, 100-108.

Hingtgen, J.N., & Bryson, C.Q. Recent developments in the study of early childhood psychoses schizophrenia. *Bulletin*, 1972, **5**, 8-54.

Hirsch, I., & Walder, L. Training mothers in groups as reinforcement therapists for their own children. *Proceedings of the 77th Annual Convention of the American Psychological Association*, 1969, **4** (2), 561-562.

Hollis, J.H. Development of perceptual motor skills in a profoundly retarded child. Part I: Prosthesis; Part II: Consequence, change and transfer. *American Journal of Mental Deficiency*, 1967, **71** (6), 941-952; 953-963.

Hollis, J.H., & Gorton, C.E. Training severely and profoundly developmentally retarded children. *Mental Retardation*, 1967, **5** (4), 20-24.

Husted, J.R., Hall, P., & Agin, B. The effectiveness of time-out in reducing maladaptive behavior of autistic and retarded children. *Journal of Psychology*, 1971, **79** (2), 189-196.

Husted, J., Wallin, K., & Wooden, H. The psychological evaluation of profoundly retarded children with the use of concrete reinforcers. *Journal of Psychology*, 1971, **77** (2), 173-179.

Ilg, F., & Ames, L. *Child behavior*. New York: Dell, 1960.

Irwin, O. Infant speech: Development of vowel sounds. *Journal of Speech and Hearing Disorders*, 1948, **13**, 31-34.

Itard, J. *The wild boy of Aveyron*. New York: Appleton-Century-Crofts, 1932.

Jedrysek, E., Klapper, Z., Pope, L., & Wortis, J. *Psychoeducational evaluation of the preschool child*. New York: Grune & Stratton, 1972.

Jorgenson, H.A. Effects of contingent preferred music in reducing two stereotyped behaviors of a profoundly retarded child. *Journal of Music Therapy*, 1971, **8** (4), 139-145.

Katz, E. *The retarded adult in the community*. Springfield, Ill.: Charles C Thomas, 1968.

Kephart, N. *The slow learner in the classroom*. Columbus, Ohio: Merrill, 1960.

Kirk, S.A., McCarthy, J.J., & Kirk, W.D. *Illinois test of psycholinguistic abilities*. Urbana: The University of Illinois Press, 1968.

Kluppel, D.D. Language Training. In B. Stephens (Ed.), *Training the developmentally young*. New York: John Day, 1971.

Kolburne, L.L. *Effective education for the mentally retarded child*. New York: Vantage Press, 1965.

Larsen, L.A., & Bricker, W.A. A manual for parents and teachers of severely and moderately retarded children. *IMRID Papers and Reports*, 1968, **5** (22).

Lavatelli, C. *Teacher's Guide: Early childhood curriculum–a Piaget program*. Boston: American Science and Engineering Company, 1970.

Leath, J., & Flournay, R.L. Three year follow-up of intensive habit training program. *Mental Retardation*, 1970, **8** (3), 32-34.

Lemke, H., & Mitchell, R.D. Controlling the behavior of a profoundly retarded child. *American Journal of Occupational Therapy*, 1972, **26** (5), 261-264.

Levine, M.N., & Elliott, C.B. Toilet training for profoundly retarded with a limited staff. *Mental Retardation*, 1970, **8** (3), 48-50.

Lewis, M.M. *Language, thought, and personality in infancy and childhood*. London: G.G. Harrap, 1963.

Luckey, R.E., & Addison, M.R. The profoundly retarded: A new challenge for public education. *Education and Training of the Mentally Retarded*, 1974, **9** (3), 123-130.

Lyle, J.G. The effect of an institution environment upon the verbal development of imbecile children. *Journal of Mental Deficiencies*, 1960, **4**, 14-23.

Malloy, J. *A communication shaping program. Pinecrest State School handbook for aides*. Pineville, La.: Pinecrest State School, 1970.

Malloy, J. *Trainable children: Curriculum and procedures*. New York: John Day, 1972.

Malpass, L.T. Motor proficiency in institutionalized and non-institutionalized retarded children and normal children. *American Journal of Mental Deficiency*, 1960, **64**, 1012-1015.

Manfredini, D. Understanding social and emotional development. In B. Stephens, D. Manfredini, and M. Malcotti (Eds.), *Training the difficult retardate*. Philadelphia: Temple University, 1972.

Martin, C.L., & Travis, J.T. *Exceptional children: A special ministry*. Chicago: La Grange Area Department of Special Education, 1968.

Martin, G.L. An operant analysis of response interactions during meals with severely retarded girls. *American Journal of Mental Deficiency*, 1971, **76** (1), 68-74. (a)

Martin, G.L. Operant conditioning in dressing behavior of severely retarded girls. *Mental Retardation*, 1971, **9** (3), 27-31. (b)

McCarthy, D. Language development in children. In L. Carmichael (Ed.), *Manual of child psychology*. New York: Wiley, 1954.

McCarthy, J.J., Stevens, H.A., & Billingsley, J.F. *Program development for severely retarded institutionalized children*. Madison: University of Wisconsin, 1969.

Mecham, M.J. Developmental schedules or oral-aural language as an aid to the teacher of the mentally retarded. *Mental Retardation*, 1963, **1**, 359-369.

Melton, R.S., Charlesworth, R., Tanaka, M.N., Rothenberg, B.B., Busis, A.M., Pike, L., & Gollin, E.S. *Cognitive growth in preschool children*. Princeton, N.J.: Educational Testing Service, 1968.

Minge, M.R., & Ball, T.S. Teaching of self-help skills to profoundly retarded patients. *American Journal of Mental Deficiency*, 1967, **71** (5), 864-869.

Morlock, D.A., & Mason, B. Outdoor education for the mentally retarded. *Education and Training of the Mentally Retarded*, 1969, **4**, 84-88.

Mulhern, T., & Baumeister, A.A. An experimental attempt to reduce stereotype by reinforcement procedures. *American Journal of Mental Deficiency*, 1969, **74** (1), 69-74.

Musick, J.K., & Luckey, R.E. Program profiles: A token economy for moderately and severely retarded. *Mental Retardation*, 1970, **8** (1), 35-36.

Nawas, M.M., & Braun, S.H. The use of operant techniques for modifying the behavior of the severely and profoundly retarded. Part I: Introduction and initial phase. *Mental Retardation,* 1970, **8** (2), 2-6. (a)

Nawas, M.M., & Braun, S.H. The use of operant techniques for modifying the behavior of the severely and profoundly retarded. Part II: The techniques. *Mental Retardation,* 1970, **8** (3), 18-24. (b)

Nawas, M.M., & Braun, S.H. An overview of behavior modification with the severely and profoundly retarded. Part III: Maintenance of change and epilogue. *Mental Retardation,* 1970, **8** (4), 4-11. (c)

O'Brien, F., Bugle, C., & Azrin, N.H. Training and maintaining a retarded child's proper eating habits. *Journal of Applied Behavior Analysis,* 1972, **5** (1), 57-72.

O'Rourke, T. *A basic course in manual communication.* Silver Springs, Md.: National Association of the Deaf, 1970.

Painter, G. *The effects of a tutorial program on the educational development of disadvantaged infants.* Unpublished doctoral dissertation, University of Illinois, 1967.

Parker, J.L. Need for new strategies for identification and assessment of mental retardation. *Slow Learning Child,* 1971, **18** (3), 131-141.

Paul, H.A., & Miller, J.R. Reduction of extreme deviant behavior in a severely retarded girl. *Training School Bulletin,* 1971, **67** (4), 193-197.

Pearson, P.H., & Williams, C.E. (Eds.). *Physical therapy services in the developmental disabilities.* Springfield, Ill.: Charles C Thomas, 1972.

Penny, R. *Substitute parents: Training the profoundly retarded patient for return to the community.* Springfield, Ill.: Charles C Thomas, 1967.

Posternak, Y. La participation des parents et des volontaires dans nos institutions. [The participation of parents and volunteers in our institutions]. *Deficience Mental,* 1971, **21** (2), 44-46.

Riekehof, L. *Talk to the deaf.* Springfield: Missouri Gospel Publishing House, 1963.

Robinault, I.P. (Ed.). *Functional aides for the multiply handicapped.* New York: Harper and Row, 1973.

Roos, P., & Oliver, M. Evaluation of operant conditioning with institutionalized retarded children. *American Journal of Mental Deficiency,* 1969, **76** (3), 325-30.

Rosenkranz, C.I. From whom shall we serve to how shall we serve them: Extending school services to more severely handicapped children. *Bureau Memorandum.* Madison: Bureau of Special Education, 1973, **14** (4), 14-17.

Rosenzweig, L.E., & Long, J. *Understanding and teaching the dependent retarded child.* Darien, Conn.: Educational Publishing, 1960.

Ross, R.T. Fairview problem behavior record. Fairview, Calif.: Fairview State Hospital (undated).

Ross, R.T., & Boroskin, A. Are IQ's below 30 meaningful? *Mental Retardation,* 1972, **10** (4), 24.

Rybak, W.S., & Todd, B. Together we learn. *Clinical Pediatrics,* 1968, **7** (12), 705-706.

Sanford, A. *Learning accomplishment profile: HCEEAA preschool project for developmentally handicapped children.* Chapel Hill, N.C.: Chapel Hill City Schools, 1971.

Sarason, S.B. *Psychological problems in mental deficiency.* New York: Harper, 1953.

Schiefelbusch, P.L., Copeland, R.H., & Smith, J.O. (Eds.). *Language and mental retardation.* New York: Holt, Rinehart & Winston, 1967.

Scoggins, R.T. A team approach using cassette tapes. *Children Today,* 1972, **1** (4), 16-19.

Shearer, M.S., & Shearer, D.E. *Portage project checklist.* Portage, Wis.: Cooperative Educational Service Agency #12, 1972.

Shirley, M. The first two years: A study of 25 babies. *Institute of Child Welfare Monographs,* 1933, **2** (Series #7), 139-141.

Silverstein, A.B. Reliability and constancy of a new measure of intelligence for institutionalized retardates. *American Journal of Mental Deficiency,* 1971, **76** (2), 257-258.

Sloan, W. *Lincoln adaptation of the Oretsky Test.* Lincoln, Ill.: Author, 1948.

Sternlicht, M. Evaluation of a remotivation program with institutionalized mentally retarded youngsters. *Training School Bulletin,* 1971, **6** (2), 2-6.

Stephens, B. Motor learning. In B. Stephens (Ed.), *Training the Developmentally young*. New York: John Day, 1971.

Stephens, B., Manfredini, D., & Malcotti, M. *Training the difficult retardate*. Philadelphia: Temple University, 1972.

Stephens, B., Smeets, P., Baumgartner, B.B., & Wolfinger, W. Promoting motor development in young retardates. *Education and Training of the Mentally Retarded*, 1970, 119-124.

Stevens, M. *The educational needs of severely subnormal children*. Baltimore: Williams and Wilkins, 1971.

Talbot, M., & Séguin, E. *A study of an educational approach to the treatment of mentally defective children*. New York: Teachers College Press, 1964.

Tarjan, G. Classification and mental retardation: Issues arising in the fifth WHO seminar on psychiatric diagnosis, classification and statistics. *American Journal of Psychiatry*, 1972, **128** (11), 34-45.

Temptin, M. *Certain language skills in children*. Minneapolis: University of Minnesota Press, 1957.

Therapeutic recreation service and mental retardation: Special Issue, *Therapeutic Recreation Journal* 1969, **3** (3), 1-36.

Thompson, L. *Motor development of the young retardate*. Unpublished manuscript, Department of Special Education, Temple University, 1969.

Thompson, P. Keynote Address. *Proceedings from the Regional Topical Conference: The severely multiply handicapped, what are the issues*. Salt Lake City: University of Utah, 1974, 70-76.

Topper, S.T. Gesture language for a non-verbal severely retarded male. *Mental Retardation*, 1975, **13** (1), 30-31.

Tredgold, A.F. *A test book of mental deficiency* (6th ed.). Baltimore: William Wood, 1937.

Treffry, D., Martin, G., Samels, J., & Watson, C. Operant conditioning of grooming behavior of severely retarded girls. *Mental Retardation*, 1970, **4** (8), 29-34.

Uzgiris, I., & Hunt, J. McV. *Instrument for assessing infant psychological development*. Urbana, Ill.: University of Illinois, 1966.

Valett, R. *The Valett developmental survey of basic learning abilities*. Palo Alto, Calif.: Consulting Research Press, 1966.

Van Riper, C. *Speech correction: Principles and practices*. Englewood, N.J.: Prentice-Hall, 1963.

Vayda, K.G. *Issues in programming for the severely and profoundly retarded*. Personal Communication, Clarion, Pa.: Clarion State College, 1974.

Warren, S.A., & Burns, N.R. Crib confinement as a factor in repetitive and stereotyped behavior in retardates. *Mental Retardation*, 1970, **8** (3), 25-28.

Webb, R.C. Sensory motor training of the profoundly retarded. *American Journal of Mental Deficiency*, 1969, **74** (2), 283-295.

Webb, R.C. *Glenwood awareness, manipulation and posture index*. Glenwood, Iowa: Glenwood State Hospital and School, 1972.

Weir, R. Some questions on the child's learning of phonology. In F. Smith & G. Miller (Eds.), *The genesis of language*. Cambridge, Mass.: M.I.T. Press, 1966.

Wessel, J.A. *I CAN: What it is. Programmatic research project in physical education*. Paper presented at the CEC Convention, Los Angeles, 1975.

Wessel, J.A., and Associates. *Individualized physical education curriculum materials*. East Lansing: Michigan State University, 1973.

Woodward, M. The behavior of idiots interpreted by Piaget's theory of sensory-motor development. *British Journal of Education Psychology*, 1959, **29**, 60-71.

Zook, L., & Unkovic, C. Areas of concern for the counselor in a diagnostic clinic for mentally retarded children. *Mental Retardation*, 1968, **6** (3), 19-24.

TEACHER TRAINING IN SPECIAL EDUCATION: A REVIEW OF RESEARCH

Richard E. Shores
James D. Burney

George Peabody College

Ronald Wiegerink

University of North Carolina

The responsibility of special education teacher-training programs is to increase the teaching competency of trainees, which will in turn increase the level of educational services offered handicapped persons. Research in teacher education has therefore concentrated on identifying attributes, skills, and training tactics that should ultimately lead to increased teaching effectiveness. (For reviews of regular education teacher effectiveness research see Fattu, 1963; Heath & Nielson, 1974; Heitzmann & Starpoli, 1975; Kay, 1971; Morsh & Wilder, 1954; Rosenshine, 1969). The research in special education teacher training we similarly divided into two major areas: (*a*) that which concentrated on identifying characteristics and behaviors of special education teachers; and (*b*) that which concentrated on procedures to develop or evaluate teacher training. Those studies (*a*) which concentrate on teacher characteristics and behaviors were further clustered into: research on identification of competencies, research on teacher characteristics, and research on identifying critical teaching behaviors. Those studies which we reported on teacher training were clustered as to the focus for evaluating the training, i.e., pupils, teachers, or teacher-pupils.

RESEARCH ON IDENTIFYING TEACHER BEHAVIOR

Identifying teacher competencies

A question long asked by teacher trainers, What are the competencies needed for effective teaching? has recently gained even greater importance in teacher training research, owing primarily to the recent emphasis on accountability

199

in teacher education (Jones, 1973). Accountability in special education means that teacher trainees demonstrate competence in teaching and that teacher educators facilitate developing this competency. The research literature regarding competency/based teacher training has been primarily concerned with identifying competency statements.

Cooper, Jones, and Weber (1973) proposed four bases for competencies: philosophical, empirical, subject matter, and practitioner-job analysis. Others (Dodl, 1974; Popham, 1974) have recommended general competency areas that must be included. Shores, Cegelka, and Nelson (1973) reviewed some 50 lists of special education teacher competencies which were collected from programs in colleges and universities, as well as published accounts in the literature. Our general impressions of these lists were that the competency statements often were vague and seldom included references to child behavior.

A primary method used to determine competent teaching skills appeared to be some form of expert judgment. Often the procedures used to arrive at the competencies included discussions among experts in the field. For example, Cruickshank (1966) organized, conducted, and edited a report on a conference concerned with examining the competencies of teachers for brain-injured children. The areas of competency were defined by Cruickshank through "conferences with others" (p.v.). From this base, professionals in education, psychology, neurology, and medicine presented and discussed position papers. Cruickshank (1966, pp. 311-334) summarized the conference by breaking the general areas of competencies into 111 "specific competencies" discussed by the participants.

Another procedure which has been used in arriving at competencies included expert judgment with verification by other "experts" in the field. Mackie, Kvaraceus, and Williams (1957) compiled a list of 88 competencies needed by "teachers of emotionally disturbed and socially maladjusted children" from suggestions by a panel of experts. The list was organized into a questionnaire and submitted to teachers in the field to determine: (a) how they viewed the importance of each competency and (b) how they viewed their proficiency in each competency. From the results, the authors made recommendations for improving old as well as establishing new teacher training programs.

Dorwood (1963) modified the competency list of the Mackie et al. (1957) study to compare regular classroom teachers with teachers of the emotionally disturbed. The results indicated that regular classroom teachers did not differ greatly from special education teachers in their views regarding the list of competencies. Only 17 of the 100 items produced significant chi-square differences between the groups. The significant differences obtained seemed more related to the setting in which the teacher worked (e.g., regular or self-contained special class) than to differences in teaching competencies.

More recently Bullock and Whelan (1971) replicated the Mackie et al. (1957) study for the purpose of assessing how "teachers currently involved in the education of emotionally disturbed children viewed the competencies which had been delimited during the earlier stages of concern for the emotionally disturbed" (p. 486). These researchers concluded that there was a significant difference between the two groups of teachers, in that the current teachers "tended to feel that the items (competencies) were not as important as did the participants in the original study" (p. 487). In addition, they regarded themselves as being more proficient in the competencies than did the participants in the original group. The differences found in competency statements in the above study were further supported by Weisham (1972) in a follow-up study of teachers of the blind. He found that competency statements formulated earlier by the Council for Exceptional Children (1966) did not seem to meet the needs of more recently trained teachers.

What contributed to the change in teacher opinions found by Bullock and Whelan (1971) and Weisham (1972) is unknown. Possibilities include differences in training programs, sampling procedures, new knowledge regarding handicapped children, or a combination of many factors. It could also be that the validity of expert judgment is questionable in view of long-term reliability problems. Both the Bullock and Whelan (1971) and the Weisham (1972) studies seemed to agree that the experts of 1957 are not the experts of today in that, from the results of their studies, both articles made recommendations for teacher training which not only expanded those competencies recommended by earlier studies but added to them. The new recommendations included developing better remediation procedures for the different types of exceptionalities (not only for the specific categories of the visually handicapped and behaviorally disturbed) such as: competencies in working with paraprofessionals, competencies in utilizing principles of behavior in managing exceptional children, and more information regarding all exceptionalities.

A different strategy was utilized by Meyen, Connolly, Chandler, and Altman (1971) to verify competencies of curriculum consultants for exceptional children. The purpose of their project was to develop a prototype training program for the preparation of curriculum consultants for the mentally retarded. Their strategy included the typical panel of experts, but the list was also submitted to a variety of field personnel, including administrators and psychologists, as well as teachers. The major procedural difference between this project and the above studies (Bullock & Whelan, 1971; Dorwood, 1963; Mackie et al., 1957) was in terms of the multiple comparisons made among the groups of field personnel. The results indicated that the various professional groups differed as to the competencies needed by the special education consultants. We feel that the competencies derived from these experts were valid, but that varied role expectations in the field were primarily responsible for differences of opinions found in the data.

At least two major similarities in arriving at competency statements appear from the literature reviewed above: (a) experts, often through a symposium or by responses to questionnaires, agreed on a list of competencies; and (b) for validation, the lists were submitted to field personnel via questionnaire to verify or refine the experts' judgments. From (a) and (b), implications were drawn as to areas of competency in which teachers needed to be trained. The major problem with these procedures in developing training programs, as well as evaluating programs, is the validation of the teaching competencies. Expert judgment is, of course, acceptable as a starting point. However, if the primary goal of competency-based teacher-training programs is the improvement of educational services to the handicapped child, then it would seem that the validity of the competencies ultimately rests with the demonstrated effects teaching behaviors have on children's development.

Recently, verification and modification of the training programs, and therefore the competencies being trained, have been attempted by follow-up studies. Although empirical validation of the teacher-training programs is currently very difficult, there have been a few studies reported recently which have evaluated specific teacher-training programs by questionnaires to graduates of the individual programs. For example, Wood (1970) conducted a questionnaire follow-up of graduates of the University of Minnesota teacher-training program for teachers of the emotionally disturbed. Most of those returning the questionnaire felt that improvement could be made by adding "course work and field experiences focusing on developing greater practical skill in working with children" (p. 682). In addition, some questioned the importance of the course work dealing with "the dynamics of disturbed behavior and implications for education and principles of learning theory" (p. 682). From the results it appeared that this program, which trained teachers for the category of "emotional disturbance," was successful in preparing people who seem "dedicated" to teaching this category of children, but that the program could be improved by developing greater skills in applying theory to practice in teaching disturbed children.

Weisham (1972) submitted questionnaires to M.A. graduates of a program for teachers of the visually disabled. The questionnaires were directed toward four major areas: (a) specific educational and personal characteristics, (b) vocational behavior, (c) the graduates' perceptions of the preparation offered by their training programs, and (d) the value of their preparation in relation to their present positions. Weisham stated that results were indicative of the program's success in "developing and sustaining the students' commitment to the education of the visually disabled'' (p. 607). The author concluded that generic methods courses which cut across categories of exceptionality should be included in all special education teacher-preparation programs (p. 610). He also recommended that the competency statements be updated.

The results of the above two follow-up studies of graduates from categorical programs seem to indicate agreement that practical experience and course work in the technology of teaching should receive greater emphasis in training programs, regardless of the handicapping condition of the children.

There have been few evaluative reports of noncategorical or cross-categorical training programs, probably owing to the newness of these programs. Cooke and Wiegerink (1973) followed graduates from a cross-categorical program offered at Peabody College (further described by Weigerink and Currie, 1972). The results of this follow-up study indicated that the trained students found positions in special education suited to their individual training programs. This study also agreed with Wood (1970) and Weisham (1972) in that the students ranked the field work and teaching technology preparation (e.g., course work in precision teaching and behavior modification) as the training which aided them in being successful in their professional positions. Further, the data from the Cooke and Wiegerink study indicated that the course work in specific categories (e.g., Introduction to Mental Retardation) has not proven to be of great value to the graduates.

McKenzie, Egner, Knight, Perelmen, Schneider, and Garvin (1970) reported on a noncategorical consulting teacher program which emphasized applied behavior analysis skills. The data reported were possibly more unique than others reviewed, since the data demonstrated children's responses being modified by the consultative efforts of the former trainees rather than by questionnaire data from the teacher or the supervisor.

The preceding studies indicate the importance of updating the competency statements of the programs, emphasizing what may be considered technological training. In addition, the technological training (viewed either as needed or of utmost importance) seemed similar across categories of exceptional children.

This review should not be viewed as exhaustive of follow-up studies; instead it is intended to demonstrate attempts of teacher training programs to evaluate the effects of their training and thus validate the competencies being trained. Evaluative efforts have generally involved a questionnaire follow-up format with the graduates and, at times, their supervisors as respondents. Information of this type provides training programs with data regarding what the graduates and their supervisors think of the training received in the programs, thus helping the programs modify their training. However, ''think'' responses do not indicate improvements in education of handicapped children. If the purpose of the evaluative data is to aid in improving services to handicapped children, more data concerning the cause-and-effect relationship of teacher behavior and child performance must be generated.

Research on teacher characteristics

Research aimed at identifying personality and attitudinal characteristics of competent teachers has a long history in regular education (Cooper & Bemis, 1967; Getzels & Jackson, 1963). Although not investigated as frequently as in regular education, the teacher characteristics important to special education have been the subject of several studies.

Meisgeier (1965) studied characteristics which contributed to successful student teaching in special education and found several factors. Likewise, Blackwell (1974) identified 11 teacher characteristics (from the Edwards Personal Preference Schedule) related to supervisors' ratings of teaching performance. Of the 11 characteristics, only 2 seemed positively correlated. Wakefield and Crowl (1974) used a concordance procedure with the Edwards Personal Preference Schedule and found that professionals tended to agree on clusters of characteristics of the "ideal special education teacher."

Scheuer (1971) investigated the relationship between teacher personality variables, as perceived by teachers of maladjusted students, and academic gains of the students—in addition to the supervisors' ratings of teachers on a teacher competency check list. Results of this study indicated no significant relationship between the personality variables, as perceived by the teachers and students, and competency in teaching, as measured by the teachers' supervisors. The multiple correlations among the various measurements revealed a few low but significant correlations. However, with one exception, none of the significant correlations supported the hypotheses under investigation. The author explained the lack of significant relationships between the competency in teaching and the personality variables as due to "semantic difficulties concerning the terms effectiveness and competency" (p. 729). He indicated that "competencies in teaching are classroom techniques," while effectiveness was viewed as "the teacher's ability to establish a favorable emotional climate in the classroom" (p. 729), which was what he indicated the personality instruments were measuring.

Other studies have investigated special education teacher personality and attitudes as predictive indicators of successful teachers, similar in intent to the above studies (see, e.g., Dobson, 1972). The results of these studies may be best viewed as a long list of special education teacher characteristics which would include, among others, self-respect, spontaneity, sensitivity, high frustration tolerance, intelligence, emotional stability, energy, responsibility, positive attitude toward children, and openness (Rappaport & McNary, 1970).

The cumulative evidence from these studies tends to indicate that teacher personality, as measured, is at best minimally related to children's classroom performance. The lack of impressive data may be a result of the research strategies utilized. For the most part, research procedures have called for personality and attitudes to be measured via paper and pencil tests or through oral one-to-one questioning. Such procedures are open to serious questions of both validity and reliability (Nunnally, 1967). It would, therefore, appear that more accurate measurement systems need to be developed before such constructs of teacher personality and attitudes can be used effectively in teacher education.

Research on teacher behavior

Research focusing on the teacher's behavior in the classroom has often used direct observation procedures. Direct observation studies have potentially fewer problems with reliability and, therefore, validity than indirect measurements such as personality inventories (Medly & Mitzel, 1963; Wright, 1960). This is not to say that direct observation research strategies are free of reliability and validity problems. However, reliability is easier to establish because it requires only that data collectors consistently agree on the behavior(s) being observed. Therefore, observational systems can be developed to reliably quantify almost any teacher or child behavior of interest in the classroom.

Probably the most widely used method of direct observation in studies of teacher behavior is the Flanders Interaction Analysis (Flanders, 1965). For the most part this system has been applied to investigate the status of teacher and student interactions in regular classrooms with normal children rather than in special education or with handicapped children. Studies using the Flanders system have produced correlational evidence of relationships between teachers' verbal behavior and children's verbal behavior (Flanders, 1965), as well as between certain kinds of teacher-student interactions and academic achievement of children (see Schneyer, 1970, for a review of these studies). Amidon (1967) reviewed studies using the Flanders system and made several suggestions relating the results to teaching children considered emotionally disturbed. His suggestions differed somewhat from what the research seemed to indicate. For example, the research (as reviewed by Amidon and Schneyer) indicated that teachers should provide for "indirect influence" (a major category in the system) to enhance pupil academic achievement and attitudes toward school. Amidon (1967) suggested that "special education teachers probably talk more, give more instructions" (defined under category of direct influence), "use more accepting of feelings statements" (defined under indirect category), "and have greater confrontation with individual children" (generally under direct influence) "than regular teachers" (p. 19). Amidon seemed to view special education teachers as different in their behavior from successful teachers in regular education, in that they should engage in more "direct influence" behavior and less "indirect influence" behavior.

Amidon (1967) also suggested that the Flanders Interaction Analysis be taught to all teachers as a method they might use to assess and modify their own classroom behavior. There is some support for this suggestion. For example, Bondi (1970) found that student teachers in regular education who received interaction analysis feedback differed significantly on several verbal behavior categories from those not receiving such feedback. It should be emphasized that Bondi's study did not indicate that the behaviors changed in the student teachers produced concomitant changes in the children.

Rich (1974) used the Flanders Interaction Analysis to identify 10 teachers considered high on the indirect scale and 10 teachers high on the direct scale. He further identified students in the classrooms of these teachers who were high or low on several social-emotional development measurements. The general purpose of the study was to assess the possible interrelated effect of teacher style (indirect vs. direct) and student social-emotional development on several measures of student performance. The results indicated that the students and teachers who were matched (i.e., indirect teacher with high-developed children and direct teachers with low-developed children) performed significantly better on all performance measures than the mismatched group.

Fink (1972) developed a teacher-pupil interaction observation system similar to the Flanders technique but specifically designed for use in special education classrooms. Fink's method has face validity and acceptable reliability and appears to be sensitive to both teacher and student behavior. Fink's results agreed with the studies using the Flanders system (Flanders, 1965; Amidon & Giammatteo, 1965) in that feedback accounted for the largest amount of recorded teacher behavior.

Another project (Cantrell, 1973) reported a direct observation system based on the Flanders system to monitor teacher behavior. Cantrell's system required measurement both of teacher responses and of students considered to have potential learning and/or behavior disorders. The results of the observations were used to develop strategies for inservice and preservice teacher training, as well as to provide monitoring systems to evaluate the effects of the training. Recent analysis of the data from this project has supported the other studies (Fink, 1972; Alexander, 1974) in that the praise category is highly correlated with student performance (Cantrell, Wood, & Nichols, 1974).

Those in applied behavior analysis have taken a different research strategy to investigate the relationship of teacher-child interaction, with results supporting the above studies. For example, Thomas, Becker, and Armstrong (1968) systematically controlled approving and disapproving behaviors of teachers to investigate the effect these events had on children's study behaviors.

The results indicated that approving responses (e.g., praise, smiles, physical contacts, etc.) of the teachers increased appropriate classroom behavior. When disapproving behaviors were tripled, increases appeared in disruptive behaviors. Other studies using similar research strategies have found similar results, i.e., teacher attention and approval have been demonstrated to control a wide variety of children's behaviors (Broden, Bruce, Mitchell, Carter, & Hall, 1970; Hall, Lund, & Aackson, 1968; Madsen, Becker, & Thomas, 1968; Shores, 1972).

The above studies seem to contradict results of other studies of teacher-child interaction. Rosenshine and Furst (1971) reviewed 50 studies in regular education and stated that teacher approval and praise statements are not highly correlated with children's behavior (p. 55). This seeming contradiction may be the result of the different research designs and data collection procedures used. Those studies cited by Rosenshine and Furst (1971) were static designs correlating teacher responses with children's responses, while the studies cited above were for the most part applied experimental analysis of behavior designs (Baer, Wolf, & Risely, 1968), or at least designs which called for some experimental manipulations (Cantrell, 1973; Rich, 1974).

In applied experimental analysis of behavior designs, which utilize continuous data obtained through direct observation recording systems, it is possible that the data on child and teacher would not be statistically correlated but still be experimentally related. For example, it has been pointed out that the total number of teacher praise statements was often found to be unrelated to total number of children's responses (Rosenshine & Furst, 1971). However, if the teacher praise statements were made contingent on pinpointed children's responses, those responses could be controlled (Broden et al., 1970; Cantrell et al., 1974; Hall et al., 1968; Madsen et al., 1968; Shores, 1972). The studies reviewed by Rosenshine and Furst (1971) investigated the relationship of frequency of teacher behaviors to frequency of children's behaviors. The studies using applied behavior analysis designs investigated specific relationships between precisely defined teacher behavior and precisely defined child behavior by directly manipulating the teacher behavior to assess the effects of the experimental manipulation on the children's performance. The latter research procedures lead to statements of at least "influence," if not cause and effect, while the former lead only to statements of relationship or covariance.

The results of studies on teacher behavior tend to indicate that a positive approach (e.g., using praise statements) relates to increased academic responses and more controlled classroom behavior. Possibly of even greater importance is the increased sophistication of the measurement systems developed to study teacher-child interactions. As indicated by others (e.g., Fink, 1972; Rosenshine & Furst, 1971), such procedures have the potential of completely analyzing the dynamic relationships among teachers, children, and curriculum. Future research along these lines is needed which will lead to the empirical base necessary for developing true competency-based teacher training programs (Shores et al., 1973).

RESEARCH ON TEACHER TRAINING

Although the preceding section of this chapter indicates that teacher education programs are not yet operating from an empirical base in establishing competencies of teachers, teacher training must still provide students with the "best" training possible. The "best," as indicated in the preceding section, is usually defined by the training environment. However, most agree that this training should include the establishment of criteria for evaluating the performance of the trainees and, often, the performance of the trainer—as well as the performance of the children taught by the trainees (Baker, 1974; Branson, 1970; Burns, 1972; Glaser, 1963, 1971; Gorth & Hambleton, 1972; Popham, 1971). Several positions have been presented regarding teacher-training criteria. Shores et al. (1973) proposed pupil behavior change as the ultimate criterion for evaluating teacher performance. Soar (1974) concurred with Shores et al. regarding simpler, lower-level objectives of teacher training, but proposed that higher-level objectives (e.g., affective development and theoretical knowledge) and more slowly developing objectives (e.g., classroom management and interpersonal skill) were not directly measurable through children's performance. Musella (1970) also questioned reliance upon pupil growth, teacher characteristics, or classroom interaction as indicators of teacher effectiveness, suggesting rather a focus on teacher self-improvement as a primary criterion. Kauffman, Hallahan, Payne, and Ball (1973) offered a teacher effectiveness formula designed to allow (at least for the purpose of exploration) empirical evaluation among teacher, instructional methods, children, and instructional tasks. Effective teaching, according to Kauffman et al., would be a maximum "fit" of all factors, as measured by behavior change of the pupils.

From this overview of teacher-educators' positions, it appears that the criteria for evaluating training programs is determined by each training program's focus in changing or developing the response patterns of the teacher-trainees or the pupils of the trainees. The research on teacher training which follows is organized into three major areas reflecting the major focus of the research. Particularly important are the criteria referents used to evaluate teacher training activities. These three criteria referents are: pupil performance, teacher performance, and the combination of teacher and pupil performance.

Research on pupil performance

A number of special education teacher-training programs have used pupil performance as their major criterion-referent. For example, Haring and Fargo (1969) offered direct observation procedures to evaluate acquisition of specific teaching skills in terms of child performance. Their major point was that a teacher's success must be reflected in the child's increased performance level. Like Haring and Fargo, McKenzie et al., (1970) presented a consulting teacher-training program in which children's performance was the criterion for success of the training program. Their data presented demonstrated changes in children's behavior. While McKenzie et al. (1970) described the program which prepared the consulting teachers, as well as children's performance within prescribed programs, their data did not specify precisely *what* the teacher did to bring about the change in the children's behavior, nor precisely *how* the teacher trainees were taught.

Hall (1971) presented a model labeled "responsive teaching" that was similar to those of Haring and Fargo (1969) and McKenzie et al. (1970) in that the criterion of teaching was reflected in child performance. Hall's responsive teaching model incorporated three main points based on applied behavior analysis concepts: (*a*) The child's behavior is precisely defined, which enables the teacher to observe and record the behavior; (*b*) the method or teaching procedure is designed and introduced to improve or remediate the child's behavior; and (*c*) a few simple experimental designs can determine whether the procedure produces a change in the child (p. 4). Hall supported his model by presenting data on children's performances which were changed by student-teachers enrolled in his course who used the principles of responsive teaching.

Such research efforts as these which focus upon child behavior changes, provide excellent support for the success of the teacher-training program. However, without measurement and control of teacher behavior, these data do not give precise information about the cause and effect of teacher and child behavior. For criterion referenced research to be of greater value in teacher training, the trainee's behaviors need to be specified in the same manner the above studies specify children's responses.

Teacher-training research

Research focused on the teacher-trainee has been primarily concerned with procedures (e.g., microteaching, modularized and mini-course formats, and/or the general lecture method). Criterion referents of these studies are the trainee responses assessed through content testing, as well as observations of change in teaching.

Studies using microteaching approaches have indicated that such training does influence the behavior of teachers. McKnight (1971) described basic microteaching techniques and reviewed research on modeling and feedback as they relate to microteaching. Pierce and Halinski (1974) used microteaching techniques to train teachers in three methods of lesson planning. No significant differences were found among students taught using the three approaches. However, significant differences in teacher performance have been reported by others after training using microteaching. Kelly (1970), for example, studied the teaching of basic language skills to disadvantaged kindergarten children. Teachers were rated in a pre- posttraining design of 14 teaching behaviors. The training utilized microteaching techniques and the results revealed significant positive changes in teaching behavior. Douglas and Pfeiffer (1973) successfully trained undergraduates in a specific style of supervisory behavior using microteaching techniques. The results again supported the success of such techniques in training teachers, and the authors concluded that microteaching was a valuable supervisory training tool.

Another training procedure which often incorporates microteaching techniques is modularized instruction. Modularized instruction, as generally conceived, develops clusters of objectives with nearly self-contained units of instruction, allowing students to achieve the objectives on a given criterion level. Blackhurst, Cross, Nelson, and Tawney (1973) reported success in training students using a modularized approach in a cross-categorical methods course. Nelson (1974) discussed further modifications and student reports of the course, in which the students felt that the modular approach was superior to traditional approaches they had previously encountered.

Further support for modularized teaching was established by Blackburn (1974), who investigated the effects of modularized teaching in a course designed for preservice teachers of behavior-disordered children. Significantly better performance on a posttest was noted for those teachers trained using the modularized approach than for those trained using traditional lectures.

A mini-course approach to teacher training has been proposed as an alternative to traditional course structure in training teachers (Borg, Kelley, Langer, & Gall, 1970). The basic components of a mini-course described by Stowitchek and Hofmeister (1974) are: "(a) presentation of specific training techniques through filmed lessons, (b) demonstration of the skills through model films, and (c) preparation and presentation by course participants of microteaching sessions" (p. 490). Borg, Kallanbach, Kelley, and Langer (1968) reported that the mini-course was successful in changing teacher behavior in the field. Stowitschek and Hofmeister (1974) further validated the mini-course procedures by training special education teachers in mathematics instruction.

Others have reported teacher training programs incorporating various procedures, including microteaching and a modular format (e.g., Altman & Meyen, 1974; Hurley, 1971; Lilly, 1970; Rochford & Brennan, 1972; Schwartz, 1967; Tawney, 1973). These reports focused on the procedures used to develop teaching skills and related those skills to child performance. For example, Tawney's (1973) "Practice What You Preach" project collected data on prospective teachers to assess their acquisition of certain criterion tasks. The project also outlined plans to study the maintenance of the teaching behaviors after training. In addition, many of Tawney's tasks included criterion references to changing children's behavior as a function of the acquired teaching skills.

It should be noted that the such projects as Tawney's, and others which measured teacher acquisition and maintenance of skills, included a great deal of practicum work with handicapped children, and in many cases the criteria for acquisition were demonstrated in one or more practica (Berdine, Knapp, Tawney & Martinson, 1975; Brooks, 1975; Cegelka & Tawney, 1975).

The above studies indicate that teacher training is moving away from the traditional structure of lecture courses to more innovative procedures such as microteaching and instructional modules. These procedures have capitalized on instructional technology and are likely to lead to more efficient and cost-effective special education teacher-training programs.

Integration of teacher training and pupil outcomes

Recent research has combined criterion referenced performance of teachers in training with pupil outcomes. McNeil (1967) compared ratings of effectiveness, as measured by student behavior change, for teachers using behavioral objectives with student teachers who used nonbehavioral objectives. Results indicated superior performance of the students taught by those trained in the use of behavioral objectives. Similarly, Smithman and Lucio (1974) studied how pupils' math performance was affected by teacher vision. Results indicated superior performance of pupils whose teachers were evaluated through objectives, as opposed to the control group which was evaluated through a rating scale.

Cantrell et al. (1974) reported a study in which teachers were trained to criteria in a behavior management modularized course. As the teachers gained criteria, direct observation of their teaching in their individual classrooms indicated a more positive approach to the children. In addition, the pupils' academic responses increased significantly over those prior to the training.

Similarly, Cegelka and Tawney (1975) reported on a project for retraining experienced teachers to serve as supervisors of teacher-trainees. The retraining was accomplished through a modularized course structure. Evaluation data indicated that the experienced teachers not only successfully completed the instructional modules, but their classroom behavior also was significantly enhanced. In addition, an increase occured in the percentage of positive interactions with their children.

Stowitchek and Hofmeister (1974) used their mini-course format to train special education teachers in mathematics instruction. Results indicated that the pupils of those teachers who met criteria in the mini-course made significantly better mathematics achievement scores than did the control group.

Each of the above studies illustrate procedures which provide alternative strategies to the lecture course method in training teachers. Because these strategies seem to provide close ties to fieldwork activities, they are more readily evaluated by concurrent measures of teacher and pupil performance. We consider this form of evaluation of teacher education the basic ingredient that special education training has lacked in becoming accountable, not only to the trainee but, more important, to handicapped children.

SUMMARY

This review of research on the training of special education teachers has shown the interrelationship of various lines of investigation, as well as the relative strengths and weaknesses of each. In those cases where a significant research effort directly supplements or contradicts findings in special education, that research has been cited. Of special significance for further research are those studies indicating the relative weakness of teacher characteristics as predictors of teacher effectiveness. The accumulated evidence of these studies leads us to the conclusion that research efforts might be better spent in other areas. One of these areas would be the identification of specific teacher competencies. Because of the observable, behaviorally definable nature of these competencies, further research into their effects upon student learning is feasible.

The demonstrable need for identifying and empirically validating teacher competencies defines a major thrust of future research. As Shores et al. (1973) pointed out, the only way to specify cause-and-effect relationships between teacher behavior and pupil learning is to investigate pupil behavioral change as it results from identified, carefully defined teacher competencies. The challenge is clear. After reviewing personality characteristics, teaching behaviors, pupil performance, and systems of teacher training, it is time to empirically relate specific teacher behavior to specific pupil behavior change. Only by critical investigation of this ultimate teacher-pupil relationship can training programs for special education teachers achieve their ultimate effectiveness.

References

Alexander, R. Teacher-pupil behavior in classes for the emotionally disturbed: An observational analysis and intervention. In L. Bullock (Ed.), *Teacher educators for children with behavioral disorders: Proceedings of the annual fall conference*. Gainsville, Fla: University of Florida, 1974.

Atman, R., & Meyen, E. Some observations on competency based instruction. *Exceptional Children*, 1974, **40**, 260-265.

Amidon, E. An approach to the study of teaching. In P. Knoblock & J.L. Johnson (Ed.), *The teaching-learning process in educating emotionally disturbed children*. Syracuse, N.Y.: Syracuse University Press, 1967.

Amidon, E., & Giammateo, M. The behavior of superior teachers. *The Elementary School Journal*, 1965, **65**, 283-285.

Baer, D., Wolf, M., & Risley, T. Some current dimensions of applied behavior analysis. *Journal of Applied Behavior Analysis*, 1968, **1**, 91-97.

Baker, E. Beyond objectives: Domain reference tests for evaluation and instructional improvement. *Educational Technology*, 1974, **14** (6), 10-16.

Berdine, W., Knapp, D., Tawney, J., & Martinson, M. Community action teacher training in special education. *Exceptional Children*, 1975, **41**, 495-496.

Blackburn, G. Modularized and traditional teaching methods used in preservice teacher training. In L. Bullock (Ed.), *Teacher education for children with behavior disorders: Proceedings of the annual fall conference*. Gainsville, Fla: University of Florida, 1974.

Blackhurst, A., Cross, D., Nelson, C., & Tawney, J. Approximating noncategorical teacher education. *Exceptional Children*, 1973, **39**, 284-288.

Blackwell, R. Study of effective and ineffective teachers of the trainable mentally retarded. *Exceptional Children*, 1972, **39**, 139-143.

Bondi, J.C. Feedback from interaction analysis: Some implications for the improvement of teaching. *The Journal of Teacher Education*, 1970, **21**, 189-196.

Borg, W., Kallanbach, W., Kelley, M., & Langer, P. *The minicourse: Rationale and uses in the in-service education of teachers*. Paper presented at the annual meeting of the American Educational Research Association, Chicago, 1968.

Borg, W., Kelley, M.L., Langer, P., & Gall. *The minicourse: A micro-teaching approach to teacher education*. Toronto: Macmillan, 1970.

Branson, R. The criterion problem in programmed instruction. *Educational Technology*, 1970, **10** (7), 35-37.

Broden, M., Bruce, C., Mitchell, M.A., Carter, B., & Hall, R.V. Effects of teacher attention on attending behavior of two boys at adjacent desks. *Journal of Applied Behavior Analysis*, 1970, **3**, 199-204.

Brooks, B. Applied teacher training—a consumer based approach. *Education and Training of the Mentally Retarded*, 1975, **10**, 46-50.

Bullock, L.M., & Whelan, R.J. Competencies needed by teachers of the emotionally disturbed and socially maladjusted: A comparison. *Exceptional Children*, 1971, **37**, 485-489.

Burns, R. Achievement testing in competency-based education. *Educational Technology*, 1972, **12** (11), 39-42.

Cantrell, R.P. *Final report of subcontracted services for program consultation teacher training and research evaluation*, HEW-BEH Project No. 71-7248; A prevention-intervention model for students' learning and behavior problems, July 1973.

Cantrell, R., Wood, J., & Nichols, C. *Teacher knowledge of behavior principles and classroom teaching patterns*. Paper presented at the annual convention of the American Educational Research Association, Chicago, 1974.

Cegelka, P., & Tawney, J. Decreasing the discrepancy: A case study in teacher reeducation. *Exceptional Children*, 1975, **41**, 268-269.

Cooke, T.P., & Wiegerink, R. An evaluative follow-up of Project IN-STEP. Unpublished paper, George Peabody College, Nashville, Tenn., 1973.

Cooper, J., & Bemis, K. *Teacher personality, teacher behavior, and their effects upon pupil achievement, final report.* Albuquerque: College of Education, University of New Mexico, 1967.

Cooper, J., Jones, H., & Weber, W. Specifying teacher competencies. *The Journal of Teacher Education,* 1973, **24,** 17-23.

Council for Exceptional Children. Professional standard for personnel in the education of exceptional children. Washington, D.C.: CEC, 1966.

Cruickshank, W.M. (Ed.). *The teacher of brain-injured children.* Syracuse, N.Y.: Syracuse University Press, 1966.

Dobson, J. Predicting and evaluating student teacher behavior. *Exceptional Children,* 1972, **39,** 29-35.

Dodl, N. Selecting competency outcomes for teacher education. *The Journal of Teacher Education.* 1974, **25,** 194-199.

Dorwood, B. A comparison of the competencies for regular classroom teachers and teachers of emotionally disturbed children. *Exceptional Children,* 1963, **30,** 67-73.

Douglas, J., & Pfeiffer, L. Changes of supervisor behavior in a microteaching practicum. *The Journal of Experimental Education,* 1973, **42** (2), 36-41.

Fattu, N. Research on teacher evaluation. *National Elementary Principal,* 1963, **43,** 19-27.

Fink, A.H. Teacher-pupil interaction in classes for the emotionally handicapped. *Exceptional Children,* 1972, **38,** 469-474.

Flanders, N.A. *Teacher influence, pupil attitudes and achievement.* Washington, D.C.: U.S. Govt. Printing Office, 1965.

Getzels, J.W., & Jackson, P.W. The teacher's personality and characteristics. In N.L. Gage (Ed.), *Handbook of research on teaching.* Chicago: Rand McNally, 1963.

Glaser, R. Instructional technology and the measurement of learning outcomes: Some questions. *American Psychologist,* 1963, **18,** 519-521.

Glaser, R. A criterion-referenced test. In W. Popham (Ed.), *Criterion-referenced measurement.* Englewood Cliffs, N.J.: Educational Technology Publications, 1971.

Gorth, W., & Hambleton, R. Measurement consideration for criterion-referenced testing in special education. *The Journal of Special Education,* 1972, **6,** 303-314.

Hall, R.V., Lund, D., & Jackson, D. Effects of teacher attention on study behavior. *Journal of Applied Behavior Analysis,* 1968, **1,** 1-12.

Hall, R.V. Responsive teaching: Focus on measurement and research in the classroom and the home. *Focus on Exceptional Children,* 1971, **3** (7), 1-7.

Haring, N., & Fargo, G. Evaluating programs for preparing teachers of emotionally disturbed children. *Exceptional Children,* 1969, **36,** 157-162.

Heath, R., & Nielson, M. The research basis for performance-based teaching. *Education,* 1974, **95,** 298-299.

Heitzmann, W., & Starpoli, C. Teacher characteristics and successful teaching. *Education,* 1974, **95,** 298-299.

Hurley, O.L. The categorical/non-categorical issue: Implications for teacher trainers. In E.L. Meyen (Ed.), *Proceedings: The Missouri Conference on the Categorical/Non-categorical Issue in Special Education.* The University of Missouri-Columbia, 1971.

Jones, R. Accountability in special education: Some problems. *Exceptional Children,* 1973, **39,** 621-642.

Kauffman, J., Hallahan, C., Payne, J., & Ball, D. Teaching/learning: Qualitative and functional analysis of educational performance. *The Journal of Special Education,* 1973, **7,** 261-268.

Kay, P. *Performance-based certification.* New York: City University Office of Teacher Education, 1971.

Kelly, M. *Teacher behaviors that improve the pupils' use of language.* Paper presented at the American Educational Research Association Annual Meeting, Minneapolis, 1970.

Lilly, S.M. Special education: A teapot in a tempest. *Exceptional Children,* 1970, **37,** 43-48.

Mackie, R.P., Kvaraceus, W., & Williams, H. *Teachers of children who are socially and emotionally handicapped.* Washington, D.C.: U.S. Government Printing Office, 1957.

Madsen, C.H., Becker, W.C., & Thomas, D.R. Rules, praise, and ignoring: Elements of elementary classroom control. *Journal of Applied Behavior Analysis,* 1968, **1,** 139-150.

McKenzie, H.S., Egner, A.N., Knight, M.F., Perelman, P.F., Schneider, B.M., & Garvin, J.S. Training consulting teachers to assist elementary teachers in the management and education of handicapped children. *Exceptional Children,* 1970, **37,** 137-143.

McKnight, P. Microteaching in teacher training: A review of research. *Research in Education,* 1971, **6,** 27-38.

McNeil, J. Concomitants of using behavioral objectives in the assessment of teacher effectiveness. *The Journal of Experimental Education,* 1967, **36** (1), 69-74.

Medley, D.M., & Mitzel, H.E. Measuring classroom behavior by systematic observation. In N.L. Gage (Ed.), *Handbook of research on teaching.* Chicago: Rand McNally, 1963.

Meisgeier, C. The identification of successful teachers of mentally or physically handicapped children. *Exceptional Children,* 1965, **32,** 299-235.

Meyen, E.L., Connolloy, A.J., Chandler, M.R., & Altman, R. *Prototype training program for the preparation of curriculum consultants for exceptional children.* Department of Health, Education, and Welfare. U.S. Office of Education. Bureau of Education for the Handicapped, Division of Training. November, 1971.

Morsh, J., & Wilder, E. *Identifying the effective instructor: A review of the qualitative studies, 1900-1952.* Chanute Air Force Base, Illinois: Air Force Personnel and Training Research Center, 1954.

Musella, D. Improving teacher evaluation. *Journal of Teacher Education,* 1970, **21,** 15-21.

Nelson, C. An evaluation of a non-categorical competency-based special education methods course. In L. Bullock (Ed.), *Teacher education for children with behavior disorders: Proceedings of the annual fall conference.* Gainsville, Fla.: University of Florida, 1974.

Nunnally, J. *Psychometric theory.* New York: McGraw-Hill, 1967.

Ostanski, J. New dimensions and considerations in the training of special education teachers. *Education and Training of the Mentally Retarded,* 1975, **10,** 117-119.

Pierce, W., Halinski, R. An evaluation of microteaching training techniques using pupil outcomes as the evaluative criterion. *Contemporary Education,* 1974, **46,** 45-50.

Popham, W. Performance test of teaching proficiency: Rationale, development, and validation. *American Educational Research Journal,* 1971, **8,** 105-117.

Popham, W. Minimal competencies for objectives-oriented teacher education programs. *The Journal of Teacher Education,* 1974, **25,** 68-73.

Rappaport, S., & McNary, S. Teacher effectiveness for children with learning disorders. *Journal of Learning Disabilities,* 1970, **3,** 75-83.

Rich, H. The effects of teachers' styles on child behavior. In L. Bullock (Ed.), *Teacher education for children with behavior disorders: Proceedings of the annual fall conference.* Gainsville, Fla.: University of Florida, 1974.

Rochford, T., & Brennan, R. A performance criteria approach to teacher preparation. *Exceptional Children,* 1972, **38,** 635-639.

Rosenshine, B. Teaching behaviors related to pupil achievement. *Classroom Interaction Newsletter,* 1969, **5,** 4-17.

Rosenshine, B., & Furst, N. Research on teacher performance criteria. In B.O. Smith (Ed.), *Research in teacher education—A symposium.* Englewood Cliffs, N.J.: Prentice-Hall, 1971.

Scheuer, A.L. The relationship between personal attributes and effectiveness in teachers of the emotionally disturbed. *Exceptional Children,* 1971, **37,** 723-131.

Schneyer, J.W. Classroom verbal interaction and pupil learning. *The Reading Teacher,* 1970, **23,** 369-371.

Schwartz, L. An intergrated teacher education program for special education—A new approach. *Exceptional Children,* 1967, **33,** 411-416.

Shores, R. What behavior research says to the classroom teacher. *Teaching Exceptional Children,* 1972, **4**, 192-199.

Shores, R.E., Cegelka, P.T., & Nelson, C.M. Competency based special education teacher training. *Exceptional Children,* 1973, **40**, 192-197.

Smithman, H., & Lucio, W. Supervision by objectives: Pupil achievement as a measure of teacher performance. *Educational Leadership,* 1974, **31**, 338-344.

Soar, R. Accountability: Assessment problems and possibilities. *The Journal of Teacher Education,* 1974, **25**, 204-211.

Stowitschek, J., & Hofmeister, A. Effects of minicourse instruction on teachers and pupils. *Exceptional Children,* 1974, **40**, 490-495.

Tawney, J.W. Practice what you preach: A proposal to develop a contingency managed methods course, and to measure the effects of this course by infield evaluation. U.S. Office of Education, Grant No. 271712. In Progress, 1973.

Thomas, D.R., Becker, W.W., & Armstrong, M. Production and elimination of disruptive classroom behavior by systematically varying teacher's behavior. *Journal of Applied Behavior Annalysis,* 1968, **1**, 37-45.

Wakefield, W., & Crowl, T. Personality characteristics of special educators. *The Journal of Experimental Education,* 1974, **43** (2), 86-89.

Weisham, M.W. Study of graduates in the education of the visually disabled. *Exceptional Children,* 1972, **38**, 605-612.

Wiegerink, R., & Currie, R.J. Project IN-STEP: Training tomorrow's special educators, *Journal of School Psychology,* 1972, **10** (2), 135-139.

Wood, F.H. Follow-up training program graduates, *Exceptional Children,* 1970, 36, 682-683.

Wright, H.F. Observational child study. In P.H. Mussen (Ed.), *Handbook of research methods in child development.* New York: Wiley, 1960.

THE INSTITUTIONALIZATION AND DEINSTITUTIONALIZATION OF THE MENTALLY RETARDED IN THE UNITED STATES

Stanley J. Vitello

The Pennsylvania State University

A study of the literature, laws, and records of Western cultural tradition suggests a pattern of inconsistency and vacillation in sentiments and behavior toward persons perceived as mentally incompetent, often accompanied by a vagueness and uncertainty as to the nature of their status and role. (June F. Lewis, 1973, p. 164)

THE PRESENT DILEMMA

In the United States this "pattern of inconsistency and vacillation" continues. On the one hand, we have the "sentiments and behavior" of the vocal minority of advocates:

Every retarded person, no matter how handicapped he is, is first of all in possession of human, legal, and social rights. As much as possible, retarded persons, whether institutionalized or not, should be treated like other ordinary persons of their age are treated in the community. Every effort should be made to "normalize" the retarded person, to emphasize his similarity to normal persons and to diminish his deviant aspects. (Bill of Rights for Pennsylvania's Retarded Citizens, 1969)

On the other hand we have the sentiments and behavior of the silent majority who voice the opinion that the retarded should be excluded from Jefferson's category of "men endowed by their creator with certain inalienable rights: that among these are life, liberty, and the pursuit of happiness."

Eventually, when public opinion is prepared for it, no child shall be admitted into the society of the living who would be certain to suffer any social handicap—for example, any physical or mental defect that would prevent marriage or would make others tolerate his company solely from a sense of mercy. (Sackett, 1974)

Advocacy for the mentally retarded (MR) is the popular calling of the 1970s, yet it is the sentiments and the behavior of the silent majority which will ultimately determine the future well-being of the MR in the United States. The following sections trace our "pattern of inconsistency and vacillation" toward the MR in an effort to provide an historical perspective.

AN HISTORICAL PERSPECTIVE: THE PAST

The history of mental retardation in the United States has been well documented (Baumeister, 1970; Helsel, 1971; Kanner, 1964; Wallin, 1966; Wolfensberger, 1969). It has been said that mental retardation has had a long past but a short history. That is, from the beginning of human history there have always been individuals among us with limited intelligence who have found it difficult to adapt to the mainstream of society; but only in the last 120 years has the United States become so sensitive to those individuals referred to as "mentally retarded."

The American pioneers, Séguin and Howe, believed that education could improve the condition of mental retardation so as to ensure a satisfactory adjustment to the community. They held that it was society's responsibility to provide this education and habilitation. In 1855, the first community residential school for the retarded was built in south Boston. Fernald (1893) described the facility:

> It was a school—organized in the family plan. The pupils all sat at the same table with the principal, and were constantly under the supervision of some members of the family in the hours of recreation and rest as well as training. It was the belief of the managers that a relatively small number of inmates could be successfully cared for in one institution. It was deemed unwise to congregate a large number of persons suffering from any common infirmity. (p. 206)

Residential schools similar to the one in Massachusetts were shortly established in Pennsylvania, New York, Connecticut, New Jersey, and Ohio. These schools were considered temporary placements where an individualized educational program provided the resident with the necessary skills for community living. Best (1965) in describing this era states, "Probably the world has never known before or since such a pouring out of sympathy for the afflicted of society, more zealous resolve to speed their relief, nor a more ornate faith in the possibilities of education" (p. 185).

The accomplishments of these early schools did not match their expectations. After graduation many of the residents returned to the residential school because they were unable to adjust to the community. Kerlin (1888) reported:

> The experiment of the past thirty years proves that, of those who are received and trained in institutions, 10 to 20 percent are so improved as to be able to enter life as breadwinners; that 30 to 40 percent are returned to their families so improved as to be self-helpful, or at least much less burdensome to their people. (p. 100)

This meant that approximately 50% of the residents could not be habilitated to the degree necessary for them to leave school permanently. The failure of the early educators to recognize this heterogeneity of the residential school population contributed to their disappointment and frustration. Disappointment led to disillusionment as to what could be done *for* the retarded. Disillusionment turned to negativism, as people began to fear the increased number of individuals being identified as retarded and reports of their criminal involvement in the community (Davies, 1968).

These events culminated in a drastically different attitude toward the retarded at the turn of the century. Once perceived as deserving habilitation and a return to the community, the retarded came to be seen as both a threat and a menace to be removed from society. Discussions focused on what should be done *about* or *to* the retarded, rather than what should be done *for* them. Society began to institute measures to protect its own well-being rather than the well-being of the retarded. Kanner (1964) writes:

> The mental defectives were viewed as a menace to civilization, incorrigible at home, burdens to the school, sexually promiscuous, breeders of feebleminded offspring, victims and spreaders of poverty, degeneracy, crime, and disease. Consequently, there was a cry for the segregation of all mental defectives, with the aim of purifying society, of erecting a solid wall between it and its contaminators. According to Kuhlman, "the view that all mental defectives should be committed to state institutions for life grew rapidly after the momentum it had gained by 1900." In another ten years, it had become unanimous as opinion ever had been on anything concerning mental defectives. The question was apparently settled. (pp. 85-86)

Construction of a monolithic public institution throughout the United States proceeded rapidly; thus the period 1910-1930 is referred to as the "institutional era." For over a half-century the retarded were "put away in these mysterious and unknown places" (Goldberg & Lippman, 1974, p. 328). The following section describes what this public institution has become and its effect upon the mentally retarded.

THE PRESENT

Description of public institutions

Today it is estimated that there are 170 public MR institutions located primarily in the rural areas of America. On the outside the institutions are spacious and pastoral. As one writer put it, "it's as if a group spent all its savings to buy choice land for a country club, but then ran out of money and could afford to erect only army barracks" (Rivera, 1972, p. 16). Approximately 190,000 MR people reside in these institutions. The number of residents in any one institution ranges from 500 to 5,000. Of the resident population 80% is equally divided among the moderately, severely, and profoundly retarded. Residents under 20 years of age comprise 50% of the overall institutional population (Baumeister, 1970; Conley, 1973).

Between 1966 and 1969, the American Association of Mental Deficiency (AAMD) evaluated 134 institutions with its *Standards for Residential Institutions for the Mentally Retarded* (Helsel, 1971). These were some of the association's findings:

1. Sixty percent of the institutions were rated overcrowded.

2. Fifty percent of the institutions were rated as below standard, with 62% of the residents living in institutions so designated. There was deterioration of buildings endangering the safety of both residents and employees.

3. Eighty-nine percent of the institutions did not meet AAMD attendant/resident ratios. Over half the personnel employed by institutions were attendants. However, it was reported in one institution the ratio of residents to attendants was 40 to 1. Attendants were untrained or poorly trained, poorly paid, and worked under poor conditions. Eighty-three percent of the institutions did not meet overall professional staffing ratios.

4. Lack of adequate space for programming (education, vocational service, recreation) was found in 60% of the institutions. Beds occupied most of the physical space in the institution. Sixty percent of the institutions were rated as having inadequate sleeping, dining, and toileting areas.

5. Seventy-four percent of the institutions were forced to use residents as institutional workers. Only 23% of the institutions paid residents for their work though 69% had written policies to protect residents from exploitation.

Investigators (Blatt & Kaplan, 1966; Rivera, 1972) have pictorially captured for the public eye the dehumanizing effects of these conditions on the lives of the retarded. In some institutions the residents are contained by fences, barbed wire, cells, ropes, and chains. The residents are poorly fed and clothed, often walking around in the nude. They and their surroundings have the odors of urine and feces. There is no evidence of rehabilitation. At best, the programs are custodial. MacAndrew and Edgerton (1964) described the routine activities in the everyday life of the institutionalized—sleeping, washing, feeding, walking aimlessly around gloomy and sterile recreational areas. The residents may cry out from lack of attention or from physical abuse. About 3,000 residents die each year in public institutions, many from unnatural deaths. After visiting institutions for the retarded in the United States, Nirje (1969) commented:

Such conditions are shocking denials of human dignity. They force the retarded to function far below their levels of developmental possibilities. The large institution where such conditions occur are no schools for proper training, nor are they hospitals for care and betterment, as they really increase mental retardation by producing further handicapping conditions for the mentally retarded. They represent a self-defeating system with shocking dehumanizing effects. Here, hunger for experience is left unstilled; here, poverty in life conditions is sustained; here, a cultural deprivation is created—with the taxpayer's money, with the concurrence of the medical profession, by the decision of the responsible political bodies of society. (p. 56)

The effects of institutionalization have been systematically studied by a number of investigators, which the following section reviews.

Effects of institutionalization

Institutionalization has affected both the cognitive and social development of the MR. The nature of these effects has been determined using both cross-sectional and longitudinal studies of institutionalized residents, as well as comparative studies of the retarded in the institution and community (Balla, Butterfield, & Zigler, 1974; Butterfield, 1967).

The effects of institutionalization on the cognitive development of the MR has been studied by a number of investigators (Cutts & Lane, 1947; Lyle, 1959, 1960; Sternlicht & Siegel, 1968). Cutts and Lane (1947) studied the effect of length of institutionalization on measured intelligence (IQ). The performance of matched groups of institutionalized residents was compared on the Wechsler subtests. The group residing 7 years in the institution performed significantly lower on the verbal subtest than the group who resided in the institution less than a year. This finding led the investigators to hypothesize that residents institutionalized less than a year had experienced a wider range of contacts in the community, which had increased their verbal abilities, whereas the less stimulating institutional environment failed to develop these abilities. Similarly, Lyle (1959, 1960) found that the verbal intelligence of institutionalized children was 1 year behind that of a matched group of noninstitutionalized children. Sternlicht and Siegel (1968) examined institutionalized children, adolescents, and adults with four different intelligence tests over a period of 4 years beginning with the first year of institutionalization. They found that the children demonstrated a significant decline in IQ over the 4-year period. Although adolescent and adult IQ also declined, the point loss was not significant. On the basis of this finding they concluded that the intelligence of adolescent and adult residents tends to remain relatively constant following institutionalization, while children are more adversely affected. The authors hypothesized that the children were still in the formative stages of development and needed more stimulation than that provided by the institutional environment.

The effects of preinstitutional history on the cognitive development of the MR has been examined by numerous researchers. Centerwall and Centerwall (1960) matched a group of 32 Down's syndrome children placed in an institution or foster home within 1 month after birth with a group reared in their own homes until institutionalization at the age of 2½. At the time of the study the early-institutionalized group had been residents for an average of slightly over 3 years, while the home group had been institutionalized on an average of slightly under 1 year. The height and weight of the early institutionalized group fell below the 10th percentile, while the physical development of the home group was significantly higher. By the age of 2 years, 44% of the home group had started walking, whereas none of the early-institutionalized children had. On both IQ and social development measures taken when the children were 7, the performance of the home group was significantly superior to that of the early institutionalized group. The authors pointed out that at the time of the study the early-institutionalized children were functioning in the severely retarded range, while the children reared at home for 2 years were functioning in the moderately retarded range. They concluded that home care and stimulation were important during the first 2 years of a child's life.

Other findings (Kugel & Reque, 1961; Shipe & Shotwell, 1965; Shotwell & Shipe 1964) support the conclusion reached by the Centerwalls. In an investigation conducted by Stedman and Eichorn (1964), 10 Down's syndrome children, between 1 and 4½ months of age, admitted to a state hospital were compared with 10 Down's syndrome children who remained at home. At the time of their study the subjects were 17 to 37 months of age. Members of the two groups were matched on CA and sex and were evaluated with the Bayley Infant Scales of Mental Development and the Vineland Scale of Social Maturity. During their stay in the institution the 10 infants had been in a special enrichment program. Two children slept in a decorated room; they were held for feeding and exposed to a variety of toys and materials. In spite of this supplementary stimulation received by the institutional children, the home subjects scored significantly higher on both the intelligence and social scales and were physically bigger. The authors concluded that, despite the enrichment program, the institution babies did not have the benefit of maternal coaching and coaxing nor the stimulation provided by normal siblings and peers. It should, however, be noted that while the above studies indicate a negative effect on cognition as a consequence of institutionalization, a number of other studies suggest that the institutional experience may have a positive effect on retarded children from extremely deprived home environments (Kershner, 1970; Rosen, Stallings, Floor, & Nowakinska, 1968).

Institutionalization affects the social development of the individual; its influence on patterns of behavior was studied by Kaufman (1966), Francis (1970), and Stayton, Sitowski, Stayton, and Weiss (1968). The subjects in Kaufman's study were 46 retarded children, half of whom were institutionalized and half of whom were on the waiting list for institutionalization. Kaufman observed the two groups for instances of stereotyped behavior, self-stimulating behavior, social behavior, and manipulation of the environment in a purposeful fashion. The institutionalized subjects displayed significantly more stereotyped and self-stimulating behaviors, while the home group exhibited more social behavior and speech for communicative purposes. The difference between the two groups on environmental manipulation was not significant. In a similar vein, Francis (1970) observed 112 institutionalized Down's syndrome children, of different CA levels with MA's of less than 2 years, for occurrences of diffuse movement, object-oriented behavior, locomotion, rocking, posturing, and self-oriented behavior. She found that, with increasing CA, all of these behaviors increased in frequency with the exception of object-oriented behavior. The amount of socialization and interest in the outer world decreased with increasing CA, while blank staring and withdrawal increased. Francis suggested that the limited institutional environment did not provide enough stimulation to foster interest in the outside world; she contended that improvement would result from increased environmental stimulation and social contact. In another study, Stayton et al. (1968) observed 40 retarded children of mixed diagnoses residing in a state institution for a period of 20 days. Social behaviors were rated to determine a mean social interaction score for each of the subjects. The investigators found that the amounts of aggression, affection, and total social interaction were significantly correlated with length of time spent at home before institutionalization: Those subjects who had spent more time at home exhibited both a greater amount of aggression and affection than did subjects institutionalized at an earlier age.

Attempts have been made to determine the role of deprivation with regard to a retarded child's responsiveness to social reinforcement from an adult. The hypothesis behind these studies is that the more deprived the child's preinstitutional or institutional environment, the more responsive he will be to social reinforcement. Zigler (1961) tested this hypothesis among 60 institutionalized cultural-familial retardates ranging in age from 8 to 14. He presented each of his subjects with two highly similar tasks. For the first task the subjects were asked to drop colored marbles into colored holes; for the second, they were simply asked to reverse the color scheme used in the first. In both tasks the subjects could either stop when satiated or make up to 400 responses. Half of the children received support from the experimenter in the form of verbal praise, while half received his attention but no praise. Two psychiatrists reviewed the histories of each subject and rated the children on a social deprivation scale. Using the median social deprivation score as a dividing point, the subjects were then classified as high-deprived or low-deprived. Zigler found that the high-deprived subjects spent significantly more time on both marble tasks under both conditions than did the low-deprived group. He concluded that adult interaction, with or without verbal reinforcement, was more beneficial for retarded children from adverse backgrounds than it was for children whose preinstitutional histories were not marked by such extreme deprivation.

Similar results were reported in an investigation by Stevenson and Knight (1962). Further support for the hypothesis was also provided by Zigler, Balla and Butterfield (1968) who conducted a follow-up study with 50 retarded children, institutionalized for 3 years, to determine whether the effects of preinstitutional history held over time. At the time of admission there had been a significant correlation between preinstitutional deprivation and the amount of time spent on the marble game, as reported by Zigler (1961). After 3 years in the institution the high-deprived cultural-familial subjects declined significantly more on total time spent on the task than did low-deprived cultural-familial groups. The investigators concluded that the decline in need for social reinforcement demonstrated by the high-deprived cultural-familials was probably owing to the fact that their present institution was not as depriving as their previous noninstitutional environments.

Another study in the same vein, by Weaver, Balla and Zigler (1971), compared institutionalized cultural-familial retarded children, noninstitutionalized cultural-familials, and normal children on responsiveness to social reinforcement. All subjects had similar backgrounds of social deprivation, and three groups of 36 children were matched on mental age and sex. The subjects were asked to place felt forms on a form board and later to place sticker figures on a form board. In each group, 12 children received support for their performance in the form of verbal reinforcement and a warm, friendly response by the examiner. Twelve subjects received punishment in the form of negative verbal comments and a cold response from the examiner. The remaining 12 subjects in each group were treated neutrally, receiving neither verbal nor nonverbal reinforcement or punishment for their performance. The investigators found that the institutionalized subjects placed themselves physically closer to the examiner under the support condition and farther away under the punishment condition than did the members of the other two groups. During free play the institutionalized subjects remained closer to the examiner for all three conditions than did the noninstitutionalized subjects or normals. It was concluded that the depriving nature of the institutional environment led to higher approach-and-avoidance tendencies in the retarded children than those manifested by MR and normals maintained in the community. These tendencies in turn tend to create a greater motivation for adult social reinforcement and a corresponding greater wariness of punishment.

In order to compare conditions of deprivation within different institutions, Butterfield and Zigler (1965) again made use of the marble game to test for responsiveness to social reinforcement. Institution A was characterized by a homelike atmosphere. The children had meals in small living units, coed activities were conducted, and there was a large degree of freedom of movement about the facility. In Institution B a large amount of external control was imposed upon the children. They had meals in a large dining hall and slept in large, impersonal dormitories. Social activities were segregated by sex, and freedom of movement about the grounds was highly restricted. Butterfield and Zigler's hypothesis at the outset of the study was that Institution B children would be more motivated to receive social reinforcement than would Institution A children. Twenty cultural-familial retarded children were selected from each institution and were matched on MA, CA, and length of institutionalization. Half of the subjects in each group received verbal reinforcement while performing the marble tasks, while half received the attention of the examiner but no verbal reinforcement. Under both conditions the children from Institution B worked longer on the task than the children from Institution A. Butterfield and Zigler repeated the study, using two different examiners who were not familiar with the experimental hypothesis to be tested. Again it was found that Institution B subjects stayed with the task longer, both with and without verbal reinforcement, than did Institution A children. The investigators hypothesized that the different social climates in the two institutions led to the difference in performance on the motivational task. They affirmed that the greater the social deprivation experienced by a child in an institution, the greater will be his motivation for social reinforcement. Studies by Klaber, Butterfield, and Gould (1969) and Balla et al. (1974) further tested the Butterfield and Zigler hypothesis and obtained similar results.

Balla et al. (1974) point out that the different environments provided by institutions affect both the cognitive and social development of the retarded. The depriving conditions found in one institution may not be present in another which attempts to supply extra stimulation in the form of academic programs, recreational experience, and more frequent opportunities for social interaction. Skeels (1941) compared two groups of retarded children: one placed in an orphanage, and the other transferred to an institution which provided superior environmental stimulation. The members of the two groups were comparable as to CA, medical condition, and family history. The IQs of the orphanage children were initially about 20 points higher than those of the institutionalized children. The program supplied by the institution included placement in wards with older and brighter girls, where a great amount of personal contact was possible. Kindergarten experiences, games, entertainment, and other means of socialization were also provided. Because of staff limitations the group of children remaining in the orphanage received few adult contacts and little supplementary stimulation. Three administrations of the Kuhlmann or Stanford Binet were used by the experimenter to assess intellectual functioning. The first was given just before transfer to the institution, the second at the close of the experimental period (which varied in length for different subjects), and the third approximately 2½ years after the close of the experimental period. Skeels found by comparing the first and second administrations of the IQ test that the institutionalized children gained significantly, while the orphanage children declined significantly. The follow-up administration of the test revealed that the institutionalized children retained their gains over time, whereas the performance of the orphanage children indicated a nonsignificant mean improvement from the time of the second testing. On the basis of his findings, Skeels stressed the relationship between rate of mental growth and the nature of environmental stimulation. He pointed out that from the time of the first to the second testing, the institutionalized children approached the normal IQ range. During the same time period, the mean scores of the children who remained in the orphanage

225

declined from the normal to the retarded range. Skeels contended that the nonstimulating orphanage environment exerted a retarding influence on children who would have had normal intellectual development under proper environmental conditions.

However, different results were obtained by Tizard (1960) who compared two groups of retarded children matched on age, IQ, and sex. One group resided in an institution, while the other lived in a small experimental residential unit run by four staff members. An attempt was made to establish a family care atmosphere in the unit: The children had daily tasks to perform and were provided with a variety of toys, activities, and trips. Tizard noted that these children were more advanced in their social behaviors and speech than were the children in the institution. They also exhibited less crying and aggressive behavior. An intelligence test revealed that the experimental group increased an average of 8 months in MA over the course of 1 year, while the children in the institution increased only 3 months in MA over the same period. Tizard concluded that the greater amount of individual attention in the unit was largely responsible for the difference between the two groups.

Similarly, King and Raynes (1968) studied 3 groups of severely retarded children in 3 different residential settings. All subjects were matched on CA and IQ. The first setting was the ward of an institution in which 18 children slept on identical beds in a large and sparsely furnished dormitory. They were toileted and received their meals as a group. Little stimulation or interaction was provided for them, and the atmosphere was one of strict regimentation. The 16 children in the second group resided in a local authority hostel where 2 to 4 children shared a bedroom which they could decorate as they wished. The children were toileted individually and had their meals with the staff members. A great deal of social interaction was provided, in addition to outdoor play and visits to shops, parks, and other places of interest. All of these children had their own clothing and toys. The third group of 22 children lived in a voluntary home which was quite similar to the hostel in atmosphere although somewhat more regimented. King and Raynes reported that a heavy emphasis was placed upon individual independence and personal responsibility in both the hostel and the home, both of which offered a lot of flexibility in the arrangement of day-to-day routines. In comparing the feeding skills and language abilities of the 3 groups of children, the experimenters found that the ward children were inferior to the other 2 groups in both areas. The researchers contended that the greater social interaction and verbal stimulation in the home and hostel, as well as the emphasis upon independence, were responsible for the difference.

Enrichment programs have been implemented within an institution in order to test their effects on the mentally retarded. (Gray & Kastler, 1969; Mitchell & Smerglio, 1970; Vogel, Kun, & Meshorer, 1967). Vogel, Kun, and

Meshorer studied two groups of 48 retarded children, only half of whom received a program of formal education. Group members were matched as closely as possible on CA, IQ, and MA. Using the Stanford Binet as a test and retest measure 3.8 years later, the investigators found that the children in the enrichment program gained a mean of 1.40 IQ points, whereas the children not included in the program lost a mean of 9.65 points. They also noted that the initially lower functioning children in the enrichment group made the greater gains. They concluded that failure to provide educational experiences for institutionalized retardates can have a deleterious effect upon their level of intelligence.

In another study, Mitchell and Smerglio (1970) compared two groups of children using the Vineland Social Maturity Scale. One group had been exposed to a special activity therapy program which stressed social competence skills and preacademic activities; the other did not have the benefit of this enrichment program. Members of the two groups were matched on preadmission Vineland SQ and age at the time of the postadmission Vineland. The activity therapy program was conducted by full-time activity therapists who provided individualized instruction for children in groups of one to six. Especially emphasized were play and readiness activities as well as self-help skills. Field trips were provided for the children, as were a number of other stimulating experiences such as stories and games. Of the children not included in the activity therapy program, about 10% were enrolled in school classes while the others attended a recreation program. In comparing the postadmission SQs of the two groups, Mitchell and Smerglio found that the members of the experimental group did not decline in SQ. The children who were not enrolled in the enrichment program, however, demonstrated a statistically significant drop in SQ. The researchers felt that the activity therapy program resulted in further development of social competence among members of the experimental group.

Similarly, Gray and Kastler (1969) reported on a foster grandparent program in a state institution. Working with moderately and severely retarded children ranging in age from 5 to 8, the grandparents spent about 4 hours a day at the institution. During their visits they took the children from the wards outdoors and provided individualized activities. Attempts were made to teach self-help and social skills as well as academic and motor skills. After 1 year in the program, children who had been cared for by foster grandparents were compared with a control group on the Vineland Social Maturity Scale. The mean gain in SQ of the experimental group was significantly greater than that of the group not participating in the foster grandparent program. Gray and Kastler concluded that the individual attention and affection which the children in the experimental group received from the grandparents were responsible for the posttest gains.

In summary, the following are fairly conclusive findings regarding the effects of institutionalization on the retarded: (a) the earlier a child is placed in an institution, the greater his losses in both cognitive and social development; (b) the longer the period of institutionalization, the greater the decline in cognitive and social development; (c) children placed in institutions from extremely deprived environments tend to make gains cognitively and socially; and (d) institutional programs can be improved to promote cognitive and social development, yet community programs tend to be more effective.

Deinstitutionalization

The reports by Blatt and Kaplan (1966) and Rivera (1972), along with mounting research which demonstrates the detrimental effects of institutionalization, prompted protests demanding the deinstitutionalization of the MR. Deinstitutionalization encompasses three interrelated processes: (a) prevention of admission by finding and developing alternative community models of care and training; (b) return to the community of residents prepared through programs of rehabilitation and training to function adequately in appropriate local settings; and (c) establishment and maintenance of a responsive residential environment which protects human and civil rights and which aids in the expeditious return of the individual to normal community living, whenever possible (National Association of Superintendents of Public Residential Facilities for the Mentally Retarded, 1974).

The deinstitutionalization of the MR in the United States is not a recent development. In 1950, the parents of the retarded organized to protest the deplorable conditions in many state institutions and the lack of community services for the MR. The National Association for Retarded Citizens (NARC) became active in providing and securing community-based programs for some retarded children who previously were sent to institutions. The organization was urging then as it is now that *all* retarded children are by right entitled to a free public school education in the community. The efforts of NARC in the 1950s resulted in the establishment of special programs in the public schools for the group of children labeled moderately or trainable mentally retarded. There was considerable controversy over whether or not the trainable child belonged in the public schools (Cruickshank & Goldberg, 1958). Today, approximately 540,000 moderately retarded children are receiving an education in the public schools. The more severely retarded children remained in institutions to endure their dreadful and debilitating effects.

The parent movement brought to public awareness the plight of the retarded. Parent groups pressured local, state, and federal governments to provide financial support for improved and innovative MR community programs. In 1961, President Kennedy authorized the formation of the President's Committee on Mental Retardation (PCMR), charged with developing "a national program to combat mental retardation." In 1963, each of the states was delegated responsibility to develop a "comprehensive mental retardation plan." In that same year President Kennedy died, as did much of the promise for the retarded. However, under the Johnson administration, significant progress was made which included: (a) the recognition of mental retardation as a national concern; (b) federal appropriations to support research in the prevention of mental retardation and manpower training; and (c) federal appropriations to support planning efforts to develop community-based services for the retarded.

In 1968, the PCMR report *Edge of Change* recommended: (a) an improvement in standards of residential care for the retarded and the simultaneous development of a system of accreditation for residential care programs and facilities for the retarded; (b monetary awards to the states based on a plan to bring present institutions up to acceptable standards and to develop community-based residents as an alternative to institutionalization. In the present decade the judiciary has joined with the executive and legislative branches of government to hasten deinstitutionalization and improve the social condition of the MR.

The rights movement

In the United States the 1960s were marked by social unrest, as the civil rights movement gave black Americans their long denied human and legal rights. Using the courts as a vehicle to secure rights was the tactic of a number of other minority groups in the decade ahead—women, the aged, homosexuals, and the mentally retarded. In the 1970s a series of class action suits (Diana v. Board of Education, 1970; Hobson v. Hansen, 1971; Larry P. v. Riles, 1971; Spangler v. Board of Education, 1970; Stewart v. Phillips, 1974) have challenged the constitutionality of placing disadvantaged children in special classes for the mildly mentally retarded. The courts decreed that such practices were discriminatory and in violation of the Fourteenth Amendment which guaranteed the plaintiffs due process and equal protection. The use of litigation on behalf of the mildly retarded was to be extended to the severely retarded so that they too might secure their constitutional rights.

We should recall that up to 1970 thousands of severely and profoundly retarded children were excluded from the public schools and placed in public institutions which lacked educational programs. In the landmark case, Pennsylvania Association for Retarded Citizens v. Commonwealth of Pennsylvania (1972), the plaintiffs challenged the constitutionality of certain state statutes which excluded retarded children from public schools. On May 5, 1972, the court ordered: (a) free public programs of education and training for *all* retarded children between 4 and 21 years of age; (b) public programs of education and training must be *appropriate* to the child's capacity and offered in

229

the least restrictive environment; and (c) the parents of the retarded are entitled to a *due process* hearing before the educational assignment and reassignment of their children. According to Abeson and Bolick (1974) 41 *right-to-education* cases had been filed through 1974 in the United States with arguments and decisions similar to the PARC case. Many states are now changing their school codes to include all retarded children in order to prevent litigation (Bolick, 1974). As these changes occur, many of the pending and future right-to-education cases will become moot.

Yet, while access to public schooling is necessary, it is insufficient. Educational programs for the severely and profoundly retarded must be appropriate to their needs. Herbert Goldstein, one of the two masters appointed by the Pennsylvania court to oversee the implementation of the court order, made it clear from the beginning that he would not be satisfied with the opening of a classroom, the hiring of a teacher, and the installation of a seat for every retarded child. His concern was for the development of quality education. As in the 1950s with the moderately retarded child, many believed that the severely retarded would not benefit from a public school education. What was required was a new conceptualization of education, such as that offered in the Pennsylvania guide entitled *Commonwealth Plan for Educating and Training of the Mentally Retarded* (COMPET, 1972):

> Education is a life-long process that relates to human development. We can, therefore, consider education as applicable to the infant as well as the mildly retarded child. (p. vii)

A series of class action suits, referred to as the *right to treatment*, seeks to obtain for the MR appropriate educational programming. The landmark case, Wyatt v. Stickney (1972), upheld that persons involuntarily confined to MR institutions have a constitutional right to adequate treatment and habilitation. As a result of the court's action, standards for adequate treatment at the Partlow State School in Alabama were enumerated: (a) a provision against uncompensated resident labor, (b) a number of protections to ensure a humane psychological environment, (c) minimum staffing standards, (d) a provision for the individual evaluation of residents, (e) statements of treatment plans and programs, (f) a provision to ensure that residents released from the institution are provided with appropriate transitional care, and (g) a requirement that every MR person has a right to the least restricted setting necessary for treatment. At the close of 1974, nine right-to-treatment cases had been filed in the courts (Abeson & Bolick, 1974). As educational programs for the severely and profoundly retarded provided by the public schools become more clearly defined and appropriate, the need for right-to-treatment litigation will also decrease.

In the future, litigation will continue in order to secure for the MR other human and legal rights which include:

the right to just compensation for labor
the right to vote
the right not to be involuntarily sterilized
the right to fair classification
the right to housing
the right to marry
the right not to be subject to experimentation.

The possession of rights assumes that the individual is in a setting to exercise his rights, yet this assumption cannot be made with many of the retarded. Their placement in restrictive settings (i.e., institutions) denies them the opportunity to participate in community life where rights are exercised. The future must provide the retarded as normal a pattern of life as possible.

THE FUTURE

Normalization

In the United States, judicial and legislative actions reflect a return to the ideology similar to that which prevailed in the 1850s at the time of Howe and Séquin. A fundamental difference, however, gives promise for a more optimistic future for the MR. Apparently society is providing a place for the retarded in the community which is not contingent upon their becoming "normal." Fram (1974) comments on the *right to belong:*

> When a separate constitution for the retarded states, in part, that the retarded shall have the "same rights as other human beings" this act recognizes the retarded as belonging to a separate class. However, the right to belong would emphasize that there is total societal acceptance of the retarded with no special contingencies. Acceptance would come first and achievement secondary; the retarded would be seen as "normal" and no demand would be made upon them beyond their capacity. Occupants of the "lower end of the normal curve" must know that the problem of retardation is not theirs alone, but also with the people around them. (p. 32)

This "new ideology" is embodied in the *normalization principle,* developed in the Scandinavian countries and presently promulgated in the United States by Wolf Wolfensberger in his text, *The Principle of Normalization in Human Services* (1972): "Utilization of means which are culturally normative as possible, in order to establish and/or maintain personal behaviors and characteristics which are as culturally normative as possible" (p. 28). Normalization is a rational attempt to deal with the conditions which have tended to deepen and reinforce prejudice and set the retarded apart from the rest of society. It tries to effect new and more appropriate patterns of living for the retarded. Normalization refers not to a treatment but to those services, situations, and attitudes which will bring about humane care of the MR (Dybwad, 1973). Nirje (1969) captures the essence of normalization:

> When residential facilities for the mentally retarded are constructed, located, operated and interpreted as homes for children; when special schools for the mentally retarded are integrated into regular schools or looked upon as no more than schools for children and youth; and when group homes and hostels for the adult are looked upon mainly as homes for the adult; then such direct and normal experiences will result in normalization of society's attitudes toward the retarded. (p. 187)

Normalization demands not only the availability of services with equal access for the retarded but also a new level of expectation. Research has clearly indicated that people respond to the demands made on them; thus, as long as we perceived the MR as deviant, we expected deviant behavior from them. When we expected that the retarded be institutionalized, they were. As expectations have changed, so has the behavior of the retarded and the possibilities for their integration into the community. Yet, as we begin to implement the normalization principles, Mittler (1974) cautions:

> If we fail to provide schools that are properly equipped and staffed by trained teachers, we must not be surprised if [the MR] fail to learn. If we design sheltered workshops on the assumption that the handicapped need to be protected from the competitive pressures of work, we should not be surprised if they fail to adapt to the demands of a system for which they have been inadequately prepared. If we provide sheltered housing and sheltered leisure activities and restrict opportunities for the fulfillment of social and sexual needs, we must not expect handicapped people always to behave according to expected conventions. (p. 15)

The normalization principle places major emphasis on the needs of the individual rather than on a system of classification which tries to fit the individual into existing systems of service.

In order to accelerate the implementation of the normalization principle, Wolfensberger and Glenn (1973) have developed Program Analysis of Service Systems (PASS), which has the following purposes: (*a*) to provide an objective, quantified evaluation of human management services for the MR; (*b*) to use the specifications of the normalization principle as a teaching tool for service personnel; and (*c*) to define quantitatively what constitutes right to treatment. The instrument is made up of ratings within two areas which have items hierarchically arranged. The ideology area is concerned with normalization and related matters (i.e., integration, appropriate interpretations and structures, specialization, etc.). The administration area deals with manpower considerations and operational effectiveness. To date, the PASS instrument has been used experimentally in Canada, Nebraska, Pennsylvania, and Virginia. While PASS appears to be a promising device for evaluating the quality of services for the retarded, additional reliability and validity are needed.

Normalization entails the restructuring of old facilities and the creation of new facilities in the community to meet the needs of the MR. The next section considers a continuum of appropriate community services.

A continuum of community services for the retarded

Deinstitutionalization can occur without normalization. That is, the MR can be relocated in community facilities which are as restrictive and dehabilitative as the public institutions (Scheerenberger, 1974; Turnbull & Turnbull, 1975). If this is allowed to occur, we may experience a "reinstitutional era" owing to our failure to provide appropriate community resources. The challenge of the future is for our societal institutions to change to meet the needs of all retarded citizens. Deinstitutionalization needs to be complemented by normalization and will only be successful if quality community programs and services are made available (Turnbull & Turnbull, 1975). Because the process of deinstitutionalization requires the exchange of manpower, services, facilities, and leadership between community and institution (Thurman & Thiele, 1973), a continuum of community services must be provided in order to protect the right of the retarded to live as "normal" a life as possible.

> The mentally retarded person has a right to live with [his] family or with foster parents, to participate in all aspects of community life and to be provided with appropriate leisure time activities. If care in another setting becomes necessary, it should be in surroundings and circumstances as close to normal as possible. (Declaration of General and Special Rights of the Mentally Retarded, 1961)

Until recently, either living at home or placement in a public institution were the only alternatives available to the retarded individual and his family (National Association for Retarded Citizens, 1973). New service delivery systems which are appearing and the reorganization of existing systems offer the retarded more and better alternatives. It is critical both in terms of habilitation and economics that there be a match between the goals of the retarded individual and the alternative placement (Conley, 1973).

A continuum of community services for the retarded should constitute a total *developmental* program, rather than just places to put people. The continuum should be flexible and responsive to the needs of retarded of all ages. It should be recognized that comprehensive programming for MR persons means that no one program is terminal or permanent. It should be possible for an individual to move from an institution to a home to an apartment and back to the institution if necessary (National Association for Retarded Citizens, 1973).

The National Association for Retarded Citizens (1974) has laid down a set of basic principles to underlie the development of service systems for the retarded. Among these principles are the following:

1. Retarded children and adults are guaranteed the same constitutional rights as other children and adults and may not be deprived of life, liberty, or property, without due process of law; nor shall they be denied equal protection granted by the laws.

2. Retarded individuals should be treated so as to promote emotional development.

3. Programs for retarded persons must give attention to the individual's personal goals.

4. Retarded children and adults should be helped to live as normal a life as possible.

5. Retarded children and adults are capable of learning and development.

6. Specific program objectives should be tailored to meet the needs of each individual and will vary for different degrees of impairment.

7. Programs for MR persons should utilize the community's existing services to the fullest extent.

8. Community services should be strategically located throughout the state, region, or county to promote maximum social integration in the community.

There is momentum for action at the local and state levels to provide such a continuum of community-based residential services.

FIGURE 1

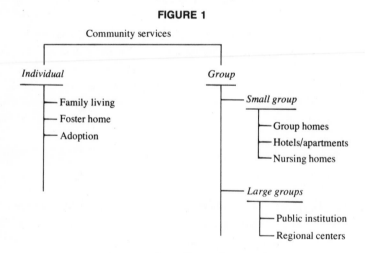

**COMMUNITY SERVICES FOR THE
MENTALLY RETARDED**

Figure 1 shows a number of alternatives (by no means exhaustive) which can make possible an appropriate placement for the retarded. The individual placements are considered more normalizing than the group placements.

The **public state institution,** as most of them operate today, violates the basic principles set down by NARC. Institutions, as described earlier, tend to be abnormal environments which prepare the retarded for nothing more than permanent residence. This restrictive institutional environment denies the retarded individual the habilitation necessary to return to the community and the opportunity to exercise his legal rights. Wolfensberger (1971) argues that there is so much wrong with our present-day public institutions that they should be dismantled. Others (Dunn, 1969; Gunzburg, 1968; Meyen, 1967) view the institution as one alternative which should be available to the retarded. They believe that conditions within institutions can be normalized and made more habilitative and humane. Agreeing with this point of view, the National Association of Superintendents of Public Residential Facilities (1974) pointed out: (a) All too often, "community back wards" and "closeting" are being substituted for institutional "warehousing." Neither community nor residential back wards or "closeting" are justified; the rights of the retarded must be respected wherever they reside. (b) Community programming should not be developed by sacrificing the quality of services for retarded persons requiring residential care. It is not a question of residential or nonresidential programming: Both are essential and both, in reality, constitute community services. (c) The conflict of persons with a common dedication to meeting the needs of the MR is unwarranted and should be resolved as rapidly as possible to insure maximum service for the retarded, both within and outside a residential environment. Residential programming must be viewed as only part of the complete range of community services which may be required by some retarded persons.

Scheerenberger (1974) adds: "By definition (and practice) a residential facility must be considered an integral part of any community. The degree to which it is a successful member of that community depends upon the degree of its involvement and interaction" (p. 4). Furthermore, for many retarded individuals the public institution will remain the only alternative for many years. But they should not be asked to endure the dehabilitating conditions in the institutions until a community placement becomes available. Immediate steps need to be taken to "normalize" the institution as much as possible to prepare the retarded for eventual return to the community. Gunzburg and Gunzburg (1971) make this realistic appraisal:

> The assumption that it is impossible to create favorable conditions for effective education and training within the institutional framework has led to the rejection of institutions and a belief that adequate results could only be attained by placing the mentally defective person in the environment of the normal community rather than abnormal institution (Tizard et al., 1967). Whatever the merits of the two approaches, there is little doubt that the institutional framework will still be with us for some time to come, even if it is only for financial reasons. It is, therefore, most important to consider what changes in outlook and approach have to be brought about and can be brought about in present circumstances, which would make living in the institution into a positive factor and would turn the institution into a legitimate alternative treatment and training facility instead of regarding it as a place of last recourse. (p. 175)

The institution can play a vital role in the deinstitutionalization process, which will occur much more rapidly and effectively if institutions assume the leadership. Thurman and Thiele (1973) suggest some new functions for the

235

institution which would give impetus to deinstitutionalization: (a) the development of prototype educational programs which can be instituted in the community ; (b) the preparation of residents for community living; and (c) the use of the institution as a training base for those who will work with the retarded in the community. Rather than serving as a facility for permanent long-term care, institutions should provide intensive comprehensive treatment (both medical and educational) in an effort to return the retarded to a family and community setting as soon as possible (Scheerenberger, 1974). In turn, community facilities can utilize the interdisciplinary staff for reevaluations, consultation, and intensive medical care. A reputable institution should maintain the best possible life-support facilities so as to ensure appropriate medical, nursing, and therapeutic services (Rowland & Patterson, 1972). Large institutions can be decentralized (Raynes, Burnstead, & Pratt, 1974). Large group activities can be replaced with small group or individual activities, and family units can be the model for small group arrangements. This may require a drastic reorganization of grouping arrangements in the institution as well as the redesigning and improved utilization of available space. But normalization of an institution entails "demesticating the atmosphere" and providing "an environment rich with opportunities." Until more appropriate community programs have been established, public institutions should perhaps be included in comprehensive state and local community planning for the MR.

Several states (Connecticut, California) have deinstitutionalized the retarded by building **regional centers** in the community (Helsel, 1971). These centers typically house no more than 200 beds and use existing services in the community to habilitate the retarded. The California centers do not provide beds; instead, they purchase community services for the retarded who live in a number of different arrangements in the community. The regional center is an improvement over the large public institution since it can provide improved care and integration because of its proximity to the community. Safeguards must be taken to ensure that the regional center does not become a mini-public institution.

There is considerable momentum in the field to establish **small group homes** in the community, and in many cases normalization has become synonymous with the building of small group homes. Houses in the community are being purchased or built for the occupancy of deinstitutionalized children. Small group homes typically have no greater than 20 residents in one facility and the home-like atmosphere provides a normalizing environment. Children attend the local public school and, like all children, come home for afternoon and evening recreational activities. Small group homes must not be established without the full range of services available to the community. Helsel (1971) warns that poor planning of group homes can result in underutilization and bad economics. Before we accelerate the establishment of small group homes across the country, we should evaluate their effectiveness. Planners of group homes in many communities are coming up against restrictive zoning regulations which do not consider group homes as single-family dwellings. Problems of community acceptance, lack of available housing, and the shortage of money to build houses may be major obstacles which thwart the small group movement.

Apartment living or **hostels** in the community are appropriate placements for employable or potentially employable retarded adults. Hostels typically house eight adult residents, a home manager, and provide opportunities to develop skills necessary for independent living and competitive employment. Community agencies offer counseling and medical services, while planned educational, religious, and recreational activities promote integration. Residents are employed in sheltered workshops or competitively in local industry. The more independent adults should be encouraged to live in apartments available in the community (Helsel, 1971; National Association for Retarded Citizens, 1973).

Many MR families are concerned for the future welfare of their children—when they become old and dependent. Placement in a community-based **nursing home** is an alternative to a return to the institution (Helsel, 1971). However, such placement may be nothing more than the exchange of one custodial situation for another. Nursing homes should provide rehabilitative programs for all the aged, including the MR. The normalization principle applies to the elderly as well as the young.

It is normal for children to live at home with their **natural families.** During these critical years intellectual and emotional development occurs in a stimulating and accepting environment provided by parents. Yet this right has been denied many MR children. Until recently parents of the retarded have been led to believe that "the best thing" for their children is institutionalization. Further, the law has made it simple in our society for parents to divest themselves of a retarded child (Wolfensberger, 1971). Such laws reflect an attitude that the retarded do not belong in "normal" families, even if the parents have the emotional and financial resources. Society stigmatizes both the family and the child, resulting in the child's removal. The right of the retarded child to be a member of a family needs to be protected, for it is more than a legal right, it is a natural right. However, Meyen (1967) cautions:

> Because of the tremendous variation in the problems presented, it is unwise to generalize with respect to the desirability of keeping retarded children in their homes. The attitude of parents on the matter ranges all the way from determination to retain a child whether or not it is wise for them to do so—to the despair that results from carrying an intolerable burden. The financial capability of families covers an equally wide range. Thus, what is "best" for the retarded child, his family, and the community can be properly determined only by adequate professional evaluation, skillful counseling, and an objective point of view on the part of local and state authorities. (p. 340)

Every effort should be made to keep the child at home before alternatives are considered. The birth of a retarded child requires that the family receive *immediate* psychological support. Counseling should be made available upon the diagnosis of mental retardation (President's Committee on Mental Retardation, 1970), a service which can be provided by the hospital as part of its follow-up of infant care. Representatives of the local Association for Retarded Citizens should be contacted to come to the assistance of the family. Immediate assistance of this kind often makes the critical difference in the family's ability to keep the child and avoid the necessity of early institutional placement. Free public school programs and family subsidies should reduce the financial burden on many families, enabling them to provide the necessary care for their children (Wolfensberger, 1971). If the child cannot be cared for at home, alternative placements should be as close to the parents as possible. There may be other members of the extended family such as grandparents who can be entrusted with the care of the child. The presence of small group homes in the community would enable parents to visit their child frequently or take him home for short periods of time.

A family atmosphere can be provided for many mentally retarded citizens by placing them in **foster homes** (Browder, Ellis, & Neale, 1974). Foster parents are paid for maintaining the child and providing supportive services. In situations where families have relinquished the legal rights to their child, the possibility of **adoption** should be considered (Soeffing, 1975).

Much remains to be done to establish the above arrangements as realistic alternatives for the MR. Continuous efforts must be made to insure them a normal pattern of life, regardless of degree of retardation and age.

Toward 1980

1980 has been designated the year in which all the handicapped will be assured of a free public school education. Another goal is to reduce by at least one-third the number of MR individuals in public institutions. While the courts have provided impetus for rapid movement toward the attainment of these goals,

> legal activity, the catalyst and leverage for necessary change, is not a final solution. Because post-litigation complacency is always a danger, persons committed to the goal that all children receive an education suited to their educational need must bear the responsibility of keeping the issue alive and moving, and seeing that the right to education is not, because of apathy, rendered meaningless. (*Basic Rights of the Mentally Handicapped*, 1973, p. 55-56)

The latter part of the 1970s will be a critical period in the history of mental retardation. Given access to public education and housing, the MR must still be assured appropriate educational and community programs. This will involve:

1. The use of citizen advocacy to further the acceptance of the MR in the community
2. The development of quality educational and community programs
3. The training of personnel to design and deliver these programs

4. Increased political activity at all levels of government to insure the legislative appropriations needed to implement the court right to education and treatment decisions.

The present climate in the United States regarding the treatment of the MR suggests great promise for the nation. It is a sign of man's compassion and sense of justice toward his fellow man. Norman Acton (1971) visualized the future in this way:

> In the ideal future, the human rights of every individual will be protected by a society of people whose education and maturity of attitude have eliminated all forms of prejudice and discrimination, and assured equal opportunity for all. Evolution towards that ideal cannot, however, be left to chance—we must depend on laws to protect human rights, and on administrative mechanisms to insure that the values set forth in the laws are promoted and, if necessary, enforced. (p. 1)

References

Abeson, A., & Bolick, N. *A continuing summary of pending and completed litigation regarding the education of handicapped children.* Reston, Va.: State-Federal Information Clearinghouse for Exceptional Children, 1974.

Acton, N. Legislation and the rights of the disabled. *International Rehabilitation Review,* 1971, 22.

Balla, D.H. Butterfield, E.C., & Zigler, E. Effects of institutionalization on retarded children: A longitudinal cross-institutional investigation. *American Journal of Mental Deficiency,* 1974, **28**, 530-549.

Basic rights of the mentally handicapped. Washington, D.C.: Mental Health Law Project, 1973.

Baumeister, A.A. The American residential institution: Its history and character. In A. Baumeister, & E. Butterfield (Eds.), *Residential facilities for the mentally retarded.* Chicago: Aldine, 1970.

Best, H. *Public provision for the mentally retarded in the United States.* Worcester, Mass.: Hefferman Press, 1965.

Bill of Rights for Pennsylvania's Retarded Citizens, 1969 (mimeo).

Blatt, B. & Kaplan, F. *Christmas in purgatory: A photographic essay on mental retardation.* Boston: Allyn and Bacon, 1966.

Bolick, N. (Ed.). *Digest of state and federal laws: Education of handicapped children* (3rd ed.). Reston, Va.: State-Federal Information Clearinghouse for Exceptional Children, 1974.

Browder, J.A., Ellis, L., & Neal, E. Foster homes: Alternative to institutions? *Mental Retardation,* 1974, **12** (6), 33-36.

Butterfield, E.C. The role of environmental factors in the treatment of institutionalized mental retardates. In A.A. Baumeister (Ed.), *Mental retardation: Appraisal, education, and rehabilitation.* Chicago: Aldine Publishing, 1967.

Butterfield, E.C., & Zigler, E. The influence of differing institutional social climates on the effectiveness of social reinforcement in the mentally retarded. *American Journal of Mental Deficiency,* 1965, **70**, 48-56.

Centerwall, S.A., & Centerwall, W.R. A study of children with mongolism reared in the home compared to those reared away from the home. *Pediatrics,* 1960, **25**, 678-685.

Commonwealth Plan for Education and Training of the Mentally Retarded. Harrisburg: Department of Public Education, 1972.

Conley, R.W. *The economics of mental retardation.* Baltimore: Johns Hopkins University Press, 1973.

Cruickshank, W.M., & Goldberg, I.I. The trainable but non-educable. *National Education Association Journal,* 1958, **47**, 622-623.

Cutts, R.A., & Lane, M.O. The effect of hospitalization on Wechsler-Bellevue subtest scores by mental defectives. *American Journal of Mental Deficiency,* 1947, **51**, 391-393.

Davies, S.P. *The mentally retarded in society.* New York: Columbia University Press, 1968.

Declaration of General and Special Rights of the Mentally Retarded, 1961 (mimeo).

Diana v. Board of Education, Civil Action No. C-70-37 (N.D. Cal. 1970).

Dunn, L.M. Small, special-purpose residential facilities for the retarded. In R.B. Kugel, & W. Wolfensberger (Eds.), *Changing patterns in residential services for the mentally retarded.* Washington, D.C.: President's Committee on Mental Retardation, 1969.

Dybwad, G. *New patterns of living demand new patterns of service—Is normalization a feasible principle of rehabilitation?* Paper presented at the International Conference on Models of Service for the Multi-Handicapped Adult, New York City, October 10, 1973.

Fernald, W.E. The history of the treatment of the feeble-minded. *Proceedings of the National Conference for Charities and Correction,* 1893, 203-221.

Fram, J. The right to be retarded—normally. *Mental Retardation,* 1974, **12** (6), 32.

Francis, S.H. Behavior of low-grade institutionalized mongoloids: Changes with age. *American Journal of Mental Deficiency,* 1970, **75**, 92-101.

Goldberg, I.I., & Lippman, L. Plato had a word for it. *Exceptional Children,* **40** (5), 1974, 325-334.

Gray, R.M. & Kastler, J.M. The effects of social reinforcement and training on institutionalized mentally retarded children. *American Journal of Mental Deficiency,* 1969, **74**, 50-56.

Gunzburg, H.C. *Social competence and mental handicap: An introduction to social education.* London: Bailbere, Tindall, & Cassell, 1968.

Gunzburg, H.C., & Gunzburg, A.L. Social education and the institution: The shaping of a therapeutic "non-institutional" environment. In *Proceedings of the Second International Congress on the Scientific Study of Mental Retardation,* 1971.

Helsel, E.D. Residential service. In J. Wortis (Ed.), *Mental retardation and developmental disabilities.* Vol. 3. New York: Brunner/Mazel, Inc., 1971.

Hobson v. Hansen, 320 F. Supp. 720 (D.D.C. 1971).

Kanner, L. *A history of the care and study of the mentally retarded.* Springfield, Ill.: Charles C Thomas, 1964.

Kaufman, M.E. The effects of institutionalization on development of stereotyped and social behaviors in mental defectives. *American Journal of Mental Deficiency,* 1966, **71**, 581-585.

Kerlin, J.N. Report of the committee on the care and training of the feeble-minded. *Proceedings of the National Conference for Charities and Correction,* 1888, 99-101.

Kershner, J.R. Intellectual and social development in relation to family functioning: A longitudinal comparison of home vs. institutional effects. *American Journal of Mental Deficiency,* 1970, **75**, 276-284.

King, R.D., & Raynes, N.V. Patterns of institutional care for the severely subnormal. *American Journal of Mental Deficiency,* 1968, **72**, 700-709.

Klaber, M.M., Butterfield, E.C., & Gould, L.J. Responsiveness to social reinforcement among institutionalized retarded children. *American Journal of Mental Deficiency,* 1969, **73**, 890-895.

Kugel, R.B., & Reque, D. A comparison of mongoloid children. *Journal of the American Medical Association,* 1961, **175**, 959-961.

Larry P. v. Riles. Civil Action No. 71-2270 (N.D. Cal. 1971).

Lewis, J.F. The community and the retarded: A study in social ambivalence. In R.K. Eyman, C.E. Meyers, & G. Tarjan (Eds.), *Sociobehavioral studies in mental retardation.* Washington: Monographs of the Association on Mental Deficiency, No. 1, 1973.

Lyle, J.G. The effect of an institutional environment upon the verbal development of imbecile children. I: Verbal intelligence. *Journal of Mental Deficiency Research,* 1959, **3**, 122-128.

Lyle, J.G. The effect of an institutional environment upon the verbal development of imbecile children. II: Speech and language. *Journal of Mental Deficiency Research,* 1960, **4**, 1-13.

MacAndrew, C., & Edgerton, R. The everyday life of the institutionalized "idiots." *Human Organization,* 1964, **23** (4).

Meyen, E.L. (Ed.). *Planning community service for the mentally retarded.* Scranton: International Textbook Company, 1967.

Mitchell, A.C., & Smerglio, V. Growth in social competence in institutionalized mentally retarded children. *American Journal of Mental Deficiency,* 1970, **74** (5), 666-673.

Mittler, P. Planning for the future. *Parent's Voice,* 1974, **24** (2), 15-16.

National Association for Retarded Citizens. *Handbook for residential service committees.* Arlington, Va.: 1974.

National Association for Retarded Citizens. *The right to choose: Achieving residential alternatives in the community.* Arlington, Va.: 1973.

National Association of Superintendents of Public Residential Facilities for the Mentally Retarded. *Contemporary issues in residential programming.* Washington, D.C.: President's Committee on Mental Retardation, 1974.

Nirje, B. A Scandinavian visitor looks at U.S. institutions. In R.B. Kugel, & W. Wolfensberger (Eds.), *Changing patterns in residential services for the mentally retarded.* Washington, D.C.: President's Committee on Mental Retardation, 1969.

Pennsylvania Association of Retarded Citizens v. Commonwealth of Pennsylvania, Civil Action N. 71-42 (E.D. Pa. 1972).

President's Committee on Mental Retardation. *MR68: The edge of change*. Washington, D.C.: Superintendent of Documents, U.S. Government Printing Office, 1968.

President's Committee on Mental Retardation. *MR70: The decisive decade*. Washington, D.C.: Superintendent of Documents, U.S. Government Printing Office, 1970.

Raynes, N.V., Burnstead, D.C., & Pratt, M.W. Unitization: Its effects on residential care practices. *Mental Retardation*, 1974, **12** (4), 12-14.

Rivera, G. *Willowbrook*. New York: Random House, 1972.

Rosen, M., Stallings, L., Floor, L., & Nowakinska, M. Reliability and stability of Wechsler IQ scores for institutionalized mental subnormals. *American Journal of Mental Deficiency*, 1968, **73**, 218-225.

Rowland, G.T., & Patterson, E.G. The developmental institution. *Mental Retardation* 1972, **10** (4), 36-38.

Sackett, R. Editorial page, *Philadelphia Inquirer*, Sunday, May 26, 1974.

Scheerenberger, R.C. A model for deinstitutionalization. *Mental Retardation*, 1974, **12** (6), 3-7.

Shipe, D., & Shotwell, A.M. Effect of out-of-home care on mongoloid children: A continuation study. *American Journal of Mental Deficiency*, 1965, **69**, 649-52.

Shotwell, A.M., & Shipe, D. Effect of out-of-home care on the intellectual and social development of mongoloid children. *American Journal of Mental Deficiency*, 1964, **68**, 693-699.

Skeels, H.M. A study of the effects of differential stimulation on mentally retarded children: A follow-up report. *American Journal of Mental Deficiency*, 1941, **46**, 340-350.

Soeffing, M. Families for the handicapped: Foster and adoptive placement programs. *Exceptional Children*, 1975, **41** (8), 537-543.

Spangler v. Board of Education, 311 F. Supp. 501 (S.D. Cal. 1970).

Stayton, S.E., Sitowski, C.A., Stayton, D.J., & Weiss, S.D. The influence of home experience upon the retardate's social behavior in the institution. *American Journal of Mental Deficiency*, 1968, **72**, 866-870.

Stedman, D.J., & Eichorn, D.H. A comparison of the growth and development of institutionalized and home-reared mongoloids during infancy and early childhood. *American Journal of Mental Deficiency*, 1964, **69**, 391-401.

Sternlicht, M., & Siegel, L. Institutional residence and intellectual functioning. *Journal of Mental Deficiency Research*, 1968, **12**, 119-127.

Stevenson, H.W., & Knight, R.M. The effectiveness of social reinforcement after brief and extended institutionalization. *American Journal of Mental Deficiency*, 1962, **66**, 589-594.

Stewart v. Phillips, Civil Action No. 70-1199F (D. Mass. 1970).

Thurman, S.K., & Thiele, R.L. A viable role for retardation institutions. *Mental Retardation*, 1973, **11** (2), 21-22.

Tizard, J. Residential care of mentally handicapped children. *British Medical Journal*, 1960, **1**, 1041-1046.

Turnbull, H.R., & Turnbull, A.P. Deinstitutionalization and the law. *Mental Retardation*, 1975, **13** (2), 14-20.

Vogel, W., Kun, K.J., & Meshorer, E. Effects of environmental enrichment and environmental deprivation on cognitive functioning in institutionalized retardates. *Journal of Consulting Psychology*, 1967, **31**, 570-576.

Wallin, J.E.W. Training of the severely retarded viewed in historical perspective. *Journal of General Psychology*, 1966, **74**, 107-127.

Weaver, S.J., Balla, D., & Zigler, E. Social approach and avoidance tendencies of institutionalized retarded and noninstitutionalized retarded and normal children. *Journal of Experimental Research in Personality*, 1971, **5**, 98-110.

Wolfensberger, W. The origin and nature of institutions. In R.B. Kugel, & W. Wolfensberger (Eds.), *Changing patterns in residential services for the mentally retarded*. Washington, D.C.: President's Committee on Mental Retardation, 1969.

Wolfensberger, W. Will there always be an institution? II: The impact of new service models. *Mental Retardation*, 1971, **9** (5), 31-38.

Wolfensberger, W. *The principle of normalization in human services*. Toronto: National Institute on Mental Retardation, 1972.

Wolfensberger, W., & Glenn, L. *Program analysis of service systems: A method for the quantitative evaluation of human services*. (Handbook). Toronto: National Institute on Mental Retardation, 1973.

Wyatt v. Stickney, 344 F. Supp. 378 (M.D. Alabama, 1972).

Zigler, E. Social deprivation and rigidity in the performance of feeble-minded children. *Journal of Abnormal & Social Psychology*, 1961, **62**, 413-421.

Zigler, E., Balla, D., & Butterfield, E.C. A longitudinal investigation of the relation between preinstitutional social deprivation and social motivation in institutionalized retardates. *Journal of Personality and Social Psychology*, 1968, **10**, 437-445.

A REVIEW OF CRITICAL ISSUES
UNDERLYING MAINSTREAMING

Charles Meisgeier

University of Houston

AN OVERVIEW

Mainstreaming is both an educational philosophy and a management system. As a concept, it is not new since it was discussed in the 1950s and advocated even before. As a philosophy, it has undergone significant change and growth in the last two decades and, in one form or another, has been endorsed as a desirable long-term goal by many educators. As a management system in public school education, however, the history of mainstreaming is short. One of the earliest attempts at what was called "progressive inclusion" was begun in Bellingham, Washington, in the mid-1950s, but broad-scale implementation in a large public school system began only in 1971.

Mainstreaming advocates the right of all children to acceptance within school programs regardless of how they may deviate from "norms" in appearance, performance, or behavior. As an educational philosophy, mainstreaming promotes acceptance of all children within the flow of school life. This is accomplished by making the school responsible (accountable) for adapting its programs to meet each child's needs rather than requiring the child to adapt to an inflexible school program designed for a hypothetical "average child." Moreover, mainstreaming shifts the emphasis of its special services from a focus on handicapping conditions and problems to a focus on learning needs. Mainstreaming as a management system is a complex array of interacting programs and support services designed to implement the changes necessary to operate a zero-reject model in the public schools.

The issues

The issues related to mainstreaming are very much in the forefront today, at a time when the breakdown of traditional patterns is causing great pressure within the schools, at the same time that social, political, judicial, and legislative activities are bringing great pressure to bear from without. In the past, public

245

schools have reacted to problems by setting up a task force here, a pilot project there, or a special classroom in the back of the building. It is now apparent that systemwide changes are urgently needed. Everywhere new strategies are being tried, new roles are developing, and new delivery systems being implemented. Nearly all of them relate in some way to one or more components of a mainstreaming management system. Why? The answer lies in the interdisciplinary base upon which the mainstreaming concept is built.

A point of convergence

Accommodative procedures such as organization development, systems analysis, aptitude treatment interaction, interaction analysis, educational renewal, cost effectiveness, task analysis, programmed learning, modularized curricula, criterion- and domain-referenced testing, applied behavior analysis, precision teaching procedures, instructional materials and media development, computer-managed instruction, diagnostic teaching, continuous progress learning, individualized instruction, and so on—all find their point of convergence in the educational management system known as mainstreaming. None of these concepts alone can be termed mainstreaming. Merely placing a child into a "regular" class must not be viewed as mainstreaming. Rather, mainstreaming programs must utilize innovative procedures such as those listed above for the successful integration of children with problems into the mainstream.

Traditional mass instructional practices are incompatible with mainstreaming concepts. The degree to which mainstreaming can occur and be successful relates directly to the accommodative ability or accommodative power of the educational environment to respond to all children in all curricular areas.

Mainstreaming has its roots in special education, but the focus of its activities is the renewal of the entire educational system. It demands the development of an adaptive or accommodative system capable of continuous renewal. Because of this, it will be growing in significance in the months and years ahead.

The issues presented and discussed here are not meant to be an exhaustive study of all aspects of mainstreaming management systems. Many books will be written about that in the years ahead. Rather, this chapter presents those issues that seem pertinent now to the development of the mainstreaming movement. A brief look at the historical antecedents of the movement is necessary to understand the current issues.

HISTORICAL ANTECEDENTS

By 1962, Reynolds (1970) had conceptualized a framework for special education in which he outlined a broad range of services that emphasized the large number of children needing services within or close to the regular classroom. A few years later, in February 1967, a landmark conference, sponsored by the U.S. Office of Education was held at the University of Maryland. Educators, psychologists, sociologists, and representatives from a number of related professions met to discuss "Variables and Categories—Exceptional Children." This was a significant conference called to discuss, and critically appraise, the system called "special education." Out of it came a move to direct particular attention to the problems of categorization, the degrading effects of labeling, the fallacies of the placement system, the misuse of the traditional predictive model, and the rejection-oriented service delivery systems for special education.

In his greetings to the conferees, Dean Anderson (1967) quoted from a note by Jean Hebeler, Chairperson of Special Education, indicating that the purpose of the conference was to "attempt to move away from systems of categorizations of kids which have their model in other disciplines and focus on learning and the educational function . . ." (p. 6). The shift of focus from handicapping conditions to a focus on learning set the stage for mainstreaming.

Evelyn Deno (1967), reacting to the major presenters, commented that "we need to be somewhat more certain about what special education is" (p. 184). She asked the assembly a question that frequently continues to be voiced today: "Are we making something special out of something that doesn't need to be special . . .?" (p. 184). Recognizing the need to involve regular educators more effectively in developing programs, Maynard Reynolds (1967) called attention to the increasingly deteriorating dividing points between regular and special education.

Many new directions, particularly the collection of events and activities comprising the trend now identified as "mainstreaming," trace their first national recognition to this conference. Since that time, the rationale and procedures of mainstreaming have become clearer and the technology and strategies for activating the concept have matured considerably.

A growing force

As a measure of the growing interest in mainstreaming, since 1967 articles in the professional journals have steadily increased. In reviewing the literature for this chapter, 121 articles related to mainstreaming concepts were identified in the special education journals from January 1970 to March 1975, contrasted with 23 such articles in the previous 5 years. In the non-special education journals, 35 articles related to mainstreaming were identified for the same period, and only 6 articles were identified for the previous 5 years. An additional 63 publications on mainstreaming have appeared since 1970, contrasted with 42 in the previous 5 years (Maier, 1975).

Those who have been most involved in developing programs in the schools or teacher-training programs for mainstreaming seem to agree that it is more than a fringe movement. Rather it appears to be a steadily growing force with the potential to change the direction of special education. It may also possibly divide the field into separate camps or create a continuing controversy. Reynolds (1973), thoughtfully reflecting on the impact that mainstream-related issues might have on the present systems, stated that "the turbulence of recent days and of those ahead will be too great for absorption in our present system of special education, and new approaches must be structured" (p. 25). Lilly (1971) advanced the same position, calling for new solutions to new problems and for a new way of thinking about exceptional children.

The commitment

In a paper entitled "Special Education as Developmental Capital," written after she studied and reviewed the principal mainstreaming programs in the nation, Deno (1971) discussed the commitment of the movement's advocates and program developers in military language.

> One army of special educators is committed to the point of view that education's mode of address must change drastically from its present forms if the precious uniqueness of each child's humanity is to be cherished. They believe that not only must regular education practice change, but that the program authorizing legislation, training program focus, service delivery systems forms, and even the structures of special education's major professional organizations must change. The viewpoint must switch from the present fix on pathology, which points the accusing finger of cause at the child, to approaches which emphasize the fact that the problem is not in the child, but in the mismatch which exists between the child's needs and the opportunities we make available to nurture his self-realization. These professionals deplore that proliferation of disability categories as a way of making better provision for children's needs. They are sure that the only meaningful category for educational purposes is the individual child. (p. 56)

Deno effectively developed this theme and, in a departure from the more traditional view, proposed that special education

> conceive of itself primarily as an instrument for facilitation of educational change and development of better means of meeting the learning needs of children who are different; and that it organize itself to do that kind of educational services job rather than organize itself as primarily a curriculum and instruction resource for clientele defined as pathologically different by categorized criteria. (p. 56)

In pursuing these points, Deno returned to the controversial question she posed at the Maryland conference several years earlier.

> Does special education need to exist at all as a separate administrative system? Further if it needs to exist now because of conditions that prevailed in education in the past and may still exist at this time, should special education assume it must always exist as a separate service delivery system? (p. 61)

This broad view is also reflected by Reynolds (1973) who, in his review of recent mainstream innovations, pointed out that the educator's commitment should be to all children. He also recognized that countermovements in defense of traditional special education would arise and that naive approaches to educational change that focus only on a single aspect of the program (such as the training of new personnel or a resource room model) will not bring about the fundamental changes required to serve all children. He called for changes that involve a host of educational personnel and programs at the level of schools, universities, and state agencies.

FORCES FOR A NEW SPECIAL EDUCATION

Systems, behavioral analysis, accountability

A common thread running through operational mainstream programs is the emphasis on what might be called (*a*) systems approaches to service delivery, (*b*) application of the principles of applied behavior analysis (which is viewed as compatible with humanistic goals), and (*c*) program accountability. Deno (1973) reported that the programs she studied reflected a common view that mainstreaming must involve more than just the subsystem of special education. "If the goal is broader learning opportunities for handicapped children then it is not enough to tinker just with the special education system" (p. 75). She called for a productive alignment of all elements which affect the educational programs of children.

A number of educators have foreseen the situation that is now evolving. In a section of their book describing administrative structures, Meisgeier and King (1970) forecast that special education in the 1970s would have to respond to new developments with more effective strategies. "Special education, functioning for the most part as a separate or sub-system, increasingly will find the need to become an integrated and essential part of the main system" (p. 122).

Segregation-integration

Although segregation of the retarded in special classes has been widely accepted and practiced, a panel at the 22nd annual meeting of the International Council for Exceptional Children as early as 1945 discussed and criticized segregation practices. They concluded that although some segregation might be necessary, the social isolation and discrimination that were its consequences created serious problems and that educable retardates should be included in the regular school environment as quickly as possible (Hobbs, 1975a).

Since that time the efficacy of special class placement has been discussed and studied again and again. The literature is full of studies, reviews, and analyses—both pro and con. It is difficult, however, to evaluate the impact these studies have had on the development of mainstream programs. While the efficacy studies have had an impact on the development of mainstream programs, much stronger forces have been at work. Court decisions mandating such doctrines as

249

"right to education" in the "least restrictive alternative" environment carry the threat of punitive action and cause school systems to adopt mainstreaming-type programs more rapidly than they would otherwise.

Forces for change

The demise of self-contained special classes and the rise of main-streaming concepts is a complex phenomenon resulting from a series of social, political, psychological, and educational developments. The cumulative, interactive, enabling effect of each of these developments has made it possible for the movement to crystallize and mature at this time.

These forces reflect increasing recognition of the needs, rights, and uniqueness of each child. New legislation and court actions are opening up negotiations with regular education, as a total system, to obtain for each exceptional child a legitimate place in the school program, in the least restrictive manner possible—an appropriate place utilizing appropriate procedures within the natural learning environment (Reynolds, 1974).

Social forces

A major development in the social area affecting attitudes toward the integration of exceptional children into the mainstream of institutional life is related to the intense racial struggle which began in the mid-1950s (Hobbs 1975b). Minority group children have filled special classes, and eventually they drew the attention of civil rights offices and the courts. Sarason (1972) equated the arguments for and against special classes to the separate but equal decisions of the Supreme Court, in which separate facilities were declared unequal and unfair to both the segregated and nonsegregated. Children from impoverished and minority group areas are diagnosed as retarded 15 times more often than are children from more affluent areas, according to findings of the President's Committee on Mental Retardation (1970). In the special class studies reported by Mercer (1975), 67% of the children with stigmatizing labels were viewed as normal by other social systems. Other writers have called attention to the widespread mislabeling that has occurred, particularly with minority groups. In California, Gilhool (1973) reported that classes for the educable retarded contained 27% black and 26% chicano, whereas only 9% of the school population was black and 13% chicano.

The mainstreaming mandate

As a result of such findings Reynolds (1974) has reported that

administrators of our largest cities are under a virtual mandate to reverse the expansion of special education programs and to eliminate the testing, categorizing, and labeling practices which are associated with placement in the programs. (p. 4)

Not all special educators are in agreement, however, with this mandate. One group continues to make a strong argument against the declaration of a moratorium on special class placement, feeling that such a move would be a serious mistake (Heller, 1972).

There is no doubt, however, that the impact of mainstreaming concepts on the schools is being intensified as a result of recent legislation and court litigation (Hobbs, 1975b). Pressure from educators, civil rights advocates, legislators, and the courts is having an impact on regular and special education practices and boundaries. The result is a mandate to educate all children in the least restrictive manner possible—a mandate that speaks not only of "right to education" and zero reject but, perhaps more importantly at this point, of the right to appropriate treatment and due process (Reynolds, 1974; Hobbs, 1975a).

Legal and legislative forces

Injunctions against group testing, modifications of tests for cultural and language subgroups, and the necessity for parental consent have resulted in a series of cases which Gilhool (1973, p. 598) called "right-to-education" cases: e.g., Diana v. State Board of Education (1970) Larry P. V. Riles, 343 F. Supp. (1972); Ruiz v. State Board of Education (1971).

In the case of Wyatt v. Stickney, Judge Johnson ruled that persons receiving treatment by the state had certain rights. Going significantly beyond the right-to-education cases, his ruling declared that it is not sufficient to place a person in a special program or facility; rather, each person must be appropriately treated in a humane physical and psychological environment. The U.S. Supreme Court subsequently affirmed this concept. This case emphasized the rights of persons to an appropriate individualized program, including treatment, habilitation, and education, with periodic review and evaluation. It also established the concept of programming in the least restrictive setting (Gilhool, 1973, p. 597) or, to put it positively, programming in the most advantageous setting (Schwartz, 1975).

Decisions by the courts on the right to education, the right to appropriate treatment, and the right to due process are securing for the exceptional person rights and programs that educators have been either unwilling or unable to provide. These actions are providing a strong base and legal sanction upon which mainstreaming programs can be built. In retrospect it is inevitable that the exceptional child would eventually have utilized the courts to achieve social change and justice in what has become a long tradition in our nation. Other minority groups have effectively demonstrated the efficacy of such approaches (Gilhool, 1973).

Gilhool felt that the common element of this and related movements appears to be the experience of being declared inferior because of age (child/senior), income, handicap, race, language, or sex. The consequences of such judgment are of course enormous. Individuals in these groups become nonpersons. They do not have to be heard, and official behavior has long been characterized by actions which are unresponsive to the needs of these groups.

The result is discrimination and the tendency to separate certain individuals and groups. What is probably worse is that the person on the wrong end of the judgment begins to believe that he *is* the way he is being treated, that indeed he is inferior. In the face of authority, he has generally failed to assert his rights (Gilhool, 1973). This, however, is changing!

The reader is directed to a monumental study on the classification of exceptional children by Nicholas Hobbs and 93 contributors. The report, sponsored by 10 federal agencies, is presented in three volumes. The first, *The Futures of Children* is a systematic summary by Hobbs of the recommendations of 31 task forces. *Issues in the Classification of Children,* Volume I, explores theoretical issues and the classifications systems. Volume II explores issues related to institutions, special perspectives, legal aspects, and public policy questions.

Parent pressures

During the 1950s organized parent groups created intense pressure on schools and institutions to develop more services for exceptional children. In concert with interested professions, they used their political power to bring about the kind of programming they thought was needed. More recently these organizations have turned to the courts to achieve their demands for inclusion of their children in a wide array of programs, for program improvement, for involvement in the decision-making process, and for responsiveness to the expressed needs of the families of handicapped children. Minority group members whose children are quite affected by special class procedures are also a part of this movement and are demanding programs that do not resort to negative labeling and isolation (Reynolds, 1974).

The reluctant victim

As in other movements that emphasize the rights of the individual, the forces for such change may be stronger outside the field than within. The case might be made that special education is following as a reluctant victim of these forces rather than providing the leadership to reshape its goals and programs. It appears that much of the support for mainstreaming has evolved from the concerns of the general society, reflected by actions and interpretations of judges and lawmakers. The new heroes of special education appear to be lawyers, judges, and legislators, rather than the educators. (Blatt, 1972).

Individualism

Reynolds (1974) summarized many of these developments in a concept he called *individualism,* a term he used synonymously with mainstreaming. In this regard, Reynolds believed that mainstreaming encompasses far more than special education in the schools. His concept of individualism encompasses serving children in their natural environment, whether that be home, school, or community. Reynolds put it another way in his statement that "fundamentally the movement reflects the democratic philosophy that equal access to societal institutions and resources is the right of all individuals, however different from the majority they may be" (p. 1).

Mainstreaming is not a retrenching or a resurrection of worn out procedures but, as Reynolds emphasized, is the result of a "trend toward the progressive inclusion of handicapped persons in all our community and educational institutions" (p. 4).

BASIC CHANGES IN ASSUMPTIONS UNDERLYING SPECIAL EDUCATION

Prediction and capacity

At a 1974 conference in Chicago before a large group of professionals developing mainstream programs, Reynolds presented a thought-provoking view of the current status of the historic predictive model. He saw a decline in its use and viewed its demise as still another enabling force for mainstreaming. Over the years, according to Reynolds (1974), the linkage of simple prediction and capacity came to be taken for granted. The predictors in the academic area were usually general intelligence tests which, early in the movement, resulted in individualized grading systems. It then became a matter of "fairness" to expect that some children would achieve more and some less and that this should be reflected on their report cards. Reynolds described the special attention given to children with so-called high capacity and low achievement, indicating that millions have been spent to support the erroneous assumption that discrepancies between mental age and achievement indicate aptitude for greater performance.

Although the discrepancies between capacity and achievement have not been carefully studied, they are, according to Reynolds, continually used to draw a distinction between a learning disability and mental retardation. If a child had high capacity but low achievement, the assumption was made that he was different from the child with a uniformly low, flat profile.

A subtle form of discrepancies analysis, using profile interpretations, involves the assumption that the general level of a profile yields some kind of capacity or "expectancy" level, and that departures from the flat median line represent needs and potentialities for remediation. By some mystical process, the average of several scores becomes the "expected" level on each variable, and presumably flat profiles are preferred over irregular ones. This form of discrepancy analysis will stand up to rigorous examination no better than simpler approaches using general intelligence as the standard. (Reynolds, 1974, p. 17)

Looking at the positive side, Reynolds felt that conceptual viewpoints emphasizing environmental variables, such as those proposed by Bijou (1963) and others, would gain more acceptance. For example, Bijou purported that "a retarded individual is one who has a limited repertory of behavior evolving from interactions with his environment and contacts which constitute his history" (p. 99). Reynolds stated that concepts which stress general capacity (such as IQ) appear to be superfluous within this type of framework. For Reynolds (1974), such classifications as retarded, learning disabled, remedial, etc. which are built upon capacity estimates and discrepancy systems are tenuous and much less fixed than they appeared in earlier years.

The diagnostic prescriptive model

Another change in the basic assumptions underlying special education relates to the controversy between those who advocate a diagnostic/prescriptive model that emphasizes a task analysis-type of approach and those who advocate an ability training model. The relationship of this issue to mainstreaming is significant. The ability-training model tends to imply that the problem is within the child, thus requiring diagnostic procedures to label and identify the child for formal training. The task analysis approach tends to make no "within-child" inference, but rather focuses on analyzing the learning task and environment rather than the child.

The efficacy studies

In a series of studies since the 1950s the adjustment of exceptional children, more specifically the educable retarded, has been examined and reexamined. Lilly (1970) suggested that these studies are inconclusive and will probably always remain so. It is difficult to apply the results of these so-called efficacy studies to the mainstreaming movement. Much time has elapsed and many changes have taken place. These studies measured a form of integration that occurred without adaptation of the mainstream. It cannot be doubted that this series of studies casts doubt on the value of special classes, and thus gave some impetus to the search for an alternative model. Still, the extent of that impact and the actual relationship of most of these studies to mainstreaming is somewhat clouded. While they did examine subcomponents in isolation from larger systems, most of these studies did not deal with the complex variables involved in most mainstreaming programs. Guerin and Szatlocky (1974) emphasized that the efficacy studies have focused on special vs. regular class placement but that "virtually none have examined the various ways of educating the retarded child with his non-retarded classmates" (p. 173).

It is helpful to examine this issue in light of a concept presented by Cronbach (1975). He called attention to the important effects of time in his statment that ". . . the explanations we live by will perhaps always remain partial, and distant from real events, and rather short lived." He continued, commenting that, "if the effect of a treatment changes over a few decades, that inconsistency is, in effect, a Treatment x Decade Interaction that must be regulated by whatever laws there be. Such interactions frustrate any would-be theorist who mixes data from several decades indiscriminately into the phenomenal picture he tries to explain" (pp. 122-123).

Thus time and change must be considered in dealing with the problem of relating the significance of the efficacy studies to the current trend known as mainstreaming. Within the context of a systems definition presented elsewhere, it must be concluded that *mainstreaming as it is defined herein has not existed in the past*. Therefore, the efficacy data previously collected cannot be viewed as definitive studies of the variables associated with mainstreaming, since most were completed in decades prior to the present and by no stretch of the imagination could the programs they describe meet the requirements of current mainstreaming definitions. In our review of the efficacy studies of regular or special class placement, for example, only a small percentage could be found to meet the test of current mainstreaming definitions: (*a*) individualization of programs for all children, (*b*) appropriate teacher training (both regular and special) to implement individualized management systems, (*c*) applications of the principles of applied behavior analysis, (*d*) appropriate support systems, (*e*) total systems analysis, and (*f*) change where needed. Thus, the earlier efficacy studies regarding achievement, motivation, self-concept, teacher attitude, peer acceptance, IQ variations, labeling effects, learning models, vocational and personal adjustment, teaching methods, parental attitudes must remain of indirect and historical interest. As such, they will not be used in this review to develop a rationale for, or a measure of, the efficacy of mainstreaming efforts in the last quarter of this century.

Changing and eroding boundaries

Returning to Cronbach for a moment, we note that the generalizations that the special education field has generated in the past obviously held true within specific limiting boundaries, in specific contexts, and at specified times. But the question remains, Can these boundaries hold for the future? Do the boundaries of the 1950s and 1960s still exist? It appears, in fact, that the old boundaries are not holding (Reynolds, 1974; Meisgeier, 1975).

The old boundaries of regular, special, vocational, and technical education—and the boundaries of community agencies and state institutions—are rapidly being renegotiated and realigned. Major changes are taking place within and without those realigned boundaries that appear to be resulting in a transition through a mainstreaming vehicle to a "new special education." This point was broached by Lilly (1970) in his new definition that stresses exceptional situations rather than exceptional students. He suggested that if his definition were adopted, it would not only require new priorities for research, training, and school practices but "most likely, it would signal the end of special education as we have known it" (p. 48).

IN SEARCH OF A MAINSTREAMING DEFINITION

An integrated systems plan for educational renewal

In developing his rationale for what was probably the most massive mainstreaming effort in the nation, Meisgeier (1973, 1974b, 1974c) was heavily influenced by the concepts of organization behavior, organization development, systems analysis and design, and applied behavior analysis. Using Sarason's (1972) concepts of programmatic and behavioral regularities, he described special education as a sub- or parallel system that developed as an alternative response to the inflexibility and unresponsiveness of the mainstream to the needs of exceptional children.

> In the past, organizations have developed sub- or parallel systems to deal with children and programs that did not fit into either the behavioral or programmatic regularities of the system. For example, one of the major effects of large-scale testing programs has been to identify behavioral irregularities, remove them from the main system, partially or totally, and place the burden of resolving the irregularities either upon the children, parents, or staff of the sub- or parallel system. Little or no adaptation or modification was made in the main system. In fact, the effect of these mechanisms was to reinforce the behavioral and programmatic regularities of the main system. (Meisgeier, 1973, p. 136)

Meisgeier's approach emphasizes analysis and deliberate modification of the programmatic or fundamental regularities (which explicitly or implicitly describe intended behavioral outcomes), resulting in either new behavioral regularities or the changing of old ones. He suggests that mainstreaming programs must acknowledge the existence of a universe of alternatives to existing programmatic regularities in all of education (the mainstream) rather than focus on change of outcomes, themselves the result of more basic programmatic decisions. Until mainstreaming evolved, special and regular education responded to problems by attempting to change behavioral regularities so as to avoid coming to grips with the rigidity and pathology within the basic system. This approach to problem solving may temporarily relieve the surface tensions, he asserts, but the unresolved basic program issues may, in fact, be causing more serious and unnecessary problems in the schools.

Meisgeier's (1974b, 1974c) systems definition emphasizes the need for education to become "an adaptive system that is responsive and relevant to the needs of all children.. . ." The focus of change should be on the basic program regularities of the main system, rather than on third- or fourth-level behavioral regularities which are functions of more basic program decisions. His solution is an "integrated system plan" that demands adaptation of all main and supporting systems. Since mainstreaming of special education pupils will never be possible without concomitant changes in related systems, "the burden for adaptation, which previously had rested unproportionately upon the child, now shifts to the system. The child is responsible only as one aspect of the environment comprising the system" (Meisgeier, 1973, p. 137). His premise requires major change and modification of the mainstream, plus a support system that provides leadership, expertise, and mechanisms to bring about or create a new mainstream in keeping with appropriate instructional strategies and emerging organizational practices. The definition demands a special education for children with learning, behavior, and physical-sensory problems in the regular environment, regardless of etiology without resorting to elaborate classification and limiting or categorizing schemes.

Other definitions

In a recent survey by Meisgeier and Newberger (1975) of state departments of education, confusion about mainstreaming was often voiced in questions posed by the respondents. "What is 'mainstreaming' anyway? We have always mainstreamed!" In view of the previous discussion and the following definitions, these questions might have more accurately stated, "We have tried in the past to put children into regular programs, but we have not tried to change the regular environment, and we have not changed the support system or methodology of special education and, as a result, we have failed in these efforts." Special education historically has had little meaningful interaction with the mainstream, and the barriers which have been erected between regular and special education had become almost impenetrable—until recently.

While citing a number of concerns about mainstreaming, Hobbs (1975a) stressed the need for individualized instructional programs for all children, special support staffing, and carefully articulated programs. He further emphasized the need for support and training in the implementation of these programs for regular teachers.

Birch (1974), reporting on a survey of state directors of special education, provided a descriptive definition of mainstreaming that suggests the following:

1. Assignment of handicapped pupils to regular classes, with the child reporting to the regular teacher at any level, preschool through secondary

2. The necessity for adaptation of regular class procedures and content

3. Assignment of handicapped in regular programs for half or more of the school day

4. A special education support system that provides space for the special education teacher and includes special teachers as team members in open-spaced schools

5. Involvement of regular and special teachers cooperatively in developing schedules, assignments, grades, etc.

6. Special teachers to help regular teachers through educational assessments and instructional consultation for ineligible pupils

7. Removal of children for special services only for short periods when absolutely necessary

8. Identification of children based on educational need—rather than categories or severity of problem—and development of mainstream capability to meet this need.

The Texas Education Agency (1972), a pioneer in mainstreaming concepts, describes its new Plan A as an acceptance of the challenge to provide educational opportunity for every child. The plan emphasizes educational experience related to the *needs* of children and precludes isolation of children from their peers and from the real experiences of the adult world of their future.

While the new Texas Plan A delivery system is based on 17 recommendations of a blue-ribbon study force, it highlights the 3 most significant, which can also be identified as essential elements of other definitions:

1. Discontinuance of labeling and categorization of children

2. Emphasis on the educational needs of the child, not on the handicapping condition

3. Emphasis on modification of mainstream programs or facilities rather than on self-contained isolation.

Summary of major definitions

A summary of the major mainstream definitions emphasizes several main components, the common thread being the emphasis on changing all the relevant systems involved.

1. Modification of mainstream delivery systems, curriculum management systems, instructional strategies, professional roles, and other environmental variables

2. Appropriate preservice and re-education programs for mainstream teachers, managers, supervisors, and other staff

3. Modification of special education delivery systems, curriculum management systems, instructional strategies, professional roles, and other environmental variables

4. Appropriate preservice and re-education programs for special education teachers, managers, supervisors, and other staff

5. Change and modification of related support and parallel systems

6. A change to a teacher training-consultation model for special education, supervising, and psychological staff with deemphasis of elaborate, irrelevant, categorically oriented diagnostic procedures and systems

7. An emphasis on continuous progress, success oriented programs for all children

8. Precision programming and daily accountability for basic program and support system interventions

9. Pro-active programming that is responsive to educational needs of all students, as opposed to programming for economic, political, or managerial convenience.

MAINSTREAMING COMPONENTS

Resource rooms

The principal difference between "mainstreaming" and efforts toward mainstreaming appears to be the degree to which a particular program or effort attempts, on the one hand, to develop its special resources for the exceptional child outside the regular classroom or, on the other hand, assists with alteration of the regular class environment. The resource approach generally removes children from the regular class for intervention during the school day, but it does not usually include *significant* support for and major involvement of the regular teacher in program planning and modifications for the child during the rest of the day. Therefore, the resource room approach alone can hardly be called mainstreaming according to previous definitions. Special education may make many significant changes within its own boundaries, including establishment of resource rooms for children who remain in regular classes, but this alone cannot be called mainstreaming (Meisgeier, 1975).

As with the efficacy studies, it is extremely difficult to evaluate the data being generated about resource rooms in terms of the efficacy of mainstreaming in general. There are many varieties of resource rooms—some are successful, some are not. If our expectation is that 1-hour daily sessions in resource rooms will magically or pervasively eliminate children's learning problems without concomitant efforts to teach children in a healthy learning environment the other 4 hours of each day, we are surely going to be disappointed. *The process must be a cooperative effort between regular, alternative, and special education to be called a mainstreaming effort.*

Because very few of the studies of resource rooms include such a comprehensive, cooperative approach to the problem, they neither support nor detract from mainstreaming concepts. Until all the components of mainstreaming programs are assembled it is difficult to evaluate the effects of individual resource programs to either validate or disprove the efficacy of mainstreaming.

Advantage of the resource room

Apart from the question of whether a resource room serving children from regular classes constitutes mainstreaming, the resource room alternative offers the advantages of program flexibility and closer teacher interaction (Reger,1973). Labeling can be reduced or eliminated, segregation can be avoided, and children can receive immediate services through a noncategorical resource approach (Hammill, 1972).

Adelman (1972) emphasized the importance of looking at the resource room not only as an alternative learning environment, but as an aid for regular education with the aim of reducing the number of children requiring more specialized instruction. He suggested the primary function of the resource teacher should be to help regular teachers deal more adequately with individual pupil needs. Although this is often voiced as a goal, most resource programs have had little impact on mainstream practices. Snapp (1972) also emphasized the need to involve specialist personnel in helping regular teachers individualize their program.

For a summary of the issues relating to the resource room approach, the reader is directed to an interesting discussion in a symposium, presented by the *Journal of Special Education,* by Sabatino (1972a) and responses by Hammill (1972), Heller (1972), Reger (1972)' Snapp (1972), Adelman (1972), Ohrtman (1972), and a rebuttal by Sabatino (1972b). While differing on specific issues, these authors seemed to agree that the resource room approach is good but that something more is required. They suggested that the resource room should be part of a continuum of alternative services that includes interaction with mainstream education in more innovative and constructive ways.

The following reports or studies are incorporated here to list descriptions of several types of resource programs. Practically all groups of handicapped children have participated in such programs. Resource rooms for the various categories are described in the articles listed below.

1. *General resource room model:* Reger (1973)

2. *Educable mentally retarded:* Hanula Resource Center, Gardner (1971); Barksdale and Atkinson (1973); integrated resource model, Miley (1973); efficacy, Walker (1974)

3. *Behavior problems:* experimental program, Glavin, Quay, Annesley and Werry (1971); academic achievement, Quay, Glavin, Annesley, and Werry (1972); follow-up research, Glavin (1973)

4. *Combination programs:* Wilcox Student Resource Activity Center, Kirby (1973); Harrison Resource Learning Model, Bruininks (1973); child oriented resource program, Reger and Koppmann (1971)

5. *Hearing impaired:* county school resource room, Bowman (1973); units for deaf children, Dale (1966)

6. *Visually impaired:* integrated resource room, O'Brien (1973)

Programs integrating various categories of handicapped children into regular classes are described by the following:

1. *Learning disabled:* Griffiths, Gillen, and Dankel (1972)
2. *Mentally retarded:* Guerin and Szatlocky (1974)
3. *Hearing impaired:* Better and Mears (1973); Fisher (1971); Garrett and Stovall (1972), Northcott (1971), Sugrue (1967)
4. *Resource teachers:* Stearns and Swenson (1973)

Resource rooms plus

What are some of the program components that need to be added to a resource room for the full implementation of mainstreaming? In addition to resource rooms, mainstreaming models usually include components designed to help the regular class teacher provide a more responsive and advantageous program for special students during the entire school day. Each model may develop slightly different kinds of resource persons to work with regular teachers. A brief overview follows of representative supporting program components as reported in the literature.

Consulting teacher model

Christie, McKenzie, and Burdett (1972) reported on a consulting teacher program that focuses on training and assistance to the regular class teacher. The program emphasizes training in procedures for individualizing instruction, adaptation of materials, and the techniques of applied behavior analysis.

McKenzie (1972), arguing for increasing the responsibilities and skills of regular teachers, felt that removing children from the regular class does not give teachers an opportunity to learn new needed skills. He further suggested that it reinforces the idea that the only way difficult children can receive adequate instruction is by removal from the class.

Perelman and Fox (1974) indicated that the consultant teacher should not remove the child from the regular class but should concentrate on the measurement of entry level skills, specifying objectives, the development of teaching-learning procedures in a behavioral analysis framework, and evaluation. Training for regular teachers is to be provided through consultation, workshops, and more formal course-work.

Clinical teacher model

Schwartz and his associates (1972, 1974) developed the clinical teacher model for the preparation of ''generic'' teachers for learning resource centers to identify levels and objectives, develop an individualized program, and to provide performance feedback. The clinical teachers focus on desired academic and social behaviors rather than on medical or psychological categories. The clinical teacher has the skills to work with the educable retarded, learning disabled, and emotionally disturbed in a noncategorical setting.

Diagnostic prescriptive teacher model

Prouty and others (1970, 1973) described a preparation program for a diagnostic/prescriptive teacher (DPT). While recognizing that a few children with multiple or severe problems may need special class placement, this program focuses on accommodation in or modification of the regular class environment. The program emphasizes that both the regular and the specialist teacher share responsibility for developing the child's programs. The operational model follows a process of referral, observations by the DPT, a referral conference, diagnostic teaching, educational prescription, prescription conference, demonstration short-term follow-up, evaluation and long-term follow-up. Although the 10 steps of the model do provide a framework to assist and support the regular class teacher, final responsibility for the child's program remains with that teacher.

The stratistician model

The stratistician model, developed at the Rocky Mountain Regional Resource Center, is reported by Buffmire (1973). The model involves behavior modeling, class screening, observation, planning, program evaluation, diagnosis, instructional and interaction skills, evaluation of interventions, and data collecting. It acts as an intermediary for resource-room and regular-room activities.

Madison School model

The Madison School plan reported by Taylor and Soloway (1973) discards traditional labels and views about IQ scores, sensory motor ability, and social functioning. The plan includes a systematic process for compulsory reintegration of children and establishes four general levels of competence: preacademic, academic, setting, and reward competence. A framework determines the readiness of the child to function in a regular classroom. A learning center provides three transitional settings: preacademic I, preacademic II, and academic I.

The Santa Monica school district, which uses the Madison School plan, destroys all special classroom rosters in June, and the children are placed in regular classes the following fall. School district data indicate that one-third of the EMR and EH children are not referred for placement again from the regular classes.

Fail-save model

VanEtten and Adamson (1973) described the fail-save program, built upon the model of the methods and materials consultant teacher who functions in the areas of diagnosis and pinpointing, development of an instructional prescription, parent training, and program monitoring. The fail-save model limits the amount of time a child spends in any of five phases:

1. Consultation (involving referral, observation and diagnosis)
2. Resource room, regular class (diagnosis of the child's basic learning process)
3. Resource room placement
4. Special class placement
5. Alternative program placement

Learning problem model

Mann and McClung (1973) describe their program to train regular teachers in learning disabilities through a common core of competencies and a diagnostic teaching approach. Using task analysis, teachers delineate critical skills in reading, writing, spelling, and arithmetic, while identifying deficits that prevent success with specific tasks.

The Houston plan

The Houston plan—an integrated system plan for education—as described by Meisgeier (1974b) has an underlying philosophy that all education should be special education. The plan emphasizes

1. Integration of special and regular education programs
2. Continuous progress learning systems
3. Specialist and materials support for regular teachers
4. A consultative model for diagnostic, resource, and other specialized services
5. Prevention strategies in the formative years
6. A continuum of services

During the 3 years the program was in operation, the new model increased the number of children served from 10,500 to over 21,000 with limited additional personnel. Precision learning centers (PLCs) were established in 135 schools and used diagnostic precision teachers and learning facilitators. The model calls for a student resources committee responsible for the educational plan developed for each child. The PLC was set up as a model for individualized instruction, team teaching, behavioral management techniques, educational planning, materials adaptation, and daily precise measurement of progress in a success-oriented environment. A PLC served 30 to 40 children per facilitator.

During the 3-year period, over 2,300 regular classroom teachers and other personnel completed a core training program that emphasized the skills and strategies necessary to maintain handicapped children in regular classrooms. A support team, operating in a consultation/training model, provided continuous training for the special education personnel in six Learning Resource Centers.

Prescriptive education model

The Prescriptive Education Program (PREP) of the Portland Public Schools is described by Frankel (1974) as a multidisciplinary effort to provide services to children with learning and behavioral difficulties. With the child's teacher as the central member, a team of diagnostic teachers, reading specialists, psychological examiners, and others work together to assess needs, formulate objectives, plan interventions, develop appropriate instructional and management techniques, put plans into operation, and assess progress. Emphasis is on prevention of and amelioration of problems in the early stages.

New skills, strategies, and delivery systems

The foregoing review of new concepts and emerging profeseional roles confirms that development and renewal are apparent in all areas of special education. Underway everywhere are: studies of the learning process itself; development of sequential learning objectives in all curriculum areas; emerging roles such as that of clinical teacher, stratisticians, diagnostic/prescriptive teachers, and learning facilitators; programs for the application of behavior modification techniques and the development of instructional materials. Mainstreaming is one system that makes education adaptive enough to incorporate such diverse activities into the operation of schools.

SUMMARY

A natural consequence of referring problems from the main system into a professional jurisdiction, or subsystem, is to reinforce the unyielding nature of the rigid main system. This has certainly been demonstrated in the past 20 years by the growth of special education. As evaluation procedures become more discriminating, it is easy to fantasize, perhaps tongue in cheek, that an increased percentage of youngsters will probably be identified as deviating from ''normal'' learning patterns so as to require an individualized learning program. Will giftedness tend to be viewed as an educational challenge to schools, one which requires unique programs? In time, is it possible that there could be more children ejected than will remain in the regular classroom? Will the logical conclusion then be that the subsystem grows and grows until it becomes the mainstream of school experience? Will what is now the mainstream become a subsystem of unexceptional children? Should this occur, the mainstreaming techniques now being implemented as special education will become the mainstream by default.

One fact is not conjecture. The courts, the Congress, and the state legislatures (along with all the psychological, educational, social, and political forces previously discussed) are converging in their efforts to bring about a nondiscriminatory, humane, individualized, and appropriate educational program for each child, focused on his unique needs or problems. Thus, special education would seem to have been appointed by circumstances to become the adaptive agent within the more rigid system of public education.

Mainstreaming is not only a new method or a reorganizational scheme. It cannot be described as only an effort to eliminate labels, replace special classes with resource rooms, or a movement to return the retarded to regular classes. To believe mainstreaming is a fad or a cylical return to some previously tried and failed procedure is to misunderstand its pervasive implications for reform, its historical antecedents, and the massive societal forces that are bringing it about. Whatever the future holds for education as a whole, it is becoming apparent now that mainstreaming may be the major interim step toward a new special education—a transition toward new roles, clients, strategies, training, and service delivery systems for the special education programs of the future.

References

Adamson, G., & VanEtten, G. Zero reject model revisited: A workable alternative. *Exceptional Children,* 1972, **38**, 735-738.

Adelman, H.S. The resource concept: Bigger than a room. *Journal of Special Education,* 1972, **6**, 361-367.

Anderson, R.C. In *Maryland special study institute* (stenographic transcript). Washington, D.C.: Ace-Federal Reporters, 1967.

Barksdale, M.W., & Atkinson, A.P. A resource room approach to instruction for the educable mentally retarded. In *Principal's training program, a book of readings.* Austin, Texas: Region XIII, Education Service Center, 1973.

Better, G.B., & Mears, E.G. Facilitating the integration of hearing impaired children into regular public school classes. *Volta Review,* 1973, **75**, 13-22.

Bijou, S.W. Theory and research in mental retardation. *Psychological Record,* 1963, **13**, 99.

Birch, J.W. *Mainstreaming.* Reston, Va.: Council for Exceptional Children, 1974.

Blanton, R.L. Historical prespectives on classification of mental retardation. In N. Hobbs (Ed.), *Issues in the classification of children.* Vol. 1. San Francisco: Jossey-Bass, 1975.

Blatt, B. The legal rights of the mentally retarded. *Syracuse Law Review,* 1972, **991**, 991-994.

Bowman, E. A resource room program for hearing impaired students. *Volta Review,* 1973, **75**, 208-213.

Bruininks, R.H. Problems and needs in developing alternatives to special classes for mildly retarded children. In *Principal's training program, a book of readings.* Austin, Texas: Region XIII, Education Service Center, 1973.

Buffmire, J.A. The stratistician model. In E. Deno (Ed.), *Instructional alternatives for exceptional children.* Reston, Va.: Council for Exceptional Children, 1973.

Christie, L.S., McKenzie, H.S., & Burdett, C.S. The consulting teacher approach to special education: Inservice training for regular classroom teachers. *Focus on Exceptional Children,* 1972, **4**, 1-10.

Christoplos, F. Keeping exceptional children in regular class. *Exceptional Children,* 1973, **39**, 569-572.

Comprehensive special education in Texas: An overview of a dynamic new education program termed "Plan A.". Austin, Texas: Texas Education Agency, 1972.

Croft, J.C. A look at the future for a hearing impaired child of today. *Volta Review,* 1974, **76**, 115-122.

Cronbach, L.J. Beyond the two disciplines of scientific psychology. *American Psychologist,* 1975, **10**, 116-127.

Dale, D.M. Units for deaf children. *Volta Review,* 1966, **68**, 496-499.

Deno, E.N. In *Maryland special study institute* (stenographic transcript). Washington, D.C.: Ace-Federal Reporters, 1967.

Deno, E.N. Special education as developmental capitol. *Exceptional Children,* 1971, **37**, 229-237.

Deno, E.N. Where do we go from here? In E. Deno (Ed.), *Instructional alternatives for exceptional children.* Reston, Va.: Council for Exceptional Children, 1973.

Fisher, B. Hearing impaired children in ordinary schools. *The Teacher of the Deaf,* 1971, 161-174.

Fox, W.L., Egner, A.N., Pavlucci, P.E., Perelman, P.F., & McKenzie, H.S. An introduction to a regular classroom approach to special education. In E. Deno (Ed.), *Instructional alternatives for exceptional children.* Reston, Va.: Council for Exceptional Children, 1973.

Frankel, H.M. Portland public schools' prescriptive education program. In P.H. Mann (Ed.), *Mainstream special education: Issues and perspectives in urban centers.* Reston, Va.: Council for Exceptional Children, 1974.

Fuller, J.W., Jr., Robinson, C.C., Smith, R.A., Vincent-Smith, L.J., Bricher, D.D., & Bricher, W.A. Mental Retardation. In N. Hobbs (Ed.), *Issues in the classification of children.* Vol. 1. San Francisco: Jossey-Bass, 1975.

Gardner, O.S. Out of the classroom: The birth and infancy of the resource center at Hanula. *Exceptional Children,* 1971, **38**, 53-58.

Garrett, C., & Stovall, E.M. A parent's view on integration. *Volta Review,* 1972, **74**, 338-344.

Gilhool, K. Education: an inalienable right. *Exceptional Children,* 1973, **39**, 597-609.

Glass, R.M., & Meckler, R.A. Preparing elementary teachers to instruct mildly handicapped children in regular classrooms: a summer workshop. *Exceptional Children,* 1972, **39**, 152-156.

Glavin, J.P. Followup behavioral research in resource rooms. *Exceptional Children,* 1973, **40**, 211-213.

Glavin, J.P., Quay, H.C., Annesley, F.R., & Werry, J.S. An experimental resource room for behavior problem children. *Exceptional Children,* 1971, **38**, 131-137.

Griffiths, A.N., Gillen, J.F., & Dankel, R. Leave dyslexics in the classroom. *Academic Therapy Quarterly,* 1972, **8**, 57-65.

Guerin, G.R., & Szatlocky, K. Integration programs for the midly retarded. *Exceptional Children,* 1974, **40**, 173-179.

Hall, R.V., & Copeland, R.E. The responsive teaching model: A first step in shaping school personnel as behavior modification specialists. In F.W. Clark, D.R. Evans, & L.A. Hamerlynch (Eds.), *Implementing behavioral programs for schools and clinics.* Champaign, Ill.: Research Press, 1972.

Hammill, D. The resource room model in special education. *Journal of Special Education,* 1972, **6**, 349-354.

Hammill, D.D., & Larsen, S.C. The effectiveness of psycholinguisitic training. *Exceptional Children,* 1974, **41**, 5-14.

Heller, A.W. The resource room: Mere change or real opportunity for the handicapped? *Journal of Special Education,* 1972, **6**, 369-375.

Hobbs, N. *The futures of children.* San Francisco: Jossey-Bass, 1975. (a)

Hobbs, N. (Gen. Ed.) *Issues in the classification of children.* Vol. 1. San Francisco: Jossey- Bass, 1975. (b)

Hobbs, N. (Gen. Ed.). *Issues in the classification of children.* Vol. 2. San Francisco: Jossey-Bass, 1975. (c)

Iano, R.P. Shall we disband special classes? *Journal of Special Education,* 1972, **6**, 167-177.

Kirby, D.F. A plan to abolish the "special class." *The Pointer,* 1973, **75**, 120-125.

Lilly, M.S. Special education: A teapot in a tempest. *Exceptional Children,* 1970, **37**, 43-49.

Lilly, M.S. A training-based model for special education. *Exceptional Children,* 1971, **37**, 745-749.

Maier, K. Five-year comparison of mainstreaming publications. Working paper. University of Houston, 1975.

Mann, L., & Phillips, W.A. Fractional practices in special education: A critique. *Exceptional Children,* 1967, **33**, 311-315.

Mann, P.H., & McClung, R.M. A learning problems approach to teacher education. In E. Deno (Ed.), *Instructional alternatives for exceptional children.* Reston, Va.: Council for Exceptional Children, 1973.

Mann, P.H. (Ed.). *Mainstream special education: Issues and perspectives in urban centers.* Reston, Va.: Council for Exceptional Children, 1974.

McKenzie, H.S., Egner, A.N., Knight, M.F., Perelman, P.F., Schneider, B.M., & Garvin, J.S. Training consulting teachers to assist elementary teachers in the management and education of handicapped children. *Exceptional Children,* 1970, **36**, 137-143.

McKenzie, H.S. Special education and consulting teachers. In F.W. Clark, D.R. Evans & L.A. Hamerlynk (Eds.), *Implementing behavioral programs for schools and clinics.* Champaign, Ill.: Research Press, 1972.

Meisgeier, C.H., & King, J.D. *The process of special education administration.* Scranton, Pa.: Intext, 1970.

Meisgeier, C. The training needs of regular educators. In P.H. Mann (Ed.), *Mainstream special education: Issues and perspectives in urban centers*. Reston, Va.: Council for Exceptional Children, 1973.

Meisgeier, C. Alternative delivery systems for special educational services. In G. Ragland & J. Hughes, *Proceedings of the Special Study Institute on the Right to Education Mandate*. Chapel Hill: University of North Carolina, 1974. (a)

Meisgeier, C. The Houston plan—retraining of regular classroom teachers to work with handicapped children within the regular classroom setting. In P.H. Mann (Ed.), *Mainstream special education: Issues and prespectives in urban centers*. Reston, Va.: Council for Exceptional Children, 1974. (b)

Meisgeier, C. *Mainstream education*. Address presented at the annual meeting of the Mississippi Association for Children with Learning Disabilities, Biloxi, February 1974. (c)

Meisgeier, C., & Newberger, D. State department mainstreaming survey. Working paper, University of Houston, 1975.

Mercer, J. Psychological assessment and the rights of children. In N. Hobbs (Ed.), *Issues in the classification of children*. Vol. 1. San Francisco: Jossey-Bass, 1975.

Miley, B. An integrated resource model. *The Pointer*, 1973, **18**, 149-151.

Northcott, W.N. The integration of young deaf children into ordinary educational programs. *Exceptional Children*, 1971, **38**, 29-32.

O'Brien, R. The integrated resource room for visually impaired children. *New Outlook for the Blind*, 1973, **67**, 363-368.

Ohrtman, W.F. One more instant solution coming up. *Journal of Special Education*, 1972, **6**, 377-381.

Perelman, P.F., & Fox, W.L. Training regular classroom teachers to provide special education services: The consulting teacher program. In P.H. Mann (Ed.), *Mainstream special education: Issues and prespectives in urban centers*. Reston, Va.: Council for Exceptional Children, 1974.

President's Committee on Mental Retardation. *The six-hour retarded child*. Washington, D.C.: U.S. Government Printing Office, 1970.

Prouty, R.W., & Prillaman, D. Diagnostic teaching: a modest proposal. *The Elementary School Journal*, 1970, **70**, 265-270.

Prouty, R.W., & McGarry, F.M. The diagnostic/prescriptive teacher. In E. Deno (Ed.), *Instructional alternatives for exceptional children*. Reston, Va.: Council for Exceptional Children, 1973.

Quay, H.C., Glavin, J.P., Annesley, F.R., & Werry, J.S. The modification of problem behavior and academic achievement in a resource room. *Journal of School Psychology*, 1972, **10**, 187-198.

Reger, R., & Koppmann, M. The child oriented resource room program. *Exceptional Children*, 1971, **37**, 460-462.

Reger, R. Resource rooms: Change agents or guardians of the status quo? *Journal of Special Education*, 1972, **6**, 355-359.

Reger, R. What is a resource room program? *Journal of Learning Disabilities*, 1973, **6**, 609-613.

Reynolds, M. In *Maryland special study institute* (stenographic transcript). Washington, D.C.: Ace-Federal Reporters, 1967.

Reynolds, M.C. A proposal conceptual framework for special education. In C.H. Meisgeier & J.D. King, *The process of special education administration*. Scranton, Pa.: Intext, 1970.

Reynolds, M.C. Categories and variables. *Exceptional Children*, 1972, **38**, 357, 366.

Reynolds, M.C. Critical issues in special education leadership. In R.A. Johnson, J.C. Gross, & R. Weatherman (Eds.), *Decategorization and performance based systems*. Vol. 1. Minneapolis: University of Minnesota Press, 1973. (a)

Reynolds, M.C. Reflections on a set of innovations. In E. Deno (Ed.), *Instructional alternatives for exceptional children*. Reston, Va.: Council for Exceptional Children, 1973. (b)

Reynolds, M.C. *Educating exceptional children in regular classes*. Paper presented at the meeting of the Leadership Training Institute, Chicago, October 1974.

Sabatino, D.A. Resource rooms: The renaissance in special education. *Journal of Special Education,* 1972, **6**, 335-347. (a)

Sabatino, D.A. Revolution: Viva resource rooms. *Journal of Special Education,* 1972, **6**, 389-395. (b)

Sarason, S.B. *The culture of the school and the problem of change*. Boston: Allyn and Bacon, 1972. (a)

Sarason, S.B. The special child in school—report on a paper. *Bulletin of the Orton Society,* 1972, **22**, 117-122. (b)

Schwartz, L., Oseroff, A., Drucker, H., & Schwartz, R. *Innovative non-categorical interrelated projects in the education of the handicapped*. Tallahasee, Fla.: Florida State University, College of Education, Department of Habilitative Sciences, 1972.

Schwartz, L., & Oseroff, A. Clinical teacher model for interrelated areas of special education. In P. Mann (Ed.), *Mainstream special education: Issues and perspectives in urban centers*. Reston, Va.: Council for Exceptional Children, 1974.

Schwartz, L. Personal communication, April 29, 1975.

Snapp, M. Resource classrooms or resource personnel? *Journal of Special Education,* 1972, **6**, 383-387.

Stearns, K., & Swenson, S.H. The resource teacher, an alternative to special class placement. *Viewpoints,* 1973, **49**, 1-12.

Sugrue, T.J. New York City's high school program for the deaf. *Volta Review,* 1967, **69**, 247-252.

Taylor, F.D., & Soloway, M.M. The Madison plan: A functional model for merging the regular and special classrooms. In E. Deno (Ed.), *Instructional alternatives for exceptional children*. Reston, Va.: Council for Exceptional Children, 1973.

Texas Education Agency. *Plan A: What, who, why, where, when and how?* Austin, Texas: Texas Education Agency, 1972.

U.S. Commission on Civil Rights. *The excluded student: Educational practices in the southwest*. Report no. 3. Washington, D.C.: U.S. Government Printing Office, 1972.

VanEtten, G., & Adamson, G. The fail-save program: A special education service continuum. In E. Deno (Ed.), *Instructional alternatives for exceptional children*. Reston, Va.: Council for Exceptional Children, 1973.

Walker, V.S. The efficacy of the resource room for educating retarded children. *Exceptional Children,* 1974, **40**, 288-289.

Ysseldyke, J.E., & Salvia, J. Diagnostic-prescriptive teaching: Two models. *Exceptional Children,* 1974, **40**, 181-185.

INDEX

Citations of authors and studies in this index have been limited to those discussed in detail.